the New Challenge to Capitalist Globalization

THE BATTLE OF SEATTLE

Eddie Yuen, Daniel Burton Rose, and George Katsiaficas, editors.

D1227710

The Battle

of Seattle:

The New Challenge to Capitalist Globalization

**Eddie Yuen,
Daniel Burton Rose,
and George Katsiaficas,
Editors**

Soft Skull Press, 2001

ISBN:1-887128-66-2
The Battle of Seattle: The New Challenge to Capitalist Globalization
© 2002 Eddie Yuen, Daniel Burton Rose, George Katsiaficas. All rights for
individual articles and art remain with the authors and artist.

First Edition
Printed in Canada at Kromar Printing Ltd.

Book Design/Production: David Janik
Editorial Coordination: Nick Mamatas
Cover Art: Eric Drooker (www.ericdrooker.com)

To Carlos Guiliani, and all those who fight against global capitalism:
No Estamos Solos.

Acknowledgements

Eddie Yuen would like to thank Laura, James Davis, David Martinez, Iain Boal
and Nick Mamatas. Special thanks to Daniel Burton Rose for finishing the man-
uscript and to my mother, Betty J. Yuen.

dbr would like to thank: Candace, Bo, Punani, my mother and father and Billy
for support; Ronica, Sonja, Paul, Jess, Laura, Clea, and Georgia for camaraderie;
Trevor, Tiffany, Crystal, Alexis and Erik for your help—without you I couldn't
have done it, really; Scott Fleming and the people at the Prison Activist Resource
Center (www.prisonactivist.org) for letting me in their space; Michael Albert for
the tremendous resource he maintains with ZNet (www.zmag.org); AK Press for
patience; ditto Prison Legal News (www.prisonlegalnews.org).

gk thanks Sander and Nick for their spontaneity and vision, Allison, Brian, Joe,
David and EPICA for their continuing commitment, Kwangju people for their
sacrifice and optimism, Billy for his friendship and engouragement, and Daniel
and Eddie for staying focused in the trenches.

to order this book and other great Soft Skull titles at a big discount, visit
www.softskull.com

Soft Skull Press, Inc.
107 Norfolk St.
New York, NY 10002

Table of Contents

I. A Gathering Storm

Revolt of the Globalized

Roots of the Movement

Reclaiming the Streets, Then the World

II. N30 Aftermath

Rebellion and Repression

III. Uneasy Alliances

Together with the Right Against Globalization?

IV. The Movement So Far

V. Watershed: Towards a New Movement

New Movements

part I:

A GATHERING STORM

A
GATHERING
STORM

Introduction

Eddie Yuen

9/11 Prologue

As this book was heading to press, the world came to a halt with the horrendous terrorist attacks of September 11th. The radical political space which had been opened up by the anti-globalization movement was instantly pulverized (especially in the US), and the world since then seemed enveloped in a new Cold War between a vengeful American empire and a vicious right wing Islamic fundamentalism. This project, which started out as a practical compendium of articles for use by a nascent movement, feels, as I write this prologue, like a work of history, depicting a long ago time. We can only hope that the movement is able to regroup and articulate an anti-war politics that incorporates the imagination, hope and theoretical insights learned from the struggles portrayed here.

While it may seem tempting for the anti-globalization movement to simply remind the public that the attacks were the predictable result of miseries wrought by capitalist globalization, and that the death toll by preventable starvation, disease and war mandated by the neo-liberal project is far greater daily than the several thousand entombed at the World Trade Center, such an approach in and of itself would be both callous and wrong-headed. My experience talking with others on the streets of New York in the wake of the attacks is that only by starting with the shared experience of anguish and terror can people be reached—compassion, not cerebral arguments, must be the starting place for any effort to counter war fever and xenophobia. The fact that anti-globalization activists were acutely aware of the suffering of the world's majorities prior to the 9/11 attacks, and that it has only been some feminists and Leftists who have consistently opposed right-wing Islamicists (even as the US government spent billions of dollars supporting them), is of little help to the Movement in the current climate of trauma and confusion. As Naomi Klein says, we must not engage in a "calculus of suffering"—what happened on 9/11 is a heinous criminal act the gravity of which is not lessened by prior or subsequent atrocities of whatever magnitude. The movement must not allow the meaning of September 11th to be monopolized by jingoists and marketers.

In fact, the attacks and the subsequent anthrax panics have been doubly calamatous for anti-globalization activists, and even more so for Muslims and Arab-Americans. Not only have activists dealt with the anguish and fear common to society at large, but they also find themselves the targets of a criminalization of dissent not seen since McCarthyism. Coming just six weeks after the unprecedented police violence at Genoa, the terrorist attacks will undoubtedly be used as a pretext to repress anti-globalization activists everywhere in the world. In this climate, many of the debates within the pages of this book seem somewhat eclipsed. For example, the prioritizing of tactics over politics must, it seems to me, be reversed at least for the time being, as the atmosphere of fear gives an unprecedented advantage to the state. In particular, the reification of militancy in some quarters of the movement must be reconsidered in the present context, since property destruction and the wearing of disguises will now symbolize not rebellion but terror for huge sections of the public. The escalation of rhetoric, in which activists participated in the overall societal devaluation of language ("We declare war on the G8,") seems also to be anachronistic at a moment when claims on the sincerity of words seem temporarily feasible.

In general, the movement must find a way to articulate that it is for Peace *and* Justice, and against terrorism of all kinds. This is a challenging project, since the anti-globalization movement must now complexify that which appears to be simple (good vs. evil, civilization vs. barbarism) while previously its task was to simplify that which appeared to be complex (the WTO, neo-liberalism, economics). This project is necessary, since the prospects of the movement - and the global majorities that it represents—being reduced once again to spectatorship, while History is decided by equally ruthless and dystopic contending forces, is too horrible to contemplate. Only a principled global social movement, committed to direct democracy and bearing compassion and intelligence in equal measure, can oppose the hijacking of anti-imperialist causes by right wing movements of the South.

We now confront a race to the bottom for basic freedoms and civil liberties as well as for environmental and working conditions. To survive and prevail, the movement must return to its vision, its imagination, its compassion and its courage. Mere words, yes, but through action their meaning can be restored.

October 31, 2001

From Seattle to Genoa

In the months since the Seattle demonstrations occurred, their historic significance has become increasingly clear. The business press has become obsessed with the "antiglobalization" movement and has backed away from its previously triumphalist position, while almost every magazine and newspaper of note has sent reporters scurrying to interview activists who had been previously shunned. November 30, 1999 (N30) is seen as a turning point—for capital, the media, activists of all stripes, and millions of ordinary people around the world who had previously not thought of the global economy as a matter which was relevant to their lives or, more importantly, alterable by their actions. Seattle, then, is not simply a specific historical event but is symbolic of the antiglobalization movement as a whole, in the same way that May '68 in Paris represented the New Left or Soweto in 1976 represented the struggle against apartheid.

This book focuses primarily on the history, composition, tactics and politics of the new movement against global capitalism; it is not a detailed analysis of the specific horrors of the WTO, the World Bank and the IMF. Nevertheless, we do not wish to convey a false distinction between theory and practice; one of the most striking things about this movement is that the issue is the issue. Activists around the world are increasingly challenging the Experts on the great mystifications of the Economy and the Market. Corporate managers and political leaders are awakening to the fact of multitudes around the world educating themselves as to the reality of capitalist globalization and rejecting it on its own terms. Nor is all the theorizing on the part of the movement negative or merely diagnostic. The myriad radical forces opposing capitalist globalization, whether in Chiapas, Ogoniland, or Papua New Guinea, have consistently demonstrated a vision of a different world through praxis, and this was abundantly clear in the streets and jails of Seattle.

On N30, the conduct of the WTO, its corporate backers, and the city of Seattle all revealed the violence, intolerance of genuine dissent, and fundamentally impoverishing nature of the neoliberal project. The WTO was exposed as secretive and wholly undemocratic in its internal practice; the elite nations met in the "green room" for important decisions while the poor nations were symbolic window dressing. The debates within the Ministerial revealed that it is not the demonstrators but rather the capitalists who are living in a dream world: after all, what could be more utopian than the neoliberal ideology that reduces everything human and natural to the status of a commodity. The liberal city of Seattle dropped its façade of tolerance when faced with determined resistance, and initiated a high tech police riot that sent shock waves around the world. Corporations, politicians and governments were faced with a wave of popular scrutiny of their actual policies that no amount of media spin-doctoring could neutralize. It was a moment of clarity in which the illusions of democracy and corporate benevolence were exposed, and "the violence inherent in the system," as Monty Python humorously phrased it, was revealed. (To put the same idea in the deadly serious words of Thomas Friedman, the "iron fist" is sometimes necessary to support the "invisible hand" of the free market).

The style and practices of the street movement in Seattle could not have been in sharper contrast to those of the WTO and its defenders, and were equally reflective of their respective visions of the world. The top-down decision making of the bureaucrats and politicians was contrasted with direct democracy and consensus decision making on the part of the demonstrators. The authoritarian militarism of the police was opposed by decentralized yet disciplined nonviolent resistance. Even the militant elements of the protest were far more focused and conscious in their choice of targets (corporate stores) than were the police who indiscriminately gassed huge sections of Seattle. Finally, the protesters embodied genuine political (if not racial) diversity; labor, environmental and human rights organizations were out in force, reformist, socialist and anarchist politics were all present, and grassroots social movements from around the world were represented. This authentic (and necessarily tense) diversity was in sharp contrast to the homogenizing project of the WTO, which subordinates all "interest groups" to the universal interest of capital. In short, the movement represented in its practice a politics not only deeply oppositional to capitalist globalization, but also prefigurative of something else. While it is unarguable that this politics must become more articulate, it is important to remember Seattle as a moment in which the horizons of the possible were greatly expanded.

How to Use This Book

This volume is an attempt to bring together under one cover some of the most interesting debates and commentaries from within the antiglobalization movement. While the contributors may disagree with each other over a variety of issues, they are all nevertheless part of the same political phenomenon—something that has been described by one commentator as "already the largest international social movement in human history". It is precisely because certain politics within this movement have been marginalized while others have been legitimized that we have brought out this collection.

Although we have organized the material into five parts (with many subheadings) this book, like the movement it describes, is perhaps best read as a network or rhizome rather than as a linear train of information. Thus, while we organize the essays topically and chronologically whenever possible, the authors inevitably range over a variety of issues which intersect in an unruly and hopefully productive way. For example, many authors deal with the question of racial diversity in the movement, but we have not "ghettoized" them in one chapter (as is tempting) on the grounds that this question is so important that it must be present throughout each and every section of the text. This introduction will attempt to point out some of the connections, overlaps and debates among the authors. Finally, as a reading guide (and also as a fascinating essay in its own right) we include a glossary of keywords by Iain Boal at the end of the book. We recommend it as a reference (along with the more orthodox index) to decode whatever terminology, jargon, cliches or ideology the reader may encounter in the book and in media coverage of the movement.

Part I, "A Gathering Storm," consists of materials intended to provide background information and historical context for the "Seattle movement". The most important point here is that the recent upsurge against capitalist globalization has its origins in the countries of the global South. This is illustrated in our graphic: "Internationalism Against Globalization: A Map of Resistance" which enjoins us to think of the struggle in a unified (though not totalizing) way. George Katsiaficas, in his piece "Seattle Was Not the Beginning," traces a line between the protests against IMF Structural Adjustment Programs (SAPS) which have rocked the world from the late '70s, peaking perhaps in the uprising in Caracas in 1989, to the battles in Seattle, Melbourne, Prague, and Genoa. Manuel Callahan, in "Zapatismo and the Politics of Solidarity," focuses on the inspiration that Chiapas has given to the form and content of the new movement. Jaggi Singh, in his piece "India, the WTO and Capitalist Globalization," offers a glimpse into the widespread resistance within that society. By understanding these antecedents to Seattle, the movement in the overdeveloped world may be less seduced by illusions of its own centrality and will perhaps see more clearly that the global majorities are not merely passive victims of "free trade" and structural adjustment. Acknowledging this historical trajectory does not imply a return to the "Third Worldism" which enraptured much of the Western left from the '60s to the '80s and which was often woefully uncritical of leaders and parties claiming to represent the Third World masses. Rather, it demands that new forms of solidarity emerge to accompany the new forms of organization, communication, strategy and analysis that characterize the new movement. More than anything that the movement has yet done, it is this possibility of a deepening global alliance of workers, students, farmers, youth, indigenous people, immigrants and "marginals" whose potential is most alarming to the capitalist globalizers. We conclude the first section of Part I with excerpts from "The Age of Clandestinity" by the Italian Associazione Ya Basta!, a group which has become renowned for its tactical innovations (Tutti Bianchi or "white overalls") but whose penetrating analysis of the connection between neoliberalism and the dehumanization of immigrants deserves a much broader hearing.

Part I continues with several pieces on the origins of the new movement in the overdeveloped world, principally Europe and North America. This too is vital, since the Seattle demonstrations revealed a deep historical amnesia both on the part of the mainstream media, and, unfortunately, many activists themselves. Despite the novelty appeal of such angles as "a new generation takes to the streets" or "turtles and teamsters united in protest," the media have on the whole characterized the antiglobalization movement as a shallow and anachronistic echo of the '60s. According to this narrative, the outbreak of unrest in Seattle was like the reawakening of a mastodon trapped in amber since the days of Kent State. The rich history of American dissent ranging from the wildcat strikes and GI resistance of the '70s, through the AIDS activism and Central American solidarity of the '80s and the wilderness defense and environmental justice movements of the '90s are all effectively erased. In fact, as Barbara Epstein points out in her article, "Not Your Parents' Movement," the differences from '60s protests are more striking than the similarities. This is true both in terms of the political analysis of the demonstrations (targeting corporations/capital rather than the state) as well as the social constituencies of the demonstrators—think of the coalition of left and environmental activists with labor, unheard of in the '60s. Since many comparisons with '60s movements have been either strained (Michael Albert's comparison of the Black Bloc to Weathermen), or slanderous (Franklin Foer's contention that the antiglobalization movement is dumber than the New Left), we hope that the pieces by Epstein, Katsiaficas and David Kubrin help both to debunk certain myths and to rediscover lost connections. Part I concludes with a second essay by Katsiaficas on European autonomous movements in the '80s, and two pieces on anti-G8 protests in Europe in '98 and '99. These pieces, along with later essays by L.A. Kauffman on radical environmentalism and anarchism, Andrew Hsiao on recent movements of people of color, Liza Featherstone on the campus antisweatshop movement and Jay Griffiths on Mayday in London, provide further documentation of the historical roots and global synergy of the new movement.

Part II, "N30 Aftermath," documents the debates which took place during and after the WTO protests in Seattle, particularly around questions of tactics and organization. The emphasis in this collection is on the "direct action" street movement, and not on labor unions or the environmental and human rights organizations which were also a key part of the Seattle coalition. Throughout the book we do include much discussion on the relationships between these different sections of the movement—notably the pieces by Stanley Aronowitz, Naomi Klein, James Davis, Alexander Cockburn and Jeffrey St. Clair and O'Connor. Events since 1999, however, have made it quite clear that it is the direct action "street warriors" (as Cockburn and St. Clair call them), and not the NGOs or unions but who are on the cutting edge of opposition to capitalist globalization in the rich countries.

One of the most influential strands of the new movement is the tradition of mass civil disobedience commonly known as Non-Violent Direct Action (NVDA). This tendency can trace a direct lineage from Mahatmas Gandhi and Martin Luther King Jr., but was manifested in Seattle in a form that crystallized in the peace and antinuclear movements of the '70s and '80s. This iteration of NVDA is characterized by two principles that have long been assumed to be inseparable but which may in fact be linked by historical contingency. The first of these is the adoption of a strict nonviolence code that was a response to a macho fascination with revolutionary violence in the '60s. The second is the commitment to direct democracy, specifically the organizational forms of the affinity group, decentralized spokes-council meetings and consensus process. This commitment was a response to the preponderance of charismatic (and almost always male) leadership cults as well as the increasingly authoritarian organizational forms that became popular during the late New Left. Ideological nonviolence and a deep commitment to direct democracy can thus be seen as twin responses to the negative model of authoritarian Marxist-Leninist parties intent on seizing state power which had appeal to many radicals in the last century. The notion of prefigurative politics—in which the means for attaining a nonviolent, noncapitalist and truly democratic society must be consistent with the goal—remains at the core of the direct action movement. Many activists in the new movement, however, appear interested in decoupling radical democracy and ideological nonviolence, wholeheartedly embracing the former but arguing for more strategic flexibility with the latter, particularly with regard to collective destruction of corporate property. Activists in the US remain overwhelmingly opposed to harming any human beings (including cops) and would therefore be considered completely nonviolent in many other parts of the world. But, as Neumann, Ehrenreich, Kauffman and others make clear, some young activists have come to the conclusion that it is only through "breaking the spell" that ascribes greater rights to private property than to living beings that a genuinely liberatory society can be prefigured. In this regard, the American movement may be coming more in sync with its sibling movements around the globe that do not share the same fetishization of private property, particularly the conflation of personal property with corporate property that is the basis of US law.

Direct Democracy

Much greater unity may be found around the theory and practice of direct democracy within the new movement. This may in large part be due to its astonishing success as an organizing strategy; even Time, Newsweek and The Economist have grudgingly acknowledged how the "ostentatiously nonhierarchical" activists have run rings around the compulsively hierarchical police forces of London, Seattle, Melbourne, Prague, Quebec City, Gothenburg and several other cities. This recognition has not stopped the corporate media from resorting to their familiar strategy of elevating certain street activists as "leaders" (for example David Solnit of Direct Action Network and John Sellers of Ruckus Society) and certain intellectuals (notably Noam Chomsky and John Zerzan) as "gurus". Fortunately, most everyone in the movement knows the game here, and has declined the honor, with its inevitable subsequent discrediting, character assassination or co-optation. On a more comical, though sinister, note, during the Republican National Convention protests in July 2000, the Philadelphia Police Department was apparently operating with the "intelligence" (offered by a right wing thinktank) that the demonstrations were masterminded by Russian communists. On the whole, though, it is one of the great successes of the new movement that its decentralized and radically democratic nature has been undeniable, and utterly distinct from the economic institutions and civil authorities that it challenges. In this book, the pieces by Klein and Stephanie Guilloud provide the most detailed accounts of how direct democracy works within the movement.

This extraordinary emphasis on democratic process has its roots in the direct democracy of the Civil Rights Movement and the early New Left, and was kept alive principally by radical counter-culturalists and feminists in the late '60s and '70s. It also resonates with much older currents of anarchism and council communism, particularly the workers' and soldiers' soviets of Petrograd and Kronstadt in the Russian revolution, the affinity groups of the Spanish revolution of the '30s, and the worker and student councils of Paris in 1968 and Italy in 1969—traditions which have been rediscovered by many activists in recent years. Elements of radically democratic self-organization have also been present in more recent struggles, notably the Kwangju uprising in South Korea in 1980, the Chinese student movement of 1989 and the South African township uprisings in the '80s. Finally, the turn towards radical democracy owes much to the influence of neopaganism and nonwestern political theory (particularly that of indigenous people), although at times these elements are thrown together in problematic or even culturally imperialist ways. More than anything, though, the increasing appeal of participatory democracy has to do with the failure of the alternative. Bitter experience with the channeling of movement energies into centralized and undemocratic structures and leaders, ranging from the dismantling of the Rainbow Coalition by Jesse Jackson in 1988 to the corporate restructuring of the anarchist-founded Pacifica Radio Network by Democratic Party operatives in the '90s, has led many activists to realize that popular power is too important to be delegated or surrendered.

Nevertheless, although it is empowering, prefigurative and effective, radical democracy is not without its problems. Before activists become too self-satisfied with their antiauthoritarian process, they should consider the fact that much of the rhetoric of radical democracy and decentralization is being utilized by decidedly nonradical political and social forces. This is most evident amongst über-capitalist cyber-libertarians such as Wired Magazine, but can also be seen in the proliferation of management books invoking Taoism and, most perniciously, the adoption by some neonazi groups of anarchist inspired "leaderless resistance". Empowering though it may be, it is sheer reification to think that decentralization and democratic process always carries within it an inherently liberatory politics. Just as the new radicals must be careful not to merely replace the fetishism of nonviolence with a cult of militancy (specialized, theatrical and a mirror of the state), so too must they beware the fetishization of process. After all, prefigurative politics must mean something more than a vision of life as an endless meeting.

An even more serious problem facing the direct action movement and its process of radical democracy is that of "the tyranny of structurelessness". Since at least the '70s consensus process has been criticized as being tacitly exclusionary towards working class people due to the fact that it is excessively time consuming and privileges bourgeois oratorical conventions. For many of the same reasons, consensus process as it is currently practiced in the US movement is also overwhelmingly white and "countercultural," although this is also connected to the question of which issues are politically prioritized. Just as the vaunted "cyber-democracy" of the new movement often looks more like a "geek adhocracy," the practice of direct democracy in the new movement often appears to outsiders to be insular. These problems may not be as intractable as they seem, however, since many young activists of color are increasingly interested in reclaiming their legacy of direct, participatory democracy.

The New Politics of Direct Action

The remainder of Part II deals in more detail with the debates over tactics that have swirled around the movement since Seattle. As Ehrenreich points out in her article "Anarkids and Hypocrites," by the time of the Seattle protests some aspects of the Non-Violent Direct Action tradition had become ossified, as witnessed at the Nevada Test Site and School of the Americas "cross-the-line-and-get-cited-out" exercises of the late '80s and '90s. Furthermore, the idea that offering up one's body to the state is the highest form of political commitment has been increasingly criticized as a politics based on white-skin privilege which is incomprehensible to many people of color who are involuntarily sacrificed every day. Most significantly, the state has increasingly failed to uphold its part of the ritual, and will now more likely than not engage in violent beatings and gassings regardless of how pacific its supplicants may be. With this in mind, then, N30 in Seattle represented a dramatic reinvigoration of this protest tradition due to the presence of several new protest tendencies.

As Kauffman documents in her article "Who Are Those Masked Anarchists," the '90s Earth First! milieu shaped a cadre of forest activists who transformed the calcified rituals of nonviolent direct action into a creative and effective ensemble of tactics. The Earth First-ers raised the stakes of blockading with both technical innovations (tripods from the Penan people's struggle in Sarawak, lockdown devices, tree sits) and a fearless commitment to making the defense of wilderness more a literal endeavor and less a media event. Having honed their tactics in the isolated forests of the Pacific Northwest, and having suffered beatings, intimidation, pepper spray torture and, in the case of David "Gypsy" Chain, death, many forest activists would not be content with a merely symbolic blockade. Seattle was a laboratory for a new repertoire of flexible and militant direct action tactics never before seen in an urban context on such a large scale.

Crucial to the success of the new blockading tactics were the elements of surprise and mobility. While thousands of demonstrators were holding their ground surrounding the WTO Ministerial and bearing the brunt of the police violence, hundreds more were roaming the newly liberated sectors of downtown Seattle as "flying wedges," keeping the police off balance and effectively shutting down the city. Of course, improvisational and mobile demonstrations are nothing new; some examples include the "snake dances" of the Japanese New Left (which were imported to Berkeley during the Third World Strike of 1969), the corporate war chest tours at the Democratic National Convention in San Francisco in 1984, and the Critical Mass bicycle happenings of the '90s. But in Seattle, the conjunction of mobile and territorial tactics proved to be uniquely complementary. The particularities of Seattle are not reproducible, if for no other reason than that the element of surprise is currently unthinkable for large demonstrations. Nevertheless, the shift from static to flexible demonstration tactics is clearly significant, as Klein and Hakim Bey discuss in their pieces. "Flexibility" is matched only by "globalization" as a key buzzword of neoliberalism, and many theorists suggest that, just as "our opposition must be as global as their capitalism" so too must our tactics be as mobile as their financial flows. Since globalized and flexible capital prides itself on being "nimble" and even "virtual," and thereby impervious to such "old economy" forms of resistance as sit-down strikes or factory occupations, it is imperative that the movement continues to creatively expose the weaknesses of the new global regime of accumulation.

The proximate source of inspiration for the flexible protest style of the new movement has been the extraordinary developments in Britain during the '90s. As Griffiths and Katherine Ainger describe in their essays, the Reclaim The Streets (RTS) and anti-roads demonstrations have been central in reimagining a global "carnival against capitalism." Although characterized as a "terrorist group" by the FBI, the subversiveness of RTS lies not so much in direct confrontation with the state but in temporarily occupying capitalist spaces through music and dance and, in so doing, exposing certain truths. First, by emphasizing the essential pleasure of resistance, RTS exorcized the legacy of the hairshirt left while simultaneously critiquing the empty satisfactions of consumer culture. Second, by literally "reclaiming the streets," the movement has drawn attention to the almost total privatization of public space which has taken place in the overdeveloped world. The British movement has maintained initiative in the streets through continuously evolving and flexible tactics.

Finally, the most dramatic "new" political tendency that burst into the media spotlight in Seattle were the militant punk-inflected anarchists falling loosely under the rubric of "the Black Bloc". Contrary to its sensational media profile, this tendency is not synonymous with anarchism, since the movement includes a wide range of anarchist politics. The Black Bloc tendency can be traced to the European Autonomist Marxist tradition which originated in Italy in the '70s and continued into Holland, Denmark, Germany, Switzerland and Greece in the '80s and '90s. It takes its name and style from the German Autonomen—a somewhat confusing import given the different semiotics and demographics in America. African Americans looking for the "Black Bloc" in Washington, DC on April 20, 2000, would perhaps have been surprised to find a group of predominantly white youth dressing in black. Autonomist and anarchist politics are very much a part of the direct action milieu and have been present in the US since at least the mid '80s. This is so despite the assertions by some anarchists (such as Zerzan in this volume) that their movement has nothing to do with leftism, a claim which has its complement in the denunciations of militants by certain mainstream leftists (such as Lori Wallach and Carl Pope). Militant anarchism must be understood as being on a continuum with the larger movement, in the same way that Malcolm X and Martin Luther King Jr., while at times denouncing each other, simultaneously opened up the shared space necessary for both to operate. Unfortunately, due in part to the subcultural isolation that the punk-anarchist milieu has deliberately constructed for itself, the Black Bloc's theoretically well worked out attacks on corporate property are easily written off as mindless vandalism. Broken windows are not self-explanatory, particularly in a society that conflates corporate property with personal property in the same way that it equates socialism with the loss of individual freedom and shared toothbrushes. It is one of the goals of this volume to open up a dialogue between militants and the broader movement, rather than denying that articulate militant politics even exist, as other collections have done.

The common ground is literally the shared space of the demonstration itself. Because the Black Bloc actions in Seattle were done collectively and in public, they were part of the larger politics of creating a festival of resistance to demonstrate that neoliberalism and the commodification of the world is not a fait accompli. Had these actions been done clandestinely, they would have articulated a very different politics, one of vanguardism rather than participation in the broader movement. Clandestine activity invariably brings about a climate of spectatorship, repression and paranoia that is anathema to movement building— and much more manageable by the state, not only logistically but ideologically, through the powerful discourse of "terrorism". By keeping it in the streets, the Black Bloc are engaged in the same project of radical democracy that activists around the world are rediscovering.

The danger for the new militants is that they begin to reify property destruction or street fighting in much the same way as some in the '70s and '80s fetishized nonviolence and turned it into a religion. This is especially perilous in the USA, where nihilistic violence is a frightening fact of life and where the language and imagery of violence has been firmly staked out by the right. The ball is squarely in the court of the militants to explain their actions lest others claim them. This means going beyond simply contrasting violence against corporations with violence by corporations and articulating a positive strategic rationale for trashing and militant self-defense. Thinking this impossible, George Lakey, in his piece "Mass Action Since Seattle: Seven Ways to Make our Protests More Powerful," argues that the only way for the movement to maintain the moral high ground in the face of a hostile media and state is to explicitly disavow violence and property destruction. Lakey takes the controversial position that "tactical diversity" is effectively impossible in a mass action, since more militant activities always trump less militant ones, thereby erasing the impact of NVDA and potentially endangering the nonviolent majority without their consent. Since the corporate media can always be counted on to emphasize "violent" actions, however minor, to the exclusion of all other forms of protest (let alone political content), Lakey's point that militants have a greatly disproportionate influence on the public perception of the movement must be grappled with.

The media infatuation with "violent anarchists" compounds the dangers of tactical reification by making it possible for militants to overestimate the actual material threat they present to the system. Although some militants might delude themselves into believing otherwise, window smashing is every bit as symbolic as nonviolent blockading, and causes far less economic damage. As the Zapatistas have demonstrated, even guerrilla war is guerrilla theater in the current era, so the real measure of the damage done by trashing is not literal but symbolic. On this count, the corporate potlatches of Seattle, Prague, Nice and elsewhere may indeed be damaging to corporations like Nike, Starbuck's and McDonald's whose profits are increasingly based on the symbolic power of their logos. It remains to be seen, however, whether the image of "rebellious youth" actively repudiating the sovereignty of the commodity sign will itself be co-opted by marketers and rendered consumable. While there are other less risky and more inclusive ways of rejecting corporate branding (boycotts, corporate campaigns, satire), it is must be conceded that the Black Bloc has acted out the political libido of an ad-saturated society.

This brings us to the tricky question of the extent to which militant tactics alienate the movement from its potential base of support. Geov Parrish, in his piece "Imagine," is undoubtedly correct in arguing that the trashing in Seattle was alienating to many Americans. But it is also true, as Neumann and the ACME Collective suggest, that the property destruction inspired many others, especially people of color, youth and the disenfranchised who may be turned off by the perceived masochism and naiveté of pacifism. Will these two trends balance each other out? Since polls show strong support from Americans on most antiglobalization issues, it seems likely that the relatively small numbers at US protests since Seattle can be partly explained by the alienation of some potential supporters due to fears of violence. The view that "protester violence" marginalizes the movement appears to be subscribed to by many governments, as is evidenced by the way in which the Italian police and media instrumentalized the Black Bloc in Genoa (see the pieces by Ramor Ryan and George Caffentzis and Sylvia Federici). It does not follow from this fact, though, that militants "do the work of the state," as some pacifists might argue. After all, the police have shown in every instance that they will use massive violence regardless of the behavior of demonstrators. Nevertheless, the question remains as to whether the movement's de facto commitment to "tactical diversity" will be a help or hindrance to its growth.

In the end, this debate may be resolved pragmatically. As Jim Redden documents in his essay "Police State Targets the Left," the penalties for being arrested and convicted of any crime against property (let alone resisting police officers) have become so high that such tactics may be effectively impossible in all but the largest actions. With the ever more draconian anticrime and "antiterrorism" laws constantly being passed in the USA, the possibility of emulating a European style militant youth culture (as seen in Prague, Genoa and even Quebec City), is unrealistic and potentially suicidal. Ramor Ryan's piece "Holidays In the Sun," documenting a police assault on woefully unprepared militants in Cancun, Mexico, may in fact be singularly instructive here. From the police attack on a Black Bloc in Long Beach, CA on Mayday 2001, to the use of live ammunition against demonstrators in Gothenborg and Genoa, it is clear that the antiglobalization movement cannot hope to match the real violence of the state with empty displays of militant bravado. As Juan Gonzalez points out in his piece, "From Seattle to South Central," young white radicals in America are still a long way off from learning what people of color already know—that the price of defiance in American democracy is often one's freedom or one's life. In my view, the movement needs to demilitarize its rhetoric and tactics and return to the creativity, humor and political focus that remain its most powerful traits.

Race and the Antiglobalization Movement

The debates over tactics, while important, have threatened to overshadow many other vitally important political issues that the movement must confront. This is of course not to say that the tactical is not political (since prefigurative politics are the order of the day), but that the politics of the movement cannot be reduced to questions of street tactics. In Part III, entitled "Uneasy Alliances," we present articles on three of the important issues that face the burgeoning movement: first, the relationships between the street movement and organized labor, established environmental groups and NGOs; second, how to deal with right wing political forces vis-à-vis antiglobalization; and third, the question of racial diversity within the movement. As mentioned earlier, the "race question" is so important that the articles addressing it directly (Colin Rajah, Wong, Gonzalez, Guilloud and Hsiao) are interspersed throughout the collection, rather than "added on" to the book in a way that would mimic its treatment in the movement so far.

The glaring whiteness of the new movement has been probably the greatest source of self-examination and regret within its ranks. The movement's lack of racial diversity stands in sharp contrast to its deep engagement with patriarchy and homophobia or even its tentative negotiations with representative organizations of the working class (i.e. unions). But neither seeking to "recruit" people of color into the pre-existing movement (a strategy that Wong and Guilloud both document in their essays) nor retroactively creating a mythology that Seattle was, in fact, racially diverse are adequate responses to this dilemma. A more promising starting point would be a recognition that there is, parallel to the antiglobalization movement, a growing and vibrant movement of young people of color who are waging fierce struggles against institutional racism, the prison-industrial complex and, above all, police brutality. This is especially true on the coasts, as Hsiao documents in his essay "Color Blind". In New York City in the '90s, there have been significant mobilizations against the rollback of open admission at the City University of New York, and mass protests against the police torture of Abner Louima and the police murders of Amadou Diallo and Patrick Dorismond. In California, there have also been huge mobilizations of young people of color, especially Chicanos and Latinos who have staged high school walkouts and demonstrations at college campuses across the state since the early '90s to protest a variety of racist and anti-immigrant policies. On other fronts in the last decade, demonstrations in support of political prisoner Mumia Abu-Jamal have become increasingly diverse, environmental justice struggles have reaped many important victories for communities of color, and resistance to the rollback of affirmative action has become a truly mass movement. Moreover, it is simply not true, as some white activists assume, that Capitalism and Globalization are at too high of a level of abstraction for working class communities of color to be able to find meaningful connections to their daily lives. After all, American inner cities were among the first laboratories for "structural adjustment" during the fiscal crises of the '70s and African-Americans have been disproportionately affected by capital flight and deindustrialization over the last three decades. Furthermore, millions of the new immigrants to the USA are effectively refugees from the "civil" wars of recolonization, asset stripping, privatization and enclosures demanded by the economic experts. Many of these immigrants also bring with them militant labor traditions (as European immigrants did in the last century) and, increasingly, direct experience with struggles against the IMF and neoliberalism. In short, people of color in the US provide an experiential link with the raw violence of capitalist globalization that would deepen immeasurably the level of critique and political power of the movement. These multitudes, along with a militant rank-and-file labor movement, are the social forces that the politicians and managers would least like to see at the forefront of the antiglobalization movement.

While the movement is definitely taking the question of racial diversity seriously and has made significant progress since Seattle, three especially vexing problems stand out as obstacles to alliance. The first two have to do with the relative "whiteness" of the antiglobalization movement's culture and organizational forms, respectively, while the third revolves around the vastly different experiences of repression that people of color face in the USA.

As noted in several pieces here, the demographics of the direct action movement against globalization are predominantly white, middle class, youthful, and countercultural ("extravagantly bohemian" according to one media commentator), with a politics of what George McKay calls "affinitive liberal anarchism". All of these characteristics are possible impediments to communication with anyone outside the radical milieu, especially the working class people of color who could potentially form the most potent alliance. With regard to demographics and culture, there is no point in the left flagellating itself for being what it is. Long before the 60s stereotypes of radicals were institutionalized, George Orwell said of the 1930s British Left: "One sometimes gets the impression that the mere words socialism and communism draw towards them with magnetic force every fruit-juice-drinker, nudist, sandal-wearer, sex-maniac, Quaker, Nature-cure quack, pacifist and feminist in England." Orwell's prejudices aside, it is important to remember that eccentricity and cultural rebellion seem to have always been a core component of radical movements in the West. Although cultural rebellion in the US and Western Europe has been co-opted to the point where it is no longer nearly as polarizing as it was in the '60s , it may still, as Hsiao and Wong point out, strike other constituencies as self-indulgent acting out by white kids. Rather than adopting a strategy of "cutting your hair and going to the factories," as some '60s radicals did, the antiglobalization movement at its best does not disingenuously seek to misrepresent itself to society at large. Instead, many white radicals fully embrace their prefigurative cultural rebellion while at the same time trying (with mixed results) to be aware of their own privilege and potential subcultural isolation as they seek to enter into alliances with other social forces. How successful this strategy will be depends in large part on the skepticism of American society at large, and people of color in particular, to the growing effort by the corporate media to marginalize the antiglobalizaton movement as dilettantes, "eco-terrorists," and unthinking "globaphobics." Finally, white activists in the movement must be careful not to essentialize the cultural divide (which in any event is at least as much a function of age and class as it is of race), and fancy themselves as inherently more avant-garde than their potential allies. The idea of "counterculture" itself has strong African-American roots. As Michelle Wallace says of "the great American whitewash" of the histories of '60s counterculture:

Afro-American culture was instrumental in forming the aspirations of the New Left, as well as minority revolutions—not so much by its considerable political activity, but precisely by its counterculture. While this 'minor' culture may sometimes be difficult to link directly to political protest, it was always clearly formed in the spirit of subverting a majority culture that tried to choke it at the root. Precisely in its sex, drugs, dance, music, and style, it kept the record of its discontents accurately and well. Perhaps this counterculture is the site where mainstream culture is still most forcefully challenged, even as revolutions come and go.

In future alliances (especially among youth), the cultural divide within the movement may be more over which counterculture is predominant, rather than whether or not the movement is culturally subversive. This is so because, despite the hegemony of hip-hop within urban youth culture, white activist culture often still tends to be hippie, punk or (in Europe) raver/techno in style, (although these categories are not mutually exclusive).

The second divide between the direct action anti-globalization movement and urban movements of people of color is centered on organizational style. There is a common sense understanding that middle class white activists have an affinity for decentralization, direct democracy and anarchism while people of color are dependent on charismatic leadership and enamored of hierarchical organizations. In fact, these assumptions are very far from the truth historically and serve to reinforce some self-appointed non-white "leaders" as well as some white activists who are relieved of the challenge of having to work on equal terms with people of color. As we have already mentioned, much of the repertoire of NVDA and the theory and practice of direct democracy originated with people of color and is now being reclaimed by younger activists. Recent scholarship by authors such as John Brown Childs, Robin Kelley and George Lipschutz has pointed out that the political actions of communities of color cannot be reduced to their formal organizations, and that the "great man" narrative of Third World politics is ripe for re-evaluation. Many of the tensions between the predominantly white antiglobalization movement and organizations of color in fact have more to do with the conflict between NGOs and street movements generally (see the Wong, Davis and Cockburn articles), although these tensions may be compounded by race. In conclusion, Gonzalez, Rajah and Hsiao point out that there have been some hopeful signs of cross-racial alliance building since Seattle, particularly in Philadelphia, Los Angeles and Cincinnati, but much more work needs to be done.

Finally, the most significant divide that the antiglobalization movement must deal with is the fact that the consequences for being involved with direct action politics are much higher for people of color than for whites. African Americans and Latinos in particular have borne the full brunt of the police state that white activists have briefly tasted in Seattle, Philadelphia and Genoa, and

A Gathering Storm

are unlikely to be persuaded to join in demonstrations that seem foolhardy or sacrificial. The legacy of the massive prison expansion of the last two decades cannot be overestimated, not only in terms of the 2 million people who are locked up but also when we consider the chilling effect on hundreds of thousands more who are on probation or parole, have "2 strikes" or are eligible for deportation under the Clinton "antiterrorism" laws. An example of tension around this issue is that which emerged at the Democratic Convention in LA between the Direct Action Network and the Bus Riders Union. In this case, the predominantly immigrant workers of the latter group were wary of DAN's confrontational tactics because they could not risk being arrested and possibly deported for minor offenses.

Beyond Left and Right?

The second major question that we want to draw attention to in Part III is the relationship of right wing political tendencies to the antiglobalization movement. As Schoenmakker and Krebbers point out, the far right has long maintained positions against free trade agreements and the "New World Order" on nationalist and, often, racist grounds. While the Southern Poverty Law Center is completely wrong in asserting that the antiglobalization movement in the US has been significantly infiltrated by far-right elements, it is true that some neofascists do see the movement as a potential site for recruiting and spreading their theories. To understand this phenomenon, the movement must reject the "centrist/extremist" model that is used by many liberal hate-crime watchdog groups, and instead develop a nuanced critique of the versions of "antiglobalization" on offer. James O'Connor, in his piece, "On Populism and the Anti-Globalism Movement," provides an useful taxonomy of populisms left and right, North and South, which we hope will help make clear the real issues at stake here. In the US, far right forces often advocate for the working class (as long as it is white, male, and American) and increasingly cast themselves as Green, thereby making themselves alarmingly congruent with much of the rhetoric of the antiglobalization movement. The best solution to this problem is, of course, a genuinely diverse movement; one committed to combating racism, sexism, homophobia and nationalism wherever they may be found. Although some on the left may be weary of the more narcissistic and superficial forms of identity politics which have emerged in recent years, this doesn't mean that it is possible to return to speaking of "universal" class and environmental subjects unmarked by race, gender and sexuality. As long as xenophobia, white supremacy and patriarchy are normative for American society they must always be overtly and even stridently denounced. Additionally, the logic of right wing thinking must be challenged with solid radical analysis, for it is through the proliferation of paranoia and conspiracy theory that right wing elements are most likely to infiltrate the antiglobalization movement.

Keeping It In the Streets

Finally, we want to take note of the tension between the street movement and the Non-Governmental Organizations (NGOs) which have been greatly empowered by Seattle and its aftermath. As the business press has made very clear since Seattle, the possibility of co-opting some NGOs into the negotiating process over free trade and globalization is a high priority for capital and the state. This raises profound questions for the integrity and longevity of the new movement. Activists must be careful not to let the debates over tactical differences overshadow discussion of the political differences that the direct action movement may have with some NGOs who view street demonstrations as a bargaining chip rather than a site for the development of popular power. As James Davis warns in his piece, "This is what Bureaucracy Looks Like," the professionalization of activism may have a similar effect to the ritualization of NVDA tactics that Ehrenreich describes elsewhere; it can rob the resistance of its vitality and edge. The lesson here is that the movement is more than the sum of its organizations, however valuable these organizations may be, and that at the present historical moment it is again possible to imagine something more than "a seat at the table."

Two, Three, Many Seattles

Part IV is entitled "The Movement So Far" and consists of accounts from various actions since Seattle—notably Washington DC, Philadelphia, London, Cancun, Prague and Genoa. This section is fairly self-explanatory, although it is worth remarking on the astonishing velocity of movement knowledge as it travels across national frontiers; Boris Kagarlitsky is particularly insightful on this point. It is easy to take for granted all that has happened since Seattle, and we hope that this section serves to document some of the high points of the antiglobalization movement so far.

Part V "Towards a New Movement" brings together a broad range of theoretical perspectives in order to show the genuine diversity of thought that is currently in ferment. Media pundits such as Thomas Friedman ceaselessly disparage the antiglobalization movement as being strictly negative or subtheoretical; any truth to this assertion would, however, in no way validate the dogmatic tripe that passes for neoliberal theory. It is certainly easy to see why the movement might be theory shy, given the disastrous attempts to find the Maoist or Trotskyist "correct line" in the '60s and '70s, the tortured gymnastics of academic postmodernism in the '80s and '90s, or the savage polemics between anarchists in recent years. But most activists also understand the need to probe deeper into the workings of capitalism and to understand the historical antecedents of the struggle. The contributors throughout the book offer a return to theorizing, if not Theory; the task is seen as framing the right questions and seeking answers both on the ground and through an engagement with movements past. Not doing so would be to turn our backs on the projects grand and modest, practical and intellectual, which constitute the radical legacy. As James O'Connor says, turning Hegel inside out, "the owl of Minerva folds her wings at daybreak"—his ironic point being that at precisely the moment when Marx's theory is most relevant, it is declared safely dead.

Naomi Klein points out in her article, "The Vision Thing," that there are really many antiglobalization movements—"one no, many yesses" as the Zapatistas would say. But this radical plurality is, for her, a sign of strength, not weakness, as the power of the movement is expanded through its accretion of collective wisdom, its imagination and flexibility, and the continuous invention of new forms of solidarity. One area in which the movement's theoretical engagement is most evident is in its relationship to media. The proliferation of

Independent Media Centers (IMCs) since Seattle has become the trademark of the antiglobalization movement and has shaped its organizational forms and modes of communication in profound ways, as both Klein and Perlstein point out. This has given the movement a wider forum for finding its own voice since the heyday of the underground press of the '60s, with the significant difference that it is now far more international and participatory. At the same time, the movement is constantly being belittled and attacked by the corporate media, just as every significant struggle for justice and freedom prior to it has been, and is under pressure to find new ways to get its message out to the uninitiated. The movement must face this challenge squarely and not succumb to the illusion that it is literally threatening the state and capital through its actions so far. After all, one irreducible purpose of guerrilla theater, "summit hopping," and popular protest generally is to "demonstrate" a presence that registers on the streets and ultimately in the corporate media and popular culture. The option of withdrawing utterly from the glare of the spectacle, or of simply acting as if the media-scape did not exist and instituting in the street an ideal polis of unmediated face-to-face communion is as fanciful in its own way as the Robinson Crusoe myths of primitive capitalism.

Politics, then, is not reducible to its mediatization, but neither can the mills of the spectacle be finessed. There is no outside now, if there ever was. The antiglobalization movement is already the subject of pop culture exploitation, whether playfully sympathetic (Lisa as starstruck tree-sitter in the Simpsons), relentlessly clueless (Glamour magazine's offer to activists to pose for a "Girls of the WTO" photo shoot) or vapidly malicious (the anarchoterrorist villain in the James Bond film "The World is Not Enough"). With this at times amusing attention comes a poison pill of obsolescence; anarchists, tree-sitters and giant puppets, unknown to the TV-watching public a few short years ago, will soon be dismissed as yesterday's icons.

Hail and Farewell

But this dance of co-optation plays against the backdrop of mounting carnage, and the totality of capitalism's conquest of the world is ultimately the bitter source of the movement's strength and perseverance. At the mid-point of the last century, Max Horkheimer and Theodore Adorno wrote "the fully enlightened world radiates disaster triumphant." Now the dawn of the new century offers us disasters undreamed of. As the apologists of capital celebrate the billions spent on bioengineering research to "improve nutrition and medicine," they silently watch the depopulation of the African continent by preventable diseases such as AIDS, malaria, and dysentery due to the absence of an "effective market" (money) on the part of the Africans. An elite team of population biologists, economists and geographers have calculated that the earth is greatly undervalued; they estimate that the real worth of the combined ecosystems (excluding the moon and satellites) to be $28 trillion. Meanwhile, as the diversity of consumer choice has never been greater for the world's rich, with all manner of world cuisine, world music, world travel, or world literature available to the discerning customer, actual lived diversity is ground to dust under the global commodity sign. One telling symptom is the extinction rate of human languages; according to best estimates, every two weeks on average one of the world's 6,000 remaining languages dies somewhere , while the ones we use are so degraded as to make speaking of compassion, love or authenticity seem a banal joke. Each year, thousands of species go extinct and millions of "units" of forest, fishery and other "resources" are harvested for the market. Each year millions of rural people leave their ancestral homes for the megalopolis, thousands of indigenous people have cultures shattered by missionaries and multinationals, their temporal sensibilities replaced by clock-time and their myriad aesthetics pasteurized by Spielberg and Disney. The more diversity is talked about, said Jacques Ellul, the more we can be sure that the opposite is the case. Worst of all, in the absence of radical democratic visions, countless oppressed people around the world are turning to self-destructive despair, religious fundamentalism and right wing populism, further compounding the crisis.

In the face of all this, it is well to acknowledge that the antixglobalization movement is a reality. It exists, and because of this there are new possibilities of hope in the world. We offer *The Battle of Seattle* both as evidence of that hopeful vitality and as bearings for the journey.

Who Needs the WTO?

The Surrealist Movement in the U.S.
Leaflet distributed in Seattle November 1999

In ancient times the word tyrant signified not simply a figure of oppressive authority, noted for extreme cruelty and injustice, but more precisely one who dared not appear in public without bodyguards. The vast interlocking tyrannies of our own time suggest that this strange period which flatters itself as "post-modern" might perhaps more aptly be called neo-ancient, and in any case qualifies as an example of barbarism at its goriest. Courtesy of the "free enterprise" system, the U.S. has created the most spied-on, billy-clubbed, tear-gassed, and locked-up society in the history of the world.

Today, however, it is not only top government officials, captains of industry, mobsters, and religious potentates who surround themselves with cops and more cops (public and/or private), but also celebrities, stars of stage and screen, athletes, talk-show hosts and hostesses, radio personalities, brokers, bankers, gamblers, gurus, and all manner of high-profile non-entities. So inflated has the tyrants' network become in the past hundred years that our whole society is now afflicted with cops everywhere: in the street, of course, and the workplace, on the beach, and wherever young people and people of color assemble, but also in schools, in libraries, at concerts and other places of entertainment.

These reflections came to mind as we read media reports implying that, at the World Trade Organization's highly publicized plot-and-plunderfest in Seattle this month, the number of cops, soldiers and paid informers may well exceed the combined total of WTO conference attendees and protestors.

It should not be overlooked that the WTO itself is a kind of cop, or rather a kind of tyrants' watchdog—a symbolic hyper-watchdog at the portals of the new, improved, postcolonial, multicultural, genetically modified, low-fat imperialism. Organized in 1995 with specifically antilabor motives in mind, the WTO has also manifested from the start a total contempt for even the most basic ecological concerns, and an obsequious eagerness to obey each and every command issued by the stage-managers of commodity fetishism.

It is in fact the avowed aim of the WTO to help coordinate U.S. capital's current scramble for Africa and Asia, as well as the restructuring of a freshly rebalkanized Europe, now conveniently dominated by the U.S.A.'s own NATO. More generally, the WTO's task is to oversee U.S. capital's worldwide campaign to lower wages, destroy unions, restore sweatshop conditions, shield corporate polluters and wilderness-wreckers, facilitate the commercial annihilation of endangered species, and above all keep the profits soaring. Another important but more covert purpose of the WTO is to prepare the way for the globalization of slave labor.

The WTO's function, therefore, is not simply to maintain existing inequality but to expand it, indeed to globalize it—in other words, to make an already intolerable situation infinitely worse for everyone except billionaires.

For us surrealists, the WTO represents everything loathsome and disgusting in this world, and inspires only our revulsion. Almost to the point of caricature, it epitomizes contemporary civilization's disastrous hatred of the Marvelous. The WTO not only exemplifies the fear of poetry and love, the fear of human freedom, and the fear of wild creatures and places, it also broadcasts those fears, exacerbates them, and merges them into the Great Fear that paralyzes such a large portion of the U.S. population today: the fear of being "different," of being oneself, of being alive.

The WTO's stupid, boring, empty apologetics—its "booms," options, clout, profits, Prozac, diplomatic victories, accords, telecoms, Normal Trade Relations, "services," deals, tariffs, "futures," deficits, rapid growth, incentives, deregulation, ventures, market values, and "development" (i.e., covering the Earth with cement): all this truly makes us sick. (WTO rhetoric, like that of its confederates—the World Bank, the International Monetary Fund, and President Clinton himself could serve as a manual for students of the devaluation of language.)

Such words and phrases are no laughing matter, any more than the deeds they document. Sixty-five years ago, W. E. B. Du Bois described just what horror the strokes of a pen can bring: "Flames of jealous murder sweep the earth, while brains of little children smear the hills." Make no mistake, the WTO can sign no agreement which is not a death sentence. Its reason for being is to make learning and youth, poetry and desire, solidarity and joy, poverty and weakness, wildlife and old growth—indeed everything not serving the crimes of capital—into a capital crime.

Clearly, as a bureaucratic embodiment of Patriarchy, Capital, Statism, White Supremacy, Genocide, and Ecocide—in short, the globalization of all forms of misery and miserabilisim—the WTO is a veritable emblem of the sum of all villainies today.

Is there really anything to argue about here? Isn't it frightfully obvious that the WTO is a thoroughgoing abomination? That its whole agenda boils down to domination and devastation? That we'd all be much better off without it?

Here, then, are three simple, straightforward, reasonable demands:

Abolish the WTO!
Defend the Marvelous, by any means necessary!
Free Mumia Abu-Jamal!

Revolt of the Globalized

Kevin Harris

Internationalism Against Globalization:
A Map of Resistance

James Davis and Paul Rowley

Capitalist globalization is of course nothing new (see glossary), but if we periodize the current moment of "globalization" as beginning in the early 80s, corresponding to the implementation of IMF Structural Adjustment Programs (SAPS) in the Third World and former Second World, a distinct pattern of resistance emerges. This map is an effort to depict this resistance graphically, to give shape and gravity to events that are generally portrayed by the corporate media as random, inchoate singularities (when they warrant mentioning at all).

This map is not intended to be a comprehensive account of struggle and unrest around the world, even of those events that can unambiguously be claimed as anti-capitalist. Instead, we have limited ourselves here to demonstrations, riots and events that are specific responses either to SAPS or summits/fulcrums of capitalist globalization. Even allowing for these limitations, the density of events on this map (especially in the global South) suggests that a web or matrix of anti-globalizing practices has been steadily taking shape over the last twenty years. The fact that it has only been "discovered" as a worldwide movement after Seattle in 1999 is an indication more of Eurocentric blindness in the North than of theoretical under-development in the South.

The differing icons represent the qualitatively different nature of resistance between the under-developed and over-developed world. The crosshair icon represents rebellions, ranging from spontaneous uprisings to general strikes, against the neo-liberal policies that have been described by critics as "the third world war". These policies include the displacement of communities due to the privatization of land and water, the clearcutting of forests to pay off foreign debt, the murderous immiseration of urban populations through fuel and food staple price increases, and the dismantling of public health care and education. The global majorities have courageously resisted these measures, and have developed increasingly sophisticated theories and practices in the process.

The coffin icon represents fatalities; the numbers of people known to have

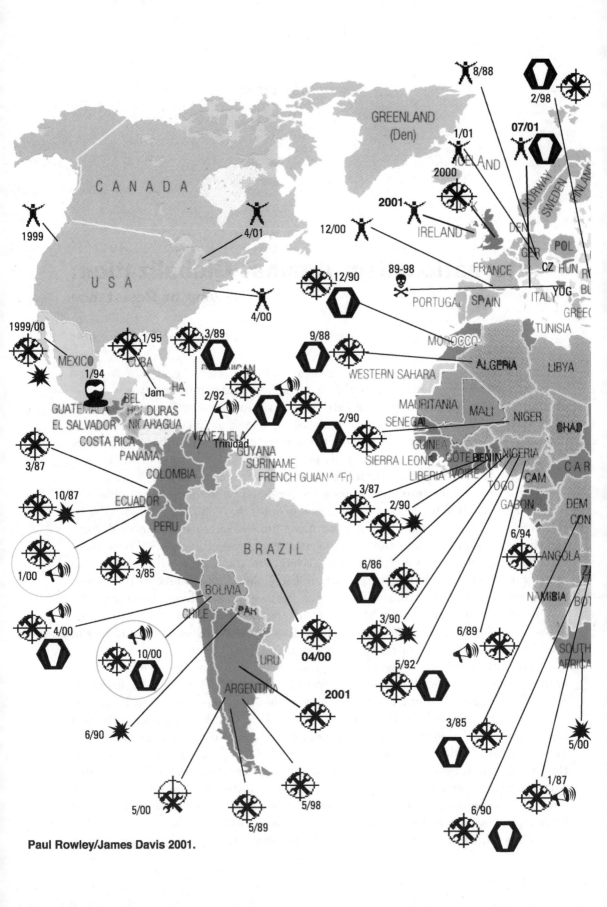

Paul Rowley/James Davis 2001.

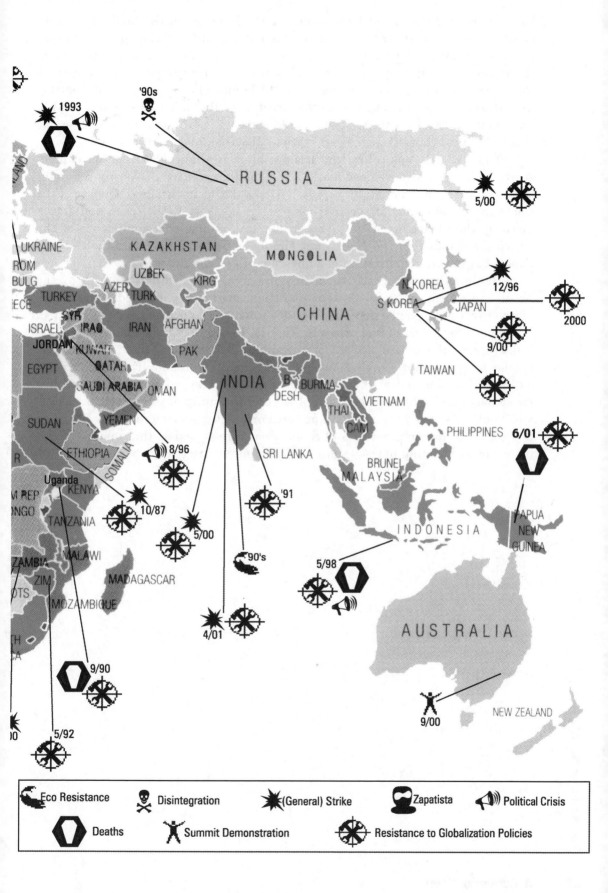

been killed by government forces (serving the interests of the IMF and capital generally) in these struggles. While we have not quantified the number of casualties killed by the governments of the South in the name of globalization, even the incomplete tally depicted in the map numbers in the thousands (topped by the 600+ slaughtered by Venezuela in 1989) and shows no signs of abating. (Needless to say, the amount of deaths directly attributable to SAPS and neo-liberalism number in the millions, but would show up in UN statistical registers as due to "natural causes" such as starvation, disease and crime).

There is only one coffin icon beside the icon of anti-globalization demonstrations in the overdeveloped world. This should serve as a sobering reminder that, as egregious as state repression has been in Prague, Quebec City, Gothenborg and Genoa, it does not compare in savagery to the social liquidation faced by the global majorities. This is not to diminish the significance of the growing resistance in the North, but simply to underline the fact that, as the Zapatistas put it, globalization is a question of life and death.

But another difference separates the anti-globalization protests of the North and South. In the South, demonstrations are usually directed at the immediate effects of a specific neo-liberal policy, such as the privatization of water in Bolivia or the raising of fuel prices in Nigeria. In the North, demonstrations typically target the entire project of capitalist globalization, and consequently appear to operate on a higher level of theoretical abstraction than the "primal outbursts" of the South. It is our hope that this map will undermine such a mind/body duality by demonstrating the potential unity of the movement North and South. As was demonstrated at the Porto Allegre Conference in Brazil in 2000, an international network of connections already exists that insists on giving common meaning to the seemingly fragmented struggles depicted here.

Seattle Was Not the Beginning

George Katsiaficas *

In the months subsequent to the now legendary battle of Seattle, the leaders of the World Bank, the International Monetary Fund and the Trilateral Commission all defined the antiglobalization upsurge as having begun in that city—and therefore as following in the glorious tradition of Microsoft and Starbucks. No less an authority on world economic affairs than Alan Greenspan, chair of the Federal Reserve Board under four U.S. presidents, recently commented that: "...the arguments against the global trading system that emerged first in Seattle and then spread over the past year arguably touched a chord in many people..."[1]

Did the current wave of antiglobalization protests begin in Seattle? No, the movement emerged first outside the United States—in Venezuela, South Korea, India, Germany and dozens of other countries. Even if we define the movement narrowly, as Greenspan has—i.e., as only being against the global trading system and not against the entirety of the capitalist world system—it is hardly of American origin. In fact, the Seattle protests themselves involved some thirteen hundred civic, social movement, and trade union organizations from over eighty countries. And furthermore, on N30, there were major demonstrations in 14 US cities; twenty thousand people marched in Paris, eight thousand in Manila, three thousand in Seoul and thousands more around the world. In Mexico City a few days later, ninety-eight people were arrested and tortured for demanding the release of arrested Seattle demonstrators. Yet U.S. activists don't include those people as part of the "Seattle" action. The Mexicans who demonstrated in solidarity with the arrested protesters in Seattle acted because they felt it was the best thing to do. For us not to recognize their actions as part of our movement is to fly in the face of the solidarity they demonstrated. Our blindness is conditioned by media silence and a host of other conditions. We need to make more of an effort to overcome the systematic fragmentation of our movement.

The anti-WTO protests in Seattle have had an immense impact on the antiglobalization movement around the world. Yet in our celebration of this action, several problems arise. I notice blindness to pre-Seattle forerunners; a failure to pose international solidarity as an alternative to globalization; underestimation of the efficacy of tactical diversity.

As a symbol for the hundreds of thousands of people around the world who have demonstrated against the neo-liberal agenda of the institutions of global capital, Seattle is vitally significant. But disregarding antiglobalization movements in other countries, particularly those at the periphery of the world system, reproduces the biases and distortions of the very system being opposed. Such disregard slyly reinforces one of the world system's central ideas: the life of a human being in the United States or Europe is worth more than the life of a Third World person. For the IMF, World Bank and giant multinational corporations, an American life is far more valuable than the life of a Venezuelan or a Vietnamese—hence in their view the protests against globalization began in Seattle. But progressive and radical history must be qualitatively different than the history of the neoliberalist champions and their corporate masters. Our history must reflect the notion that all human life is of equal value.

The best known of Seattle's precursors is the Zapatista uprising in Chiapas, Mexico. The preponderant influence of the Zapatistas on the activists in Seattle was evident in the many protesters who carried their flag, their posters, and wore masks. The Zapatistas have been key organizers of the People's Global Action Against "Free" Trade, an umbrella for movements on five continents including the Landless Peasants' Movement of Brazil and India's Karnataka State Farmer's Movement. Besides these organizations, antiglobalization uprisings in dozens of Third World countries predated the Seattle confrontation. Of these many popular responses to conditions of economic hardship dictated by global institutions, the Venezuelan uprising in 1989 was the most significant. In a few days beginning on February 27, thousands of people rose up against the imposition of IMF-ordered austerity measures. The police and army shot to death more than three hundred people and wounded thousands of others. More than two thousand people were arrested. Because of its importance, let me take a closer look.

Venezuela

Consider the following: the structural imperatives of the existing world system have resulted in poor Latin American countries paying billions of dollars in interest *each year* to rich countries' banks. Total indebtedness of the region was approximately 420 billion dollars in 1989. Of all the countries of Latin America, Venezuela had long enjoyed one of the highest standards of living, no doubt because of the exploitation of its vast oil reserves. When president Carlos Andres Perez, a longtime social democrat, came peacefully to power, few suspected he would preside over a bloody imposition of IMF-dictated austerity measures. Yet in order for the IMF to grant his government the power to avoid an economic meltdown (i.e., $1.5 billion in badly needed credit so he could lift the ceilings on interest rates and let the currency float), they required him to raise prices for food, gasoline and bus fares. On February 16, the new austerity program was announced and on February 27, it was to take effect. That day, however, rather than peacefully submitting to hardship and misery, poor people in the shantytowns that ring Caracas's modern center rose up to smash the imposition of the

The Battle of Seattle

IMF's orders.

All at once, everywhere there was resistance. In the eastern shantytown of Petare, seventeen people were killed in pitched battles with the forces of order. Shotguns and even machine guns were used by the government against rocks and an occasional sniper—not much of a match, but a heavily contested one. Snipers in the El Valle neighborhood south of Caracas killed an army major; in response, at least twenty people were shot and killed. In sixteen other Venezuelan cities, including Maracaibo, San Cristobal, Valencia, Puerto LaCruz, Barquisimeto, Carora, Merida, Puerto Ordaz, and Guarenas, the poor rose up. For days they refused to submit. On March 3, troops were still looking for snipers. On the 9th, the *New York Times* reported up to 375 deaths; the Venezuelan media counted more than 600 throughout the country. Even after calm had apparently been restored, the insurgency reappeared in other forms. In April thousands of high school and university students protested against the withdrawal of government subsidies. In May, the first national strike in thirty-one years erupted. In the wake of the uprising, Venezuelans reconfigured their country's political system and swept Hugo Chavez into power.

The rulers of the world economy can hardly plead ignorance of the Venezuela events. Greenspan had already begun his tenure in office and world financial institutions were directly involved. Indeed, within days of the fighting, on March 9, the US government began to shift its policy, easing repayment provisions on the debt. In concert with the IMF, World Bank and a cluster of other governments and global institutions, the U.S. loaned more than the amount Venezuela needed (some $2 billion in emergency loans).

Although protests in the periphery are mounted against specific grievances in their own national territory, their character is as clearly against capitalist globalization as much as the protests in Seattle. They arise against the global system and their institutional masters—economic dictators who make slaves of entire countries and regions. The free market model imposed on Venezuela in the '80s and '90s left eighty percent of the population living in slums and on the threshold of utter poverty. They turned to Chavez to pull them out of their collective misery. In 1998, his newly formed party won fifty-six percent of the vote.

Why is this international precursor of Seattle unknown to North Americans? In the US, we pride ourselves on our free press. How could such an uprising occur and leader after leader profess to know nothing about it? Similarly, food riots in the Dominican Republic in 1985, Brazil in 1986 and dozens of countries have been wiped from memory. What of the seventy-five thousand people who marched in Berlin in 1988 when the World Bank and International Monetary Fund held their meetings? Protesters there were very powerfully influenced by the outbreak of earlier riots in the Third World, and their massive and militant presence compelled thousands of bankers and monetary experts to depart Berlin a day earlier than planned.

The attempt to depict the antiglobalization movement as a US phenomenon is the other side of the more general invisibility of the rest of the world for many Americans. Setting Seattle as the starting point of a new global upsurge is part of the system's counteroffensive. Instead of seeking simply to repress and condemn the movement, leaders of the world's major financial institutions are seeking to turn the protests into socially acceptable and even systemically beneficial avenues of action. (This apparent openness from the institutions of power does however present the opportunity for the development of inside-outside strategies.)

Paying attention to the protests of young people in the capitalist metropolis while rendering invisible activists in other countries is one way of maintaining the superiority of the wealthy countries of the world. Maintaining the hegemony of the USA is also critical to the maintenance of the existing order. For a long time now, defining social movements along national lines is one way in which historians and world leaders have stripped activists of their radical antisystemic politics. Our alternative to the top-down globalization of huge multinational corporations and their militarized nation-states is an internationalism founded upon autonomous nuclei of popular participation. Protests against the meetings of the leaders of globalization concretely enunciate our critique of their policies. Clarifying the internationalism of autonomously organized revolts helps develop the self-conscious formulation of a planetary alternative to globalization.

Eros and Internationalism

As is becoming increasingly clear, militant antisystemic actions build upon one another, a phenomenon I have elsewhere described as the eros effect.[2] Through the power of exemplary peoples' actions leading to involvement by others, small groups are able to detonate social explosions in which millions of ordinary people unexpectedly take the direction of society into their own hands and make long overdue changes. Ordinary people acting together can force a president of a country, even a brutal and long entrenched dictator, out of office. They can neutralize the armed forces. Last year, for example, a few days after the Serbian people overthrew Slobodan Milosevic, the people of the Ivory Coast overthrew their dictator, Robert Guei, when he attempted to stop the counting of votes in an election he was losing. Thousands of Ivorians took to the streets, and although Guei's presidential guard fired on them and killed hundreds of people, the crowd refused to disperse. Instead they continued marching on the presidential palace. Guei fled and "people power" (a term that originated in the Philippines in 1986 after the overthrow of Marcos by thousands of people who refused to leave the streets) won another victory. the *New York Times* quoted one student, Alfred Tohouri, saying: "The mistake Guei made was to let us watch scenes from Belgrade."[3]

Because of the power of the media and the global village character of the world today, the eros effect has become increasingly important. Social movements are less and less confined to one city, region or nation; they do not exist in isolation in distant corners of the globe; actions are often synchronically related. Social movements in one country are affected sometimes more by events and actions outside their own national context than they are by domestic dynamics. The international embeddedness of N30 is evident enough in the autonomously organized global wave of resistance events in the year after it. The protests in Seattle helped define and motivate the antiglobalization movement. Inspired by N30, protests erupted in the streets of Bangkok in February 2000, Washington, D.C. in April, and subsequently in Melbourne, Prague and Davos. In the Czech Republic, one of the most popular chants was "Prague, Seattle, Continue the Battle!" (Although it is not as well known, activists in Prague were as successful as their Seattle predecessors in compelling leaders of the world's financial architecture to change their meeting plans.)

We speak so often of internationalism. But then why do we define antiglobalization struggles nationalistically? Greenspan, Wohlfenson, the Trilateral Commission, and the World Bank have characterized the upsurge against globalization as parochial, as nationalistic, while portraying themselves as progressive and global. Are progressives against globalization because we are nationalists? In Venezuela today, the answer might be yes. The Chavez government embodies the antiglobalization impulse but Chavez has to relate to his national context since he is president of a country. His activism has been global—he organized OPEC to raise world oil prices and thereby bring a greater share of the world's economic output to the oil producing countries. Ominously, US intervention in Colombia and the regionalization of that war loom on the horizon of globalization's future for Venezuela.

Should progressives in the US also think and act nationalistically? Do we share anything with the Pat Buchanans and other US nationalists who oppose globalization? No. In opposition to the globalization of corporate control by the IMF, World Bank, WTO and their governments, our internationalism calls for grassroots, autonomous political participation and mutually agreed connections between people, not connections dictated by the market or political demands of those with power and money. The progressive antiglobalization movement is not against international ties, it wants to see ties that are fair and decent. It is against ties that force people off land, against the kinds of global economic relations that make it possible for the corporations to profit greatly from degrading the world. Billions people must struggle mightily and suffer daily simply to obtain the bare necessities of life.

The *Intelligence Report,* a publication of Morris Dees' Southern Poverty Law Center, wrote that the neo-Nazis and WTO protestors in Seattle are cut from the same cloth.[4] Because the Seattle protests focused only on global institutions and not on the US government's role in all of this, the movement is open to that charge. So putting forth internationalism as our politics—not just opposition to globalization—is critical to differentiating us from the antiglobalization forces that are pro-US.

South Korea, the Power of Autonomy and the Dialectic of Social Movements

Diversity of tactics, organizations and beliefs is one of the great strengths of autonomous social movements. Using a creative variety of tactics—including militant street demonstrations—as a part of our arsenal, we can change societies in ways that parliamentary efforts or more established movements cannot. In South Korea, autonomous movements overthrew a repressive military dictatorship and established democracy. Autonomous trade unions not tied to the chaebols—huge corporate concentrations such as Hyundai and Daewoo—were also won, and both governments of Korea were pushed toward reunification.

The Kwangju uprising of 1980—an upheaval in which as many as two thousand people were killed—was the pivot around which these movements ascended. After the brutal imposition of martial law by thousands of elite paratroopers and police, the people of Kwangju drove the military out of the city and held it for almost a week. Although many people were massacred when the Army retook the city, Kwangju has become a symbol motivating action in many other countries.[5]

South Korean social movements can teach us significant lessons. In the past few years, the IMF has intoned that South Korea will have lower economic growth if it won't break up the chaebols. Ironically, South Korean President and Nobel Peace Prize winner Kim Dae Jung, once held on death row by the military dictatorship for his alleged role in the Kwangju uprising, is now leading the neo-liberalist penetration of the Korean economy. Winning democracy and getting Kim Dae Jung elected were amazing feats that we can attribute to the power of millions of ordinary people who took to the streets. Yet today with some kind of democratic structure in place and autonomous trade unions struggling for more rights for working people, the Kim government uses repression against its former allies, breaking up workers' protests with helicopters and police violence. When Kim Dae Jung, hero of the last phase of popular struggles in South Korea, turns into his opposite, history's dialectical character is revealed. No doubt, his opening to North Korea and defusing of the half-century state of war on the Korean peninsula are historic accomplishments; his government's more recent repression of workers' demonstrations speak to history's rapid pace and inner irony.

While in Korea force has been widely used for decades to maintain the status quo, in the US media manipulation and consumerism have largely been sufficient to assure corporate rule. Nonetheless, as in Korea, today's activists are often tomorrow's authorities. Both the mayor and police chief of Seattle were Sixties people. While the mayor prides himself on having been an antiwar activist during the Vietnam war, police chief Norm Stamper was a product of San Diego State University's humanistic police training program. The program distilled the Sixties model of community policing, which came about in response to demands for community control of the police. Such co-optation of the Sixties— i.e., its use to provide new ideas and leaders for the system—is very common in Europe. The Greens in Germany are but one example of leadership inside governments who are used to legitimize a new military role for Germany as well as to repress militant movements (because that's the role they are compelled legally to play as part of the government).

The aura of the Sixties is being used against the antiglobalization movement in another way. An exaggerated Sixties diminishes contemporary movements. Movements today are written off as shadows, imitations or lesser siblings. Seattle is recognized as highly significant, but movements between the Sixties and the present are forgotten. Glorification of decades (or of great events and individuals) diminishes the importance of continuity and everyday activism in the life of social movements. As a social construction, the myth of the Sixties functions thereby to discourage people from having authentic movement experiences now, in the present.

Finally, Sixties activists themselves, speaking as representatives of those halcyon days of yesteryear, intervene today as critics of militant popular struggles. Using their legitimacy as Sixties activists, they interject the authority of the Sixties into the current movement. Sixties veterans were valuable and significant parts of the Central American anti-intervention movement in the '80s.

Thirty years ago, we paid dearly for the absence of sufficient elders. However, when the legitimacy of the past is used as a weapon to argue for a particular position rather than to inform a discussion, the effect can be deleterious, often undermining creative exploration and fresh thinking. I think here of the some of the post-Seattle debates around violence. (Some of which are reprinted in this book).

For me, Seattle was a chance to connect with people from different generations of activists. I was invited to come and talk during the protests by someone I had never met, whom I think of today as a friend. Ironically, my scheduled speech at Left Bank Books the night of N30 had to be cancelled because of the declaration of martial law. Thanks to the "No Protest Zone," we had the space to go off and get acquainted, and as a result we decided to work together on this book.

Ho Chi Minh City
January 31, 2001

* This is a revised version of a talk given at Evergreen State College in Olympia, Washington on November 17, 2000. Thanks to Daniel Burton Rose, Billy Nessen and Eddie Yuen for their comments.

1. The New York Times, November 15, 2000, p. C2.

2. I first developed this concept in relation to an understanding of the global imagination of 1968. See The Imagination of the New Left: A Global Analysis of 1968 (South End Press, 1987).

3. The New York Times, October 26, 2000, p. 14.

4. "Morris Dees' New Scam," Counterpunch, March 16-31, 2000, p.2.

5. For an analysis of this vitally important event, news of which has largely failed to enter the consciousness of most Americans (activists included), the best source is Kwangju Diary: Beyond Death, Beyond the Darkness of the Age by Lee Jae-eui (UCLA Asian-Pacific Monograph Series, 1999). Also see my article "Remembering the Kwangju Uprising," in Socialism and Democracy, Spring-Summer 2000 (Vol. 14 No. 1).

Emily Abendroth

Zapatismo and the Politics of Solidarity

Manuel Callahan
abridged

This revolution will not end in a new class, faction of a class, or group in power. It will end in a free and democratic space for political struggle.
—EZLN, Second Declaration from the Lacandon Jungle

Not long after the Ejército Zapatista de Liberación Nacional or Zapatista National Liberation Army burst onto the world stage on January 1, 1994, in the southern Mexican state of Chiapas, Octavio Paz concluded that "the conflict has been the cause of little spilt blood but much flowing ink."[1] Some less charitable onlookers dismissed the Zapatistas as either "armed reformists" or hopeless nationalists.[2] Even intellectuals sympathetic with "the wind from below" were quick to simply celebrate the Zapatistas as a "postmodern rebellion" carried out by a small, poorly armed guerrilla army whose successes have been mostly confined to the "war of words."[3] Despite the brutality of a six-year, low intensity war and the Zapatistas' impact on an increasingly militant movement of global resistance to neoliberalism, analysts insist on limiting the impact of the Zapatistas to their clever and provocative interventions in the alternative press and their sophisticated negotiation of the "electronic fabric of struggle," executed by the highly literary, theoretical, and witty screeds of Subcomandante Marcos, one of the EZLN's spokespersons.[4]

Immediately following the "Battle in Seattle" Jorge Castañeda abandoned his early dismissal of the Zapatistas' historical significance when he remarked that "part of the Zapatista rebellion's legacy lives on, if only through its promise, in recent events in Seattle: the demonstrations and riots during the World Trade Organization meeting."[5] A link between the Zapatistas and the global mobilization against the WTO actually had been suggested much earlier when one pundit worried that "there are even whispers among the free-trade foes that the

Emily Abendroth

Zapatistas, southern Mexico's peasant-based rebel group, are coming by cara-van."[6] Although many of the organizations that were active in planning the direct actions, protests, and gatherings in Seattle, such as People's Global Action, Direct Action Network, Independent Media Center, Black Bloc, and Global Exchange, to name just a few, had solidarity links to the Zapatistas, the initial fears that the Zapatista rebels would leave their jungle and mountain strong-holds to storm Seattle proved excessive.[7] Nevertheless, Zapatistas and Zapatismo animated the street battles and solidarity during the "the birth of a global citi-zen's movement for a global democratic economy."[8] Amparo Reyes, a single moth-er who works at a *maquiladora* over seventy hours a week for less than a dollar per hour, took her place among other comrades at the AFL-CIO rally shouting, "Long live the Zapatistas!"[9] The red *paliacates* or bandannas that have come to be associated with the Zapatista rebels from the Lacandon jungle and highlands of Chiapas were ubiquitous in the streets of Seattle and the confrontations with police. In Seattle paliacates covered the faces of anarchists, autonomists, and environmentalists linked with a variety of affinity groups, as well as other activists long associated with the conflict in Chiapas who claim Zapatismo as a politics and Zapatista as an identity.

The Zapatistas did not coordinate the global days of action and protests that disrupted the ministerial conferences of the WTO and IMF in London, Seattle, Washington, D.C., Prague, and Davos, but they "activated millions of discontents, which quickly organized politically effective coalitions, with one sin-gle word: Enough!"[10] The awesome series of global actions, including Seattle, emerged, in part, as a consequence of a series of critical *encuentros* or encounters and *consultas* or plebescites with civil society that the Zapatistas convened as part of their strategy to defeat neoliberalism. Seattle was not just a "protest event" in solidarity with "third world" struggles, but a street battle at home. If, according to Vandana Shiva, "there was no mastermind" for an organized attack on the machinery of neoliberalism in Seattle, but rather "an invitation" to be a

Emily Abendroth

part of a global resistance, the Zapatistas were the first to write it.[11]

1. Octavio Paz, "The Media Spectacle Comes to Mexico," *New Perspectives Quarterly* 11:2 (Spring 1994): 59.

2. Immediately following the Zapatista's rebellion on January 1, 1994, Jorge G. Castañeda dismissed them as "armed reformists." See Jorge G. Castañeda, "The Chiapas Uprising," *Los Angeles Times* (January 3, 1994).

3. Roger Burbach, "Roots of the Postmodern Rebellion in Chiapas" *New Left Review* 205 (May/June 1994): 113-124. For the exchange that followed between Burbach and Daniel Nugent regarding the designation postmodern, see Daniel Nugent, "Northern Intellectuals and the EZLN" *Monthly Review* 47:3 (July/August 1995): 124-138; Roger Burbach, "For a Zapatista Style Postmodernist Perspective" *Monthly Review* 47:10 (March 1996): 34-41; Ana Carrigan, "Chiapas, The First Postmodern Revolution," in Juana Ponce de León, ed. *Our Word is Our Weapon: Selected Writings of Subcomandante Marcos* (New York: Seven Stories Press, 2000): 417-443.

4. Harry Cleaver has written consistently and cogently about the Zapatistas' use of the internet and the critical role of electronic communications networks in circulating struggle. See, for example, Harry Cleaver, "The Zapatistas and the Electronic Fabric of Struggle," in John Holloway and Eloína Peláez, eds. *Zapatista! Reinventing Revolution in Mexico* (London: Pluto Press, 1998): 81-103. For an alternative analysis of the Zapatista uprising that defines the

Manuel Callahan

success of mobilizations that make use of electronic networks as "social netwar," see David Ronfeldt and John Arquilla, *The Zapatista Social Netwar in Mexico* (Santa Monica: Rand Arroyo Center, 1998).

5. Jorge Castañeda, "Seattle's WTO Legacy Has Links to Chiapas," *Seattle Post-Intelligencer* (January 18, 2000).

6. Helene Cooper, "Seattle—Mike Dolan is Mobilizing Against Globalizing," *Wall Street Journal* (July 16, 1999).

Migrants

Associazione Ya Basta!
Excerpted from The Age of Clandestinity

1. The fourth world war has begun This conflict is the cause of the new waves of migration. They are migrations typical of the new, post-Fordist age. The migrants, whether they are greeted as political or environmental refugees or, as happens with increasing frequency, as prisoners and/or unwelcome aliens, are the victims of what Marcos has described as the fourth world war, that of neoliberalism against humanity. From 1975–1995 the number of political refugees has risen from approximately 2 to 23–36 million. This is a figure that is leading to a tightening of European laws on the right of asylum: over the last four years the number of requests for asylum has dropped considerably. Yet, as the restrictions regarding requests for asylum become tighter the number of migrants continues to grow massively: today, they're estimated at about 120 million. In most cases these migrants are attempting to move from the south of the world to the north. They are fleeing poverty and wars brought to them by the "developed" world. They are fleeing impoverishment caused by the murderous and genocidal policies of the World Bank and the International Monetary Fund which, largely by means of their Structural Changes, have starved the poorer people. In addition, all the free trade treaties, which have extended to agriculture over the past few years, are destroying local markets, causing more and more poverty, abandonment of the land and a desperate flight to the cities in search of a salary, which is hard to come by. The city, but even more the North, is a mirage—the only possibility for avoiding the poverty caused by the neoliberist empire. The flight from Mexico towards the States is just one example. All migrants are political refugees from the fourth world war and, as such, they should be welcomed.

The right to hospitality must be respected!
No distinction between migrants and refugees, goodies and baddies!

A welcome for all the victims of the IVth world war!

2. Neoliberism shows its true repressive face There are no laws to welcome these migrants, we are told. New ones must be invented, argue the left-wing politicians. But the truth lies elsewhere: at the end of the millenium neoliberism is showing its true colours: human rights are only the rights of "legal" citizens and can be acquired only by bloodshed or inheritance. Those who have the wrong skin colour do not have the same rights. Freedom of movement and domicile are permitted to capital and to goods, but not to all human beings. Our answer to inherited blood rights is the right to the soil. Our answer to the free movement of goods and capital is the free movement of people. The new laws legitimizing expulsion camps throughout the Europe of Schengen and the funds for creating centres around the edges of the Schengen borders, bought and sold by means of bilateral agreements, show a serious trend towards a police state— people are imprisoned without having committed any crime. People are imprisoned because they were born elsewhere and they want to come to the north. They end up in prison without even seeing a judge or a lawyer. Detention by the authorities is, in fact, a violation of Article III of the Italian constitution: detention and the resulting arbitrary expulsion amount to deportation. These are the universal human rights that the West has been imposing on the world for five hundred years now and which it now barbarically applies in its own home territory, against the very principles of its constitutions.

Stop expulsions! Immediate closure of the prison camps! Real equality of rights without racist discrimination! Revoke racist laws! Documents for everyone! A passport for all European nomads, the former victims of the Nazis! No quotas and no limits on migration!

3. The symbol of the fourth world war is one enormous wall
Just as the symbol of the third world war was the Berlin wall, the symbol of this one is the enormous wall that starts at the Rio Grande and runs through to Turkey, passing Gibraltar and then north, leaving out Eastern Europe; it divides Australia and Japan from the rest of East Asia. This wall is an insult to humanity. Figures showing the victims along the American border come to over 1,300 from 1993 to 1998; in 1998 alone, the police shot at 89 people. The estimated number of victims along the borders of Schengen is between 2,000 and 3,000 and there is documentary proof of 1,365 between 1993 and 1998: drowned in the sea or in rivers, blown up by mines, their craft sunk by navies, shot by the police, hung on the other side of the borders in the bilateral prisons...In only five years, the American walls and those of Schengen have each caused five to ten times the number of deaths caused by the Berlin wall in thirty years. The Schengen police force means having a central records office, files on all new arrivals, an extension of the already inhuman criminal treatment to all migrant travellers, including children. The numbers of victims on entry are swollen by the victims of expulsion; these are crimes by the state, premeditated and using a variety of tactics

(death by suffocation with a pillow or a blindfold, for example, or by anaesthetic, with the new Fascist doctors and nurses as accomplices). In the USA the Pentagon has provided bullet-proof vehicles, infrared equipment, and men, and the Border Patrol is supplemented by US Army troops. The Italian, Spanish and German states make the same sort of use of their armies.

Against borders, action along the borders!
Trials for State murders and those responsible for them!

4. A war waged by criminal and state powers The criminalisation of foreigners adds to the power of organised crime. The strategy of criminalising foreign women and men—a strategy which the European states are following by means of their mass media and their unions—is extremely dangerous. Hospitality cannot be associated with safety, neither can every outsider be regarded as a potential criminal. The Europe of Schengen is extending police control along the borders, bringing in armies and dispatching the navy to threaten and sink approaching ships; police control and police powers then spread from the borders inland, throughout the territory. All this is done by creating laws that turn our potential guests into clandestine immigrants, treating them like criminals. These are the laws of the Italian state that make every outsider clandestine: to have a stay permit you must have a job and to get a job you must have a stay permit! The European police state is attempting to involve society in its general policing plan: more and more people are forced to ask people with different coloured skins for their documents, to demonstrate a legal status arbitrarily imposed by the state: at work, in hospitals, in public offices, in taxis. . . (The German state has punished taxi drivers for having transported *sans papiers*). For the state it is a crime to come from the south or east of the world. And all this is happening while the Italian mafia groups share out the business of human transport from Albania and the government refuses to provide the means for taking control of immigration away from the mafia—control that makes a profit from everything and everybody. This is how journeys to the borders, arrival and accommodation in Europe are managed by criminal organisations and the migrants become goods, in all senses.

Stop the mafia boats in the Otranto channel! No human being is illegal! We are all clandestine!

5. A race war The only race that exists is the human race. The only important colour is the colour of your eyes. White people—said Fanon—invented the race of the nonwhites. European policies against immigration are promoted by the neoliberalist left wing, the heirs of European social democracy, which preached colonialism to give jobs to the working classes and labourers of Europe and to guide the world towards Progress. Race itself is economic dominion. The damned of the earth are the victims of this neoliberalist plan. The fourth world war is the last war of Capital but it is also a racist war. It is based on the lie that it is the West which must civilize the rest of the world. In actual fact, it is the

Associazione Ya Basta!

foreign workers who are most at risk of barbaric treatment. The criminalisation of foreign workers aims to limit their organisational potential against the concentration of capital. In any case, Capital itself derives from the natural resources and labor extracted from the mines, fields, and factories of the global south. Today the arrival of a new labour force is convenient for industrialists because it is of use in the social and industrial organisation of work in the post-Fordist era. This "flexible" labor force is exploited as temporary workers in important economic sectors and to fill servile positions such as house cleaning and sexual services. We mean to counter the race war, a safety valve for class conflict, by means of social conflict which attacks profits and their unjust distribution, redistributing riches and creating a sense of community. Our answer to the war amongst the poor is the fight for dignity and against the impoverishment of the world.

Let's unite the struggles of immigrants and those of temporary workers!
Universal citizen's income (housing, food, transport, income)!

6. A financial war Before the first world war, passports did not exist. Between the first and the second world war, America started to control immigration. Again, during the third world war, there were greater obstacles to the movement of capital as opposed to those limiting the movement of people, than there are today. Neoliberalism preaches free markets but closes and controls the labour market by means of its armies.

The relationship between human beings and goods has been turned upside down: goods move freely, as do electronic dollars, but people are stopped! The markets are free but the labour market is controlled by the armies of all the rich nations: neoliberalism does not allow free trade on the labour market—it must have control! Nonsense has been made into common-sense by means of force and propaganda by the mass media. The developed countries go on announcing recipes for development, grants and little discounts on debts but refuse to open their borders; moreover they explode financial bubbles every year in a different country. And yet multiethnic society is destined to take over. This is a fact. Arms are useless against armed reason.

For the multiethnic communities of the third millennium! Equal rights!
Freedom of movement and domicile!

7. A TV war The control of people by means of armies and the persuasion of society to accept this Fascist point of view, where every white citizen has to keep an eye on the nonwhites, depends on the ability of the owners of the mass media to spread lies. These terrorists spread fear, individualism and discouragement amongst people—by means of xenophobic campaigns that speak of the arrival of immigrants in terms of "never-ending hordes," "invasions," "landings," and other expressions taken from the vocabulary of warfare. They speak of public order but they create public fear. Once identified with criminals, the outsiders are finally shut away and deported to the prison camps, where there is no trace of the legal guarantees foreseen by the law but confined to paper; no trace of any right to communicate or to see a lawyer. Television isolates, adumbrates communication and steals time from action and rebellion, giving the illusion of knowledge. We Italians, fifty percent of whom are internal migrants, are forgetting our own history, the insults and the suffering experienced in northern Italy (where signs used to read: "We do not let rooms to southerners"), as in the other parts of the world. Television chat is repeated in the streets and provides the terrain on which right-wing opinions flourish: "There are no jobs, so why let foreigners in?" asks the television. The safeguarding of memory is a daily struggle of truth against lies, here at home, as in Chiapas. The death squads are border armies supported by television. But we shall not lose our memories as migrants—at least one of our relatives has been one: our answer to the fear spread by the mass media is the truth of direct contact and the reasonableness of people fighting to destroy profit and the exploitation of the world.

Citizens' consultations in every district!
Universal citizens' income! Universal general strike by people of all colours!

Kevin Harris

Resisting Global Capitalism in India

Jaggi Singh

The official Indian government delegation to the Seattle WTO Ministerial took a hard-line stance, at least publicly, against linking trade to labour and environmental standards. It was a position supported by all the major parliamentary factions, including the so-called left parties. Indeed, the government's view not only echoes that of other governments in the "Third World," but is critically supported by the majority of progressive opponents of globalization in India and the rest of South Asia.

It's not that activists here are "soft" or relativistic about labour standards, the environment or human rights; nor are they naïve about whom the Indian government really represents. Rather, they see Western governments' apparent discovery of universal human values and standards as a ploy to ensure a competitive advantage for their own multinational companies. This view is widespread in countries like India, with its own historical context of colonialism, and contemporary context of neocolonialism (with which the "holy trinity" of the WTO, International Monetary Fund and World Bank are considered synonymous).

According to Sanjay Mangala Gopal, the co-coordinator of the National Alliance of People's Movements, which represents some 125 grassroots organizations: "We will define our own way of development and we are capable of doing it. Who are you to teach us about child labour or anything else?"

Gopal insists that voices from the South—where the majority of the world's marginalized peoples live and survive—should provide the leadership to the international resistance to globalization (by definition, this includes those pockets of the Third World in the North, such as many indigenous and minority communities in North America). The analysis emanating from diverse sources in the Third World—not just the communists—revolves around the "Three Aunties."

They're not talking about a kindly trio of female relatives who pamper their nephews and nieces, but an analysis of the WTO and related institutions that is "anti-imperialist," "anti-colonial" and "anti-capitalist," phrases which are seemingly alien to most mainstream antiglobalization movements in the North. As Gopal puts it, "If you want real change, you have to abolish the capitalistic mode of development."

In the forceful words of R. Geetha, a union and women's rights activist based in Madras, "Who are they [the West] to impose conditions on Third World countries? People are starving here! Why the hell should they tell us what kind of economy we should have?"

Meanwhile, Medha Patkar, a leading organizer of the Narmada Bachao Andolan, a more-than-decade long mass movement against destructive development and displacement in the Narmada River Valley of India, is not shy in saying: "The ultimate goal is to say no to the WTO. We're against the whole capitalist system."

As for the clear emphasis by major Western labour, environmental and consumer organizations that the WTO needs to be reformed—the "fair trade" crowd—activists here respond with varying degrees of diplomacy. In the carefully chosen words of Patkar, "The context of developed and developing countries is different. Those who are for reforms [will] realize over a period of time that these institutions [WB, IMF and WTO] are beyond reform."

In Geetha's view, "I think the organized American working class is worried about American capital going to the Third World to exploit conditions there." She adds, "That's an indirect fight."

Meanwhile, one small independent Bombay monthly (which describes itself as "a monthly that challenges the ideas of the ruling classes") writes that "[t]he big labour unions and environmental groups" were those "whose demands almost mirrored that of the US government."

Geetha insists on having a "direct fight" against globalization, while Gopal feels that many opponents of globalization "are looking at this issue with one eye," by ignoring, or downplaying, the voices of the South.

While there is a strong basis of analytical unity by India's numerous activist groups and movements, their tactics in action are diverse, reflective of the complex—cliched but true—diversity of the subcontinent itself. The actions range from Gandhian-style nonviolence to more militant forms of direct action (including property destruction) to armed struggle in certain rural pockets of the country. To a large extent the tactics are complementary, but it would be too idealistic to assert they're not also at times at odds with each other. However, there is often a strong sense of solidarity expressed between movements. It's what Patkar describes as "different strategies, but same goals" which is to be preferred to "same strategies, but different goals" (after all, right-wing fanatics also employ nonviolence, property destruction or armed struggle as tactics).

One group directly connected to the international antiglobalization movement is the KRRS, the Karnataka State Farmer's Movement, representing thousands of peasant farmers in the southern state of Karnataka. In recent years, the KRRS has physically dismantled—with iron bars—a Cargill seed unit, trashed another office of the same multinational agribusiness, burned Monsanto's field trials of biotech cotton, and trashed a Kentucky Fried Chicken outlet in Bangalore.

The KRRS has also been a major component of the People's Global Action against "Free" Trade movement, which unites peoples' movements on five continents (including the Zapatistas of southern Mexico and the Landless Peasants' Movement [MST] of Brazil). The PGA's "hallmarks" are a clear rejection of the WTO and similar institutions and agreements, a confrontational attitude, a call to nonviolent disobedience, and decentralization and autonomy as organizing principles. The PGA also added a fifth hallmark at their recent meeting in Bangalore which "rejects all forms and systems of domination and discrimination including, but not limited to, patriarchy, racism and religious fundamentalism of all creeds."

According to the recent PGA bulletin, "The denunciation of 'free' trade without an analysis of patriarchy, racism and processes of homogenization is a basic element of the discourse of the right, and perfectly compatible with simplistic explanations of complex realities, and with the personification of the effects of capitalism (such as conspiracy theories, anti-Semitism, etc.) that inevitably lead to fascism, witch-hunting and oppressive chauvinist traditionalism." In the Indian context, the new hallmark serves to distinguish progressive internationalist opponents of globalization, like the KRRS, NAPM and NBA, from the Hindu Right who also employ much of the same rhetoric of the antiglobalization movement.

And so, on November 30, while a state of emergency was declared in Seattle, and various militarized police forces proceeded to brutalize thousands of anti-WTO demonstrators, the KRRS organized its own demonstration in Bangalore. Several thousand farmers, along with their allies, issued a "Quit India" notice to multinational food and biotech conglomerate, Monsanto.

In the spirited words of one speaker at the rally: "We don't want to grow and feed poisonous food by using the genetically modified seeds of Monsanto. It is our responsibility to protect our natural resources. I would like to tell the police to be prepared! We will attack Monsanto unless it quits India."

The KRRS action on N30 is just one example of the spate of recent antiglobalization oriented protests on the subcontinent (although mobilizations against the World Bank and IMF started in earnest in the mid-1980s). For example, also on N30, activists of the NBA organized a thousand-strong nonviolent procession in the Narmada Valley "protesting against the anti-human agreements and institutions that are pushing India and the rest of the world into the destructive process of capitalist globalisation."

One week earlier, three hundred *adivasis* (indigenous peoples) from the state of Madhya Pradesh stormed the World Bank offices in Delhi. They proceeded to block the building and cover it with posters, graffiti, cow shit and mud (yet again, more violence to property!). The protesters left a letter, which reads in part, "We fought against the British and we will fight against the new form of colonialism that you represent with all our might."

Other *adivasi* activists are also currently engaged in a six-month long procession (*padyatra*) from one end of Madhya Pradesh to the other in order to highlight the ever-hastening process of land displacement in the name of globalization.

Meanwhile, just two days ago, the nonviolent protesters of the NBA converged on the Maheshwar dam (one part of the Narmada dam system) and proceeded to illegally occupy the dam site. About four thousand took over the site, while fifteen hundred were eventually arrested by the police who responded by

Jaggi Singh

attacking some demonstrators.

The protests show no sign of ending, and these examples don't even account for other ongoing movements of indigenous persons, fisherfolk, farmers, labour activists, low caste and Dalit (former "untouchables") organizations, youth and individuals in all parts of India.

Roots of the Movement

Not Your Parents' Protest

Barbara Epstein
Dissent, *Spring 2000*

The unexpected size and militance of the recent mobilization against the World Trade Organization in Seattle, the police attack on overwhelmingly nonviolent demonstrators, the tear gas in the air, all invite comparisons with the movements of the sixties, especially the antiwar movement of the late sixties and early seventies. It is tempting for those of us old enough to remember that period to see in the Seattle mobilization, and what follows it, an opportunity to replay the movements of the sixties. In fact there are major differences between the two, and many of those differences are to the advantage of the new movement.

The most important difference is that movements of the sixties, especially the anti-war movement, were directed against the state; the Seattle mobilization was directed against the global corporations. In the sixties, the civil rights movement blamed the US government for the discrepancy between the rhetoric of democracy for all and the actual denial of the rights of citizens to blacks, especially in the South. The civil rights movement demanded that the state ensure equal rights. Many left activists of the sixties understood that the state was intertwined with the corporations; in 1966 Carl Oglesby, then President of the Students for a Democratic Society, described the system that the movement opposed as "corporate liberalism," and pointed out that liberals in power were pursuing policies designed to protect the interests of the corporations. Radical intellectuals traced corporate influences on government policy. But it was the liberals who held state power who were the focus of the movement's attack.

The enmity of sixties radicalism to the liberal state had some unfortunate side effects. Though at first Oglesby and others carefully distinguished between the liberal rhetoric used by the state to manipulate popular consent and the authentic liberal values of reformers, as the war in Vietnam expanded and anger at the government rose, these distinctions tended to slip away. Antiwar activists began to use "liberal" as a term of abuse and to measure their own radicalism in terms of how far they had moved from their own recently liberal politics. The movement's tendency to cast radicalism and liberalism as polar opposites made alliances between radicals and liberals difficult. But despite these problems, the movement's view of the liberal state as the enemy made sense. The war in Vietnam was being conducted by liberals in power who defended it in terms of liberal Cold War rhetoric. One of the contributions of the movements of the sixties was to expose the hollowness of Cold War liberalism.

The coalition that opposed the WTO in Seattle was held together by a common perception of the global corporations as the main threat to environmental standards, labor and human rights, and to democracy generally. There were differences among the various constituencies in Seattle over how far the critique of the corporations should go, and what solution should be proposed to growing corporate power. Radicals in the direct action movement and left-leaning environmental and human rights groups argued that the WTO should be abolished; more mainstream environmental and human rights organizations, and trade unionists, argued for reforming the WTO, demanding that its powers be restricted. The WTO has enormous power over the policies of not only its member nations but any nation that hopes to be admitted to the circuits of global trade. The question of what demands the movement should make on the WTO has important consequences. But in the debate between abolition and reform among the groups at Seattle, the WTO also stood as metaphor for the global

In the streets of Seattle people felt what it is like to be part of a movement.

corporations that it serves, and for a global capitalist system that the radicals want to dismantle and which others hope can be brought in line with democracy. In the sixties, especially as anger about the war intensified in the late sixties, differences between radicals and liberals tended to be hostile and divisive, with each side digging in its heels.

The differences in Seattle over what should be done with the WTO and, by implication, the global corporations were friendly and fluid. Many of the people whom I talked with, from labor, mainstream environmental movements, and the direct action movement, agreed that no one has the answer to the question of how the global economy should be reorganized, and discussion of these issues must continue. Kevin Danaher of Global Exchange, a left-leaning policy organization in San Francisco, argues that the movement must drive a wedge between the state and the corporations, and put pressure on the state to defend democracy against corporate power. This approach was exemplified in Seattle, where Clinton felt compelled to move from statements expressing vague support for the protesters to a statement to the *Seattle Post-Intelligencer* in which he called for a code of labor rights and sanctions against nations that violated them. Clinton's aides quickly denied that he meant what he had said, but his waffling added to the legitimacy, and no doubt the influence, of the protest.

The second major difference between the mobilization in Seattle and the movements of the sixties, especially the antiwar movement, is that the mobilization in Seattle involved a coalition between progressive groups, including young radicals, and labor, while labor was for the most part absent from the progressive movements of the sixties, and supported the war in Vietnam, creating the deepest rift between labor and its sometime progressive allies in US history.

There has not been a labor-left alliance in the US since the thirties, when Communists played a major role in organizing the C.I.O. and leftists, liberals and trade unionists joined forces in demanding greater rights for poor and working people, and together put sufficient pressure on the government to shift the New Deal to the left. The left/liberal/labor alliance of the thirties created a national political culture in which there was room to promote egalitarian values. The movements of the sixties had something of the same effect despite its rifts with labor and liberals, because its critique of the war, and of racism and sexism, struck responsive chords especially among youth, but also among many older people. But since the end of the war in Vietnam the divisions between progressive groups and labor, and for that matter among progressive groups, have weakened the left and allowed the right to dominate public discourse. The mobilization in Seattle holds out the hope, for the first time in decades, of a broad and potentially powerful coalition for a more egalitarian social order.

In Seattle, relations among trade unionists, environmentalists and direct actionists seem to have been governed by a spirit of respect and mutual support that I do not remember from the sixties, especially from the antiwar movement of the late sixties. The spirit of unity that pervaded the mobilization was partly a result of the brutal police attack on the nonviolent protesters blockading the Convention Center where the Ministerial was to take place. The direct action groups had announced their strategy of blockading the Convention Center and filling the jails with protesters. The police, apparently, decided to foil this attempt to attract press coverage by refraining from making arrests. Confronted with many more protesters than they had expected, the police appear to have panicked, and attacked the nonviolent protesters. By the time the labor march passed by the blockaded intersections around the Convention Center the air was full of tear gas and police were clubbing protesters and passers-by. Some people broke away from the labor march and joined the blockaders. The streets near the Convention Center became simultaneously battleground and liberated zone: the police could attack protesters in particular locations, but the protesters controlled the streets. Members of direct action groups, trade unionists, environmentalists, and people who belonged to none of these groups but had come to protest the WTO found themselves part of what was for the moment a united movement. Trade unionists joined the blockaders and were clubbed along with them. On Wednesday, when the National Guard was called in and arrests began, some trade unionists and mainstream environmentalists were arrested along with those from direct action groups. The blockaders showed sensitivity to their allies. Emma Neumann, a participant in the blockade, told me of a meeting of members of the direct action groups at which a press conference to be held by the trade unionists was announced. Someone pointed out that the trade unionists might not appreciate the presence of a group of scruffy radicals at their press conference. It was decided that the trade unionists would be consulted before a delegation was sent.

The exhilarating spirit of solidarity among the protesters in Seattle was not only a response to the police attack but also an expression of the ties built between labor and environmental groups over several years of joint opposition to free trade legislation. Trade unionists put on sea turtle costumes; the ILWU shut down the West Coast ports from San Diego to Vancouver in support of the protest. The mobilization also drew on a widespread anger at the WTO and the corporate power that it represents, attracting many more protesters than the sponsoring organizations had expected. In the streets of Seattle people felt what it is like to be part of a movement. Those who participated in the Seattle mobilization are not likely to forget that acting in coalition enhances collective power. The Seattle mobilization linked labor and environmental demands; it is unlikely that these will be set against each other again. The willingness of trade unionists to ally themselves with young radicals suggests that the days when the fear of association with radicals can be used to divide a movement may be over.

There is one difference between the Seattle mobilization and the movements of the sixties, especially the antiwar movement, that weighs against the prospects of a new mass movement. The war in Vietnam forced itself on the attention of the American people. Young people especially could not ignore it. The growth of corporate power has not yet created the sort of crisis that thrusts whole sectors of the population into collective action in the way that the war in Vietnam did. Over the last few decades the division between the rich and everyone else has widened and most people have found themselves working longer hours, in many cases at less secure jobs. But the large amounts of money that some people earn have led many to fasten their hopes on upward mobility and construct lives oriented around consumption. Many of those who took part in direct action in Seattle are part of a youth subculture that opposes corporate power, and capitalism generally, because it has created a society in which virtually everything has become a commodity. These young people want community, and they want meaningful lives in the context of an egalitarian society. There is no guarantee that these views will spread, but the fact that there is a youth culture that holds such values is one of the most encouraging lessons of the Seattle mobilization.

The Vietnam war brought together a range of progressive movements previously concerned with separate issues. Among others, it brought together northern white students and black activists, many of them veterans of the civil rights movement, around a shared opposition to the war. Today's progressive movements may not come together as easily. The Seattle mobilization represented the whiter wings of both the environmental and labor movements. The environmental justice movement is mostly made up of people of color, but the sector of the movement that has been concerned with trade issues in recent years is largely white. The labor unions that played the largest role in the mobilization, the Steelworkers, the Auto Workers, the Teamsters and the Longshoremen, are also largely white. These unions represent the industrial workers whose jobs are directly threatened by the efforts of corporations to transfer operations to nations of the South where labor is cheap and environmental regulation is weak. It is impressive that the memberships of these unions, often thought of as resistant to social change, have come to see the need to ally with workers in the South and with environmental and human rights movements at home. But the relative absence of people of color from the Seattle mobilization points to an important weakness of the emerging anticorporate movement.

If the Seattle mobilization was behind the movements of the sixties in respect to racial diversity, it was ahead of those movements in respect to the diversity of protesters by age. The movements of the sixties were almost exclusively movements of young people in their teens, twenties, or at most early thirties. The Seattle mobilization drew protesters from high school students through seniors, with the largest numbers in their teens through middle age. Each of the movements in the anti-WTO coalition included people of a range of ages, but the fact that most of the blockaders were young, and the larger numbers of middle aged people among the labor and mainstream environmental organizations, meant that the mobilization was not only a coalition of organizations but an alliance of generations. If an anticorporate movement emerges from Seattle it seems likely that young people will be at its forefront but that it will include people of all ages.

Scaling the Heights to Seattle

David Kubrin

The one thing we were denied in Seattle was a vision of what the downtown area must have looked like from above—intersection after intersection immobilized in a crazy-quilt pattern of different kinds of lockdowns, standing lines of arms-linked militants, giant inflatables, and other large structures that for one reason or another proved too difficult to move. The State owned the air space, having issued new regulations prior to November 30 reserving for itself the right to fly overhead and look down on us. No one from our media or theirs apparently thought to take an elevator to some central thirty-third floor to take a picture of the streets from above. Hence, no media images. So the glorious sight of a city under siege from the globalized forces of outrage during the Battle of Seattle was seen only by the spy satellites and various other agents of the State.

For a great many observers, of course, the obvious question was how all this had come to pass? What precedents, what processes, what essential pieces had to be in place to account for the fact that after boasting since at least 1970 that we were going to "stop business as usual," we actually did? How did we come to know what had to be done?

What follows is a prehistory of Seattle, looking at some of the principal themes and elements of the direct action and nonviolence that formed the core of the Seattle actions of November 30 and after. It reflects my experiences as an activist in the Bay Area for the past thirty years and what I was able to find out about campaigns and actions in other critical arenas over the past several decades. Given the brevity of my essay, I will necessarily focus almost exclusively on events and patterns in the United States.

Although 1960s activism was firmly rooted in both direct action and nonviolence, by the end of the decade a sharp fall-off of both could be seen. A recently developed movement dynamic of establishing an individual's or group's revolutionary credentials by continually raising the ante of militance was part of it, so too the widespread feeling that purposely courting incarceration, in the circumstances of large numbers of activists being setup, entrapped, or assassinated, was perhaps not wise. This was especially true for black activists, even though nonviolent direct action had been responsible not only for the first of the lunch counter sit-ins at the beginning of the decade, but by the middle had created, in the Mississippi Freedom Summer, the first substantial fissure in the critical edifice of black belt racism. In Northern cities, too, by the late '60s the Black Panther Party—and Malcolm X earlier—were disparaging the notion that one should love one's racist oppressor.

Not least, large numbers of New Left activists turned to many older models of Leninist organizing, which made the traditional arguments advanced to justify civil disobedience appear naive. A professional revolutionary certainly did not hope, as Southwestern Georgia Student Nonviolent Coordinating Committee field workers in 1963 had, to establish "a beloved community," nor did the Ghandhian notion of breaking the law as a form of *sàtyagraha*, or truthforce, make much sense to cadre who, in most instances, were convinced that they had to keep any revolutionary affiliations hidden. Establishing in COINTELPRO a systematic way of targeting—and hopefully eliminating—left activists, the government in the late '60s and early '70s had reacted to the movement's mounting militance with ever-increasing use of court injunctions, stretching out of sentences, and sustained efforts to dry up the cultural ponds in which the would-be US insurgent guerrilla freely swam.

In the face of government repression and the splintering of the left, many activists in the early '70s turned to project-based organizing reflecting the plethora of issues and oppositions the early black liberation and antiwar movements had inspired in their wake: women's liberation, Native American and Latino liberation, free health clinics and food co-ops/conspiracies, prison support collectives and printing coops, gay liberation and legal collectives, back-to-the-land communes and anti-rape projects. As the movement began to lay down the infrastructure of resistance, if not revolution, less energy seemed available for direct action or jail time.

Despite these many obstacles, centers had existed from the 1940s on from which a politic of civil disobedience and direct action radiated, especially among veterans of the World War II conscientious objector. camps and in parts of the movement based on forms of religion or spiritual beliefs. Through the American Friends Service Committee, Quakers maintained their tradition of radical pacifism, as, for example, in their sailing a small ship, the Golden Rule, into the Pacific nuclear test site in 1958. Catholic Workers similarly engaged in defiant actions to disrupt public air raid drills in New York City in the mid-'50s. Other groups doing radical direct action in the '50s included the Committee for Nonviolent Action, the Fellowship of Reconciliation (which for two years held vigils at Fort Detrick, where the US perfected chemical, biological, and radiation weapons and warfare), and the anarchist-inspired War Resisters' League.

Movement for a New Society, an organization with roots in Quaker activism, arose in the turmoil of the '60s and emphasized the central role of consensus decision-making and nonviolence in direct action. MNS was to play particularly significant roles in the early organizing efforts around nuclear power and weapons in the mid- and late '70s.

A strong tradition of direct action was evident among Native American and Latino activists in the late '60s. Early American Indian struggles around issues of sovereignty and land, such as the Long Walk, the occupation of Alcatraz in 1969, and support work for Big Mountain must have particularly alerted government officials to very deep strategic implications, for during the 1973 occupation of Wounded Knee, the federal government quickly demonstrated their eagerness to respond to such challenges with a military siege. Though not perhaps expressed in the language of consensus politics, there was a tendency in these struggles to pay close attention to how the issues were framed not just by the militants, but by elders or women in the community. In New Mexico, important land struggles and protests in relation to uranium mining involved establishing road blocks, among other tactics; here, too, self-defense against armed attacks was found necessary.

Reliance on direct actions, such as boycotts, vigils, and fasting as mobilizing techniques, and on the principles of nonviolence was instrumental in the successful organizing of migrant workers by the United Farm Workers in the late '60s and early '70s. From early on the struggle for justice and organizing among the farmworkers involved the larger community and frequently featured agitation by radical theater performances; it also built on a long tradition in that community of pilgrimages and processions. For both Native American and Latino struggles, protests often began with ceremonies or prayers.

In urban areas, housing struggles erupted in squats and occupations in the mid-'70s and early '80s. In San Francisco, many hundreds of activists from the Asian community and from numerous other organizations across the city mobilized on numerous occasions to show support for the elderly, mostly Filipino, tenants of the International Hotel when its owners threatened to raze it; they put in place a plan to establish a (symbolic) human barrier against the sheriff when the expected eviction actually occurred. Militant struggles around public housing in Boston resulted in the establishment of a Tent City.

Some of the actual political and ideological trends, and a great deal of the spirit that was so central in Seattle, were already manifesting themselves in the antinuclear campaigns that emerged in the mid and late '70s. A big push to bring on-line or begin actual construction of a wave of new nuclear power facilities across the country caused some of the scattered embers of long-standing local opposition to flare up. In 1976 in New Hampshire a handful of local activists, impressed by the occupation of a nuclear construction site in Germany by opponents and inspired by '60s civil rights direct actions, cut the fence surrounding the future site of the Seabrook nuclear facility, entering and climbing a construction crane. Moved by their civil disobedience, a couple of thousand protesters converged a year later for a Clamshell Alliance sponsored sit-in at the Seabrook site. Participants at Seabrook were organized by affinity groups and had received training in nonviolence before the sit-in. About fourteen hundred of them were arrested by the New Hampshire police.

As the Seabrook opposition rapidly grew, a serious conflict arose, some activists proposing to turn towards large legal rallies as a way of demonstrating the breadth of opposition to the facility, while others argued that abandoning direct action at that point would be a critical mistake. This latter group, which eventually would become the Coalition for Direct Action at Seabrook, demanded that civil disobedience continue as the focus of their opposition. They called for a massive civil disobedience for the fall of '79, and over six thousand people

arrived, prepared to assault the fences around the Seabrook site. Many beatings, gassings and macings, assaults with high pressure water hoses, along with attack dogs held at the ready by State Police, however, kept activists at a standoff.

In the face of such State repression, the CDAS was persuaded that complete autonomy of affinity groups could not always work. Coordinating committees and decision-making by an eighty percent (by 1980, this was down to seventy percent) "consensus" were introduced for actions. Even so, neither the CDAS nor the larger original Clamshell Alliance were able to sustain the high numbers and determination of the earlier actions. Some of those originally mobilized around Seabrook, on the other hand, broadened their aim, a number of them shifting to the related issue of nuclear weapons, now seen as bigger, more global dangers. They went on to organize direct actions at the Pentagon. Still other veterans of Seabrook organized mass civil disobedience on Wall Street, targeting banking, energy, and manufacturing firms, the real beneficiaries of nuclear power

Around the same time as the mobilizations at Seabrook, a parallel antinuclear movement was sprouting up in the Midwest. As if the nightmare visions of mushroom clouds in our skies evoked a metaphorical mushrooming of resistance, opposition sprang up in scattered locations, notably in the mountainous terrain around Denver. As in New Hampshire, some of the early opposition to the Rocky Flats nuclear facility, where plutonium triggers for US thermonuclear warheads were produced, was led by longtime nonviolent activists and veterans of the '60s protests against racism and the Indochinese War. Over several years, '60s activists and some Vietnam veterans organized local opposition to the facility. Early in 1978, a mass rally was scheduled at Rocky Flats, which was to end in a symbolic direct action and arrests. When authorities made no arrests, a spontaneous move to establish a long-term occupation of the railroad tracks leading to the plutonium facility drew wide support. It was only after a week of continuous presence that police began arresting the occupiers, but their places were taken by others. Support from the Denver area, at least initially, was strong. As at Seabrook, those intent on building a broad-based movement, particularly among the Rocky Flats workforce, were opposed to the occupation; this pitted the AFSC and Mobilization for Survival, which had both done some of the initial organizing against Rocky Flats, against the Rocky Flats Truth Force. Nonetheless, a continuous presence on the tracks, punctuated by periodic arrests and temporary removals by periods of particularly foul weather, continued for a number of years.

On the West Coast, several other nuclear sites became staging grounds for direct actions, sometimes with the groups sponsoring protests at one site emerging out of prior actions at another nuclear facility, as was the case with the Livermore Action Group, which mobilized activists against the lab where nuclear weapons are designed. Initially it was among those jailed after an action at Diablo Canyon Nuclear Power Facility that LAG began.

Though there were differences in the actions at Diablo Canyon (led by the Abalone Alliance), Vandenberg Air Force Base (Vandenberg Action Group), Livermore National Laboratory (LAG), and the Nevada Test Site (American Peace Test), the similarities were more striking. As at Seabrook and Rocky Flats, protests were organized around affinity groups, participants were required to take nonviolence training prior to the action, and action handbooks were issued describing the politics, history, logistics, legal matters, first aid, etc., of the upcoming action. A strong commitment to decision-making by consensus persisted, unlike at Seabrook, where it unraveled as activists were unable to resolve the serious political differences between advocates of moderate forms of protest and those insisting on continued civil disobedience. Though tensions over these differences continued, for the most part they were not as divisive as they had been at Seabrook.

In 1983, a blockade of the Livermore Lab by several thousand protesters on Summer Solstice ended with over a thousand activists under arrest. Prior to the action, activists had debated a strategy of "jail solidarity" as a way of demanding equal treatment of all those arrested. Thus, most of the one thousand arrestees refused for two weeks to go to their arraignments until the court finally agreed, with great reluctance, to sentences that were equal for all (first, second, or multiple offenders alike) and did not include probation.

Here, however, a characteristic dynamic emerged. In the face of this tremendous political victory, the Bay Area antinuclear movement was plagued by strategic confusion, unclear where its priority should now be, whether to plunge ahead or shift to a new route. By then, however, the Reagan Administration had pushed other matters to the fore. The heating up of the Cold War by the rhetorical and strategic posturing of President Reagan refocused much of the energy of activists against his counter-revolutionary policies in El Salvador, Nicaragua, Hondurus, and Grenada. The liberation theology that was such a potent weapon in the Latin American liberation movements inspired many US Christian activists to take very active roles in the solidarity actions in support of the Salvadoran and Nicaraguan uprisings and in the establishment of sanctuaries for those fighting deportation from the US back to homelands where their lives were in danger. Witness for Peace worked among Nicaraguan villages as a form of protection for them and to bear witness against US policies. The Pledge of Resistance in 1984 solicited public commitments to engage in civil disobedience should US troops invade Nicaragua. Even earlier, Catholic militants had begun "Plowshare" actions involving destruction of military weapons and lengthy periods of imprisonment, and Christian activists had been responsible for direct actions aimed at the nuclear submarines, missiles, or other forward weapons of nuclear war.

In the mid-'80s labor militants, students, and black activists engaged in a variety of direct actions, including the building of shanty towns on university campuses to call attention to their institutions' support of apartheid in their investment policies, so as to isolate and economically and politically cripple the South African apartheid regime. The same fight was taken up by communities that pressed public institutions to divest.

The war of aggression against Iraq by US and allied forces in the early '90s evoked a storm of opposition in the first phases of the Gulf War, including, in California, huge marches and rallies and many instances of activists blocking bridges and interstate thoroughfares. One Bay Area anarchist group blocked downtown streets on several occasions with funereal processions consisting of activists dragging "dead" automotive parts.

Certain strategic bridges also were erected. A critical gap was crossed when Greenpeace and others began emphasizing the vital import of environmental justice issues. Another was the opportunity that the fights against NAFTA, GATT, and MAI offered to establish vital connections between environmental groups, NGOs, and trade unionists.

Activists had begun experimenting with reshaping protests into forms of processions, incorporating pageant, dance, costumes, and types of theater, building on traditions begun in the '60s by Bread and Puppet Theater, El Theatro Campesino, and the San Francisco Mime Troupe. A San Francisco Three Mile Island Memorial March in 1980 ended with a tug-of-war between marchers representing Air, Water, Fire, and Earth elements, pulling apart a cooling tower nuclear float that had been the focus of an ongoing skit during the procession, depicting a nuclear facility undergoing a melt-down. A couple of years later an anarchist "Hall of Shame" tour of the San Francisco headquarters of the corporate benefactors of nuclear weapons and power, sent small roving groups from corporate site to corporate site during lunch hour for simultaneous teach-ins, where indictments, theater, or corporate histories were presented. Incantations, spells, and other forms of magical power raising were woven into many of these actions by the increasing numbers of self-identified pagan and witch activists, similarly at Diablo Canyon, Vandenberg, and Livermore and at the women's actions at the Pentagon in 1980 and '81 and at the Seneca Women's Peace Camp in 1983. Comparable approaches were used by activists as part of the 1984 protests at the Democratic Party national convention in San Francisco.

In the course of these varied actions, the movement was to change its scope and its vision, as if all the mushrooms and LSD consumed by many activists in the '60s and later were now having a delayed effect, leading militants to branch out, and eventually up, taking protest to new levels and domains and giving it wholly unpredictable shapes and textures. As early as the Diablo blockade, a Peace Navy was afloat, so that the blockade might truly encircle the site. As with the Sea Shepherds, Greenpeace, and others, the boats blockaded ports and sealanes to nuclear transport or, later, whaling expeditions.

It was, perhaps, especially in taking to the skies that the direct action movement was able to transcend former ideological constraints and overcome earlier limitations. Earth First!'s defense of ancient trees brought many activists up into the branches, and from that perspective it was a simple step to begin hanging the giant banners bearing slogans and images from the trees and bridges, skyscrapers, dams, or cranes, reclaiming the use of the "airways" accessible to those without capital. Greenpeace, Rainforest Action Network, and then the Ruckus Society perfected the tactics of a "Peace Airborne"—as in the US

Armed Forces, considered somewhat of an elite division. Greenpeace also experimented with variations of lockdown devices that could enable a few determined activists to immobilize strategic locations for hours at a time.

The build-up to the Gulf War also brought giant puppets into play on a more prominent scale, embodying phantasmagorical images of the oppressors and their puppets and depicting the multifaceted forces increasingly arrayed against them, thus able to project the many-sided opposition to global capital large against the sky and powerful in our imaginations. Building on traditions, techniques, and images from Bread and Puppets and from the Women's Actions at the Pentagon, the giant puppets presented allegorical motifs in outrageous imagery, and helped provide the flavor of a street festival, bringing out activists' senses of play and fantasy and turning the new mobilizations into spontaneous theaters of resistance. Prior to the 1996 Democratic Party convention in Chicago, a weekend workshop to train activists in puppet making and related aspects of street protests was given by Wise Fool Puppet Intervention and other organizers and led to the formation of the first of the Art and Revolution Convergences.

Had she been alive, Emma Goldman could easily have danced at these kinds of actions.

In the final analysis, however, we have capital itself to thank for our successes. Since the splintering of the left in the late '60s, legions of organizers have been relentlessly preaching that salvation was ours if only we could achieve unity. Though coalitions were assembled on numerous occasions, often the groups entered into agreements with others not much deeper than the willingness to share a common sound system and some of the flyers advertising the event on issue. Capital, however, was able to force us to overcome many previous hurdles.

Everywhere, "the market" trumpeted its victories—over communism, over history, and, with biotech, over life itself. In a word, capital overreached itself. Its triumphant claim to have now integrated every activity in the most remote villages into the overall global marketplace revealed a critical weakness: highly integrated structures are not only highly intrusive, they are also extremely vulnerable. Perturbations that might readily be absorbed in a more flexible structure can readily result in system-threatening crises in rigid ones, so that the collapse of the Thai economy can bring chaos to the markets of Brazil and Mexico and threaten havoc even in the economies of the rich, industrialized countries. The unprecedented extent of capital's present reach has stretched thin the fabric of mystification that in normal times has been used to hide the realities of capitalism—stretched it to the point of transparency. Globalization has revealed not only the global aspirations of capital, but its inexorable drive to transform all things, all processes, and all relationships into commodities. In so doing, it created for us the material conditions for our coming together in a spectacular orgy of global opposition.

My thanks to Jim Haber, Marian Daub, Bob Thawley, Steve Nadel, David Creighton, Starhawk, K. Ruby, Kelly Quirke, Mishwa Lee, and Iain Boal for many fruitful and provocative conversations.

David kubrin

Reclaiming the Streets, Then the World

Oakley

Germany's *Autonomen*

George Katsiaficas
excerpted from Z Magazine

Tens of thousands of militant demonstrators were on hand to greet the conventions of the International Monetary Fund and the World Bank in Berlin at the end of September 1988, compelling thousands of bankers to leave a day earlier than they had planned. When the conventions opened, more than 75,000 protestors were on hand. Although the 12,000 police and 4,000 private bodyguards were able to maintain order, spontaneous protests erupted throughout Berlin during the convention's first four days. While the Greens met to discuss alternatives to the existing world financial system, the Autonomen (or independent radicals) surprised everyone by mobilizing thousands of militants from Germany, Italy, Holland, Denmark, and the United States. Reports from Berlin indicated that the Autonomen won a victory of sorts largely because of the police overreaction against them. As members of the international press corps and local residents were brutalized by roaming police squads, public sympathy for the Autonomen grew.

As part of the movement's massive mobilizations, whether those of the peace movement, the contestation of nuclear power plants at Brokdorf and Wackersdorf, or the prolonged attempt to shut the Startbahn West runway in Frankfurt, the role of the Autonomen was to provide the militant cutting edge to popular struggles. In Hamburg, Amsterdam, and Copenhagen, however, the central thrust of the Autonomen was to occupy houses for the movement to live in – to create a free space for everyday life – and there were long and bitter struggles to defend those houses from police attacks.

In the 1980's Autonomen's international focal point was undoubtedly the set of houses first occupied in 1981 in Hamburg's Hafenstrasse. At the same time as the squatters' movement reached its high point in Berlin, several empty houses in the St. Pauli district of Hamburg were occupied. Those eight houses on the harbor became the focus for the most significant single struggle waged by the

Autonomen. Repeated attempts by the city government and police to dislodge the squatters failed as the Hafenstrasse squatters mobilized thousands of sympathizers and hundreds of street fighters to protect their liberated space. They enacted elaborate defense plans in the face of repeated police assaults; put together lightning-like retaliatory raids on city offices and corporate targets after assaults on the squatted houses; dealt with severe internal problems; and walked a thin line between the state's programs of legalization and criminalization. Moreover, they hosted international Autonomen gatherings in their houses, thereby strengthening the movement's international vitality.

As the squatters' movement elsewhere had suffered a series of defeats, the Hafenstrasse's capability to remain intact made it a struggle of almost mythic proportions among Europe's Autonomen. As one leaflet put it: "Everything is present in this struggle: militant resistance, the fight to live together in communes, internationalism, the struggle for self-management and collective structure. The Hafenstrasse has shown that resolute struggle can become the path for many." Unlike their counterparts in Berlin and elsewhere who were very often ex-students or of "respectable" working class origins, the Hafenstrasse drew heavily from the lumpenproletariat (the criminal element and black market entrepreneurs). Part of the squatters' murals painted on the side of one of the houses transformed Marx's famous call into "Criminals of the World, Unite!"

Klaus Dohnanyi, formerly mayor of Hamburg, was unable to control the Hafenstrasse "Chaoten." He sent his police to clear out the houses four times without success. In 1986, after the Hamburg electrical utility documented a yearly "theft" of more than $50,000 worth of services by the squatters, hundreds of police were called in and were able to clear out a few of the buildings, although the eight houses clustered together remained in the hands of the Autonomen. In response to those attacks, the movement unleashed its own counteroffensive, marching more than 10,000 strong around a "black bloc" of at least 1,500 militants carrying a banner reading "Build Revolutionary Dual Power!" At the end of the march, the black bloc attacked the police, sending 93 of them to the hospital. The next day, fires broke out in 13 department stores in Hamburg causing damages estimated at almost $10 million. On "Day X," April 24, 1987, small groups of Autonomen again retaliated, attacking houses of city officials, court buildings, city offices, and radio Hamburg. In all, more than 30 targets were hit in a 15-minute period.

The city then declared the occupied houses "Public Enemy Number 1," and the squatters braced themselves for fresh attacks. Steel doors were installed, bars were mounted into the windows, and barbed wire was hung on the sides and roofs of the buildings. In early November, the city promised to clear out and tear down the houses within 14 days. The squatters painted a new slogan on the side of one of the houses: "Don't count our days, count yours!" and barricaded the houses. Rumors spread that a network of underground tunnels had been dug for resupply and/or escape. Netting was hung on the second stories of the houses to ward off the use of ladders, and armed patrols on the roofs guarded against helicopters landing. Four thousand police arrived from all over Germany, and at the same time, the borders were closed to "suspicious" looking tourists headed in the direction of Hamburg.

On Friday, November 13, the squatters' radio station began broadcasting for supporters to join the fight. Police helicopters were chased from the rooftops by a few shots from flare guns, and loudspeakers blasted the song "It's war, war in the city," as the fight began in earnest. After a night of fighting, the barricades were still standing and rush hour traffic had to be rerouted because part of a nearby bridge had been borrowed to help build one of the barricades. The banner hung on the outside of the houses said "No pasaran!"

Over the next week, as the Autonomen celebrated their victory and built support for the future, 2000 police reinforcements arrived, promising an even uglier confrontation than on November 13. Mayor Dohnanyi, however, had had his fill, and he succeeded in averting a final battle by mobilizing support for a new plan: legalize the Hafenstrasse squatters by creating a corporation composed of liberal city council members and some of the squatters. The building was then leased to the squatters, and the city provided funds for renovations, thereby creating needed "alternative" housing and, of course, ending the illegal occupation of the Hafenstrasse. Although Dohnanyi's plan left the same people living in the Hafenstrasse, he vowed to clear out any new squats within 24 hours.

Conservatives resisted Dohnanyi's plan, but it was ultimately approved by the city government. In jubilation, the Autonomen dismantled the street barricades, stripped the houses of their defenses, and sent the mayor a bouquet of flowers. Dohnanyi even won the prestigious Theodor Heuss medal for his efforts at reconciliation. In May 1988, after six months of peace, conservatives blocked the legal registration of the new corporation. Rather than participate in a new round of fighting, Klaus Dohnanyi resigned as mayor, leaving his political future, and more significantly, the future of the Hafenstrasse in doubt.

Although they were victorious, seven years of continuous resistance exacted a high price on the Hafenstrasse squatters. The children who were among the earliest occupants were long gone, and the internal relationships among those remaining had their ups and downs. One of the lowest points was reached in June 1984, when three squatters (two women and a man) beat and raped a visitor in one of the buildings. The occupants decided to take matters into their own hands: the three were beaten up; their heads were shaved, and they were thrown out in the street. In a leaflet explaining their response, the residents wrote: "It was clear that we could not work with the bulls (the police) and the judges in order to deal with the problem. If we had, that would have meant going to precisely the same forces that never missed an opportunity to trick us, and with them in control, they would have tried to do us in." Because they exercised their own brand of revolutionary justice, however, the squatters were accused of creating a space outside the law, a charge which resurfaced many times over the following years in an attempt to justify the massive use of force against them.

There is a constant alertness and the willingness of hundreds—possibly thousands—to fight for their free space. Costs of clearing out the houses were unacceptably high by European standards.

The government's inability to defeat the squatters in the streets led to a tactical innovation: legalize the squatted houses in the large cities, thereby depriving the movement of a focus for action and, more importantly, of a sense of fighting against the existing system. Legalization meant that those previously living an everyday existence of resistance to a repressive order were suddenly—without any change of heart or location on their part—transformed into guests of a tolerant big brother, someone who not only provided them with a house but also with a low rent and money to repair it.

Of course, in the smaller cities and towns where the movement's activist base was small, the government's tolerance was never known. Squatted houses were simply cleared soon after they were occupied, and the local authorities were able to contain what militant opposition there was.

In the larger cities like Berlin, Hamburg, and Frankfurt, however, legalization was an important factor in the depoliticization of the movement, although the consciousness of thousands of activists and their practical refusal to throw in the towel meant, in many cases at least, that the legalized houses became base areas from which to organize. In Hamburg, the new nuclear reactor at Brokdorf became the focal point of opposition; in Frankfurt, the new airport runway; in Lower Saxony, the nuclear waste dispossal site at Gorleben; and in southern Germany, the nuclear reprocessing plant at Wackersdorf (which would have had the capability of producing bomb-grade plutonium, a fact which provided the antinuclear and peace movements with a unifying focus). In Berlin, the movement entrenched itself in Kreuzberg, where it developed an organized network of alternative institutions which served as a model for similar networks in 36 other cities.

World Trashed Organization!

Festivals and Riots Against the G8 and the WTO

SchNEWS, *May, 1998*

Revised by editors for clarity

Birmingham, UK

People dance in a ten thousand strong street party in front of a canary yellow army of conscripted police. Tripods tower against the Birmingham skyline. Only blocks away, inside the secure walls of Birmingham's G8 conference hall, Clinton, Blair and the global summit team are dancing away to "All you need is love."

Geneva, Switzerland

By Monday the G8 globalisation tour has moved to the Palais des Nations in Geneva for World Trade Day. On the street, hundreds of protesters are being arrested, beaten and deported by the Genevan authorities.

For four days this small city is under siege as the leaders of the 132-nation World Trade Organisation meet at the United Nations building. Clinton, Blair, Castro, Mandela, and other attendees leave the city in shock after the worst riots here since 1932. The opposition is led by People's Global Action.

The city erupts before the Ministers even step off their planes. Five thousand people come to Saturday's Street Party: by midnight it's a full scale riot. One car is set alight and thousands of police charge the main encampment of protesters, firing tear gas into the crowd. The demonstrators smash hundreds of windows, mainly of banks and corporate offices, until 5 AM. They cause over half a million pounds damage.

Genevans awake on Sunday to a city resembling a warzone. On pavement, phone boxes and walls the graffiti message is clear: "WTO ASSASSIN". . . "WTO vs. THE PEOPLE". . . "REVOLUTION '98." From the moment the world leaders sit down on Monday morning to the conclusion on Wednesday evening the streets are filled with riot police and demonstrators, with the constant noise of sirens and low-flying helicopters.

May 18

The offices of Lockheed, a multinational arms trader, are occupied by one group while a spontaneous street demo stops traffic and sets off smoke bombs. By lunchtime the United Bank of Switzerland is forced to close and police keep back while roads after roads are blockaded by protesters. The group continues up to the UN building, which is surrounded by armed police. The crowd chants in French, Spanish and English. By nightfall there's a highly-charged stand-off as a party kicks off next to the University.

May 19

Activists from Colombia, India, South Korea, Mexico, Nicaragua, Argentina, Aotearoa/New Zealand and across Europe, continue to network and organize direct action under the banner of PGA. In a deliberate display of nonviolence, hundreds march gagged and bound through town, to call attention to the global muting of human rights that the WTO regime imposes. At a prominent statue of Rousseau they enact a burial of his "social contract" between people and their rulers. Meanwhile, the director of the WTO, Renatto Ruggiero, tells the conference that everyone must drive faster towards globalisation, or face the danger of crashing. His Mercedes is later overturned.

> The director of the WTO, Renatto Ruggiero, tells the conference that everyone must drive faster towards globalisation, or face the danger of crashing. His Mercedes is later overturned.

As darkness descends, so do the people. A crowd of around five hundred, many "L'Hiphop" kids from nearby council estates, confront police at Plain Palais. Protestors systematically trash the nearby McDonald's and Pizza Hut. Police fire CS gas, so the angry mass smash more shops, overturn cars and run through the city in diffuse groups. Plainclothes police on mopeds give chase to troublemakers. At 1 AM police surround Artamis, a huge squatted alternative center, and arrest everyone they can. Between Monday and Tuesday 287 are detained.

May 20

Hundreds assemble outside the UN for a final push. They attempt to enter the building and stop the General Assembly. They walk, Gandhi-style, headlong into a line of riot police. There's a blur of truncheons and the ambulances begin to arrive. According to hospital staff over sixty people are treated that day, some for major injuries.

May 23

The squatters organize a demonstration against police brutality and the inhumane treatment of those arrested (strip-searches, medical neglect, and psychological abuse). The conference is over, and for now Geneva is quiet.

"This is without doubt a popular uprising against the issue of globalisation," one activist told SchNEWS. "Not just in Geneva but in cities all over the world people are beginning to realize the consequences of this crazy process and the *importance of resisting by any means necessary.*"

SchNEWS, PO Box 2600
Brighton, East Sussex, BN2 2DX
schnews@brighton.co.uk

>> Friday June 18th 1999
>> RECLAIM THE STREETS
Carnival!
"...collapse of the global marketplace would be a... ...with unimaginable consequences. ...imagine ...than the ...of the present regime."
—George Soros, financial speculator, predator

12 noon, Liverpool Street Station, London EC1

June 18th : An international day of protest, action and carnival aimed at the heart of the global economy – the banking and financial centres. Actions in : Argentina Austria Australia Bangladesh Basque Country Brazil Canada Chile Colombia Czech Republic England Finland France Germany Greece India Indonesia Ireland Israel Italy Malaysia Malta Mexico Netherlands Nigeria Poland Portugal Russia Scotland Senegal South Korea Spain Sweden Thailand Uruguay USA Zimbabwe

A Global Carnival of the Dispossessed

Katherine Ainger
Z Magazine, *September 1999*

As G8 leaders met to shape the agenda for the global economy at the summit in Koln, Germany on June 18 this year, five thousand protesters carrying signs saying "We ate the G8" and "It's Stupid, the Economy" were turning London's financial district upside down in a Carnival Against Capital. Bankers and traders watched from behind tinted windows as protesters played volleyball with inflatable globes and danced to samba rhythms in the spray of a waterspout from a damaged fire hydrant.

The protest—the most dramatic London had seen in ten years—seemed to come out of nowhere. By the end of the day a group of the protesters had invaded and trashed the ground floor of the London International Financial Futures Exchange, three McDonald's had their windows broken, two people had been run over by police vans, and riot police were charging in. The sight of anarchy hitting the world's largest financial center prompted newspaper headlines that denounced the protesters as "evil savages," an ignorant "unwashed horde" hell-bent on turning a "carnival into a riot."

Many of the scenes were undoubtedly ugly. But in dismissing the protesters as an inarticulate British subculture, the media were missing the biggest story of the day. The carnival-goers in London—the majority of whom had been nonviolent in actions and intent—were members of a far larger, invisible, but international constituency organizing around a common enemy: globalization. The events in London were only one of many during the June 18 "international day of action, protest and carnival aimed at the heart of the global economy," when simultaneous protests against global capitalism, the international financial system, and corporate power took place in forty-three countries around the world.

The response to globalization has resulted in some extraordinary new coalitions. For example, this summer four hundred Indian farmers invited by local antiglobalization activists went on a month-long protest tour around centers of power in Europe. The president of the All India Farmers Union, Vijay Jawandia, said, "Those in the North have to understand our struggle and to realize it is part of their own. Everywhere the rich are getting richer, the poor poorer, and the environment is being plundered. Whether in North or South, we all face the same future."

New communications technology such as the Internet and email has played an integral part in the process of economic globalization, but they have also fuelled a parallel globalization of resistance. The idea for June 18 was proposed by British eco-activists Reclaim the Streets, who organize illegal street parties against car culture and capitalism. Circulated on international email lists and through the Internet, the proposal caught on and gathered momentum.

The June 18 events were as diverse as the groups taking part. In Barcelona "street reclaimers" invoked the slogan of the rebellious Paris students of 1968, "Sous les paves, la plage" ("Under the sidewalk, the beach") and, dressed in swimming costumes, put out towels and sun-bathed on the road, handed out French fries to commuters in their cars, and later took part in a seven hundred strong street party. Music and dancing also hit the streets of San Francisco with "art attackers" who, armed with giant puppets and candy, lobbied those working for multinationals that exploit sweatshop workers to take the day off work and "join the revolution." In Melbourne, Australia, Kim Beazely, leader of the opposition, received a custard pie in the face for speaking at a global trade conference sponsored by Shell, while thousands of partygoers in Sydney held up traffic as a massive street festival got underway.

The National Alliance of People's Movements in India, a coalition of two hundred grassroots organizations, made a statement declaring they were taking part because so many in India have "been marginalized by the market economy and World Trade Organization policies," while in Pakistan union leaders risked their lives to come out of hiding to protest for "bread, not nuclear bombs."

Most dramatically, ten thousand people in Port Harcourt, Nigeria gathered to welcome back Dr. Owens Wiwa, younger brother of the executed Ogoni activist Ken Saro-Wiwa, from a four-year exile. The crowd, led by a coalition of indigenous activists, held a Carnival of the Oppressed against corporate imperialism and the military dictatorship, during which they unofficially renamed a main street Ken Saro-Wiwa Road, and blockaded the Shell office headquarters. The singing and dancing in the streets brought the petroleum capital of Nigeria to a standstill for the day.

A "virtual sit-in" on behalf of the Zapatistas, prompted by a group called Electronic Civil Disobedience, led to thousands of hits "flooding" the website of the Mexican embassy in the UK. Meanwhile in Montevideo, Uruguay, protesters took part in a parade through the Stock Exchange and McDonalds, accompanied by a PVC jockey riding a giant Pollution Plastisaurus made of plastic rubbish, and ending with the ritual burning of a cardboard television as the "agent of consumer-culture." A diverse coalition of religious groups took to the streets in Brazil as part of the June 18 network to call for the cancellation of Third World debt.

Street protests of various kinds—many targeting corporate headquarters and stock exchanges—also took place in Tel Aviv, Minsk, Madrid, Valencia, Prague, Hamburg, Koln, Milan, Rome, Siena, Florence, Ancona, Amsterdam, Madrid, Glasgow, Edinburgh, Lancaster, Zurich, Geneva, Toronto, Vancouver, Ottawa, Washington, New York, Los Angeles, Austin, Boston, and Eugene. The website for June 18, which streamed live video images from Australia and London declared, "Our resistance is as transnational as capital."

These new coalitions have been building since 1996, when Mexican Zapatistas held an international *Encuentro* in Spain. Social and environmental movements in North and South met and were strengthened by their common rejection of their assigned role as "the expendable members of the global economy."

By February 1998 an international meeting in Geneva had attracted over four hundred people from seventy-one countries involved in grassroots activism, from Argentinean teachers hunger-striking against privatization to Canadian Postal Union workers to landless peasants in Brazil to Indian farmers to indigenous groups such as the U'wa to European anti-road protesters. Together they launched a loose network called People's Global Action Against Free Trade and the World Trade Organization. They wrote, "Despite the huge material differences, struggles in privileged and under-privileged parts of the corporate empire have more and more in common, setting the stage for a new and stronger sort of solidarity... Scattered around the world again, we will not forget. We remain together. This is our common struggle."

The energy gained from that meeting was tremendous. A Global Street Party took place in twenty different countries during the G8 summit in Birmingham in May last year. Two days later, eight thousand people erupted onto the streets of Geneva in an anti-World Trade Organization protest, fifty thousand Brazilians participated in a "Cry of the Excluded" march, and two hundred thousand Indian farmers and fisher folk took to the streets of Hyderabad demanding India's withdrawal from the WTO.

By September that year, John M. Weekes, chair of the General Council of the WTO was pointing out that "trade is no longer seen as an arcane subject of no interest to the public," and the chair of Nestle, Helmut Maucher, was criticizing "single-issue" protest groups afflicted with "Globaphobia."

The United States has so far not witnessed the kind of mass antiglobalization protests that have taken place in Europe and the Third World. But all eyes are now on the millennium meeting of the World Trade Organization in Seattle, November 30 to December 3. Pirellis Perissich stressed at the Geneva Business Dialogue last year that the next round of trade liberalization "is going to be very difficult—resistance will be bigger than before." One U.S. trade official predicts that Seattle 1999 will be "like Chicago in 1968." As the agenda of free trade and liberalization comes into increasing conflict with realities of job insecurity, exploitation, unemployment, and social and environmental breakdown, more and more of the dispossessed will have little to lose in joining the insurgent carnival.

Katherine Ainger

N30
AFTERMATH

part II:

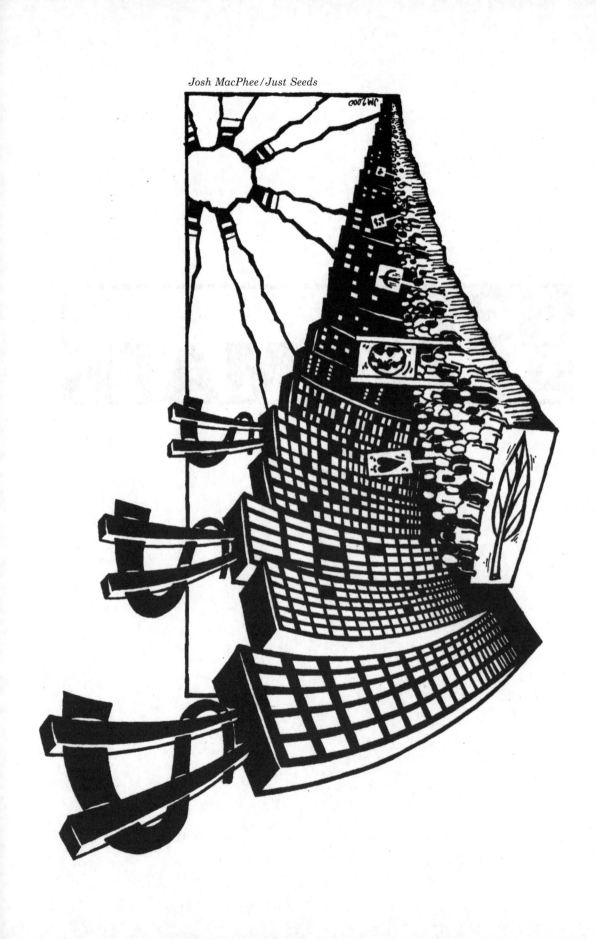

Josh MacPhee/Just Seeds

The Globalization Of Resistance

N30 International Day Of Action

Mark Laskey

N15

Amsterdam, Netherlands: Dutch activists from the Mayday Action Group occupy a replica of a 17th Century Dutch East India ship. They hang a giant banner reading "Stop the WTO" between the masts.

N16

Geneva, Switzerland: The World Headquarters of the WTO is occupied by 27 people aided by three dozen supporters blocking traffic outside. One group chains themselves to the staircase that leads to Moore's office. They unfurl a banner that reads: "No Commerce, No Organization: Self-management!" Another group makes it to the roof and drops two huge banners. They read: "WTO kills people— Kill the WTO !" and "Moore aux tyrants!" (a pun meaning "Death to the Tyrants" and "Moore to the Tyrants "). One of the protesters beams pictures of the occupation directly onto the Internet from a portable installation. Another faxes a communiqué from WTO HQ. In the third hour of the occupation, police purge the building without making any arrests or recording people's identities.

N22

Ankara, Turkey: From November 22-30 peasants, environmentalists, and trade unionists from The Working Group of Turkey Against the MAI and Globalization march over 2,000 miles in protest of the WTO and global capitalism.

N24

New Delhi, India: More than 300 indigenous people from Madya Pradesh storm the World Bank building. They cover it with posters, graffiti, cow shit, and mud, while they chant slogans and sing traditional songs. They leave the area only after the country director for the World Bank in India meets the demonstrators and receives an open letter signed by all their member organizations.

Manila, Philippines: Protesters against the Association of Southeast Asian Nations gather outside the Philippine International Convention Center, where they're beaten by riot police and sprayed with a water cannon. ASEAN is holding its third informal summit and preparatory meeting.

N27

New York City, NY: A Buy Nothing Day demonstration is held against the World Trade Organization at 44th Street Times Square. The protesters erect a two-story tripod, bringing traffic to a standstill and drawing a large crowd.

Geneva, Switzerland: Two large columns of demonstrators—2000 farmers and 3000 city dwellers—meet to march on WTO headquarters. The farmers are answering a call made by all of the Swiss farmers' associations (the Union des Producteurs Suisses, as well as the Union des Paysans Suisses and the Chambers of Agriculture). The city people were called out by a coordination against the Millennium Round. They gather in front of the United Nations building and in the heart of the banking district.

N30

United States

In solidarity with groups protesting World Trade Organization policies, over 9,000 workers from the International Longshore and Warehouse Union (ILWU) shut down ports from San Diego to nearly Canada. About three dozen ports take part in the 12-hour work stoppage. It is estimated that almost half of US trade carried on ships goes through the West Coast ports.

Atlanta, GA: A varied group of activists from the Rainforest Action Network, IWW, AIM, Food Not Bombs, Dogwood Alliance, and Earth First! gather in Woodruff Park in downtown to tell the people what the WTO is all about. There are a couple of musicians and some disjointed chanting. Food Not Bombs serves a meal.

Amherst, MA: Over 100 demonstrators meet on the town common to protest the WTO. As a diverse group of speakers addresses the crowd, a theater troupe, dressed in business suits, marches solemnly around the assembly carrying a huge chained globe. At the end of the demonstration, protestors huddle around a phone to hear an Amherst resident in Seattle describe the day's events. When they learn of the success of their co-protesters, they erupt in cheers of joy.

Austin, TX: In a demonstration organized by the ad-hoc Just Say No To WTO Coalition!, over 500 antiglobalization activists gather at Republic Square and march through downtown. Art & Revolution carry a giant WTO/octopus puppet, the radical cheerleaders entertain the crowd with some anti-corporate cheers, and a Critical Mass bicycle ride (accompanied by a number of hostile police on motorcycles) block intersection after intersection during the rush hour commute.

Baltimore, MD: A demonstration starts around 4:30 pm, but doesn't pick up speed until after 5 pm, when Critical Mass and a black bloc join, bringing the number of participants to around 125.

Louisville, KY: In protest of "increasing poverty and cuts in social services, low wages, sweatshops, meaningless jobs, more prisons, deforestation, gridlocked cities, global warming, genetic engineering, gentrification, and war" a number of anti-WTO activists meet in Jefferson Square Park for a day of celebration and resistance.

Montpelier, VT: More than three dozen activists from Bread and Puppet, Vermont Anarchist Black Cross, Institute for Social Ecology, and the Vermont Livable Wage Campaign assemble in front of the court house in solidarity with the people of the world protesting the global capitalist free market. Demonstrators perform street theater, hold signs, march and hand out literature to passersby.

Morgantown, WV: Over two dozen people from the Morgantown Anarchist Group, West Virginia branch of the Sierra Club, and others gather in front of the WVU student union in protest against the WTO. People chant, hand out leaflets, juggle, and carry signs attacking the WTO.

Nashville, TN: About forty-five protesters gather in front of Al Gore's presidential campaign headquarters. At one point, protesters enter the reception area and serenade some bemused members of Gore's campaign staff with "No, no, no WTO..."

Philadelphia, PA: One hundred and fifty activists rally outside the Banana Republic Superstore. When the weather gets too cold, they go inside the store and hold their news conference. Stunned Banana Republic workers and Philly police look on.

Santa Cruz, CA: About one hundred people gather at the town Clock Tower, a traditional spot for protests, to voice their opposition to the WTO. It is well covered by the local press.

Washington, DC: One hundred or so protestors turn out at Lafayette Park, and again at the USIA Building, to express solidarity with the Seattle protesters and their displeasure with corporate greed and the FDA's inaction with regard to genetically-engineered foods.

Canada
Edmonton, Alberta: About one hundred people hold a demonstration outside Canada Place in downtown Edmonton over the noon hour. The demonstration is sponsored by the People's Action Network.

Halifax, Nova Scotia: A Citizen's Tour of the downtown area is very successful. Protesters chant anti-WTO slogans, distribute pamphlets, and perform street theatre (including an appearance by WTO-man!). There is decent media turnout.
Ottawa, Ontario: One hundred twenty to one hundred fifty people gathered

around the Eternal Flame on Parliament Hill. Good music, lively banners and interested media make the event a success.

Peterborough, Ontario: Approximately one hundred fifty people attend the The Anti-WTO Discussion Night.

Toronto, Ontario: In solidarity with the Seattle protesters, several hundred protesters march through the streets of Toronto's financial district. They tour downtown, stopping at a number of corporations who gave financial support to the Seattle host committee for the WTO. Earlier in the month, on November 4, anti-free trade "goblins" disrupted a negotiating meeting of the Free Trade Area of the Americas in Toronto. They loosed stink bombs made from shit and rotten eggs.

Winnipeg, Manitoba: Over 300 people rally against the WTO at the intersection of Portage and Main. They shut down Portage Ave. during rush hour and march to the University of Winnipeg. The action is organized by the Manitoba Coalition Against the World Trade Organization which has also organized a month of panel discussions on the WTO. Organizations mobilizing for the rally include: CUPE Manitoba, Canadian Auto Workers, Postal Workers, Food Not Bombs, the Greens, Industrial Workers of the World, Canadian Association of the Non-Employed, and the Manitoba Young New Democrats.

Iceland:

Reykjavik: Anti-American protesters target a U.S. military base and the embassy. They demand "Yanks Out" (a promise the U.S. has left unkept since WW2).

England

Halifax: A Nestle factory is occupied and a banner is dropped outside. Sixteen are arrested.

Leeds: In the city center around fifty protestors face over three hundred cops. The protesters mill around and hand out leaflets outside of scummy companies.

London: Over 2,000 people gather at Euston Station to support striking public transportation workers and to highlight the links between the free trade agenda of the WTO and the privatization of public transport in the UK. The rally becomes more militant when about 500 people try to block a main traffic artery. They are pushed back by lines of riot police using tear gas. Some protesters fight back, using bottles and stones. They overturn a police van and set it on fire, then scatter and spread throughout the city. Occasional skirmishes continue. Thirty-eight people are arrested; both protesters and police report injuries.

Manchester: Lloyds Bank on Cross Street is occupied and shut down by about 50 activists, who then proceed to block the street outside.

South Devon: A disused garage and an old Toll House, slated to be turned into "luxury flats", are squatted in Totnes to draw local people's attention to the WTO.

Ireland

Limerick: Twenty people hold a festive protest in the center of the city outside of a McDonalds, a HMV, a Burger King and a Penny's.

Wales

Bangor: Over 40 people attend a demonstration. There is good press coverage.

Cardiff: An anti-WTO procession marches through the center of town.

Portugal

Lisbon: Nearly 300 people with giant puppets march through the streets and block traffic. During different stops there is fire-breathing and street theatre. The city Christmas tree and a McDonalds are covered in graffiti.

France

Dijon: Over 40 people chain themselves to the doors of the Chamber of Commerce and occupy the Industry and Business Institute. Activists wearing shirts reading "Enslaved By Money?" use U-locks and arm-tubes to block the entrances of the two buildings. Others throw fake blood and money on the pavement. They also glue posters on walls and shops, display banners, play drums, scream, give out free tea and coffee, as well as flyers about capitalism, anarchism, and alternative culture.

Paris: Over 20,000 people march through the streets denouncing the WTO. In two Parisian suburbs, 800 miners clash with police, ransack a tax office and burn a number of cars. Five days earlier, 5,000 French farmers with their sheep, ducks and goats, feast on regional products under the Eiffel tower in protest of the impact of trade liberalization enforced by the WTO.

Toulouse: Protesters invade the town's commercial district with a large sound system. They hang large anti-WTO signs on street lights. Anti-capitalist Father Christmases give rotten fruit—the fruit of capitalism—to passer-bys.

Switzerland

Geneva: The WTO's World Headquarters are again the target of direct action. In a pre-dawn move, saboteurs trigger an explosion in a small power supply building. They damage electrical transformers and wipe out HQ's computer links to the ministerial meeting in Seattle. For over two hours the WTO is entirely without power: computer servers are down for most of the morning. The Swiss news agency ATS reports that it has received a statement claiming responsibility for the act from a group calling itself "Green Apple".

Netherlands

Amsterdam: Over 100 activists unfurl banners in the departure hall of Amsterdam's Schipol Airport, targeting official WTO sponsors Lufthansa, Northwest Airways and United Airlines. The demonstrators hold a sit-in, demanding free flights to Seattle from the offending airlines. They maintain the sit-in for several hours, accompanied by dozens of press people and the police.

Mark Laskey

Germany

Berlin: A satirical march is held, raising banners calling for more order, more security and more police. Riot police, formed in lines in front of borgeoisie restaurants and shops, exude confusion, as if they are wondering why demonstrators aren't attacking property. The demonstration ends with a slide show on the WTO policies projected on the side of a building.

Tuebingen: Around 20 people dress as WTO delegates and show up in the pedestrian area of the town's shopping center. A big globe is enthusiastically kicked about. Some folks dressed as Death speechify about the lethal policies of the WTO. A few banners are dropped, one reading "Globalize Solidarity not the Economy". Police are obnoxious, performing identity checks on protesters. They seize film from a participant and destroy it.

Italy

Milan: Members of the Tutti Blanche ("white overalls") group lock themselves to a McDonalds, and hang enormous banners denouncing neoliberalism from it. An informational tent against the WTO is set up in the central square of Largo Cairoli. The day ends with a debate at the Social Center Leoncavallo. Andres Barreda Marin, a professor at Mexico City's UNAM, speaks on the influence of U.S. economy on capitalist globalization and on the situation in Chiapas.

Padau: A peaceful demonstration in front of a genetics exhibition is attacked by police. Top managers of companies that use genetically modified organism technology are in attendance at the exhibition.

Rome: A direct action group occupies the headquarters of the National Committee for Biosafety. They hang banners against GMOs and the WTO. The action had been promoted by various squats and grassroots unions.

Greece

Athens: Protestors clash with riot police throughout the day and into the night, following demonstrations outside the US embassy. Demonstrators protest a wide range of issues, including the tyranny of the capitalist free market and neoliberal trade policies.

Czech Republic

Prague: Earth First! Prague joins the N30 and Buy Nothing Day actions with banners, music, and masks at the city's Tesco Supermarket, while Food Not Bombs provides a meal. The event lasts two hours and is attended by about 70 people. It is covered by all the major TV stations and newspapers of the Czech Republic.

Turkey

Bergama: Protests take place against the Eurogold Corporation, which plans to operate a gold mine in the area that would use cyanide-based extraction methods. The protests are also against planned thermal and nuclear power plants.

Israel

Tel Aviv: Around 30 people demonstrate outside the US embassy in protest of the WTO. Those present include Women in Black, members of an anarcho-communist collective, and direct action Greens.

Pakistan

Muzafer Ghar: More than 8,000 people demonstrate against the WTO.

India

Bangalore: Several thousand peasant-farmers from all the districts of Karnataka province gather to protest the WTO at the central train station, then make their way to Gandhi's statue. At the end of the demo protesters issue a "Quit India" notice to Monsanto. The document is an ultimatum: the company must leave the country or suffer direct action against its installations. Another notice is issued to the Indian Institute of Science, which opened its research facilities to Monsanto, demanding that the school expel the transnational corporation from its campus.

Narmada: More than 1000 people from 60 different villages participate in a colorful procession protesting agreements and institutions that are roping India and the rest of the world into the downward spiral of globalization.

New Delhi: Hundreds indigenous people blockade the World Bank Building. Many others participate in a three day sit-in at Raj Ghat (where Gandhi's ashes are buried). At the latter location protesters burn a statue symbolizing the WTO. These actions have two specific targets: forces trying to build a massive, devastating dam in Maheshwar—Indian industrial interests, multinational corporations and the German state—and the WTO regime, for the equally vandalistic and insidious dispossession that it creates globally. Speakers at the rallies state their commitment to Gandhi's vision of a self-reliant, sustainable, solidarity-based India composed of village republics.

Korea

Seoul: Korean People's Action Against Investment Treaties and the WTO New Round hold a demo in front of government offices in Seoul. Over two dozen progressive organizations, including the KCTU and the National Farmer's Union are represented; over 3,000 workers, students, and activists take part.

Philippines

Bacolod: Thousands attend a rally against President Estrada's plans to amend the Constitution to allow for greater foreign investment.

Manila: Militants from the Proletarian Revolutionary Army perform a drive-by on Shell's headquarters, opening fire with automatic weapons and a grenade launcher. The PRA members shatter the windows and metal façade of the large shimmering building. Elsewhere in the city, roughly eight thousand union members and activists rally against Philippine membership in the WTO in front of the US embassy and near the Malacanang presidential palace. Their slogans angri-

Mark Laskey

ly state that the WTO's latest meeting could lead to unneeded food imports and a drop in local farmers' incomes.

Australia
Brisbane: Activists protest against the WTO in front of the Stock Exchange.

Melbourne: The offices of public relations firm Burson-Marsteller are occupied, in an effort to link the spin-doctors of consumerism with the neo-liberal agenda of the WTO.

D1
Boston, MA: Over six hundred antiglobalization protesters gather outside of the Boston Federal Reserve Building. A feeder march of about two hundred starts at the Park Street subway station and winds its way through the Downtown Crossing shopping district, blocking traffic during rush hour. Large puppets lead the way to the Federal Reserve. The crowd has tripled in size by the time the rally begins at 5 pm. Persevering in the face of biting winds and sub-zero temperatures, participants listen to speeches from community organizers and labor leaders, while others maintain a steady stream of cheers, jeers, and creative chants.

D2
Ljubljana, Slovenia: In solidarity with all people struggling for a better world, one hundred people gather in front of the Presern Monument to demonstrate against the tyranny of the WTO and the globalization of neoliberal capitalism.

D3
Tucson, AZ: Over fifty demonstrators gather at McDonalds near the university in solidarity with the Seattle protesters. Many protesters have plungers, illustrating the theme of the demonstration: "Flush Out Corporate Greed".

Manila, Philippines: Protesters try to force their way into the U.S. Embassy for a "lightning rally" against the violent dispersal and arrests of protesters at the WTO conference in Seattle, Washington.

D11
Mexico City, Mexico: Hundreds demonstrate in front of the US Embassy demanding the release of the protesters arrested in Seattle, as well as political prisoner Mumia Abu-Jamal. Rocks and fireworks are thrown at the embassy, resulting in several broken windows. Police charge the crowd, clubbing people and chasing them across the 14-lane Paseo De la Reforma Boulevard.

Ninety-eight protesters are arrested. Nineteen of the prisoners are minors and though told they would be released after 24 hours, they are held in prison for three days. At the same time that the minors are released a special police force transports the rest of the prisoners. The protesters are made to lay face down, are beaten, and are told that they're being moved to Military Camp #1, infamous for supposedly being the burying grounds of the massacred students of October 2nd, 1968. The police threaten to kill them and make their bodies disappear. The prisoners are shipped to the Reclusorio Norte (Northern Penitentiary), but initially believe that they are in Military Camp #1. Prison guards employ humiliation and torture tactics, including forcing prisoners to walk in "duck formation"—a squatting position and accompanied by quacking sounds. Those who do not comply are kicked and dragged. Prisoners are also forced to hold their hands in the air for an unendurable amount of time. In the beatings, guards try to not leave marks.

A bail of 2,803,200 pesos (approximately $285,000 USD) is set for the release of the prisoners. Unions, student unions, and the general public, raise the money, and the protesters are released on December 15th. Those arrested were accused of rioting, property damage, and "aggressions."

In Praise of the Seattle Coalition

Eliot Katz

They came from around the globe to change the shape of the globe
They formed a human chain and sidewalks declared their support
They led labor down unpaved roads and mountain ranges from all sides
    tipped their peaks in salute
They wore turtle caps and the Pacific roared its approval
They chanted "This is what democracy looks like" so that we who could
    not be in Seattle could watch TV & see what democracy looks like
They called for human rights and were gassed with inhuman chemicals
They insisted the food be kept clean of genetic experiment and were shot
    with rubber bullet pellet red meat welts
They demanded an end to worldwide sweatshops and were treated
    to the best nightsticks multinational business could buy
It was a coalition for the ages, of all ages, of all stages, of varying degrees
    of calm and rages
After curfew, the skies lit up & birds flew across continents to celebrate
Ancient redwood trees shook their leaves to prevent WTO delegates
    from being received
The town salmon agreed to wear union windbreakers for the week
When the mayor outlawed public gasmasks, the air sucked up to help out
It was the audible applause of the quantum that drove the police chief mad
A dog ran across the road to dispose of pepper spray containers
Stampeding cops were stopped by dolphins swimming in mid-street
I saw this every hour on the hour behind the CNN lens
In a thousand tongues, even the internet logged on the side of the young
O friends, you have jumpstarted this nation and revealed an America
    with a million human faces
Of course the corporations were defeated, any objective observer
    could see they were outmatched from the opening bell
Now come the subtle somersaults and the internationalist flips
Now the courageous maneuvers that follow a win
Now the flexible glue to keep a coalition together
Now spreading the fun so that more can participate
Now there will be more democracy and then even more democracy
Now you are welcomed heroic at the dawn of a century

12/99 NYC

So Who Did Win in Seattle?
Liberals Rewrite History

Alexander Cockburn and Jeffrey St. Clair

Hardly had the tear gas dispersed from the streets of downtown Seattle before an acrid struggle broke out as to who should claim the spoils. It's still raging. On one side the lib-lab pundits, flacks for John Sweeney and James Hoffa like the *Nation*'s Marc Cooper, Molly Ivins, and Jim Hightower, middle-of-the road Greens, Michael Moore, a recycle binful of policy wonks from the Economic Policy Institute and kindred DC think-tanks, Doug Tompkins (the former czar of sweatshop-made sports clothing who funds the International Forum on Globalization), Medea Benjamin (empress of Global Exchange). On the other side: the true heroes of the Battle in Seattle—the street warriors, the Ruckus Society, the anarchists, Earth First!ers, the Direct Action Network, radical labor militants such as the folks at Jobs With Justice, hundreds of Longshoremen, Steelworkers, Electrical Workers and Teamsters who disgustedly abandoned the respectable, police sanctioned, official AFL-CIO parade and joined the street warriors at the barricades in downtown.

At issue here is the liberals' craving to fortify the quasi-myth of Labor Revived—a "progressive coalition" of John Sweeney's AFL-CIO, Hoffa's Teamsters, mainstream Greens—poised and ready to recapture the soul of the Democratic Party. The way they're spinning it, the collapse of the WTO talks in Seattle was a glorious triumph for respectable demonstrators, achieved despite the pernicious rabble smashing windows, harassing the police, and bringing peaceful mainstream protest into disrepute.

Listen to Ivins: "Of those 35,000 people, fewer than 1,000 misbehaved by trashing some local stores. How much more coverage do the 1,000 who misbehaved get than the 34,000 who didn't? A. 35 times as much? B. 34 times as much? C. Virtually all the coverage? You are correct: C is the answer. Do the other 34,000 people get any coverage? Yes—they are referred to as 'some people concerned about the turtles'... Meanwhile the violent protesters are interviewed on national television, identify themselves as anarchists and explain to us all that owning property is wrong and that none of the earth should be in private hands."

Carl Pope, executive director of the Sierra Club, took a similar tack in an internal memo to his board of directors: "The Sierra Club was completely separate from the illegal protest, both violent and nonviolent..." Pope went on to quote Kathleen Casey, one of his staffers, to the effect that "the new coalition that worked together to thwart the WTO came out a clear winner. The Sierra Club achieved many of our goals despite the chaos and unfortunate violence that occurred in some of the actions... Some small factions engaged in vandalism and provocation, and the police sometimes over-reacted in kind."

The *Nation's* Marc Cooper announced tremulously that "the media focus on a few broken store windows should not distract from the profundity of what has happened here..." Cooper evoked "a phantasmagorical mix of tens of thousands of peaceful demonstrators... something not seen since the sixties, but in [its] totality unimaginable even then." And what is this "unimaginable" thing? "The rough outlines of the much-sought-after progressive coalition—an American version of a 'red-green' alliance."

To the fervid imagination of Michael Moore the union protests in Seattle had an effect on President Bill Clinton akin to that exercised by Jesus Christ on St Paul on the Damascus road: "He completely changed his position [he didn't] and called on all WTO countries to enact laws prohibiting trade with nations that use children in sweatshops and do not honor the rights of all workers to organize a union. "Whoa!... So, for Clinton to climb the space needle (or was he chased up it?) and then declare [he didn't] that the human rights of workers were more important than making a buck, well, this was nothing short of Paul being knocked off his horse [he wasn't] and seeing Jesus [he didn't]!...You could almost hear the collective seething of the hundreds of CEOs gathered in Seattle. Their boy Bill—the politician they had bought and paid for ... had betrayed them. You could almost see them reaching for their Palm Pilots to look up the phone number of the Jackal." In this blinding curve of balderdash Moore manages to conflate Christ, Clinton, Paul, and JFK, truly a grand slam of liberal hagiography!

To concoct the myth of respectable triumph in Seattle, divorced from dreadlocked and locked-down Earth First!ers, turbulent Ruckusites and kindred canaille, the respectable liberals have been torturing the data and the data confessed. Here's how it goes: initial scouting parties of liberal policy wonks arrived in Seattle over the weekend prior to the WTO assembly and embarked on a series of sleep-inducing debates and panels, chewing over the minutiae of proposed WTO rules and regulations. As originally envisaged, these moots were scheduled to last all week, until by a process of inexorable erosion, like the Colorado river gradually cleaving its way through the Navajo sandstone to create the Grand Canyon, the WTO would be transmuted into a wholesome compact between First World and Third, between mighty corporations and African peasants, Nike and starving Indonesian workers , for the betterment of all.

The liberal fantasy continues. On Monday battalions of clean-limbed environmentalists in their turtle necks and turtle costumes moved in a disciplined array to a [police-approved] rallying spot where they were uplifted by the measured words of that Lenin of mainstream greenery, Carl Pope. After the speechifying, the battalions redeployed in the Methodist church on Fifth which sheltered the command and control center of the progressive Non-Governmental

Organizations, aka NGOs. (In foundation-funded political wonkdom the acronym "NGO" is used constantly, often in conjunction with the phrase "civil society," to evoke non-profit organizations that mediate the public interest with governments. Oxfam is an NGO. The Interfaith Council is an NGO. World Wildlife Fund is an NGO. etc. etc.) Down in the basement of the church and rarely emerging into the light of day was Jim Hightower, the faux-populist icon of Austin, Radio Nation's Marc Cooper, and other communicators. Upstairs were the briefing rooms and mock tribunals in more or less permanent session.

It's hard to continue relating this fantasy version of history with a straight face, because it's so divorced from reality, but its official finale was the great labor march of Tuesday, November 30, when some twenty-five thousand union people rallied under the indulgent eyes of the Seattle constabulary in an old football stadium, to listen to John Sweeney, James P. Hoffa of the Teamsters, and such labor chieftains as Gerald McEntee of the AFSCME. The divorce of rhetoric from reality was best represented by McEntee, who reiterated Carl Oglesby's famous line from the 1960s, "We have to name the system." Unlike Oglesby, who was a genuinely radical SDS leader, McEntee has been among the most fervent of all Big Labor's supporters of Clinton-Gore.

To concoct the myth of respectable triumph in Seattle, divorced from dreadlocked and locked-down Earth First!ers, turbulent Ruckusites and kindred canaille, the respectable liberals have been torturing the data and the data confessed.

When the rally was over, Sweeney and Hoffa led their thousands towards downtown, where at that precise moment the street warriors were desperately but successfully preventing delegates from entering the Convention Center and Paramount theater where the opening ceremony was scheduled to take place. It was touch and go as cops steadily got rougher and the tear gas got thicker. Certainly the arrival of thousands of labor marchers on the scene would have made it much more difficult for the cops to gas, beat, and shoot the activists with wooden dowels and rubber bullets. It would have diminished the hundreds of serious injuries sustained by the street warriors.

The labor marchers approached and then. . . their own marshals turned them back. A few rebellious steelworkers, longshoremen, electrical workers, and teamsters did disobey their leaders, and pushed into downtown to join the battle. The main march withdrew in respectable good order and dispersed peacefully to their hotels, where Molly Ivins and the other scriveners began composing their denunciations of the anarcho-trashers who had marred their great event.

It would no doubt be polite to treat this myth-making as contemptible but harmless self-aggrandisement. But real social movements for change shouldn't be built on illusions, and the self-aggrandisement is far from harmless. Take Medea Benjamin of Global Exchange, an NGO that has made its name on the sweatshop issue, dickering with Nike over the pay rates and factory conditions of its workers in Vietnam, Indonesia and China. Whatever cachet Benjamin might have won by sneaking into a WTO session and being arrested after briefly addressing the delegates was swiftly squandered by her subsequent defense of

NikeTown. Benjamin and her Global Exchange cohorts stood on the steps of NikeTown and sweatshop outlets in downtown Seattle to defend the premises against demonstrators. As Benjamin herself proudly described her shameful conduct to the *New York Times:* "Here we are protecting Nike, McDonald's, the GAP and all the while I'm thinking, 'Where are the police? These anarchists should have been arrested.'" On the *Nation* website one can find an equally disgusting sample of this ass-kissing of corporate slave drivers. Stephanie Greenwood excitedly quotes the slogan of a person she describes as "her *Nation* boss," said slogan being "Capitalism, no thanks! We'll burn your fucking banks." But woe betide any demonstrator who took this slogan seriously as encouragement to inflict direct injury on capitalist property. Greenwood goes on to report admiringly a scene outside Levi Strauss where the respectable protesters "brought kids who had kicked windows in over to the cops and asked them to arrest them."

Fortunately for the kids, the cops didn't heed the invitation. Had they done so, these kids could now be facing up to ten years for "malicious mischief," which is the charge prosecutors in the Northwest are bringing against street activists. The people turned in by Benjamin and the others did endure awful treatment in jail. An early report by Amnesty International states "systematic cruel treatment was used to coerce or punish violent protesters for acts of non-compliance such as refusing to give their names in King County jail. One person was slammed against a wall, beaten while lying on the floor and his fingers forced back with a pencil. In another case guards squeezed a man's nose, almost suffocating him, when he refused to give out his name... Also at King County jail, people were allegedly strapped into four-point restraint chairs as punishment for nonviolent resistance or asking for their lawyers. In one case a man was stripped naked before being strapped into the chair. One woman was stripped naked by four women guards, while a male guard outside watched. She further had her arms and legs folded behind her and was held down on the floor with the full weight of two guards on top of her."

Aside from the baneful consequences of this on-ground-collusion with the cops, the larger political agenda of the liberals with their myth-making is far from benign. By falsely proclaiming a victory for peaceful procop protesters, they now can move on under a largely factitious banner of "unity," and hunker down with the government policy makers to rewrite the WTO treaty to their satisfaction. This is the core meaning of co-optation, and certainly the writers at the London *Economist* understand it well enough. In the wake of Seattle the *Economist* ran a long article discussing the rising power of NGOs, which successfully challenged the World Bank, sank the Multilateral Agreement on Investment, and engineered the brilliant antilandmine campaign. But, the *Economist* continued, there's hope. "Take the case of the World Bank. The 'Fifty Years is Enough' campaign of 1994 was a prototype of Seattle (complete with activists invading the meeting halls). Now the NGOs are surprisingly quiet about the World Bank. The reason is that the Bank has made a huge effort to co-opt them." The *Economist* went on to describe how World Bank president James Wolfensohn had given the NGOs a seat at the table, and now more than seventy NGO policy wonks work in the Bank's offices world-wide, and half of the bank's projects have some NGO involvement. No one should look at the NGOs without first reading Michel Foucault on co-optation and internalisation of the disciplinary function.

Finally, the myth-making actively demobilizes radical struggles against the two party status quo, since it pretends that one of the two parties—naturally, the Democrats—can actually be redeemed. Just listen to Michael Moore proclaiming the redemption and possible martyrdom of Bill Clinton. These are people who will be rallying next year outside the Republican Convention in Philadelphia but not outside the Democratic convention in Los Angeles, notwithstanding the fact that there is at least some disagreement between the Republican presidential aspirants on the WTO, whereas Gore and Bradley are in harmonious concord on this issue.

But of course it's all a myth, which can be easily popped with a simple question: if labor's legions had not shown up in Seattle the direct action protesters would have at least succeeded in shutting down the opening session on Tuesday, November 30, and they conceivably could have dominated the agenda of the entire week, as in fact they did. If the direct action protesters had not put their  bodies on the line throughout that entire week, if the only protest had been that under official AFL-CIO banners, then there would have been a fifteen second image of a parade on the national news headlines that Tuesday evening and that would have been it. The WTO would have gone forward with barely a ripple of discord except for what the African and Caribbean nations had managed to foment from the inside.

Remember, after Tuesday most of the labor people had gone back to work, and the street warriors were on their own, prompting the Seattle police finally to overreach and go berserk to such a degree that the people of Seattle and the press turned against them. People like Moore and Ivins should be taking up the cause of those protesters still facing charges. They should also be pinning the blame on those who told the cops to take the gloves off. By Tuesday night both the White House and the US Justice Department were telling the mayor of Seattle that Clinton would not come if the streets weren't cleared. Reno wanted the feds to take over the policing actions, which almost certainly would have led to a massacre.

Contrast the outlook of Benjamin and the other protectors of corporate property with the attitude of a 34-year old Oregon farmer who found himself in the midst of the downtown protest, was arrested and harshly treated in jail: "To break a window in a retail facility in downtown Seattle is nothing compared to what some of these CEOs are doing daily."

Leave the last words to Jeff Crosby, the president of a union local of International Union of Electrical Workers who flew to Seattle with 15 of his fellow union members from New England. Crosby works at a GE plant, which is about to relocate in Mexico. After he went home, Crosby put up on the web this open letter:

> The decision by the AFL-CIO not to plan direct action was a mistake. The literature and petition the AFL-CIO used for Seattle was mostly unreadable and unusable, with no edge. Despite some heroic efforts by union folks in Seattle and other places, the AFL-CIO campaign was reminiscent of the 'old' AFL-CIO's campaign against NAFTA—remember 'Not This NAFTA'? If we had run a campaign against the congressional 'Fast Track' vote with 'Not this fast-track', we would have lost that one too. Did anyone really try to bring people to Seattle under the

Alexander Cockburn and Jeffrey St. Clair

slogan, 'We demand a working group'?

This is a period when on certain issues massive, nonviolent direct action is in order, as the demonstration in Seattle shows. Every member who went on our trip reports that support for the demonstrations, even with the disruptions, is overwhelming. And not just from other workers in the shop, but family and other friends, regardless of what they do for a living. 'Since we came home, we're being treated like conquering heroes,' marveled one of our group.

Perhaps the AFL-CIO was driven by policy advisers in Washington who didn't understand how angry people are about this issue... Perhaps they did not want to embarrass Gore. Perhaps Sweeney had an agreement with Clinton to ask for inforcible labor standards. Perhaps they thought that most people would be turned off by civil disobedience, or something else, I don't know. There were plenty of people in the labor movement pushing for the labor movement to join in the Direct Action—we lost.

Fortunately the street warriors won.

Anarkids and Hypocrites

Barbara Ehrenreich
The Progressive, *June 2000*

In retrospect, it looks like a case of false advertising. Posters for the April 16 anti-IMF actions in Washington, D.C., promised a "nonviolent demonstration." But what actually happened was that thousands of demonstrators were tear-gassed, pepper-sprayed, and/or beaten with police batons.

The Midnight Special Legal Collective, which provided legal support for the demonstrators, reports that one protester had three ribs broken during his arrest. Another was beaten bloody, then tossed into a paddy wagon with the instruction that he be driven around for a few hours before being taken to a hospital. In jail, hundreds of protesters were denied food or water for twenty-four hours, leading in at least one case to a severe hypoglycemic reaction. According to the legal collective:

> One group of men was taken into a basement, put into a cage, and told by a U.S. marshal, 'There are no cameras here. We can do whatever we want.' Anyone who looked up while the marshal was speaking was punched in the face. People were being released from prison in the middle of a cold, rainy night, without jackets, shoes, in some cases without shirts, and without any money to take a bus or cab anywhere—all had been taken from them by officials.

If this is nonviolence, you'd be better off taking up extreme boxing.

The anti-IMF posters were, of course, promising that the demonstrators themselves would behave in a nonviolent fashion, but nonviolence on one side is, at least in theory, connected to nonviolence on the other. If the protesters are civil and predictable in their actions, then, it is generally hoped and believed, the police will be moved to emulate them. And if the police should fall short of perfect nonviolence, then—the reasoning goes—the poor, martyred demonstrators will at least have the moral upper hand. Hence, in no small part, the excessive reaction by organizers of the Seattle anti-WTO protests to the black-clad anarchists who threw rocks through the windows of NikeTown, Starbucks, the Gap, and a few other chain stores last November.

No humans were harmed in the rock-throwing incidents—the stores were closed at the time. Yet anti-WTO organizers from the Direct Action Network reacted as if their protest had been taken over by a band of Hell's Angels. Instead of treating the young rock-throwers like sisters and brothers in the struggle—wrongheaded, perhaps, but undeniably enthusiastic—protest organizers swept up the broken glass. They hinted that the perpetrators were agents provocateurs paid by the police. Some proudly assert—though I cannot confirm this—that Direct Action Network folks helped finger the rock-throwers for the police.

Will somebody please call Hypocrisy Watch? The same people who administered a public spanking to the anarkids featured, as one of the anti-WTO's honored guests, one José Bové, the French farmer who famously torched a McDonald's. The double standard for what counts as "violence" was never explained.

Seattle organizers also fretted that the anarkids' actions would upset the unions, although no union leaders issued a peep of complaint. It would have been odd if they had, since America has one of the most violent labor histories of any industrialized nation in the world, and not every little bit of that violence was perpetrated by the Pinkertons. Nor did the rock-throwing demonstrably "ruin" the Seattle protests in the eyes of the public. In fact, it probably doubled the media attention, with most press accounts carefully distinguishing between the fifty thousand rock-less protesters and the twenty or so window-smashers.

And it would be interesting to know how many of the anarkid-bashers ever took the time to denounce the riot that swept Los Angeles just after the Rodney King verdict in 1990. Yes, I said "riot"—including attacks on people as well as property, much of it belonging to merely middle class, mostly Korean American, citizens. But the oh-so-politically-correct, whose numbers no doubt include some of today's self-righteously nonviolent protesters, prefer to call that an "uprising."

The events in Seattle and D.C. are in many obvious ways enormously heartening, but they also illustrate how absurdly ritualized left-wing protests have become, at least on the side of the protesters. Once, back in the now prehistoric sixties, a group would call for a demonstration, with or without a police permit, and the faithful would simply show up. If you were fortunate or fleet of foot, you got away unscathed. Otherwise—well, everyone knew there were risks to challenging the power of the state.

Sometime in the early 1980s, demonstration organizers started getting smarter—or, you might say, more scientific and controlling—about the process of demonstrating. In the anti-nuclear power and antiwar movements of the day, they carefully segregated protesters who wished to be arrested from those who did not and insisted that the potential arrestees be organized into "affinity groups" that had been trained for hours or even days in the technology of "nonviolent civil disobedience." It made sense at the time. Affinity groups provided a basis for consensual decision-making among large numbers of people. The training—in linking arms, going limp, and "jail solidarity"—helped assure minimal bodily harm to the arrestees. Besides, everything gets professionalized sooner or later: why not the revolution?

But there are problems with the new liturgy of protest. For one thing, not everyone has a master's degree in nonviolent civil disobedience, and many potential protesters, even quite militant ones, would be put off by the counter-cultural atmosphere of the trainings. I can remember almost being turned away from an antinuclear action in 1982 until one of my companions had the wit to lie and claim that we had indeed gone through extensive training.

Then there is the numbingly ritual quality of the actions: Protesters sit down in a spot prearranged with the police, protesters get carried off by the police and booked, protesters get released. Sometimes safely ritualized protests can be effective, as when, in March 1999, almost twelve hundred people—including dignitaries like former New York City Mayor David Dinkins—got themselves arrested to protest the shooting of Amadou Diallo. But even one of the organizers of that protest, longtime activist Leslie Cagan, points out the irony in the protesters' harmonious relationship with the very police force whose homicidal behavior they were protesting.

Worst of all, nonviolence on the part of protesters does not guarantee nonviolent behavior on the part of the police. In Seattle, as well as in D.C., many protesters were rewarded for their civility with pepper spray, beatings, and gas. These are not crossing guards we are up against, but some of the most highly militarized police in the world. In a few decades, they have moved from terrorizing communities of color to deploying torture as a tactic against anyone, of any color, who steps out of line: starving detainees in D.C., rubbing pepper spray in the eyes of antilogging protesters in California, confining prisoners to potentially lethal restraint chairs...

> Worst of all, nonviolence on the part of protesters does not guarantee nonviolent behavior on the part of the police. In Seattle, as well as in D.C., many protesters were rewarded for their civility with pepper spray, beatings, and gas.

Clearly the left, broadly speaking, has come to a creative impasse. We need to invent some new forms of demonstrating that minimize the danger while maximizing the possibilities for individual self-expression (sea turtle costumes, songs, dancing, and general playfulness). We need ways of protesting that are accessible to the uninitiated, untrained, nonvegan population as well as to the seasoned veteran. We need to figure out how to capture public attention while, as often as possible, directly accomplishing some not-entirely-symbolic purpose, such as gumming up a WTO meeting or, for that matter, slowing down latte sales at a Starbucks.

Rock-throwing doesn't exactly fit these criteria, nor did the old come-as-you-are demos of the sixties. But neither do the elaborately choreographed rituals known as "nonviolent" civil disobedience. The people at Direct Action Network, Global Exchange, and other groups were smart enough to comprehend the workings of the WTO, IMF, and World Bank. Now it's time for them to figure out how large numbers of people can protest the international capitalist cabal without getting clobbered—or trashed by their fellow demonstrators—in the process.

Barbara Ehrenreich

The Breakdown Inside the Ministerial

Paul Richmond
Seattle National Lawyers Guild WTO Legal Group,
Waging War on Dissent, *Winter 2000*

"It is a matter of record that, despite a year of hard preparatory work by the Chairman of the General Council, delegations and the Secretariat, the Ministerial failed to reach agreement either on the launch of a new Round of trade negotiations or on the other important points which had emerged in the course of the preparatory process. Furthermore, the WTO found itself at the centre of a wave of resentment against many aspects of the global economy, for which Seattle became a focus."
— Introduction to the Annual Report of the World Trade Organization

For much of 1999 the WTO operated as a leaderless organization. Perhaps it was the earlier protests against the organization that made it difficult to find someone to act as its titular representative. But from midsummer till September of '99, a period of nearly four months, the WTO was a leaderless organization.

In September of 1999, Michael Moore, a politician from New Zealand who'd been out of elective office for almost a decade, was given the job. Moore was a long-time friend of WTO policies. He represented New Zealand at the first APEC Ministerial Meeting and as New Zealand's Trade Minister was active in launching the Uruguay Rounds that created the WTO.

Moore met with some of the citizens of Seattle in early October, speaking before the Washington Council on International Trade and at the University of Washington. During the question and answer periods Moore was belligerent. He demonstrated a superficial understanding of the issues, as well as a willingness to lie, obfuscate, talk over people he disagreed with and ignore questions.

Perhaps Moore's most ridiculous moment was when he claimed that it was a form of cultural imperialism to say that the citizens of countries with oppressive dictators might not want their despots. Moore claimed that wanting representative rather than corporate government was a form of imperialism.

It's fairly easy to see how an organization led by this individual would react when faced with pressure.

"Do you think this process broke down at any point?"
"This process didn't work at any point."
—exchange between reporter and Zimbabwe Delegate to the WTO.

"We're a democracy and understand what democracy is all about. This is not democracy. This is just ridiculous."
—Namibian Delegate to the WTO.

From conversations with and statements collected from delegates, Moore and the others in the WTO responded to these pressures by making the rules of the meetings ever more rigid. Meeting rooms were changed hurriedly and many delegations not notified. Some delegates found themselves barred from participation when they did find out about meetings.

What has been going on in Seattle is a scandal. Developing countries that form more than two-thirds of the membership of the WTO are being coerced and stampeded by the major powers, especially the host country the US, to agree to a Declaration to which they were given very little opportunity to draft or consider.

Most of the important negotiations have taken place in "green room" meetings where only a few countries are invited. Most of the developing country members of the WTO have not been able to participate. Even if a country is invited to a meeting on a particular issue, it may not be a participant in other issues. Many developing countries were not invited to any meeting on any issue at all.

As a result most Ministers have been insulted by their not being able to take part in decisions that seriously affect their countries and people. Worse, they have had little chance to even know what is being discussed, by whom or where. Nor what the results of these discussions were.

Also, the programme has been so crammed and tight that when the final draft Declaration is produced, Ministers and officials would hardly have any time at all to consider its contents.

To expect them to 'join in the consensus' through the blackmail that otherwise the Ministerial Conference would be deemed a failure, is to impose a kind of blackmail.

—Martin Khor, Director, Third World Network.

Khor's statement was echoed by two thirds of the delegates in attendance. The Caribbean Delegations, the Latin American Delegations, and the African Delegations, all issued statements and/or held press conferences where they condemned the process.

As the conference drew to a close the press came back inside. Because most of them were barred from most sessions, the twenty-five hundred WTO accredited journalists had begun covering the streets of Seattle. The tear gassings, the arrests, the no-protest zones had become the main focus of some of the world's top reporters.

General Director Moore had said there would be a final briefing on the WTO at 7:00 PM on Friday December 3. Hundreds of journalists arrived at the sixth floor Green Room. Lugging their heavy professional gear. Computers. Video Cameras. Bulky tri-pods. They staked out places and waited. And waited.

After a few hours a representative of the Ministerial rushed in. The meeting was happening right away on the fourth floor Green Room. Right away. Hurry Hurry! Run!

The hundreds of reporters packed up their bulky gear as quickly as they could. Then they made their way to the single escalator that was the only way to move between the floors of the convention center.

On the escalators, the reporters crowded together, so many grains trying to get through a large funnel. These people were exhausted from a week of breathing chemical agents on the street and receiving what seemed like little more than hot air and obfuscation inside the WTO itself. There was palpable exhaustion painted on their faces. Many of their neat professional clothes were inundated with a mixed scent of cayenne and sweat.

When they arrived at the door to the fourth floor Green Room they were stopped. They waited. After a time it was decided that this meeting was only for delegates. And so the first of the reporters made their way from the door of the fourth floor Green Room. As others continued off the single escalator they too arrived and were disappointed. This scene continued for at least another twenty minutes. To their credit, none of these reporters broke any windows.

> The agenda thus far has seen us marginalized. This morning the African Delegation has put out a statement saying if our issues are not addressed before the declaration is actually out on the table we are going to withdraw our consensus because what's the point of coming to the table in a negotiation process which is purportedly to support the development interest of all countries yet when they come to the table their interests are completely out weighed. If you really look at the agenda that some of the north countries are putting out, that's the US, the European Union, Japan and Canada in particular, they totally ignore the issues of implementation, yet they want Africa to open up its markets...
>
> Also the preamble states that the WTO is about development. For us development is about alleviating poverty, it's about insuring that human rights are upheld, it's insuring that people are able to eat, its insuring that people are employed and well employed, and not exploited and its insuring that people have rights to services.
>
> And basically what this round is suggesting and proposing is that we sign these rights away in the interests of multinational corporations. And this is really the agenda. And we can confirm that this is the agenda, because any one of these US corporations who have paid $250,000 US Dollars can have four representatives in the US delegation to actually influence the process. This system is no longer about rules, it's about who has the money to influence trade policy in northern countries and it's absolutely outrageous.
>
> —Mohau Pheko, African Woman's Congress.

The Reporters had made the escalator circuit a few times and it was getting close to midnight. Now they were told that the conference was in fact over and Mike Moore would speak with them. The location was not the sixth floor where all their equipment was set up, it was the press briefing area in the middle of the fourth floor press area. Once again, the ragtag army of the world's finest reporters funneled down the single narrow escalator.

The press area was an enormous cavern filled with rows of make shift cubicles, freestanding computers, and the like. The pathways between the obstacles were narrow and so the frenzied, hurried press was again slowed.

The small area that was designated for the final WTO press conference could have fit perhaps fifty people. The reporters pressed in filling the small side room to many times beyond its capacity. Still the majority of their number were outside the small cubicle where Moore's final remarks to the world were to take place.

To understand what happened next, it is important to understand the mindset the reporters had been put in. For most of the conference, they'd been denied access to any meeting of importance. Now, at the end of the event, they were stuck in a hallway, anxious, on assignment, and afraid they'd be scooped. And inside the small room, Moore himself was nowhere around. There were merely a lot of tired reporters, crowded together, breathing on each other.

Someone began to chant: "Mikey, come out and play."

The chant spread like wildfire. Where a few days ago had been an army of neatly clad professionals, now was a group of people outraged with what they had experienced from the World Trade Organization, and Director Mike Moore himself

Hurriedly the conference was moved back to the larger area on the sixth floor.

Once it started, the press conference quickly began to resemble the reception Moore had received at UW in October. The questions that rained down on General Director Moore from the crowd during this final conference were the same ones asked by the demonstrators outside days before and by the majority of the delegates only hours and minutes before. Moore was discomforted. Moore was confused. Every question seemed to make things worse.

Moore left the conference with many wondering if the WTO was now functionally dead.

Rebellion and Repression

Oakley

A Place for Rage

Rachel Neumann
Dissent, *Spring 2000*

There is an image from the late sixties, so famous now as to be cliché, of a young woman slipping a flower in the barrel of a soldier's gun. There's another photograph, from Paris in 1968, of a young man in a black turtleneck surrounded by running and ducking protesters. The man has a rock in his hand and his arm is pulled back, ready to throw. To these I add one from the protests in Seattle last November against the World Trade Organization: a police officer standing at attention in full riot gear, his face hidden behind a gas mask and his body buried in black padding. On the sidewalk in front of him, someone has written HUG ME in large letters with an arrow pointing to the officer. I turn these images over in my mind. The peaceful determination of a young woman confronting potential violence with a flower. The unleashed power of the rock in the young man's hand. The humor, the hope, the impossibility of putting one's arms around the police officer's heavily armored body.

The underlying question these images present is how to negotiate between violence and nonviolence as means of protest. It's a conflict that started long before the sixties, long before the struggle for Indian independence began in 1915. In the last twenty years in the United States, this question has felt less urgent. With so little visible resistance and so few enduring victories for true democracy, there's a temptation on the left to take whatever we can get, whatever its form. And yet the question flares up again now in response the possibility of building a real movement out of the actions in Seattle—how do we present ourselves? How do we press our advantage?

> "Our goals, our values, our own morality, must be visible already in our actions. The new human beings we want to create—we must already strive to be these human beings right here and now."
>
> —Herbert Marcuse

Nonviolent protest, at its best, is the enactment of the prefiguration Marcuse describes. It works on the principles of solidarity and pacifism in the face of aggression. Nonviolence defines itself, even in name, in contrast—a protester going limp in the arms of a rigid policeman, a group sitting down and singing in the path of an oncoming tank. (Without the force to counter it, pacifism becomes passivity; going limp without the policeman's presence isn't nonviolence, it's just tiredness.) The state response is officers in uniforms, tear gas, tanks, arrests. This show of force becomes, paradoxically, evidence of vulnerability; the need for the state to protect whatever it has at any cost is evidence that the current system is constructed and enforced, not natural, not self-perpetuating. Nonviolent protest is a considered way of being; in solidarity, people learn to relate to each other as part of a mutually supportive and mutually dependent community. This contradicts the social conditioning that says other people are a threat to our own success and we must each look out only for ourselves. Nonviolence is also effective theater—the media presents images of pacifism in the face of force, innocence as the victim of violence.

And at the same time, there are those who refuse to play by the rules, who smash windows, draw graffiti on walls, and shout back at the cops. Are these people outside the "morality" of progressive movements? These outbreaks aren't just adolescent rage. Aimé Césaire described the violent process of colonization: it enforces control by refusing people their own emotions and natural reactions. Our current global system is a process of colonization. It not only creates organizations like the WTO that replace national sovereignty with corporate interests, it also displaces people's human ways of relating to each other and substitutes monetary relationships in which human worth is measured in dollars.

This system would prefer that people respond to exploitation with complacency and politeness. But what becomes of people who work full-time for less than a living wage, without health care, without day care? What emotion builds up after years of work in dead-end jobs? What happens after finding out you live near a toxic-waste dump? That your son is arrested while driving for being black? Rage is a natural and required response—so repressed by the powers that be that it often becomes a lashing-out, a misdirected form of resistance.

A politics that expresses any of this messy emotion is often considered—in nonviolent circles—to be "not following process" and "acting like the enemy." But to condemn the rage by judging those who express it, without acknowledging the larger context of systematic state violence, is to strengthen the oppressor. Because rage is a natural and required response, the question is not whether it is good or bad or morally right, but what we do with it. How can we direct it into energy that creates a more just society? Traditional nonviolence is, of course, not a passive response. It is an organized attempt to confront injustice without succumbing to the violence of the oppressor. And yet, traditionally it has often been the precursor to vanguard movements impatient with both the level of violence directed at the movement and the slowness of change. Out of the civil rights movement came the Black Panthers. Out of Students for a Democratic Society, Weatherman. The system commonly tries to funnel the rage that oppression produces into other, politically acceptable, outlets—to turn aggression into sports tournaments, graffiti into sanctioned art projects—but there's something about institutionally sanctioned, structured outrage that, because of the official seal of approval, ceases to exist as rage.

> "Need I recall to any student of history the serious rioting and destruction of property which has preceded every advance in the liberties of which England is so proud."
>
> —Frances Berkeley Young, writing in the *Nation* in 1912 in response to an article describing women fighting for equal rights in England (smashing windows and "pestering public ministers") as "hysterical, crazy, and therefore irresponsible women."

Noninstitutionalized rage expresses itself in a number of ways, many of them clearly harmful and abusive. Yet if those who advocate nonviolence as the only route to social change want to create a world in which violence doesn't exist, then they must acknowledge that nonviolence and violence have been linked historically, examine the sometimes violent expression of anger and how it can be transformed into something progressive. Because of the quickness of moral judgments, many expressions of rage are conflated and immediately dismissed without being examined strategically. Property destruction is one such expression. When speaking about "violence," it's important to distinguish the rock thrown through a window from the rock thrown at another human being. This is not a semantic distinction. All expression of anger is on a continuum, but historically property destruction doesn't necessary lead to violence toward other human beings. The Luddites smashed machinery, the Wobblies closed mills and mines, the English suffragettes broke windows, and Earth First! activists tinkered with the engines and tires of logging trucks—all without injuring other human beings.

One crucial element of change (and a necessity for building a larger movement) is the visible sign of resistance. Property destruction allows for a change in landscape, a visual punctuation. The institutional response to protest in the United States in recent years has been to clean things up. Once people are arrested and silenced, there's no evidence that resistance took place. The broken window theory implies that if you can't see the smashed glass, it isn't a problem. You can't see homeless people? They must have found homes. You don't see graffiti? Must be that the anger and boredom (and creativity) behind it is gone. What if property destruction could also be creation, an added or changed image left behind? Particularly at this time—when nascent coalitions are forming against the privileging of profit over people—destruction of material things may be an apt response.

I approach these possibilities with caution. Property destruction has often been linked with larger uses of violence. Because of the way that men in particular are taught both to repress and vent their anger, it often comes out as an exaggerated representation of masculinity, reproducing instead of contradicting the existing power structure. Violent opposition in this country, from Weatherman to the Black Panthers, has often internalized violence, taking out their anger on each other as opposed to a larger target. There is always a question of control, of keeping the energy of the initial emotion and transforming its expression. Is it possible to target this anger without deflating it?

Of course there are also legitimate questions about when is the time for property destruction and when is the time for sitting in the street (and when, if

Rachel Neumann

ever, the two can happen productively simultaneously). At times it may be necessary for thousands of people to lock arms at the entrances to a Convention Center. At other times, a few people may be able to capture media attention and define an issue through targeted property destruction. Note the instant fame of José Bové, the French farmer who tried to dismantle a McDonald's. It is important to remember that these choices are, in large part, decided by media attention—they are strategic, not moral questions.

I am not suggesting property destruction is the only or even the best answer to these questions. It simply represents one expression of rage that nonviolent movements have not figured out how to either integrate or control; it has its own energy and validity. To think about the ways in which protest uses emotion in terms of strategy, not morality, shifts the debate. Much discussion of these questions has been framed by broad definitions of violence and nonviolence. The words have been thrown around so often that, like prolife and prochoice, any actual meaning becomes unintelligible. An authentic discussion requires a restructuring of language, an interest in moving beyond the oversimplified debate of Ghandi vs. Che, Martin vs. Malcom.

Clearly the rage that people feel as a result of exploitation and alienation, and the expression of that rage, is not the same as the violence committed by the overseers of coffee plantations, by sweatshop managers in New York and Taiwan, of sugar cane and pineapple field owners. A communiqué, sent out after the Seattle protests, from the ACME collective reads: "We contend that property destruction is not a violent activity unless it destroys lives or causes pain in the process. Private property, especially corporate private property, is in itself infinitely more violent than any action taken against it." They go on to distinguish between personal and private property—the things that we own that have worth because they are dear to us (books, photos, the homes we have worked on) and property that exists solely at the expense of others and with the purpose of generating more capital.

There are few enough moments these days where real change is possible. The insistence by progressive movements to protest in the morally right way is, in part, the result of the scarcity of media opportunities for progressives. But to build greater momentum requires creating a language and organizing movements that are not just part of the officially sanctioned and familiar political landscape. Traditional nonviolence, as it has been practiced in this country, has become part of familiar political behavior. Ghandi is quoted on ads for First National Bank and Apple Computer. Protesters dutifully file into protest pens and, as in the massive protests over the shootings of Amadou Diallo in New York, arrests are choreographed in advance. This last example was both effective as a media event and oddly disconcerting for some participants. Clearly in large part performance, it brought the issue to the media's attention, but didn't necessarily address the frustration and anger of those who had been brutalized by the police. How do we keep the principles of what has been traditionally been called nonviolence intact and, at the same time, nurture an authentic and growing movement? Who will see themselves in our actions? Of all the graffiti spray-painted during the protests in Seattle last November, one piece stays with me: "Don't Forget: We Are Winning." The "We" here was everybody—the union marchers, the environmentalists in turtle costumes, the anarchists in black—and the brightly-painted scrawl had a salutary effect on more than one tear-gassed protester. Even in Seattle, that "We" was not broad enough. Although not true of many of the workshops that took place the week before or the labor march, the protesters in Seattle on November 30, engaging in both nonviolent direct action and property-destruction, were predominantly white. In the evening, however, teenagers of every color were drawn downtown by the energy and filled the streets even as the police were clearing them. When I speak of finding a place and a form for rage, I am not just speaking about the emotion of those who engaged in the property destruction in Seattle, though they are included, but of the people who engage in violence and property destruction in their own homes and their own neighborhoods.

Langston Hughes was describing, not threatening, when he wrote about the explosion of a dream deferred. How do we make a place for the rage that has built up for so many years? This is something we have to do—not only in order to create a more economically and racially diverse movement of (and not just on behalf of) the most oppressed, but also so as to acknowledge our own anger and the ways we have internalized the violence around us. We all feel that rage. If there is a morality involved here, it is this: if we want the lives we envision to be prefigured in our actions, as Marcuse writes, then we must have the honesty to recognize ourselves in the anger we see on the street. To act in the world as we would like the world to be requires making a space for the fulcrum of our emotions. It is dishonest not to talk about the intangibles: the feeling in the air and the smiles on people's faces as the Nike sign was being dismantled in Seattle. It wasn't so much the rage of the people destroying the sign—they were calm and focused. It was the reflection, and the release, of the crowd's rage and a symbol of how it could be transformed into action. Without the sign, the place felt different; as if it belonged to us, the people in the streets, and not the police. We need to hold these questions close to us: how to create not only a language but a way of being that holds true to ideas of solidarity and community, that does not recreate the violence we are protesting against, and, at the same time, holds a place for rage.

Josh MacPhee / Just Seed

N30 Black Bloc Communiqué

ACME Collective
Surfaced Saturday December 4, 1999

On November 30, several groups of individuals in black bloc attacked various corporate targets in downtown Seattle. Among the targets were (to name just a few):

Fidelity Investment (major investor in Occidental Petroleum, the bane of the U'wa tribe in Columbia); Bank of America, US Bancorp, Key Bank and Washington Mutual Bank (financial institutions key in the expansion of corporate repression); Old Navy, Banana Republic and the GAP (as Fisher family businesses, rapers of Northwest forest lands and sweatshop laborers); NikeTown and Levi's (whose overpriced products are made in sweatshops); McDonald's (slave-wage fast-food peddlers responsible for destruction of tropical rainforests for grazing land and slaughter of animals); Starbucks (peddlers of an addictive substance whose products are harvested at below-poverty wages by farmers who are forced to destroy their own forests in the process); Warner Bros. (media monopolists); Planet Hollywood (for being Planet Hollywood).

This activity lasted for over five hours and involved the breaking of storefront windows and doors and the defacing of facades. Slingshots, newspaper boxes, sledge hammers, mallets, crowbars, and nail-pullers were used to strategically destroy corporate property and gain access (one of the three targeted Starbucks and NikeTown were looted). Eggs filled with glass etching solution, paint-balls, and spray-paint were also used.

The black bloc was a loosely organized cluster of affinity groups and individuals who roamed around downtown, pulled this way by a vulnerable and significant storefront and that way by the sight of a police formation. Unlike the vast majority of activists who were pepper-sprayed, tear-gassed, and shot at with rubber bullets on several occasions, most of our section of the black bloc escaped serious injury by remaining constantly in motion and avoiding engagement with the police. We buddied up, kept tight, and watched each others' backs. Those attacked by federal thugs were un-arrested by quick-thinking and organized members of the black bloc. The sense of solidarity was awe-inspiring.

The Peace Police

Unfortunately, the presence and persistence of "peace police" was quite disturbing. On at least six separate occasions, so-called "nonviolent" activists physically attacked individuals who targeted corporate property. Some even went so far as to stand in front of the NikeTown super store and tackle and shove the black bloc away. Indeed, such self-described "peace-keepers" posed a much greater threat to individuals in the black bloc than the notoriously violent uniformed "peace-keepers" sanctioned by the state (undercover officers have even used the cover of the activist peace-keepers to ambush those who engage in corporate property destruction).

Response to the Black Bloc

Response to the black bloc has highlighted some of the contradictions and internal oppressions of the "nonviolent activist" community. Aside from the obvious hypocrisy of those who engaged in violence against black-clad and masked people (many of whom were harassed despite the fact that they never engaged in property destruction), there is the racism of privileged activists who can afford to ignore the violence perpetrated against the bulk of society and the natural world in the name of private property rights. Window-smashing has engaged and inspired many of the most oppressed members of Seattle's community more than any giant puppets or sea turtle costumes ever could (not to disparage the effectiveness of those tools in other communities).

Ten Myths About the Black Bloc

Here's a little something to dispel the myths that have been circulating about the N30 black bloc:

1. "They are all a bunch of Eugene anarchists." While a few may be anarchists from Eugene, we hail from all over the United States, including Seattle. In any case, most of us are familiar with local issues in Seattle (for instance, the recent occupation of downtown by some of the most nefarious of multinational retailers).

2. "They are all followers of John Zerzan." A lot of rumors have been circulating that we are followers of John Zerzan, an anarcho-primitivist author from Eugene who advocates property destruction. While some of us may appreciate his writings and analyses, he is in no sense our leader, directly, indirectly, philosophically or otherwise.

3. "The mass public squat is the headquarters of the anarchists who destroyed property on November 30th." In reality, most of the people in the "Autonomous Zone" squat are residents of Seattle who have spent most of their time since its opening on the 28th in the squat. While they may know of one another, the two groups are not co-extensive and in no case could the squat be considered the headquarters of people who destroyed property.

4. "They escalated situations on the 30th, leading to the tear-gassing of passive,

nonviolent protesters." To answer this, we need only note that tear-gassing, pepper-spraying and the shooting of rubber bullets all began before the black blocs (as far as we know) started engaging in property destruction. In addition, we must resist the tendency to establish a causal relationship between police repression and protest in any form, whether it involved property destruction or not. The police are charged with protecting the interests of the wealthy few and the blame for the violence cannot be placed upon those who protest those interests.

5. Conversely: "They acted in response to the police repression." While this might be a more positive representation of the black bloc, it is nevertheless false. We refuse to be misconstrued as a purely reactionary force. While the logic of the black bloc may not make sense to some, it is in any case a pro-active logic.

6. "They are a bunch of angry adolescent boys." Aside from the fact that it belies a disturbing ageism and sexism, it is false. Property destruction is not merely macho rabble-rousing or testosterone-laden angst release. Nor is it displaced and reactionary anger. It is strategically and specifically targeted direct action against corporate interests.

7. "They just want to fight." This is pretty absurd, and it conveniently ignores the eagerness of "peace police" to fight us. Of all the groups engaging in direct action, the black bloc was perhaps the least interested in engaging the authorities and we certainly had no interest in fighting with other anti-WTO activists (despite some rather strong disagreements over tactics).

8. "They are a chaotic, disorganized, and opportunistic mob." While many of us could surely spend days arguing over what "chaotic" means, we were certainly not disorganized. The organization may have been fluid and dynamic, but it was tight. As for the charge of opportunism, it would be hard to imagine who of the thousands in attendance didn't take advantage of the opportunity created in Seattle to advance their agenda. The question becomes, then, whether or not we helped create that opportunity and most of us certainly did (which leads us to the next myth):

9. "They don't know the issues" or "they aren't activists who've been working on this." While we may not be professional activists, we've all been working on this convergence in Seattle for months. Some of us did work in our home towns and others came to Seattle months in advance to work on it. To be sure, we were responsible for many hundreds of people who came out on the streets on the 30th, only a very small minority of which had anything to do with the black bloc. Most of us have been studying the effects of the global economy, genetic engineering, resource extraction, transportation, labor practices, elimination of indigenous autonomy, animal rights, and human rights and we've been doing activism on these issues for many years. We are neither ill-informed nor inexperienced.

10. "Masked anarchists are anti-democratic and secretive because they hide their identities." Let's face it. With or without a mask we aren't living in a democracy right now. If this week has not made it plain enough, let us

ACME Collective

remind you—we are living in a police state. People tell us that if we really think that we're right, we wouldn't be hiding behind masks. "The truth will prevail" is the assertion. While this is a fine and noble goal, it does not jive with the present reality. Those who pose the greatest threat to the interests of Capital and State will be persecuted. Some pacifists would have us accept this persecution gleefully. Others would tell us that it is a worthy sacrifice. We are not so morose. Nor do we feel we have the privilege to accept persecution as a sacrifice: persecution to us is a daily inevitability and we treasure our few freedoms. To accept incarceration as a form of flattery betrays a large amount of "first world" privilege. We feel that an attack on private property is necessary if we are to rebuild a world which is useful, healthful and joyful for everyone. And this despite the fact that hypertrophied private property rights in this country translate into felony charges for any property destruction over $250.

Motivations of the Black Bloc

The primary purpose of this communiqué is to diffuse some of the aura of mystery that surrounds the black bloc and make some of its motivations more transparent, since our masks cannot be.

On the Violence of Property

We contend that property destruction is not a violent activity unless it destroys lives or causes pain in the process. By this definition, private property—especially corporate private property—is itself infinitely more violent than any action taken against it. Private property should be distinguished from personal property. The latter is based upon use while the former is based upon trade. The premise of personal property is that each of us has what s/he needs. The premise of private property is that each of us has something that someone else needs or wants.

In a society based on private property rights, those who are able to accrue more of what others need or want have greater power. By extension, they wield greater control over what others perceive as needs and desires, usually in the interest of increasing profit to themselves. Advocates of "free trade" would like to see this process to its logical conclusion: a network of a few industry monopolists with ultimate control over the lives of everyone else. Advocates of "fair trade" would like to see this process mitigated by government regulations meant to superficially impose basic humanitarian standards.

As anarchists, we despise both positions. Private property—and capitalism, by extension—is intrinsically violent and repressive and cannot be reformed or mitigated. Whether the power of everyone is concentrated into the hands of a few corporate heads or diverted into a regulatory apparatus charged with mitigating the disasters of the latter, no one can be as free or as powerful as they could be in a nonhierarchical society. When we smash a window, we aim to destroy the thin veneer of legitimacy that surrounds private property rights. At the same time, we exorcise that set of violent and destructive social relationships which has been imbued in almost everything around us.

The Battle of Seattle

By "destroying" private property, we convert its limited exchange value into an expanded use value. A storefront window becomes a vent to let some fresh air into the oppressive atmosphere of a retail outlet (at least until the police decide to tear-gas a nearby road blockade). A newspaper box becomes a tool for creating such vents or a small blockade for the reclamation of public space or an object to improve one's vantage point by standing on it. A dumpster becomes an obstruction to a phalanx of rioting cops and a source of heat and light. A building facade becomes a message board to record brainstorm ideas for a better world. After N30, many people will never see a shop window or a hammer the same way again. The potential uses of an entire cityscape have increased a thousand-fold. The number of broken windows pales in comparison to the number broken spells—spells cast by a corporate hegemony to lull us into forgetfulness of all the violence committed in the name of private property rights and of all the potential of a society without them. Broken windows can be boarded up (with yet more waste of our forests) and eventually replaced, but the shattering of assumptions will hopefully persist for some time to come.

Against Capital and State,
the ACME Collective
"Peasant Revolt!"

Disclaimer: These observations and analyses represent only those of the ACME Collective and should not be construed to be representative of the rest of the black bloc on N30 or anyone else who engaged in riot or property destruction that day.

ACME Collective

the Stranger

FREE EVERY ... VOL.9, NO.13 · DEC. 9-15, 1999 · MAKING THE ... CITY SAFE FOR SHOPPERS

OUR HO-HO
HOLIDAY
EDITION OF
EXCELLENT

WTO BREAKUP

SEASON'S GREETINGS!

121 CN

FEDERAL BLAST DISPERSION CHEMICAL GRENADE (CN)

WARNING... `DANGER
FOR USE BY TRAINED PERSONNEL ONLY
MAY START FIRES

NORM GOES DOWN:
RIOT-HAPPY COPS TELL ALL

PAUL IS DEAD
MAYOR SCHELL WORKS BER, THEN WTO 15

OUR TEARY-EYED FAREWELL TO THE WTO

SEATTLE'S ANEMIC PROTESTERS, WTO BLOOPERS, THE MEAN INTERNATIONAL PRESS, AND ADVICE FROM A REAL COP! P.9

Imagine

Geov Parrish

"The revolution. . . didn't and doesn't need these vitality-sucking Oregon parasites. It's not the property destruction we resent—it's the deliberate sabotaging of our work... Fuck you. Fuck everything you stand for. And stay the fuck away from our revolution."
—"Anarchists, Go Home," *Seattle Weekly,* December 9, 1999.

Okay, I was pissed. *Really* pissed. And so, I wrote a rant, published for the three hundred thousand readers of the *Seattle Weekly.* I wrote it within hours of when fifty thousand of us—mostly young, many self-identified anarchists—had an important and irretrievable part of our stunning, historic victory snatched away by the property damage tactics of a relative handful of tunnel-visioned fools. Who then actually *bragged* about their stunt.

My venue may well have been a mistake; a mainstream media outlet is usually no place to air an internal anarchist debate on tactics. The title wasn't mine; it was unfortunate, and I should have seen the possibility of it coming. (I have an uneasy relationship with mainstream media; we use each other.) But the Seattle public desperately needed to hear that anarchists were far from in agreement. And while I'm over the anger—what's done is done—I remain convinced that the Seattle property damage was, at best, one of the great tactical mistakes of U.S. protest history; at worst, a tragic, intentional act of sabotage that knowingly did the work of the corporate state more effectively than the state itself could ever have done.

To understand why I reached that conclusion instantly, and stand by it today, set aside what *was* accomplished in Seattle: the setting in motion of the possible eventual death of neoliberalism, the global inspiration for an already vibrant grass-roots movement. That was in itself beyond anything dreamed possible by the few thousand wet blockaders, determined on the morning of November 30, 1999 to deliver an antiglobalization statement more emphatic than the symbolic march later that day by the AFL-CIO. Big labor's plan was a now-forgotten attempt to petition for "a seat at the table" by lying under the table and licking the boots of power like some abused dog.

It could have been the last time.

Imagine for a second. Imagine that the American public—the folks who get their news from Tom Brokaw or Dan Rather, the folks who will never see "This is What Democracy Looks Like," or even hear the phrase—had never heard the media myth, induced by endless footage of the same six broken windows and a flaming dumpster, of Seattle "riots" that desperate police and National Guard had to stop by whatever means were at hand. Imagine that they had instead taken away from Seattle the story that ordinary citizens, folks just like you and me, can stop global power dead in its tracks. That we have the power, not by voting every four years, but by knocking over the table and refusing to settle for scraps. Were it not for the property damage and its ready-made images, for all the venal bias of corporate media, that is the story the networks and pundits would have had to address—with or without the self-interested response of the corporate state and its heavily armed goons. And it could have forever changed politics in the heart of the beast.

Now imagine that fifty-one million Gore voters, witnessing an obvious, semi-sanitized coup d'etat one year later, had absorbed that lesson, and the subsequent lessons of D.C., Philly, L.A., Prague, et al. What could have, what *would* have happened?

Any good anarchist, of course, can sneer with self-righteous validation at the bankruptcy of the 2000 (or any other) Presidential elections. But for most Americans, it's their most passionate engagement with political life. What did we lose?

All that was at least possible on the morning of November 30, when the black bloc could have looked around the streets of downtown Seattle and realized, with the cops hopelessly outnumbered and the meetings of one of the world's most powerful groups obviously paralyzed, that this was no time to upstage the "pathological pacifists." Everyone on the streets that day—blockader or black bloc—understood the significance of breaking windows, understood that it would completely change how the world viewed the event. That's why so many protesters were inanely screaming "No violence!," and that's why the black bloc acted as it did. But whether out of contempt for the often ineffective tactic of civil disobedience, or a simple inability to let go of a plan, an opportunity to inspire tens of millions of people in the heart of the most destructive society in global history was missed. We may never get another opportunity like that in our lifetimes.

That's why I was so pissed at the black bloc—not because I'm philosophically opposed to property damage (many of the same activists who hated the broken windows adored José Bové), but because it was so obviously and critically the wrong time and place, and because we lost so much we'll never get back.

There were other losses and gains. On the minus side, tens of millions of people "learned" what an "anarchist" was. ("It's a mindless young criminal who burns things to the ground for no apparent reason. Right?") For some reason, a lot of black blocers seem giddily triumphant on this point. Hello? Do you ever actually talk with anyone outside your circle of friends, anyone who doesn't agree with you? In Washington state, we have a guy named Robert Yates, who was

Congress Scraps One F22
Decides to build
20 thousand
schools instead
EDUCATION/B1

Mumia Freed
Tens of thousands celebrate
in the streets
JUSTICE/D1

Jordon gives
Nike the boot
Joins world wide
Nike boycott
SPORTS/E1

Seattle Post Intelligence
THE VOICE OF THE PEOPLE
Tuesday Morning • November 30, 1999

Boeing to move overseas

By JOE HILL
NEWS CORRESPONDENT

Clinton pledges help for poorest nations

By Ken Saro-Wiwa
P1 AGRICULTURE CORRESPONDENT

arrested in 2000 for a string of over a dozen gruesome rape/murders of young
women over the course of many years. Yates is loathed and despised here, as he
should be. The "Eugene anarchists" (which overlaps slightly with actual anarchists from the actual city of Eugene) are loathed and despised more. Thanks a
whole helluva lot. I've got to organize in this community.

Also on the minus side, we got a ready-made excuse for police repression.
Yes, I know, that part would have happened anyway, but because downtown
Seattle burned to the ground (that's the national myth), a broad swath of the
public that might have been outraged by the state's thuggish reaction instead
thinks it's just fine.

(Memo to those privileged white "revolutionaries" who think it's righteous
to set in motion the apparati of a police state: "The People" aren't down with it.
"The People"—that is, the folks who knew the reality long before you, who risk
first hand each day the gauntlet of our police state's underside—didn't want or
need the additional hassles, and hate *you* for instigating them. What do you
think will be done with all those new high-tech weapons when there's no international conference in town?)

On the plus side, the same myths of widespread destruction that horrified
Americans inspired much of the rest of the world. They already knew that the
WTO and other instruments of American dominance were evil—but they didn't
think we had it in us. They're right, for the time being—we don't—but it's a nice
myth to have.

Finally, on the plus side, the black bloc itself learned from Seattle. At D.C.
and subsequent demos, the black bloc has done a lot to restore its reputation
among other activists, providing a flexible, creative, and constructive role. At
many of these events, the bloc is agreeing to respect other organizers' desires for
a nonviolence code for the scope and duration of the action. (According to a number of sources, such an agreement was also in place in Seattle, and was ignored.)
For all the black bloc's contempt for the ideological inflexibility of "pacifists," in

Geov Parrish

Seattle it was the bloc's ideological inflexibility that proved tragic. That lesson was noticed, all to the good.

There is another lesson, too, one that is so far learned incompletely. I learned it, or at least tried to, after my unfortunate quote that began this piece; it is to accept the assistance of anyone who would help weaken a corrupt global system, move on from the mistakes, and persevere at alliance-building—the only way we will ever achieve the critical mass necessary for a legitimate revolution.

But much of the radical anarchist press clearly hasn't learned that lesson. Too much of it still uses "pacifist" like an epithet (and an inaccurate one, applied to anyone who practices civil disobedience), ignoring the long and storied history of anarcho-pacifism. Nor has it been learned by the largely white, largely privileged radical Left, looking down its collective nose at those it would so graciously help (but not allow to help define the movement); looking down still further at the increasingly desperate SUV-driving middle-class folks who could also swell our ranks; refusing to accept the help of the radical Right on issues like civil liberties or NATO bombings when we might make common cause; using language too obtuse to make sense to anyone outside the choir; and on, and on. We're not strong enough to topple global capitalism by ourselves. We don't have to be. We could have a lot of friends. But we have to know our audience, and we must speak and act intelligibly.

Seattle was a tremendous start, but as Alexander Cockburn so correctly notes, we're not going to surprise the corporate state again. The challenge now is to move beyond the tactic of surrounding convention centers; to reclaim, in our local communities, the opening for revolutionary possibility among disengaged, cynical (North) Americans that we could have had, but lost, in Seattle. The Bush years will provide lots of chances to demonstrate—now even to disbelieving Democratic Party loyalists—that there is a class war underway, and that the only way to end that war is to respond as though we are under attack. Because we are, and it will be far more obvious now than it was under Clinton, or would have been under Al Gore. In the end, the mantra is no different for anarchists than for anyone else who wants to see a more just, less bloody world: organize, organize, organize.

Who Are Those Masked Anarchists?

L.A. Kauffman

Looking back at Seattle a year after we shut down the WTO, I'm struck by the extent to which the issue that was foremost in many activists' minds at the time—the split between the direct-action blockaders and the window-smashing Black Bloc—now seems almost like a nonissue. I don't mean that the heated tactical and philosophical debates about what constitutes nonviolence have gone away: they never will, for these are questions that every protest movement must eventually face. But many people organizing against corporate globalization in the United States decided, in the wake of Seattle, not to allow our movements to be divided and conquered over the question of property destruction. On several occasions since then, most dramatically during the A16 protests against the World Bank and International Monetary Fund in Washington, D.C., Black Blocs have agreed to respect nonviolence guidelines set by larger coalitions, while the coalitions in turn have adopted less stringent guidelines that permit, for example, the dismantling of police barricades.

That said, the Black Bloc remains perhaps the least understood component of the Seattle protests. The corporate media quickly labeled them "violent" (indeed, my own account for Salon.com was edited so that it did, too—teaching me never again, no matter how bad of a pepper spray-induced migraine I have, to give an editor the green light to edit as she pleases). Many clueless journalists, looking for a leader of the leaderless group, declared that anarchist writer John Zerzan was the rioters' guru—after all, his name turned up when they did a Nexis search for "Eugene" and "anarchist." Most accounts, moreover, missed the fact that most of the direct-action blockaders considered themselves anarchists as well: The century-old stereotype of anarchy as mayhem defined the media coverage.

The Black Bloc concept—a group of anarchists who dress in black, mask their faces, use militant tactics, and watch each other's backs—was borrowed from the German *Autonomen* and first used in North America, to my knowledge, in the early 1990s. "It was focused on an idea of solidarity," explains Lesley Wood, a Canadian activist who has participated in some Black Bloc contingents, "that you were a unit and you operated as a unit, and you protected anybody from out-side attacks."

The roots of Seattle's Black Bloc, however, lie in the tempestuous forest activism on the West Coast from the middle of the 1990s onward. In 1995, President Bill Clinton signed the "Emergency Salvage Timber" rider into law, which permitted a logging free-for-all on public lands. This sell-out radicalized many environmentalists and galvanized a new set of militant and savvy Earth First! protest campaigns throughout the West, especially in Oregon and Idaho.

The most important and influential of these was the campaign to preserve a forest in Oregon's Warner Creek watershed that had been torched by an arson-ist, rendering it eligible for logging under the salvage rider. When the cutting was about to begin, a group of protesters blocked the main logging road—and maintained the blockade for an astounding 343 days. "There were these two signs on the gate, white and red striped signs like candy canes with reflectors on them," remembers a young man named Cloud, who took part in the encampment. "So we wrote 'Cascadia Free State' and claimed it as our own."

The eleven month Cascadia Free State was an unprecedented experiment in anarchist principles of self-management, a "temporary autonomous zone" where activists enacted their dreams of the good society. The experience of cre-ating such a world for themselves, and then seeing it destroyed by Forest Service bulldozers, fostered a rare fearlessness and audacity, which came to define the activist climate of nearby Eugene. When four young women who took part in the blockade were jailed in the summer of 1996, dozens of activists stormed the jail, causing a formidable ruckus and smashing one window before being arrested themselves. Later, someone torched a nearby Forest Service ranger station, burning it to the ground. Their encampment was demolished, but the activists ultimately won; the timber sale was canceled and the forest remains untouched.

Part of the reason why the Cascadia Free State lasted as long as it did was because the blockade employed "lock down" devices, which make it more difficult and expensive for the authorities to remove protesters from a site. Any barricade or fortification that activists create is ultimately symbolic; the police will always have more force at their disposal, and the equipment to knock it down or tear it apart. But if a person is attached to it, and would be injured if the blockade were simply demolished, it's a whole different game.

Lock down devices were first developed by radical environmentalists in Australia in the 1980s, and soon spread, first to England and then to North America. The simplest of them are called "lock boxes," and are made of steel or PVC pipes with a cross bar welded at the midway point inside them. The activists who are going to lock down place a chain bracelet around each of their wrists with a clip or carabiner hanging from it. Then they insert their arms into the pipe and clip onto the cross bar inside. In this way, they can lock themselves to, say, the axle of a logging truck, or link together with others in a circle. To remove them, the authorities have to cut the pipes off without cutting the demonstrators, which can take hours.

But the authorities came up with an alternative approach to dismantling the blockades: try to force the protesters to unclip through pain compliance.

Police first began using pepper spray against demonstrators on the West Coast for this purpose. In the most widely publicized incident, in 1997, four Northern California Earth First! activists who were blockading the office of an anti-environmental congressman in Eureka had pepper spray applied directly to their eyes with cotton swabs. The incident was videotaped, and on it you can hear the blood-curdling screams of the young Earth First!ers as the caustic chemical—which according to manufacturers' guidelines should not be used within two feet of a person's body—burns their eyes.

"When you lock yourself to something, you're subjecting yourself to a reaction—a reaction to your action," explained John Bowling, an Earth First!er who has trained activists in lock down techniques, a few days before the WTO protests began. "And we've seen an overwhelming, unconscionable expression of police brutality, just sheer torture, used on people who are peaceful in their intent, who are not a flight risk. I think what that has done is radicalized people, and actions are gaining in intensity as a result of that."

Bowling was alluding in part to the Black Bloc action that was being openly advertised at that point, well in advance of the WTO meetings. It was no secret that people were planning to destroy property on the day set aside for blockading the trade talks. Rioting had broken out at a Reclaim the Streets protest in Eugene, Oregon the previous summer, on the occasion of the June 18, 1999 global day of action. In the intervening months, anarchist militants had been circulating apocalyptic manifestos promising more fights to come. A pre-WTO article in a Eugene 'zine called the *Black-Clad Messenger* warned, "Tilting at the excesses of the system never gets down to the rotten, death-culture foundations of the system. . . . Anarchy says it is time to face reality and destroy the global (and local) machine. Phony half-measures and pseudo—critiques and submissive demos are no advance at all. SEE YOU IN SEATTLE!"

During the week-long activist convergence before the Seattle protests began, there were sharp disagreements over the nonviolence code that the newly forming Direct Action Network had adopted for its November 30 blockade. The dissidents, angered that property destruction was prohibited under the guidelines, organized discussions of Ward Churchill's *Pacifism as Pathology*, a text with a far greater influence on Black Bloc anarchists than anything written by John Zerzan. They also circulated small leaflets that advertised the meeting time and place—11:11 AM at 4th and Pine Streets—for those who wanted to "fight the system." Throughout the Convergence Center at 420 Denny Street, handwritten stickers questioned, "Will your 'resistance' be contained?" and declared, "Fuck the civil—let's get disobedient!"

Contrary to many people's assumptions, the activists who organized Seattle's Black Bloc were not mostly male. Young women have been some of the most outspoken and influential figures in the activist scene from which the rioters arose. Their prominence goes back to the movement's Earth First! origins, particularly to the 1990 split between macho deep ecologists like Dave Foreman and those activists—of whom the late Judi Bari was the most prominent—who were looking to fuse radical ecology with the agenda of the cultural and social left. The departure of the Foreman faction led to what's been called "the feminization of Earth First!" Since that time, women have been in the forefront of many of the local and single-issue campaigns that were the building blocks of

L.A. Kauffman

Seattle.

One young woman—a principal force behind the Seattle Black Bloc, whom I knew slightly through Earth First! circles—handed me a manifesto some days before the WTO protests whose words haunted me long afterwards. It read, "Let's not train the thousands of people who gather in Seattle to do no more than be herded by the police, hold signs, and offer themselves up as sacrificial lock-down lambs. I'm not advocating a riot. The ground between violence and pacifism is wide, much larger than the ivory tower of either. Meet me there."

On the big day of action, many of the blockades were secured by lock downs, and the locked down folks were indeed mercilessly pepper sprayed by the cops. That night, I talked to Yarrow Rain King, a young woman from Humboldt County in Northern California who was part of a circle of twenty-odd protesters locked together in an intersection. Her hands were shaking so badly that she could hardly light a cigarette. She described how the police came and went around the circle spraying everyone directly in the face—not once but a brutal four times. Despite the burning pain, no one unclipped. "It's become something that we expect, when we lock down we risk getting pepper sprayed," she quietly explained. "It's been a long time since they've been cutting us out of lock boxes."

While these events were unfolding, and locked down blockaders around the whole perimeter of the convention center were being subjected to similar abuse, the Black Bloc was some distance away, smashing the windows of corporate businesses and decorating downtown Seattle with radical graffiti. (My favorite, on a Banana Republic store: "We are winning—don't forget!") Then as now, I didn't have a problem with what they were doing: It's refreshing to see the sanctity of private property directly challenged. But I had a big problem with when they did it, and I still do. With five days of WTO meetings to choose from, I thought it was petulant of the Seattle Black Bloc to insist on holding their action on the same day as the blockade, despite requests from the Direct Action Network that they not do so.

But this dispute no longer seems very relevant. "Some day," said one of the window breakers last year, identifying himself rather wittily as a member of the Eugene Brick Throwers Union Local 666, "we're all going to be dancing on the graves of all these corporations together, and we're going to forget about this whole argument." A year after the protests, that day seems no closer, but the most striking thing is the sense of hope that Seattle has awakened among activists of many kinds. The divisions that seemed so momentous outside the WTO have faded from view.

There's a fair bit of talk these days about whether having Black Blocs at every big action turns them into a one-note samba, organized not for any strategic reason but because there was one at the action before. Many people are moving toward using the tactics without the costume: In Philly, some folks ran in circus get-ups as the Revolutionary Anarchist Clown Bloc (with the brilliant chant: "Hey hey, ho ho, hee hee!"), and the idea of a Pink Bloc is in the air. Meanwhile, some are saying that the era of lock down devices is coming to an end; the police successfully confiscated most of them before A16 in D.C., and used them as a pretext to raid the puppet warehouse at the Republican Convention protests in Philadelphia and arrest everyone inside.

The central issue facing the U.S. movement against corporate globalization today, however, is not tactical but racial: whether this predominantly white movement will make the connections between global corporate power and the criminal injustice system here at home, and whether it will build productive alliances with movements of color, directly confronting institutionalized racism in the United States.

Josh MacPhee / Just Seed

Jail Solidarity in Seattle

Kari Lydersen

"Two people seized my arms and twisted one of them behind my back and upwards. They twisted some more, cuffed me with metal and lifted me into The Chair, a raised steel compliance device with velcro restraining straps. They wheeled me into an elevator, all the while telling me to shut up, enough already, they were tired of hearing my whining. We went up. They wheeled me into a tank and then past several cells that had women peering out of slender windows. They stopped me in front of the last cell in the row. Opened the door, unstrapped me and asked me if I was going to cooperate."

This is how Mary Oliver describes her experience in the King County Jail after being arrested during the massive protests that shut down the World Trade Organization's meeting in Seattle Nov. 29–Dec. 2, 1999. Oliver refused to cooperate.

Like several hundred other arrestees, she refused to give her name except as Jane Doe. Thousands of protesters on the outside surrounded the jail, blocking its entrances for twenty-four hours and demanding the prisoners' release and an apology for the excessive force of the cops gone berserk. The Direct Action Network (DAN), one of the major organizers of the protest, held extensive workshops ahead of time schooling activists in the concepts and practice of nonviolent civil disobedience and jail solidarity, the tactic in which a large group of prisoners all refuse to give their names, ideally clogging the jail system and forcing the city to release them without charges.

"DAN Legal" promised to represent everyone who was arrested. Katya Komisaruk, the leading force behind DAN Legal, pledged to uphold the all-for-one, one-for-all motto of jail solidarity, promising that everyone would leave the jail together. DAN Legal representatives handed out cards with their number on it for protesters to call from jail.

Everything didn't go as planned, however. For starters, relatively few were actually arrested during the major action on Tuesday, November 30. That's when protesters blocked the roads leading to the WTO meeting and hell broke loose as police attacked crowds with rubber bullets, tear gas, and night sticks. Though many came away with injuries, there were no mass arrests. It was the next day, after martial law had been declared, that police swept through whole areas putting people in handcuffs and throwing them in paddywagons. Many tourists, journalists and residents who weren't involved in the protests were arrested—"I was in the brig with a 17-year-old who skipped school to watch the protests and a guy who was trying to clean up the mess with a broom," said Thomas Sellman, a Capitol Hill resident who was arrested after handing out copies of a *New York Times* cartoon in a no-protest zone to make a First Amendment point.

These arrestees were shipped to the Sandpoint naval detention center in buses, where they were held for hours without food, water, or bathrooms. While on the buses and in cells at Sandpoint, protesters started spreading the word about jail solidarity. Most were then transferred to King County Jail, where the confusion and human rights abuses that occurred on the streets were mirrored.

Protesters report being roughed up, threatened, sexually abused, doused with pepper spray at close range, stripped, denied medication and food and water, and other abuses. Access to lawyers was virtually denied, with most people waiting ten or more hours before being allowed one phone call. Komisaruk said she had briefly been allowed to talk to protesters on the buses and at Sandpoint, but then was barred once authorities realized she was doing nothing to calm protesters down.

The people practicing jail solidarity and otherwise not cooperating received particularly harsh treatment. Sellman described seeing six or more people who were considered leaders strapped in restraint chairs, sprayed with pepper spray, hooded, and then pushed down hallways out of sight of their cellmates. "We saw an older sister who was being searched flinch and then be brutally thrown to the ground," said Franchezska Zamora, a thirty-year-old L.A. resident who was arrested. "Another sister was stripped down, chained and beaten, and put in a confinement chair."

Ryan Mehan, a twenty-two-year-old Washington resident, described a guard repeatedly spraying pepper spray in a middle-aged man's eyes from three feet away as the man was practicing nonviolent noncompliance, refusing to get up from his seat at Sandpoint.

After three days, with up to fifteen thousand protesters outside completely blocking access to the jail, DAN Legal lawyers had still not been allowed to see prisoners. The public defender's office, meanwhile, had filed a lawsuit demanding access to the prisoners.

At this point Komisaruk negotiated a deal with city attorneys wherein DAN reps were let into the jail if DAN dispersed the crowd of protesters outside. Komisaruk described the process as a switch from jail solidarity to court solidarity, meaning protesters would be processed in the court system and then try to band together to have cases dismissed there.

"We have two main topics, jamming the jails and jamming the legal system," said Komisaruk, forty, an Oakland-based lawyer who got her first exposure to jail solidarity and other activism tactics during the antinuclear demonstrations of the early 1980s. "At this point it was clear jail solidarity was not going to work, because a lot of the people arrested were ordinary Seattleites who hadn't gone through the trainings. We knew that by Monday a lot of them would have to get out and give their names, so the numbers for jail solidarity would be dwindling. I had done research on the Seattle legal system and I knew that if everyone gave their name and demanded a jury trial, we could jam the legal system."

Others described the deal as an abandonment and betrayal of the idea of jail solidarity, or said they were confused about what was actually going on at all.

Within the next few days the majority of protesters were released with no charges or with misdemeanor charges that were later dropped. About 210 people were released through dismissals, guilty pleas, and diversions. On January 4, City attorney Mark Sidran announced the dismissal of 280 misdemeanor charges. The felony charges are dealt with in a completely different system, not under Sidran's jurisdiction, so jail solidarity would have little or no impact on their outcome.

The Seattle Police Department reported that of 601 arrests made during the protest and 30 arrests in the following weeks, the District Attorney pursued misdemeanor charges against 51 people and felony charges including burglary and malicious mischief against at least 26 people.

The felonies were all settled out of court, while five or so misdemeanors went to trial. Most were resolved with fines, probation, and time served. A year later, many hold up Seattle as an example of successful jail solidarity, where people remained strong in the face of vicious physical and mental abuse and misinformation; where hundreds were in fact released with no charges and where people held out for days giving their names only as John or Jane Doe. "Everyone's trying to recreate Seattle," said Tara Herivel, a law student who served as a legal observer during the protests.

Jail solidarity has also been practiced by protesters arrested at the International Monetary Fund's meeting in Washington, D.C. on April 16, 2000; at the Republican National Convention in Philadelphia in July 2000; and at the Democratic Convention in Los Angeles in August. Organizers of those jail solidarity movements, which had varying degrees of success, point to Seattle as an inspiration.

"We'd gone into it hearing the success stories of Seattle," said Danielle Redden, a DAN Legal team member who spent six days in jail in Philadelphia. But many Seattle prisoners as well as progressive Seattle public defenders who worked tirelessly throughout the protests say the jail solidarity action and specifically DAN Legal's leadership has left a sour taste in their mouth. They say that just as the Seattle police were caught off guard and overwhelmed by the scope of the protests, DAN Legal was biting off more than it could chew in urging hundreds of people to practice solidarity and, with scarce resources, promising to defend them all.

"Because I believe strongly that direct action participants need excellent, aggressive and well-prepared legal assistance, I offer my view that DAN Legal did not provide that effectively in Seattle," said Lisa Daugaard, a Seattle public defender who has represented people arrested in the protests. Daugaard and a number of other local attorneys have said that while DAN Legal may have been well-meaning, they were unequipped to handle felonies or the vast number of arrestees, and that they were unscrupulous in leading protesters to make choic-

Kari Lydersen

es with possibly severe implications. By DAN Legal, the attorneys are largely referring to Komisaruk. Komisaruk spent two years in federal prison after breaking into the Vandenberg Air Force Base in California in 1988 and destroying a million dollar computer with a crowbar. She left cookies, flowers and a poem for the guards, and scrawled writing on the wall explaining that her act was aimed at preventing nuclear war. That arrest was her thirty-first for acts of civil disobedience and protest.

"Jail solidarity is something I've sort of grown up with," said Komisaruk, who did antinuclear actions as part of the Clamshell Alliance and the Abalone Alliance based in California in the late 1970s and early 1980s. "In the 1980s a lot more lawyers were trained in jail solidarity actions. Then there was a slow period and the knowledge kind of laid dormant. Now much of the expertise is lost."

Daugaard noted that Komisaruk, a member of the California bar since 1993, is not licensed to practice in Washington. She said Komisaruk did not have the necessary knowledge of the local system to effectively negotiate with prosecutors. Daugaard said it was her impression that few or none of the handful of other DAN Legal lawyers were certified in the state. "Real opportunities were lost to get folks out of jail and back on the streets using procedures such as writs of habeas corpus after arrestees had been detained more than forty-eight hours, the limit under local court rules," said Daugaard. "Public defenders were prepared to bring such writs, but the DAN legal team had never considered them and was unprepared to take advantage of that option."

Komisaruk said that DAN Legal had thirteen or fourteen lawyers in Seattle, including some local and some out-of-town lawyers; she did not give exact numbers. She said that out of town lawyers are allowed to try cases if they are substituting for a sponsoring local lawyer. Daugaard also blames Komisaruk and the rest of DAN Legal for asking the thousands of protesters surrounding the jail to leave.

"Thousands were prepared to continue barricading the jail, for several days if necessary," she said. "Many more were marching toward the jail to strengthen the force when the amazing word came that DAN Legal was asking people to leave."

Herivel said that Komisaruk went back on her word by making a deal with prosecutors.

"Promises were broken," she said. "People were abandoned in the system because deals were being brokered. First DAN said they would represent everyone, then they said they wouldn't represent people with felonies. They never should have promised to do things they couldn't do. People were caught up in the moment without being informed about how these things would affect them in the long-run. They were taken advantage of for just being bodies." Komisaruk said that she did promise DAN would represent everyone, but that she never meant for felonies to be included in the jail solidarity action. She said committees of people in the jails, not DAN Legal, made the decision to leave, and that the detainees with felony charges supported those decisions.

"The people with felonies were in communication with the others, and they basically said, 'It's better for you to be out on the street and doing fundraising,'" said Komisaruk. "Everyone felt OK about leaving because they knew the people with felonies supported them."

It ended up being local public defenders and private lawyers, not DAN Legal attorneys, who got many of the protesters out of jail and represented them in court, Daugaard and other public defenders said. Komisaruk said that DAN Legal lawyers handled "quite a few cases," but didn't actually go to court with many of them since charges were dropped.

"I was planning to try a case myself," said Komisaruk. "I was kind of hovering in the background following them and looking for a juicy one. But as charges were dropped, they kept disappearing one by one." Neill Fox, a public defender who represented protesters, described the whole situation as one of confusion and misinformation.

"There were people being held incommunicado," he said. "It wasn't clear who our clients were. A lot of the things that happened were because of the lack of communication. The political movement was very scattered."

Fox didn't think DAN Legal's emphasis on jail solidarity was a good idea to start with, considering there were hundreds of people who hadn't done the trainings and hadn't planned to get arrested, not to mention people with medical problems and young children who couldn't afford a long stay in jail. "Part of the friction between DAN and lawyers in this office was the fact that people here felt jail solidarity wouldn't work for their clients," he said. "Jail solidarity works if it is very well organized, but we had a lot of people in there who didn't have the luxury of doing jail solidarity." Fox added that it is hard to judge whether the jail solidarity really had any positive effect.

"The jail solidarity didn't necessarily lead to the dismissal of charges," he said. "The dismissals were because of the city's lack of evidence. The jail solidarity didn't do what it was initially meant to do, which was to convince the city to release people without charges in a few days."

Dimitri Iglitzin, a lawyer from a private firm who negotiated with the city on behalf of the protesters, said that, "Overall, it's not clear to me that DAN's emphasis on jail solidarity, followed by its abrupt change of tactics on Sunday, did anything to achieve equal treatment of those arrested or to further the success of the anti-WTO action in general. In retrospect, it might have been better to have everyone cite out and return to downtown Seattle for further actions." He said that he was "shocked" at the lack of an organized decision-making structure for DAN.

"There has to be a separation of powers between the legal team and the organizing team," he said. "My deepest objection was that you had legal making the decisions for the defendants. That's not legal's job. DAN, not DAN Legal but DAN, should have created a decision-making structure that could handle mass arrests. There should be a committee that is making decisions on the inside."

Seattle has an unusual set-up in which there are four public defenders offices that cover different parts of the city. Komisaruk blamed the public defenders' animosity toward her on competitiveness between the offices.

"I think people's territorialism interfered with their work," she said. "As some of the public defenders started working with DAN Legal, that rivalry created a difference in the way the different offices responded to us. Some decided they loved DAN Legal, and some decided we were out of town busybodies interfering with their work."

She also said the public defenders received pressure from their higher-ups not to support jail solidarity.

"An absolute mainstay of criminal law is you are responsible only for your client, and the goal is to screw the other defendants to help your client if you have to," Komisaruk said. "As a result defense attorneys often have a hard time shifting gears to understand jail solidarity, where it's everyone standing together."

Sellman, the Capitol Hill resident who had no previous political history and had no plans to participate in the protests until he was pepper sprayed on his way to work, said he was happy with DAN's representation. Sellman had never heard of DAN before, but he was given a yellow flier listing their number, and when he was allowed his one phone call after ten hours in jail he called them.

"There wasn't really that much they could say," he said. "Just because I called didn't mean they could get me out of jail. But it reassured me to know they were doing something on my behalf. I didn't feel completely isolated." When he went to his court date, Komisaruk was there. He said she convinced him to plead innocence instead of having his case thrown out "without prejudice," meaning the defendant is not completely exonerated and prosecutors can collect more evidence and retry the case.

"There's no way I would have known what those terms meant if she hadn't explained it to me," he said. "The local attorneys didn't do that. I think what Katya was doing was very valuable. She really made herself available."

In Philadelphia, several hundred of the 480 protesters arrested practiced jail solidarity for about a week, again largely orchestrated and supported by the DAN Legal team, which had changed names to the Midnight Special Law Collective (after the folk song) or the R2K Legal Collective. But after a week had gone by and there were still no offers from the district attorney's office and suffering a "media blackout," DAN Legal rep Danielle Redden explained, "we decided that jail solidarity just wasn't working."

Many people faced bails of $100,000 or even $1 million, and rampant physical, sexual, and psychological abuse was being reported in the jail. Protesters began to give their names, and were released with a multitude of charges. Trials started in the fall on over three hundred misdemeanor charges and over thirty felonies.

Jail solidarity actions in Washington D.C. for the IMF meeting did meet with more success on a small scale.

In D.C., over twelve hundred people were arrested over several days of actions, including a surprise pre-emptive round-up of peaceful marchers on the Saturday before the IMF meeting. The over five hundred people arrested during this march against the prison industrial complex included tourists, journalists and residents who were begging to be able to leave the area. Prosecutors in D.C. refused to negotiate with the several hundred protesters who were practicing jail solidarity. When they tried to force activists into court, many resisted by stripping naked and tying themselves to the beds in their cells. A number of protesters were transferred to the jail general population, where guards made a point of saying that "you white boys" would be raped by black prisoners and contract AIDS. A judge eventually ordered prosecutors to negotiate with protesters, and eventually all were released and all charges were dropped to $5 jaywalking fines.

Overall, it is obvious that every protest situation is different and any efforts at jail solidarity need to take this into account. For jail solidarity to work, it must be well-coordinated, well-thought out and rooted in the local community. Seattle should not be celebrated as an unqualified success, but examined as a working model of do's and don'ts for the coming mega-protests.

"I am at a loss to understand what DAN, or its legal team, believes was the success of the legal strategy used in Seattle," said Iglitzin. "I have great affection and respect for the dedicated members of DAN's legal team, who worked extremely hard under quite harrowing circumstances, but I think that further analysis of what went wrong is appropriate."

Oakley

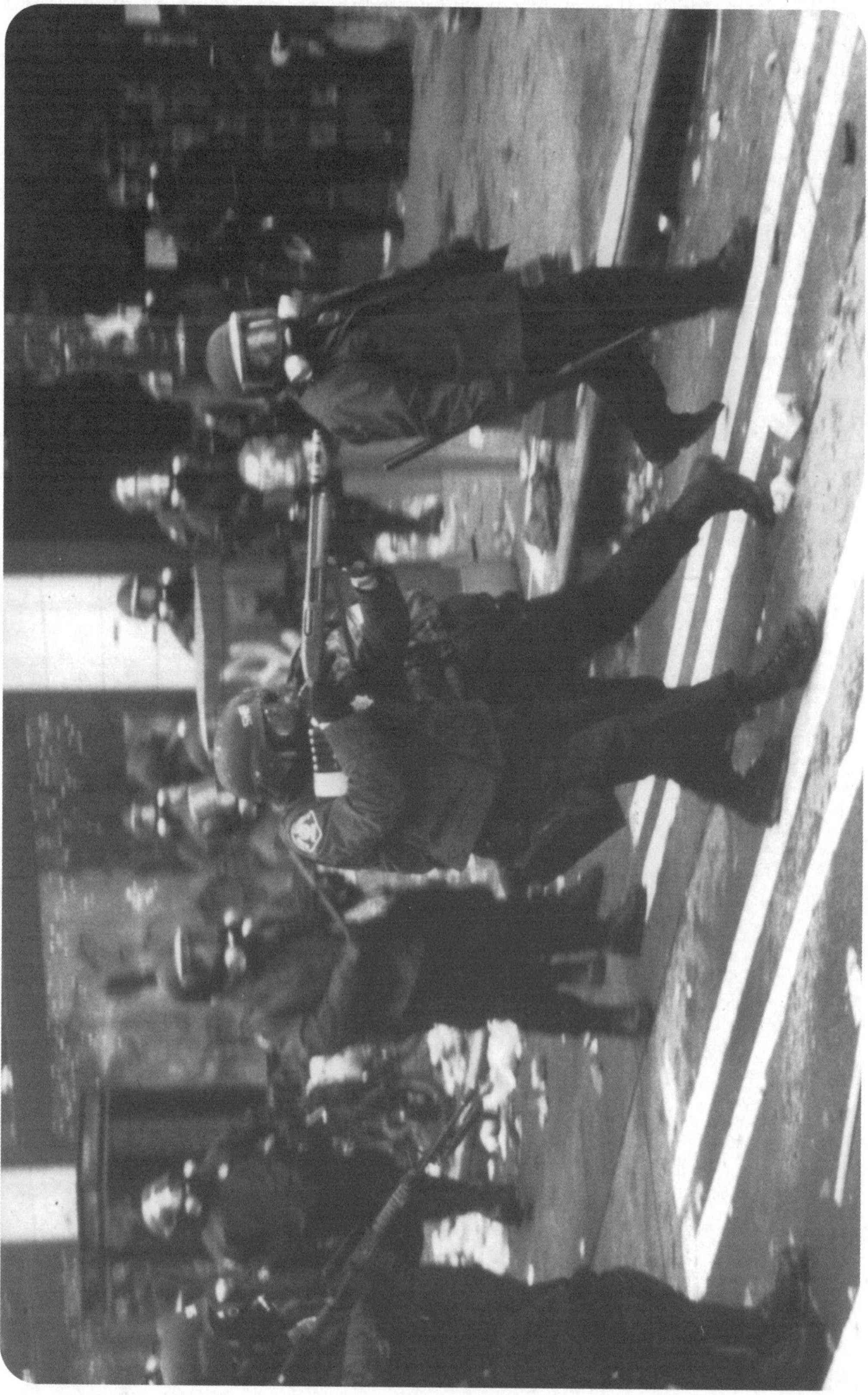

Police State Targets the Left

Jim Redden
Excerpted from Snitch Culture

The sound of breaking glass signaled a dramatic change in the focus of the government's political surveillance programs in late 1999. After spending most of the decade spying on the right wing neo-Patriot movement, law enforcement agencies abruptly shifted gears and declared brick-throwing anarchists to be the newest threat to the American way of life. By the dawn of the new Millennium, the government was running COINTELPRO-style operations against a coalition of radical labor, environmental, and human rights organizations opposed to corporate control of the global economy. Police were photographing suspected activists and entering license plate numbers in their computer databanks. Undercover operatives were infiltrating meetings and disrupting protests. Even the Pentagon was involved, dispatching its Delta Force antiterrorism commandos to identify and secretly videotape suspected leaders. By early August, calls were underway for a full-blown federal investigation into the movement, raising the specter of government-orchestrated Green Scare along the lines of anti-Communist witch hunts of the 1950s.

The shift was the direct result of the massive protests which disrupted the World Trade Organization conference in Seattle. Over fifty thousand demonstrators jammed the streets, snarling traffic and preventing WTO delegates from reaching their meetings. When the authorities tried to break up the protests, a small group of the most militant activists struck back, vandalizing businesses in the downtown core and clashing with police throughout the city. Much like the urban riots of the early 1960s, the intensity of the confrontations caught political leaders and law enforcement officials off guard, prompting the most significant change in the direction of the government's domestic surveillance operations in the past twenty years.

Throughout the 1980s and '90s, the FBI and other domestic law enforcement agencies focused their political intelligence-gathering programs on militias and other Far Right organizations. But, by the summer of 1999, federal authorities were beginning to look at the emerging antiglobablization movement. Tipped off that large numbers of protesters were preparing to travel to Seattle for the December WTO meeting, the FBI began spying on environmental, labor, and anticorporate activists. As the *Seattle Weekly* reported on December 23, 1999, "Sources say. . . that police and 30 other local, state, and federal agencies have been aggressively gathering intelligence on violent and nonviolent protest groups since early summer (FBI agents even paid personal visits to some activists' homes to inquire about their plans)."

Even the military got involved. According to the *Weekly,* the Pentagon sent members of the top-secret Delta Force to Seattle to prepare for President Bill Clinton's arrival. As the paper put it, "the elite Army special force, operating under its cover name of Combat Applications Group (CAG), was in Seattle a week in advance of the Clinton visit to scope out possible terrorist acts. Under the control of the Joint Special Operations Command (JSOC) at Fort Bragg, North Carolina, the contingent took up residence in a Regrade motel and fanned out downtown dressed as demonstrators, some wearing their jungle greens."

The preparations didn't work. Thousands of protesters overwhelmed the police on the opening day of the conference, shutting down the center where the main meetings were scheduled to be held. The police overreacted and began macing and tear-gassing the protesters who were preventing the WTO delegates from entering the center. A small group of the most militant protesters retaliated by attacking such corporate icons as McDonald's, NikeTown, the Gap, and Starbucks; smashing windows; toppling shelves;, spraying graffiti; and provoking a massive police crackdown.

The mayor of Seattle declared a state of "civil emergency," essentially a local version of martial law. Washington's governor called out three hundred state troopers and two divisions of the National Guard to secure the blocks around the downtown convention site. A "Protest-Free Zone" was declared around the conference headquarters, allowing the police to exclude anyone merely wishing to express their First Amendment rights. Police dressed up in military-style riot gear chased protesters through the streets for the next few days. Thousands of people were sprayed with pepper gas, clubbed with ballistic batons, and shot with rubber-coated bullets and steel pellet-filled "beanbag" shotgun rounds. Many of the victims were innocent bystanders and business owners who simply didn't get out of the way fast enough.

The chaos was broadcast around the world. TV viewers saw police firing at protesters at point blank range. One cop went out of his way to kick an empty-handed protester in the groin. Another cop ripped a gas mask off a pregnant foreign reporter and struck her.

Delta Force troops were in the middle of the confrontations, working to identify protest leaders. "Some Deltas wore lapel cameras, continuously transmitting pictures of rioters and other demonstrators to a master video unit in the

motel command center, which could be used by law enforcement agencies to identify and track suspects," the *Weekly* reported.

The WTO conference ended in disarray, a victory for the protesters and a major embarrassment for the Clinton administration. Four days later, Seattle Police Chief Norm Stamper resigned in disgrace.

The corporate media immediately fell into line behind the government, portraying all anticorporate protesters as violent thugs to justify the coming crackdown. Although the police shot demonstrators with tear gas canisters at point blank range, images of black-clad anarchists smashing windows dominated the postriot news reports. The December 13 issue of *Newsweek* linked the anarchists to Ted Kaczynski, the Unabomber. *60 Minutes* traveled to Eugene for a story on the new domestic terrorists. "They came to Seattle with violence in their hearts and destruction on their minds," the CBS News show warned viewers sternly.

The government's abrupt shift from right to left wing activists was accompanied by a wave of false alarms and bogus reports. A rumor spread that the Eugene anarchists were planning to drive up the freeway to Portland and disrupt that city's downtown New Year's Eve party. The local police went on high alert, fencing off the site and installing security gates to detain and search party-goers. The U.S. Marshals Office opened a number of temporary holding cells in an old downtown federal building. The FBI set up a command center in the basement of the nearby Mark O. Hatfield Federal Courthouse. Heavily-armed federal agents gathered in the basement on New Year's Eve. Police in full riot gear patrolled the perimeter. None of the anarchists showed up. The informant was wrong.

Another bogus tip sparked a similar panic in Tacoma, Washington a few months later. The local steelworkers union had called for a March 25 rally at the Kaiser aluminum plant. Labor and environmental activists from throughout the Pacific Northwest were planning to attend. Then Eugene authorities contacted

Jim Redden

the Tacoma police and reported that some of the anarchists were allegedly heading their way with a bomb. The police contacted union organizer Jon Youngdahl, who called off the protest. No bomb-carrying anarchist was ever found.

Anarchy fever gripped the Portland police again in late April. A few hundred local activists were planning a May Day march and demonstration. An unnamed informant told the police that the Eugene anarchists were coming up to cause trouble. According to one police report, they "have little regard for the laws of society" and were expected to engage in civil disobedience. Police Chief Mark Kroeker, a former deputy chief from the Los Angeles Police Department who had only been on the job a few months, dispatched over 150 officers in full riot gear, including black body armor and helmets with plastic face shields. Police spent hours chasing demonstrators through the streets, spraying them with mace, clubbing them with ballistic batons, and shooting them with "beanbag" rounds. Nineteen people were arrested, mostly on minor charges. None were anarchists from Eugene. Kroeker later apologized to the city council for the actions of his officers.

These incidents occurred as federal authorities were bracing for the next major antiglobalization protests, set for the World Bank and International Monetary Fund meetings scheduled to begin on April 16 in Washington, D.C. As the activists began planning their demonstrations, they were targeted by federal, state and local law enforcement officials. Their meetings were infiltrated, their public gatherings disrupted, their phones tapped, and police were posted outside their homes and offices. Even the corporate media took note of the harassment. "Some protesters think they are being watched. They are correct." the *Washington Post* reported on April 10, quoting Executive Assistant Washington Police Chief Terrance W. Gainer as saying, "If it's an open meeting and it says, 'Come on over,' then anybody's welcome."

Three days later, *USA Today* reported government agents were going undercover online to thwart the protesters. "[T]hey have been monitoring seventy-three internet sites where the groups have been exchanging messages to learn more about their plans. Sometimes, officers have even gone online posing as protesters," the paper said, adding that police were physically following suspected anarchists throughout the capitol city. "They have been monitoring the movements of nearly two dozen self-proclaimed anarchists who have arrived in Washington."

As a result of this surveillance, all thirty-five hundred D.C. police officers were put on alert, along with an unknown number of law enforcement agents from at least twelve federal and state agencies, including the FBI and the Bureau of Alcohol, Tobacco and Firearms. The authorities spent over a million dollars on new body armor and bullet-proof shields. They set up three mass detention centers where arrested protesters would be taken. They removed sixty-nine mailboxes where bombs could be hidden.

"They ain't burning our city like they did in Seattle," Police Chief Charles Ramsey told *USA Today*. "I'm not going to let it happen. I guarantee it."

The authorities started cracking down on the activists the week before the

IMF/World Bank meetings were scheduled to begin. On April 13, seven activists driving to a planning meeting were pulled over and arrested. Police seized 256 PCV pipes, 45 smaller pipes, 2 rolls of chicken wire, 50 rolls of duct tape, gas masks, bolt cutters, chains, an electrical saw, and lock boxes. According to a *Washington Post* account of the incident, a Secret Service agent frisked one passenger, showing him a photo that had been taken of him earlier.

The police justified the arrests by saying the materials and tools found in the van were "implements of crime." The accusation struck NLG President Karen Jo Koonan as absurd. "These activists construct signs, puppets, sound stages, and other tools for expressing their political views," she wrote in a letter to U.S. Attorney General Janet Reno. "They were in fact arrested for possession of implements of First Amendment activity. We have been told by an MPD officer that the FBI directed them to make this arrest."

Josh MacPhee / Just Seed

The police claim was made for a specific purpose—a purpose which would soon become clear. It is illegal for the police to spy on people simply because of their political beliefs. But political activists can be monitored if the police believe they are planning to commit crimes, no matter how petty. The police claimed the items seized from the van were 'instruments of crime" to justify their surveillance. It was a claim that would be heard repeatedly in the days, weeks, and months to come.

On the morning of April 15, law enforcement authorities unexpectedly raided a warehouse that served as the demonstrators' headquarters. According to eyewitness accounts, the agencies involved in the raid included the BATF, the Washington Metropolitan Police Department, and the Washington Fire Department. Saying the warehouse violated fire codes, the authorities threw all the activists out and closed the building. Then the authorities claimed they found weapons in the warehouse, physical proof that violent crimes were being planned. According to the police, the evidence included a Molotov cocktail, balloons filled with acid, and a lab for producing explosives and pepper spray. In a later retraction, the police admitted they'd only found oily rags and a kitchen, but the admission came after the ware-

Jim Redden

Oakley

house was shut down. Police also kept all the signs, banners, and giant satiric posters under construction inside, depriving the demonstrators of their most effective means of communicating their causes.

By the morning of Saturday the 16th, the police had cordoned off fifty blocks around the headquarters of the World Bank and the International Monetary Fund. The first mass arrests happened that afternoon when thousands of protesters marched toward the headquarters of the two financial institutions. The police blocked their way, then isolated and arrested approximately 635 activists, more than the total arrested during several days of rioting in Seattle. "What makes the situation all the more maddening is that such actions are apparently being taken based on the ridiculous view that every protester or activist is an anarchist time bomb waiting to go off—a view apparently buttressed by unspecified police 'intelligence' that may or may not be true," reporter Jason Vest wrote in the online SpeakOut.com website.

The authorities quickly revealed that they were obsessed with identifying the protesters. Those who provided identification were fined $50. Those who didn't were fined $300.

Demonstrators clashed with police during the next few days. The federal government gave all non-essential employees in Washington, D.C. the day off on Monday, resulting in a partial government shut-down, which is far more than the neo-Patriot movement was able to achieve at any point in the 1990s. By the time it was over, even the IMF had released a communiqué acknowledging the protesters had made its policies a matter "of growing public debate." As the ABC Evening News reported on Monday, "The demonstrators outside the building did their best to be heard. The delegates inside the building said they got the message."

The full extent of the government's surveillance operation was not revealed until May 4, when the Paris-based *Intelligence Newsletter* carried a story titled "Watching the Anti-WTO Crowd" which reported that U.S. Army intelligence units were monitoring the anticorporate protesters. Among other things, the newsletter discovered that "reserve units from the US Army Intelligence and Security Command helped Washington police keep an eye on demonstrations staged at the World Bank/IMF meetings. . . [T]he Pentagon sent around 700 men from the Intelligence and Security Command at Fort Belvoir to assist the Washington police on April 17, including specialists in human and signals intelligence. One unit was even strategically located on the fourth floor balcony in a building at 1919 Pennsylvania Avenue with a birds-eye view of most demonstrators."

The newsletter also charged that much information being collected about the protesters was being fed into the Regional Information Sharing System computers used by law enforcement agencies across the country. According to the report, the government is rationalizing this surveillance by claiming the protesters are terrorists. As the report put it, "to justify their interest in antiglobalization groups from a legal standpoint, the authorities lump them into a category of terrorist organizations. Among those considered as such at present are Global Justice (the group that organized the April 17 demonstration), Earth First!, Greenpeace, American Indian Movement, Zapatista National Liberation Front and ACT-UP."

In early May, *In These Times* confirmed the government spy operation. The progressive newspaper quoted Robert Scully, executive director of the National Association of Police Organizations, as saying that federal, state, and local law enforcement agencies were "successful in infiltrating some of the groups. . . and had firsthand, inside information of who, when, why, and where things were going to happen."

Even before the Washington, D.C. protests began, organizers began planning to bring their message to the Republican and Democratic Presidential conventions, scheduled for July and August in Philadelphia and Los Angeles. Police representatives from both cities traveled to the nation's capitol for the April demonstrations, consulting with federal authorities on how to identify and handle the demonstrators. Federal officials also traveled to the convention cities, setting up surveillance operations in advance of the arriving demonstrators.

By late May, the corporate media was openly writing about the intelligence-gathering operations. Previewing the Republican convention, the *Philadelphia Inquirer* said, "The Secret Service is checking rooftops. The FBI is monitoring the Internet. And city police are getting ready to play cat and mouse with protesters... 'Virtually every resource that the FBI has available will be put into play,' said Thomas J. Harrington, the assistant special agent-in-charge in the FBI's Philadelphia office."

The Reuters news agency confirmed the FBI's role in June 2, saying, "The U.S. Secret Service is running security inside the convention and at main hotels, the FBI is handling intelligence, and state police are providing escorts for dignitaries. That leaves Philadelphia's 6,800-strong police department to keep the

Jim Redden

streets of the 5th-largest U.S. city safe for delegates and clear of unruly crowds."

Throughout June, activists from several groups reported at least five instances in which unidentified men were seen photographing people entering and leaving protest planning meetings. On June 29, a reporter with the *Philadelphia Inquirer* observed two men dressed in casual clothes watching activists arrive for a meeting at the offices of the Women's International League for Peace and Freedom. The pair sat on the hood of a maroon Plymouth, taking pictures of the activists as they came and went. Both men refused to answer any questions from the reporter. Police spokeswoman Lt. Susan Slawson flatly denied her agency was doing anything that would violate its policy against political intelligence-gathering, saying, "[W]e are in no way violating it." But then the reporter traced the license plates on the Plymouth to the police department. Confronted with proof of his agency's role in the surveillance operation, department spokesman David Yarnell reluctantly admitted the activists were right. "We were watching. We were making surveillance efforts. It's just prudent preparations for anything," he confessed. "This is just outrageous," responded organizer Michael Morrill. "If this is in fact going on, and city officials are lying about it, I wonder what else they're doing."

Philadelphia police officials openly talked about having the protesters under surveillance when the Republican National Convention began on July 31, with Police Commissioner John Timoney specifically saying his troops were watching "the anarchists." The first serious confrontation occurred on August 1, after police unexpectedly raided a warehouse where activists were painting posters and building puppets. Before the raid, police claimed the activists were storing weapons in the building, in this case C4 explosives and acid-filled balloons. No explosives, acid, or other weapons were found. But seventy activists were arrested, and all their signs and puppets were seized.

The raid set off street protests, during which fifteen police officers were injured in scuffles, and more than twenty-five police cruisers and other city vehicles were vandalized by protesters who also overturned dumpsters, smashed windows, and sprayed graffiti on downtown buildings. Before the end of the day, more than 350 people were arrested, including nineteen who were charged with such felony offenses as assaults. Most were jailed and kept imprisoned on high bails. Hundreds were still behind bars days after the convention ended, complaining of deplorable conditions and brutal treatment.

The day after the delegates went home, Timoney called a press conference and announced that he and his intelligence officers had uncovered a vast left wing conspiracy. In language reflecting the anti-Communist hysteria of the Red Scare, the Philadelphia police commissioner claimed outside agitators had conspired to cause violence and property damage at the convention. He called on the federal government to investigate this subversive plot, saying, "There is a cadre, if you will, of criminal conspirators who are about the business of planning conspiracies to go in and cause mayhem and cause property damage in major cities in America that have large conventions or large numbers of people coming in for one reason or another."

CITIZENS,
THE POLICE OF THE... MEETING IS UNLAWFUL, WE ...BLIC LET YOU KNOW AS YOUR UP PEACEFULLY. IF YOU DO NOT OBE.T AND INVITE YOU TO BREAK THE RISK THE POLICE ORDER FORCES WILL TA... ITATION YOU RUN GAINST YOU. ...EASURES

BÜRGER,
DIE POLIZEI DER TSCHECHISCHEN REPUB DASS IHRE VERSAMMLUNG GESETZWIDRI UND FORDERT SIE ZUM RUHIGEN AUSEIN WENN SIE DIESER AUFFORDERUNG NICHT DER GEFAHR AUS, DASS DIE ORDNUNGSE EINGREIFEN WIRD.

Tim Russo

One of the alleged conspirators was John Seller, director of Ruckus Society, a Berkeley-based organization which trains political protesters in civil disobedience tactics. He was arrested while walking down the street and talking into a cell phone outside the Police Administration building. Although all of the charges filed against Sellers were misdemeanors, one of them was carrying an "instrument of a crime," the police excuse for spying on him. His bail was set at $1 million, far more than all but the most dangerous felons are required to post.

In seeking the high bail, District Attorney Cindy Mertelli produced a twenty-seven page "dossier" on Sellers. She called him "a real risk of danger to the community," noting he had been "involved in Seattle, a situation with almost dead bodies." Although none of the charges levied at Sellers involved violence or even vandalism, Mertelli said he "sets the stage to facilitate the more radical elements and intends to do the same in L.A.," where the Democrats were set to meet in early August.

Shortly after bail was set, CBS News reported that Philadelphia police had pinpointed the "ringleaders" of the most violent protests against the Republicans and had been stalking them throughout the day. Sellers was identified as one of the ringleaders that were stalked.

"We know they had a list of things they were going to do, and they set about doing it," Timoney said at an August 2 news conference, signalling that at least some of his information came from infiltrators. "I intend on raising this issue with federal authorities. Somebody's got to look into these groups."

Although a judge soon lowered the bail, the local news media immediately embraced the police version of events. The day after Timoney's press conference, the *Philadelphia Inquirer* congratulated the police for their restraint, crediting their excellent intelligence-gathering work. The paper also said that what appeared to be a spontaneous melee on August 1 was in fact a carefully choreo-

Jim Redden

Oakley

graphed assault, the result of a conspiracy.

Timoney's conspiracy theory got a boost when it was embraced by Bruce Chapman, president of the Discovery Institute and a former U.S. Ambassador to the United Nations Organization in Vienna. Writing in the *Washington Times,* Chapman claimed several left-wing political organizations had conspired to cause violence in Seattle, Washington DC, Philadelphia, and Los Angeles, including the Direct Action Network, Global Exchange, the Rainforest Action Network, the Foundation for Deep Ecology, and the International Forum on Globalization, which he described as "an umbrella group for 55 organizations opposed to globalization and high technology." Chapman said several of the most prominent organizations were funded by Douglas Tompkins, who he described as "a businessman who nurses an intense anger at modern technology and international trade." Chapman ended his piece by calling for a federal investigation of Tompkins, the organizations, and "the rioters."

Although the most serious charges against Sellers were eventually dropped, protesters faced a similar surveillance and harassment campaign in Los Angeles. On July 13, the *Los Angeles Times* printed a guest editorial by Mayor Richard Riordan which warned of violence by "international anarchists." In the piece titled "A Fair Warning to All: Don't Disrupt Our City," Riordan said the protesters coming to town had attended "training camps where they have learned strategies of destruction and guerrilla tactics." Before too long, the authorities and media were talking about the protesters in terms which had previously been reserved for domestic terrorists. On July 23, the *Los Angeles Times* reported the Secret Service and other government agencies were warning that a biological agent might be released in or around the Staples Center, where the convention was scheduled to be held. "We have purchased a lot of equipment, specialized masks and gowns," said Dr. Robert Splawn, medical director of the California

Hospital Medical Center, the closest hospital to the center.

The police also began visiting businesses near the center, showing them videos from the Seattle protests and advising them to consider boarding up glass walls and windows, hiring additional security guards, and stocking up on emergency provisions like flashlights, food, and water. "It's almost like a tornado," said LAPD Detective Darryl. "You can see it coming, but you don't know where it's going to go."

On August 7, the Southern California chapter of the ACLU wrote a letter to Police Chief Bernard Parks and Deputy City Attorney Debra Gonzales on behalf of several groups coordinating the upcoming demonstrations, including the D2K Convention Planning Coalition, the Rise Up/Direct Action Network, and the Community Action Network. In the letter, ACLU attorney Dan Tokaji complained that police were watching the four-story protest headquarters building around the clock, constantly videotaping the building and recording license plate numbers of cars used by protesters. The letter also alleged police were selectively enforcing traffic laws near the building, and had repeatedly entered it without producing search warrants. "They've crossed the line separating legitimate security preparations from unlawful harassment that violates protesters' first and fourth amendment rights. The mere potential for a disturbance does not justify the suspension of our constitutional rights," the letter said.

When the city didn't respond, the ACLU went to federal court on August 11 and obtained a temporary restraining order prevent the police from raiding the building without a warrant. In their complaint, ACLU lawyers cited twenty-two separate incidents of surveillance and harassment, including random police visits without warrants, low helicopter overflights, and people being followed and searched after leaving the building. Although U.S. District Court Judge Dean Pregerson granted the injunction, he did not bar police from keeping the protest headquarters under surveillance if they had "probable cause."

But the injunction didn't stop the police from infiltrating the protest organizations. On August 12, a group called The Youth Are the Future! We Demand a Better World! held a meeting at Luna Sol Cafe. They were planning to participate in the next day's Mumia Abu-Jamal protest march. Shortly after the meeting broke up, uniformed police officers rushed through the cafe's door and threw three of the main speakers up against a wall. Several of the meeting's participants also jumped up and helped with the arrests, revealing themselves to be undercover officers. After checking the identities of the three activists, the officers let two go and hauled the third one away in handcuffs.

By the time the Democratic National Convention began on August 18, federal, state, and local law enforcement agencies were running an untold number of undercover officers and other infiltrators among the protesters. The infiltrators included members of the LAPD's Anti-Terrorism Division who were already spying on political dissidents in the Los Angeles area. As reported by the *Los Angeles Times,* "[S]ome of these undercover officers met before going out on the streets in their work clothes: T-shirts and shorts, bandannas, thong shoes and sneakers. They even were allowed to break department policy by wearing beards and keeping their hair long. One wore a 'Free Mumia' bandanna, a reference to a Pennsylvania inmate on death row for killing a police officer. His face was unshaven, his hair tousled."

Among other things, these "scouts" mingled with protesters at the various demonstrations, using cell phones to file continuous reports and allowing commanders to make "real time" decisions on deploying riot gear–equipped squads around town. Intelligence officers working in several downtown command posts took information from the undercover officers, then immediately shared it with commanders and lieutenants. Police used tips provided by these infiltrators to justify arresting forty-two animal rights protesters on August 15. Authorities claimed the protesters had materials which could be used in "homemade flamethrowers," a charge strongly denied by the activists. A Superior Court judge released forty of them after a hearing two days later.

"It's standard operating procedure: infiltrate and disrupt," protest organizer Lisa Fithian told the *Times*. "They are potentially trying to incite problems in the midst of our demonstrations. We're not doing anything illegal; we're not doing anything wrong."

The undercover agents helped police arrest hundreds of demonstrators during the convention. By the time the Democrats went home, even the protesters were beginning to concede the snitch-fueled tactics were beginning to hurt the antiglobalization movement. "Anyone who has been involved in the mass protest movement through a major event of the last six months has friends who have been brutalized at the hands of the system," activist/journalist Tim Ream wrote in an August 10 dispatch from Los Angeles, noting that nearly twenty-five hundred protesters had been arrested since November 30, 1999.

But the repression wasn't merely happening in America. In recent years, the FBI has opened more than forty satellite offices around the world. In August 2000, the *Central and Eastern European Review* reported that FBI Director Louis Freeh and Czech Interior Minister Stanislav Gross met to discuss launching a joint operation in advance of the annual meeting of the World Bank and the International Monetary Fund, set for September 26 in Prague. At the time, thousands of anarchists, socialists, communists and other left-wing European activists were planning to protest the gathering, and Czech Prime Minister Milos Zeman had declared that the "largest threat to stability in the country is the extreme left."

As *Freezerbox* political writer Ezekial Ford put it, "The Battle of Seattle— followed by Mayday demonstrations around the world and the IMF protests in Washington—was a wake up call to those interested in seeing popular struggle against the reign of capital stunted or reversed. We must remember that the 1960s were viewed by elites not as a flowering of consciousness or a period of liberation for subjected groups, but constituted a 'crisis of democracy,' according to the Trilateral Commission, the collective voice for elites in the US, Europe and Japan. Networks of activists involved in the struggle against the investor-centric model of globalization may become future targets of state repression, just as they were in the '60s and '70s. And the FBI is apparently doing the preparatory fieldwork."

Indeed, some American protesters reported that they were prevented from entering the Czech Republic. The FBI had apparently provided their names to border guards, who used the information to turn them away.

The New Millennium is suddenly looking a lot like the '60s.

ACCIÓN DIRECTA

**RETA A LOS PARTIDOS REPUBLICANO Y DEMÓCRATA
ESTE VERANO EN PHILADELPHIA Y LOS ANGELES**

**THIS SUMMER IN PHILADELPHIA & LOS ANGELES
CHALLENGE THE REPUBLICAN & DEMOCRATIC PARTIES**

DIRECT ACTION

Mass Action Since Seattle

Seven Ways to Make Our Protests More Powerful

George Lakey
www.trainingforchange.org, *October 2000*

Seattle, Washington, D.C., Philadelphia, Los Angeles: each of them were experiments in mass direct action for justice and environmental sanity. Each has drawn thousands of committed people who care deeply about a better world, for their own back yard, and for the planet. Each has involved risk, pain, and suffering, as well as moments of profound connection, creativity, and community. Historians will mark 1999–2000 as a time when the river of change ran more quickly.

Each city's action has also invited controversy and debate about tactics and strategy. In the "morning after" period in which people lick their wounds and organize legal defense against continued state repression, it's easy for resentments to flare and defensiveness to flourish. The challenge is: how to be honest about differences of views, how to allow the authentic debates to happen, and still not lose ourselves in divisiveness?

However much we may need to disagree as we dialogue about our future, two points of unity stand out for most activists: 1. The System needs major change, and compared with those who consciously fight us to preserve the unjust status quo, we activists objectively are allies of each other; 2. We will all benefit from a rapid learning curve in which we learn the most possible from each round of struggle and stay flexible and ready to give up what doesn't seem to be working.

In that spirit, I write about some ways to sharpen future mass direct action scenarios. We can fully appreciate the hard work and sacrifice that has gone into each of these recent experiments (and others, such as Windsor, Eugene, Minneapolis) and still act on our freedom to make different choices for next time as we learn more about how to make social change in the twenty-first century.

And even though this article is about the future and uses some of this year's examples, I'll also weave in direct action examples from the past in order to honor our ancestors and to reduce the near-sightedness that comes from only knowing about the activist culture immediately around us.

1. Create more "dilemma demonstrations"

This form of direct action puts the power holders in a dilemma: if they allow us to go ahead and do what we intend to do, we accomplish something worthwhile related to our issue. If they repress us, they put themselves in a bad light, and the public is educated about our message.

Many examples can inspire our creativity. Most readers will know that some campaigns to save old-growth trees have set up these dilemmas. If, for example, the protesters are allowed to sit in the trees, the trees are saved. If the protesters are stopped violently, the public is educated and new allies can be won.

During the 1992 power holder celebration of the anniversary of the Columbus horror, an informal group of us decided to take advantage of a visit of replica ships Nina, Pinta, and Santa Maria. We paddled canoes into the middle of the harbor crowded with sailboats and media and raised our banners against racism and slavery. Police boats pursued us immediately, which turned the attention of the crowd to the drama of watery arrests of us and our signs. The corporate media coverage turned out to be centrally about our message rather than reverence for Columbus. For the power holders, whether to arrest was a dilemma: if they let us protest, we spoiled the party, but arresting us got the message out to even more people!

African American students in the South were very creative with such tactics, for example sitting at the lunch counter asking for coffee. If they were served, racism took a hit. If they were either attacked by civilians or arrested, racism also took a hit. The sit-inners didn't even need the signs they brought in order to make their point. The power holders were repeatedly put in a dilemma: whatever they did resulted in lost ground for the status quo.

I wouldn't say that it is always easy to create such tactics, and there are times when stopping traffic may be our best idea. The difference, however, is very clear if we take the point of view of the bystander or the television camera. When the police drag away protesters who are blocking a city intersection, what is the message of the protesters? The World Bank has policies that hurt people? Maybe, if the bystander or television viewer is willing to make several logical steps or leaps of imagination. There's no reason to expect that bystanders and TV viewers will work hard to make those connections, especially when the excitement is in the physical conflict itself between arresting officers and activists.

One way to spur our creativity, so more of our tactics actually put the power holders in a dilemma, is to picture to ourselves what the actual point of confrontation will look like to curious bystanders who are not already on our side. The scenarios we then develop will have more power and clarity of message.

One place to look for dilemma demonstration ideas is the community work that activists are already doing. Community gardens, for example, might be planted in places which need reclaiming. In the midst of the Seattle action some activists did guerrilla gardening in the median strips of downtown streets and

Tim Russo

avenues along the wharf.

2. Decide specifically whom we're trying to influence

Using a term like "the public" is too simple a way to think about strategy (even though I just referred to the public in the previous section). "The public" includes many subgroups, some of whom are very important to the success of a campaign, some less important, and some not important at all. If we create a map of the political territory and decide whom we most need to influence in what ways, we will create tactics that more frequently have the force that's needed.

For example, a small group in the Movement for a New Society once threw a monkey wrench into a U.S. foreign policy objective by correctly figuring out who to influence through direct action. The U.S. was supporting, as it often does, a military dictatorship that was killing thousands of people. In fact, Pakistani dictator Yayah Khan was killing hundreds of thousands of people in East Bengal who wanted independence. The U.S. government lied about its support, but the activists learned that Pakistani ships were on their way to U.S. ports to pick up military supplies for the continuing massacre. The group also realized that if longshoremen refused to load the ships, the U.S. government would be foiled.

The problem was, the East Coast longshoremen were, if anything, politically inclined to support the government, and wanted to feed their families. The activists repeatedly tried to persuade the longshoremen to act in solidarity with the East Bengalis, without success. It was time for direct action. The group announced a blockade of the port which was expecting the next Pakistani freighter, and began practicing "naval maneuvers" with sailboats, rowboats and the rest of its motley fleet. The media gave ongoing coverage, and longshoremen witnessed on television as well as in person the strange antics of protesters who seemed to believe they could stop a big freighter with tiny boats. The tactic raised the longshoremen's motivation to listen and discuss, and they agreed that, if the activists created a picket line, the longshoremen would refuse to cross it!

George Lakey

Tim Russo

When the campaign succeeded in that city, the activists took it to other port cities and finally the International Longshoremen's union agreed workers would not load Pakistan-bound weapons anywhere in the U.S.! The blockade, initiated by a small group, succeeded because the group crafted direct action tactics specifically geared toward the part of the public that most needed to be influenced. [1]

As we design campaigns focused on the World Trade Organization or capital punishment or the sex trade we need to create a political/cultural/economic map of "the public" and decide who we want to influence in what ways. Part of our power is in fact through making such choices.

3. Use campaigns more often, to become proactive rather than reactive

Sometimes a strong reaction to a move of the power holders can be very powerful, as it was in Seattle. By mobilizing around the WTO meeting and disrupting it, tremendous gains were made. The negative side of globalization was put on the public agenda for the first time, something which all the organizing against the North American Free Trade Agreement failed to do. New ongoing alliances became tantalizing possibilities. The very unleashing of rebel energy itself was positive.

Occasionally reacting is one thing; remaining in a position of reaction is something else. A good word for continuous reaction is "disempowerment." Mohandas K. Gandhi's first principle of strategy was to stay on the offensive. Having our action agenda dictated by where and when the power holders want to have their meetings is not staying on the offensive.

Campaigns put us on the offensive. A campaign is a focused mobilization of energy with a clear objective, over a time period that can realistically be sustained by our constituency. Often the objective is in the form of a demand which a targeted entity can make a decision about.

The United Students Against Sweatshops movement mostly works through campaigns, which is one reason why it is meeting with success. When these students choose their objective and identify the power holder whose position needs to change, a lot else starts to become clear. Who is going to oppose them most strongly? And who are their greatest potential allies? In the early part of the campaign they can open communication with the allies and have them already half on board by the time the campaigners start direct action.

This is not a new idea. The victories of the civil rights movement that are now part of our activist lore were won through campaign—the Montgomery bus boycott, for example, or the Birmingham struggle of 1963 in which a major industrial city was dislocated in order to force the federal government to pass an equal accommodations bill. [2]

Running a campaign is like taking a magnifying glass and holding it between the sun and a piece of paper. By focusing the energy of the sun, the glass ignites the paper. Successful campaigns focus on their target over time—nine months, two years, even more if they have the people resources—with a specific demand that seems achievable.

One of the biggest victories of 1980s U.S. grassroots campaign organizing has been kept a secret from most younger activists. In fact, the collusion of the media and the schooling system has been so successful that I've rarely met a young activist in the current movement who knows about the successful fight against nuclear power in this country.

The antinuclear struggle of grassroots groups was against an amazing array of power: the federal government (both civilian and military), the banks which were making major profits from loans to utilities, the utilities themselves, the huge companies like General Electric and Westinghouse which made the nuclear plants, the construction companies, and the building trades unions. The struggle was also against "conventional wisdom in the U.S.," which believed, in the beginning of the '70s, that nuclear energy was safe and cheap.

Grassroots activists beat the combined power holders! There's not room here to describe the struggle, which often used mass direct action in brilliant ways to stop U.S. utilities from ordering any new nuclear power plants by the late '70s. The grassroots groups used a variety of tactics, from testifying at official hearings to civil disobedience. A favorite tactic was mass occupation of the site where the plant was to be built. The movement remained decentralized, yet each local area expanded through designing and implementing campaigns. [3]

4. Shift our understanding of the role of mass media

The mass media have certain patterns of behavior which are fairly predictable, and our movement needs to learn to use those patterns to our advantage.

We need to understand that the mass media have always reflected the biases of their owners. This is not a new phenomenon. The white-owned media have historically been biased against people of color, straight-owned media against sexual minorities, and so on. I find it difficult for many middle class activists to empathize with working class people and their unions—why? Middle class activists have been conditioned by the systematic bias of media owned by the wealthy.

We free up our creative energy when we simply acknowledge that these

George Lakey

biases exist, rather than go into righteous indignation every time we read or see a new piece that puts us in an unfavorable light. Once we acknowledge the reality, we can decide: for the next campaign we design, do we need favorable media coverage, or not?

If we don't need it because, for example, the group we want to influence through direct action can get our message in other ways, then we can save ourselves some aggravation. We may be able to rely on the independent media, on the Internet—even on street speaking and mass leafleting. It depends on who we need to reach. The Chinese students during their prodemocracy uprising in 1989 were facing a totally controlled mass media, so they used word-of-mouth and middle-of-the-night posterings and supplemented with faxes!

If we do need some positive media coverage, we can learn how to get it. There's a whole art to this and some allied media professionals willing to lead workshops on it, but I'll state a few principles here.

1. Media usually show what is most dramatic. If a thousand people sit in lockdown and three people smash a window, the campaign will be presented as smashing windows. Organizers need to handle that reality; avoidance of that reality just leads to confusion and demoralization in the movement. (More on this later.)

2. Liberal media pundits, who might be expected to be "on our side," usually start out confused. Early liberal commentators on the civil rights movement were often full of advice on how nonviolent action was a bad idea and sweet reason would be better. The first women to picket the White House for the right to vote were criticized harshly by liberals in the media. Let's face it. To many people of goodwill, an uproar is upsetting. A ruckus is confusing. Most middle and upper class people dislike conflict, however liberal or even radical their political views. If they are media commentators, they will find fault with our direct action.

3. Mass media generally prefer to ignore direct action if they can. The struggle against the School of the Americas, for example, has often found its increasingly large direct actions to be all but ignored. Media will sometimes make exceptions if the action is particularly novel, creative, or includes humor. For example, the campaign against military aid to Pakistan got television coverage in Philadelphia twenty-seven days out of thirty, because the organizers found creative and photogenic ways of dramatizing the blockade, and there was such a strong local tie-in. There was also a narrative in the anti-weapons campaign, a story with build-up of suspense. Media have a harder time resisting a campaign with a story-line and an unpredictable "ending." This is another limitation of organizing events rather than campaigns.

Many of us who saw "Billionaires for Bush (or Gore)" at the conventions in Philadelphia and Los Angeles may not know about their stunt during candidate Forbes' presidential primary race in New England. The group (affiliated with United for a Fair Economy) went to the 1999 kick-off Forbes news conference in "Republican drag," which included dark suits and conservative ties for the men. At the point in the news conference when the reporters were most bored, the

Tim Russo

group suddenly unleashed their signs "Millionaires for Forbes" and cheered Forbes in the name of greed. The media coverage was a victory for the movement and embarrassing for the electoral charade.

4. Just because a creative tactic got media attention once doesn't mean it will get it again. Media editors often find it easy to ignore whatever has been done before. In September, 2000, at Carleton College in Minnesota demonstrators realized this truth and switched tactics. Charleton Heston, president of the National Rifle Association, came to speak on behalf of a Senator, and the protesters decided not to block the entrance to the hall or rally outside and chant. Instead, about half the students in the audience wore black and, when the other half of the audience gave Heston a standing ovation, the protesters sat impassively in their chairs. The public radio report of the event was unusually detailed and vivid.

    This tactic may work again and again, but to increase our likelihood of coverage in a tough media environment, it pays to go to our creativity and invent new tactics. Creativity is one of the biggest strengths of our movement—let's use it!

5. Because the reporting side of mass media often ignores or downplays, and the liberal pundits usually start out confused and critical, a movement that needs the media needs to use sustained campaigns rather than episodic uproars. The organizers in Dr. King's Southern Christian Leadership Conference practically had this down to a science: they could predict how many days of a campaign before coverage would appear in local papers, how many weeks until regional papers started covering, how many weeks until national media paid attention, and how long until the liberal columnists changed their minds and saw merit in the protests. These campaigns were

George Lakey

Tim Russo

often successful in achieving concrete victories, with media coverage as one ingredient of their success. People of color, working against white-owned media bias, successfully used the media as a resource in their struggle. Readers who have seriously explored the power of racism have an idea what an amazing feat that was!

Today's activists can learn how to do that when we need corporate mass media for achieving our campaign objectives.

5. Heighten the contrast between protesters and police behavior

One of the great things about our movement is that it understands the importance of drama in the social change process. The confrontations of Seattle and since assume what every playwright knows: the heart of drama is conflict.

I don't want to downplay the value of other kinds of social change work: day-in, day-out educational outreach; culture work; developing alternatives that show better, more community-centered ways of functioning; and so on. In my study of societies where social movements accomplished progressive change, though, nearly all of them required at some point major confrontations. Drama does what nothing else can do: it arouses the attention of otherwise occupied parts of the citizenry, it educates them on a gut level, it motivates them to find ways of acting that make sense in their terms, and it even attracts many of them into the movement itself. [4]

Drama in the streets is, however, different from an off-Broadway play. A sophisticated theater audience might prefer characters to be multifaceted, without a clearly-defined "good guy" and "bad guy." The social change drama of the streets cannot be so subtle: it really does come down to "the goodies" vs. "the baddies"—in our case, those who stand with oppressed people vs. those who stand with greed, privilege, and domination.

Of course political radicals already know who are on the right side in this play, but when we plan we can forget that most people don't make our assumptions! The moderate audience in the mainstream watching the drama in the streets is surprisingly open-minded about who are the goodies and who are the baddies. Maybe the goodies will turn out to be the protesters, and then again, maybe the police will be. Since drama motivates, some in the audience are curious to see who will turn out to be who.

The protests at the Republican National Convention in Philadelphia provide a clear example of this. Some widely-publicized police violence prior to the convention damaged the police image. Those of us organizing the Convergence training in the week just before the Convention did effective media outreach, receiving highly favorable publicity. The result was that, going into the Convention, the burden of proof was on the police to re-establish their credentials as responsible and controlled, and the protesters occupied the moral high ground. A succession of three clearly peaceable marches in three days sustained this, even though the marchers on the third day had been promised arrest. The group organizing that third march, the Kensington Welfare Rights Union, also took care not to be politically isolated, so that their civil disobedience would bring allies out in support. The police felt they had to back off the arrest threat on the third day, lest they confirm their image as "the baddies."

The second phase of the Convention actions, beginning August 1, reversed roles. The police did not have to be lambs; in the context of public fears and expectations, they only needed to show restraint, flexibility, and control. This they did, avoiding tear gas, major pepper spray, rubber bullets, and charges with or without horses. Protesters were caught without a style that would put them in stark contrast with the public behavior of the police. The protesters looked . . . well . . . disruptive. (Which we'd said over and over was our goal!) And the police were helping the public by getting traffic moving again. The police chief, who had on national television been on the defensive, became a folk hero. The Philly mainstream could breathe a sigh of relief that "our hometown police are much better than those brutal, out-of-control Seattle police, and where did these protesters come from, anyway?"

The great lesson to be learned here is that the drama of the streets cannot carry a complex analysis that requires long dissection and persuasion. The drama in street confrontations needs the simplicity of contrast between the protesters' behavior and that of the police.

The symbols used to heighten contrast depend on the situation. Black student sit-inners wore dresses and coats and ties, and remained calmly seated at the counters while hysterical white racists hit them. Gandhi designed a raid on a salt works in which demonstrators calmly walked across the boundary where they were beaten down by soldiers.[5] Vietnamese monks sat in meditative positions in the streets of Hue, in front of tanks, to help bring down the dictatorship in 1963. Philippine participants in "people power" mass action overthrew a government partly with flower necklaces for the dictator's soldiers.

Again, our power lies in our choices. We can choose to design our confrontations using appropriate symbology so that the part of the public we most want to influence will see us as the people standing up for justice. It's our choice.

The Republican National Convention in Philadelphia again shows how much we need to learn about this dimension of direct action. The reaction of the membership of a largely African-American activist group of poor and working class people to the direct action was significant. These Philadelphians use civil disobedience themselves, and are experienced in tactics of blockade and occupation. They also have their own experience with media distortion and police brutality. Nevertheless, the members felt no empathy or solidarity with the Convention disruption. The Convention direct actionists didn't set up the contrast between ourselves and the police to be clear and dramatic. Chanting "police state" is utterly unconvincing to bystanders who see with their own eyes an unusual degree of police restraint, especially if the bystanders know personally how bad brutality can get.

Police are sometimes sophisticated enough to be quite intentional in reducing the contrast. The Albany, Georgia police chief defeated the African American 1962 civil rights campaign led by the Student Nonviolent Coordinating Committee (SNCC) and Martin Luther King by carefully restraining his police and reducing the contrast. He astutely used his police to prevent Ku Klux Klan and other forces from beating up demonstrators, again to hinder black people from gaining the moral high ground. Dr. King applied the learning from this lesson in the following year's Birmingham, Alabama campaign, and SNCC's most dramatic use of this lesson was in 1964 in Mississippi.

The police strategy of lessening the contrast between their behavior and ours is one more challenge to our creativity. The British Empire tried a similar strategy during the mass direct action campaign in India called the Salt Satyagraha. Tired of beating and jailing demonstrators, they massed their police in the road in front of the marchers and did a nonviolent sit-down blockade! The marchers stopped and a stalemate ensued. After hours of uncertainty, night fell and allies of the marchers went off in search of food and blankets. When they returned, the marchers took the food and blankets and passed them over to the police. This proved too much for the police, who abandoned the street, and the marchers proceeded to a midnight victory celebration. It was another example of Gandhi's emphasis on staying on the offensive; when confronted with nonviolent resistance, the marchers escalated their nonviolence! [6]

6. Take a powerful attitude toward the prospect of state repression

Obviously, the purpose of repression is to induce fear, so people will give up fighting injustice. The power holders have a range of tactics up their sleeves: one example is setting a million dollar bail on Philadelphia protesters charged only with misdemeanors. Power holders are counting on the feeling inside us—our fear—to change our behavior so as to make us less effective.

That's why one of the most fundamental choices any social movement makes is what kind of attitude to have toward repression.[7] It's natural for us to fear punishment, deprivation of liberty, losing our jobs—we're only human, after all. It is so natural to be fearful in the face of repression that we may not know movements make choices about how to counteract the threats of the state. In the workshops for the Republican Convention protests, many participants didn't know that there was a choice. They believed that all movements have the same attitude toward repression, which is far from true.

The Battle of Seattle

Tim Russo

Some movements see power holders inviting them to play what I call "the Fear Game": authorities punish and threaten so that activists will respond fearfully. These movements choose a different strategy.

For example, during the Montgomery bus boycott the power holders decided to play the Fear Game by leaking the word that they had a list of black leaders who were going to be arrested. The leaders decided to take a powerful, proactive attitude; they went to City Hall as a group and demanded to be arrested at once. They carefully expanded their numbers so that, more than likely, some individuals would not be on the list and could indignantly demand to be arrested rather than be insulted by not being considered a leader. More recently labor unions in Decatur, Illinois made a similar move: hundreds of workers filled City Hall and refused to leave until the intended arrests were actually made.

Consider the difficulty this puts the power holders in. If the people refuse to fear them, the power holders have lost one of their most powerful weapons! Another example comes from Poland, where after many years of Communist dictatorship a radical group of workers and intellectuals decided to depart from their activist tradition and create an open, above-ground organization for human rights. The move was a breakthrough which supported the growth of the mass Solidarity movement, resulting by the end of the '80s in the nonviolent overthrow of the dictatorship.[8]

The choice to adopt a discipline of secrecy in which activists work may at some times and places be useful, but it is a choice that needs careful thought, especially when we consider that it is often not necessary even in full-blown police states. In the US., playing the Fear Game seems to be hurting the movement.

One consequence is the withholding of trust. To win, movements need to expand. To expand, activists need to trust themselves, each other, and the people they want to convince. Think of the last time someone succeeded in persuading you to act. Did you pick up a vibe that they didn't trust you? You probably picked

Tim Russo

up the opposite energy—optimism and confidence that, once you got the information, you'd want to participate.

A major dynamic I've personally seen in our movement is trustlessness. The Fear Game operates in worries about who might be an agent, who might betray us, who cannot be relied on. People don't tell their names, censor their interactions, hold back. The wariness is toxic because activists feed each other's fear. I've seen a black man on his way out of a movement in disgust because of what he perceived as white racism; the hostile vibe he perceived might instead have been "He might be an agent!" This example shows how secrecy complicates movement life. White racism does of course exist where white activists gather, because we have been socialized by a racist culture. When white activists put up other barriers to entry into the movement, like fear of strangers, the barriers can easily be perceived as racism (which is also connected with fear of strangers!).

Even within the boundary of color, trustlessness reduces the movement's growth. A woman of color cried as she told me about the refusal of a meeting of people of color to proceed until each new person, including her, had been vouched for by two others—an institutionalization of trustlessness. When trustlessness is institutionalized, a movement is very easy to contain because it can't recruit outside the circles of those who define themselves as victims. Since many talented and effective people don't find it useful to define themselves as victims, they are unlikely to stuff themselves into the confining circles of conspirators however radical their views.

The Fear Game also reduces the ability of direct actionists to develop and sustain alliances. Successful direct action movements develop an ability to attract allies. The role of ally is different from the role of campaigner. The job of campaigners is to take the initiative, to get the ball rolling. The job of allies is to come in and help push once it's rolling. In the U.S. we find a lot of activists who simultaneously are campaigning on one issue and are allies to other campaigns around other issues. This flexibility works well.

Because the Fear Game generates trustlessness, protesters have a harder time trusting allies. They sometimes enter the confrontation stage politically isolated, having failed to reach out and open up the communication channels with people busy on other projects. Where all this comes crashing down is at the moment of state repression, which is when allies are often the most needed and also when there is most confusion in the air. That's when activists, who refuse to trust the allies, say to the allies: "Trust us and do X, Y, and Z!" Then the protesters become disappointed and even furious when the allies don't immediately come to attention and salute!

If playing the Fear Game initiated by the state reduces the internal morale of the movement, reduces its growth potential, and hurts relationships with allies, what's the point of the secrecy and stealth? For one thing, it makes possible certain direct action tactics that rely on surprise. We may be reluctant to give up those tactics. I also enjoy the emotions that go with plotting and scheming, and I may not be alone on that! Another reason why secrecy and stealth may appear in our movement is that they strengthen the boundary between Insider and Outsider.[9]

Unfortunately, the security agencies also know the negative impact of secrecy on the movement, and work it to their own advantage.[10] They start out with abundant resources to put into spies and electronic surveillance, and the more covert we are, the more resources they can demand (thereby increasing the already obscene size of the security state). Not only is it an advantage to them in terms of increasing the power and affluence of their apparatus, but it also justifies their putting more people in our ranks, who help make decisions and sometimes exercise leadership. And the more aware we are of this, the more scared we become and the less we can trust each other, which is wonderful from their point of view. The basic reason they like the Fear Game so much is that they know they are sure to win it.

Fortunately, we can make other choices. We can draw inspiration from the choice of the Student Nonviolent Coordinating Committee (SNCC) in 1963–64 to organize openly in Mississippi, perhaps the most violently racist state in the U.S. at the time. The largely-black SNCC workers dealt with men who were police by day and KKK by night; SNCC often lived in Freedom Houses that were unprotected in the countryside; they had no guns and everyone knew it; the federal agents refused to protect them; the Mississippi media were against them as were most clergy. SNCC knew they would be hurt, jailed, tortured, and some would die; they were not naive in choosing their attitude toward repression.

At the very beginning of the 1964 Freedom Summer, three SNCC workers were murdered—James Chaney, Michael Schwerner, and Andrew Goodman—to scare away others who had volunteered. SNCC refused to go underground; they had a better strategy. SNCC's choice expanded the movement dramatically both in Mississippi and nationally, won powerful allies, and broke the political stranglehold of racism in that state. I would challenge anyone in today's movement to study SNCC's attitude toward repression in Mississippi in the summer of 1964 and then explain why our movement should play the Fear Game. The more powerful choice is openness.

George Lakey

7. Fully commit to strategic nonviolent action explicitly

The vast majority of protesters in this current wave of mass direct action want to be nonviolent and see no reason to do anything else. The dilemma facing the designers of a campaign is: do we fully commit and be explicit about that, or do we soft-pedal the nonviolence? Choosing for a campaign is more important than for these short actions we've seen in Seattle, etc., because the stakes are greater in the course of a campaign of months or years. Before his Chicago campaign, for example, Dr. King and his organizers spent months negotiating with forces in the community to get agreement on nonviolence. King's organizer who was liaison to the gangs was personally beaten up many times by gang members to test his fidelity to nonviolence before they would seriously discuss and finally make an agreement.

It is tempting not to take a stand on nonviolence. There may be moralistic pacifists around, mired in the past and more interested in preaching than acting; their obnoxiousness encourages organizers to just want to move on to the next agenda item.

Some white activists hesitate to take a stand on nonviolence because they mistakenly believe that "it's a white thing." That would be a big surprise to the hundreds of thousands of people of color in the U.S. who have used nonviolent direct action in campaigns for over a century. (In 1876 in St. Louis African Americans were doing freedom rides against discrimination on trolley cars, to take one of thousands of examples.) Not to mention the role of nonviolence in the anticolonial struggles in Africa and Asia. When we think of nonviolence, why do the names of Gandhi, King, and Cesar Chavez so easily leap to mind? They are only the tip of the iceberg. Actually, a far, far higher proportion of people of color have engaged in nonviolent action in the U.S. than have white people, and continue to do so year in and year out.

The mass media and social studies courses haven't given us this information. What else is new? Only the study of social movements will return our heritage to us. (I won't even start with the myth that nonviolent action is inherently middle class—that's even more off base than the myth that it's white.)

It may help to remember that this discussion is not about pacifism, but about strategic nonviolent action. Many pacifists don't do direct action because they want to avoid conflict, and most people who do nonviolent action aren't pacifists. So the question is not on a philosophical level but on a strategic level: what makes sense for making change?[11]

Some activists may fear that taking a stand could alienate some friends of ours who are radical and brave. And what about tolerance—who are we to lay down the law? Isn't the movement to proceed by consensus, and there isn't consensus on this issue!

Alienating our more militant friends is a tough issue, but dialogue would help. I've heard the Black Bloc, for example, referred to by protesters as if it is a rigid monolith which will always believe the same thing and to which we must defer. Another possibility is that the Black Bloc wants as much as anyone to be more effective, can evaluate what's working and what isn't, and has internal diversity of opinion.[12] The approach in the African-American community during the civil rights movement was useful. When a mass direct action campaign was being organized in a Southern city and consensus wasn't reached about strategy

Tim Russo

and tactics, people agreed to disagree, and respected each other's right to conduct their own operation. During the recent Democratic National Convention in Los Angeles, an agreement like that was worked out for a planned action.

Everyone "doing their own thing" in a mass action doesn't work because it's self-contradictory. If those who organize the action base it on strategic nonviolent action, they aren't being allowed to "do their thing" if others come in and do violence or even property destruction. The advocates of violence or property destruction are, when it comes down to it, being intolerant by not letting their comrades carry out their intentions. The only way that tolerance can work is by mutual understanding that different strategies will be used at different times or in different places—sufficiently different that the police cannot use one kind of action as an excuse to bash another kind.

Tactical disagreement is another diversity challenge that faces our movement. If some of our more militant friends aren't willing to "agree to disagree" but instead use confrontational tactics that endanger others without their consent, then the issue is no longer about strategy and tactics, it is about respect and needs to be tackled on that level.

Doubt about our legitimacy in setting policy needs to be addressed ourselves, first of all. Is it OK for me to take initiative in working for change? Initiative is a kind of leadership. As I take initiative I do set a tone, and my words and actions attract some people and turn off others. I can't actually take initiative without finding that I have some responsibility for consequences. So if I'm willing to empower myself to act for change, then I might as well be mindful of the results of what I do and don't do. If I do (with friends and comrades) create a policy of strategic nonviolence, that has one set of results. If I don't, it has another set of results.

I want to leave aside the question of armed struggle for another time, even though I find it fascinating and sometimes work in situations where it is a very real option. In fact, I've taught social change in the middle of a guerrilla encamp-

George Lakey

Tim Russo

ment in the jungles of Burma; my students were soldier revolutionaries. The very different situation in the U.S., however, is: "If most of us want to be nonviolent anyway, how can we make the most of it?"

The option to make a fuller and more explicit commitment to nonviolence has several advantages. For one thing, it takes the wind out of the sails of the state, which wants us to be violent and, if we're not willing to do violence ourselves, will pay people to do it in our name. There are too many sad stories of groups that learned this the hard way. In Philadelphia, for example, a group of youthful activists believed itself set up by the police because of its growing effectiveness. The police raided the house where the leaders lived communally; while the activists were being handcuffed in the living room the police "discovered" dynamite in the kitchen. The activists complained later, "We have never advocated violence." But the group had been unwilling to take a credible stand for nonviolence, for reasons similar to those advanced today. Mississippi police didn't even try to set up SNCC in 1964 because, as SNCC's Mississippi coordinator Robert Moses told me, "We don't have guns in our freedom houses and everyone knows it."

It may be, as some of today's Philadelphia activists believe, that police agents were responsible for the property destruction which handed the moral high ground over to the police during the Republican Convention. Again, the movement was fairly defenseless against this kind of tactic because it could not achieve consensus on a stand against property destruction. As much as we'd like to blame police, in all honesty we have to look at how we helped to set ourselves up.

Leaving the issues of nonviolence and property destruction ambiguous may not matter too much for the kind of event organized in Philadelphia or L.A., where most people fairly quickly return to the rest of their lives. People doing a campaign over time which is working to accomplish an objective,

Tim Russo

however, may have too much at stake to be wishy-washy about something that could undo all their hard work.[13]

Some activists with a long-term commitment are also attracted to nonviolence as a basic personal/political ethic and way of life. One version of this is called "nonviolent revolution": a personal politics that loves life enough to struggle and loves liberation too much to dominate or violate others.

The biggest advantage of all to adding depth to our commitment to nonviolence is related to the flexible and decentralized character of the action style which worked so brilliantly in Seattle and replayed again in Washington, Philadelphia and Los Angeles.[14] The flexibility and decentralization can bring added power to mass direct action; it also brings chaos. The new physics teaches us that chaos can accompany system change. Easy for the physicists to say; they are theorists and not personally one of the atomic particles buzzing around! We protesters are the particles; we are the ones in motion and are faced with the challenge of how to stay centered in the midst of chaos.

If we do manage to stay centered, we'll make better choices and stay more loving; when we're disconnected we easily get upset or scared or stuck in attitudes of hostility. An advantage of nonviolent action is that it is easier to stay centered while doing it.[15] Of course we'll still experience a roller coaster: flashes of anger, chills of fear, highs of elation, and other strong emotions. Centeredness is the ability to handle the feelings without becoming attached to them; it's letting them run through us rather than letting them run us.

Doing violence or even the nonviolence called property destruction doesn't support being centered. We need ways of participating in chaos with eyes wide open, minds fully aware, feet on the ground, creativity pulsing, and readiness to connect.

There are no guarantees: chaos is still chaos. My experience is that going into chaos with a nonviolent commitment increases the chance of being centered, which ultimately benefits everyone.

George Lakey

Mass Action Since Seattle 169

NOTES

These are the views of George Lakey and not necessarily those of the organization he works with, Training for Change.

1. This campaign, which has more to teach us about direct action than there's room to go into here, is described blow-by-blow by Richard K. Taylor, *Blockade* (Maryknoll, NY: Orbis, 1977). This campaign in solidarity with Bangladesh happened in 1971–72.

2. One of my favorite books by Martin Luther King, Jr., is *Why We Can't Wait,* the behind-the-scenes story of the Birmingham campaign. The book also includes his "Letter from a Birmingham Jail." (Book available in various editions.)

3. There are trainers who can lead workshops on campaign design. For more information on the successful antinuclear struggle, see Bill Moyer's paper which is a must-read for direct action strategists, "Movement Action Plan,"available from the Social Movement Empowerment Project, 721 Shrader, San Francisco, CA 94117. Bill's model has been picked up by a number of movements, for example the whole issue of World Rainforest Report for Sept. 1994 in Australia is devoted to MAP. You'll find a summary in chapter two of *Grassroots and Nonprofit Leadership: A Guide for Organizations in Changing Times,* by Berit Lakey, George Lakey, Rod Napier, and Janice Robinson (Gabriola Island, B.C., Canada: New Society Publishers, 1995).

4. More on this dynamic is in my book, *Strategy for a Living Revolution,* which was revised as *Powerful Peacemaking* and published by New Society Publishers in 1986.

5. The historically accurate version in the film *Gandhi* is worth watching repeatedly.

6. A good source for learning from the master strategist Gandhi is the television documentary *A Force More Powerful,* which also includes the cases of Danish resistance to German Nazi occupation, Polish resistance to Communist dictatorship, and the Nashville sit-in movement. Available from Public Broadcasting System, which aired the program in September 2000.

7. To read about one choice, called security culture, go to the website: security.tao.ca or nocompromise.org. The article "Security Culture" states its basic assumption at the beginning: "To minimize the destructiveness of this government harassment, it is imperative that we create a 'security culture' within our movement." Some movements, operating in much more dangerous situations than the U.S., Canada, or Western Europe, have found that security culture maximizes rather than minimizes the destructiveness of government harassment.

8. This is one of a long list of dictatorships that have been overthrown by nonviolent "people power," despite the state's using military repression to defend itself. Just in the past few decades mass nonviolent action has played a decisive role in ousting one-party states and dictatorships in: Bolivia, Haiti, Argentina, East Germany, Czechoslovakia, Hungary, Poland, the Philippines, the Baltic States, Mali, Malawi, Madagascar, and Benin, and prevented military-backed coups in Thailand and Russia. See Stephen Zunes, Lester R. Kurtz, and Sarah Beth Asher (eds.), *Nonviolent Social Movements: A Geographical Perspective* (Malden, MA: Blackwell Publishers, 1999).

9. Fortunately we can create many, many tactics that do not rely on surprise. One resource to jump-start our creativity is Gene Sharp's book *The Politics of Nonviolent Action,* where he describes 198 tactics that have been used historically (Boston: Porter Sargent, 1973).

10. During the movement against the Vietnam War, F.B.I. documents included a discussion of the importance of making activists believe there was "an F.B.I. man behind every mailbox." During a spokescouncil meeting preparing for the protests at the Republican National Convention, an activist took a break to call an anarchist house in West Philadelphia and learned from activists there that, when they randomly took their phone off the hook,they heard the spokescouncil meeting!

11. Actually, I believe that a healthy movement includes a lively discussion of pacifism, too, because it represents such a dramatic break from the dominant cultural theme of violence/militarism/sexism/imperialism that we see everywherfrom playgrounds to movies.

12. An example of Black Bloc interest in dialoguing with the movement is the statement put out by the Bay Area Black Bloc dated October 7, 2000. Their email address: BlackBloc@ziplip.com

13. I don't mean that violence and property destruction are the same discussion. Principled pacifists and nonviolent actionists Daniel and Philip Berrigan are well known for their use of property destruction, for example. On the other hand, believers in assassination might not consider property destruction valuable.

14. Betsy Raasch-Gilman emphasizes the freshness and innovation of this approach in her paper, "A Trainer's Report on the WTO Protests in Seattle," available from Training for Change. Her paper is also on the Training for Change website: www.TrainingforChange.org

15. Barbara Deming develops this theme and applies it to macro-level change in her important and practical book, *Revolution and Equilibrium* (NY: Grossman, 1971).

UNEASY ALLIANCES

part III:

HUMAN NEED
NOT CORPORATE GREED

ENOUGH IS ENOUGH!

NO GLOBALIZATION WITHOUT REPRESENTATION

MARCH FOR OUR LIVES
MONDAY AUGUST 14, 2000
4PM PERSHING SQUARE · 7PM STAPLES CENTER
MOBILIZE FOR JUSTICE AUGUST 14-17

This Is What Bureaucracy Looks Like

NGOs and Anti-Capitalism

James Davis

"I'm aware that it's a lot more glamorous to be on the barricade with a handkerchief around your nose than it is to be at the meetings with a briefcase and a bowler hat, but I think that we're getting more done this way." —Bono

This essay takes a critical look at the role Non-governmental Organizations (NGOs) play in the growing movement against global capital. The movement, which made its spectacular US debut in Seattle, has lent NGOs unprecedented political influence. Leading thinkers and institutions of capitalist planning are desperate for allies to appease their critics. As we will see, the impulses of the NGOs and those of the movement are politically at odds. While much discussion has concentrated on tactical differences, a more profound problem lies beneath. Lacking in imagination and caught between the many-headed street movement and an impulse to negotiate directly with power on its behalf, the specter of NGOs as a device for the containment of political dissent arises.

The government's friend

There is no doubt that NGOs do vital work in any number of places around the world. From famine relief to bringing clean water to rural communities throughout the South, many such groups are at the front line of people's struggles to survive and gain a modicum of political rights. NGOs have inherited a tradition of charity work that has been around since the earliest days of colonialism. More and more of them have abandoned the sorry history of proselytism and missionary work in favor of a human rights agenda and, more recently, a clear political and economic critique. In this regard the contribution of NGOs to the creation and maintenance of a space for political discourse in many places is inestimable. The experience of Chiapas is one example where NGOs, among others, organized in support of the Zapatistas and made an overt military solution an untenable option for the Mexican State. In Seattle and Quebec groups like Public Citizen and Global Exchange made enormous organizing contributions, mobilized formidable resources and infiltrated the corporate media with articulate and provocative spokespeople and sound bites. But it is precisely for groups like this that the contradictions of institutionalized radicalism become most apparent. To understand why this is the case we must consider the changes in the terrain of struggle that Zapatismo and Seattle have wrought.

After having been denounced in the South for decades as an incubus, the World Bank, the IMF, and their even more odious offspring the WTO, are now pilloried even in the business press which feels it must distance itself from them or risk contagion. The WTO has effectively put the overdeveloped countries on notice that their turn to be 'structurally adjusted' has come and hence expanded resistance to the 'first world' also. George Soros, the swashbuckling knight-errant of speculative financial flows, has even criticized the institutions and neoliberal ubereconomist Jeffrey Sachs is back-pedaling madly. A legitimation crisis is brewing for international capital. The only question is, who will save them and how? Recent demonstrations in Seattle, Prague, Davos, D.C., Melbourne, and Quebec City, escalating in fierceness, and increasingly articulate have left the capitalist planned *coup du monde* a shambles.

To the media it seems that NGOs and protestors are virtually interchangeable and synonymous. In reality elite decision-makers evaluate the NGO world with a quick and pragmatic eye and see potential allies in the delicate work of diffusing this new opposition. *The Economist* took note of this in pointing out that when "assaulted by unruly protestors, firms and governments are suddenly eager to do business with the respectable face of dissent." Legitimation strategies are everywhere. In *Business Week*, "A double backlash is generating skepticism about the ability of globalism to do good." All of a sudden we witness the recruitment of a moral philosophy absent from the economist's dictionary since the nineteenth century and along with it a pantheon of do-gooders to show the way.

Among the re-imagers we find Bono, narcissistic Irish pop star, cultural carpetbagger, and supremely cynical carer whose current promotions include a campaign to 'forgive' Third World debt. He has become a roving ambassador for Jubilee 2000, an NGO which advocates debt relief as good business. Bono (born again) has met the pope (a fan), Jesse Helms and 'Jim' Wolfensohn, the former World Bank boss. He has been coached in the intricacies of global capitalism by Harvard's Jeffrey Sachs. In recent years Sachs has changed his colors and jumped ship from his hard line of the 1980s and early '90s. Having factored in political crisis he is now the liberal neoliberal barely recognizable as one of the primary architects of 'shock therapy'. That policy succeeded in prising the collective wealth of Russia away, laundering it through the Mafia and the banking system, and recycling it as investment dollars in the US and Western Europe. The shock has contributed to a fall in the life expectancy of Russian men by six years in the 1990s, among other calamities.

Bono is an extreme example of those with whom the institutions would like to be associated. His naivete about why he was at the Prague WTO meeting is almost endearing; at least other opportunists in the NGO industry appreciate that without the demonstrations and the ensuing legitimacy deficit there would be no seats at the table for any of them. Some of them will have read as much in *The Economist* who was in no doubt as to why "groups such as Oxfam were all but co-opted into designing debt relief strategies."

The ideal for capitalism would be to create and co-opt a "responsible" leadership who could then negotiate on behalf of the hordes and diffuse the movement while recuperating it. "Horst Kohler, the IMF's new boss has been courting NGOs. Jim Wolfensohn, the [World] Banks boss, has long fawned in their direction." Surely, they imagine, there are some reasonable types who understand that we can't go back to the stone age and that progress will continue. Stephen Hellinger, president of Development Gap, one of the organizing NGOs of the "Fifty Years is Enough" campaign , was successfully recruited by the World Bank. He works with them to review the effects of Structural Adjustment and reflects on his experience in the *Financial Times*. "Wolfensohn has yet to take the critique that is coming out around the world," he says and adds that, "It has been six years, the hopes we had for him have yet to materialize." Incredibly Hellinger finds Wolfensohn to be the impediment to change—a different boss and perhaps we could get somewhere. Ironic then that Wolfensohn got the chop for being too reform minded.

Is it mere coincidence that the implementation of the neoliberal project in the form of privatization, trade feudalism and the attempted elimination of the welfare state occurred simultaneously with the emergence of NGOs as central to its explanation and narrative? While neoliberalism as conceived by the Chicago boys (Sachs among them) Thatcher, Reagan et al, was a strictly conservative strategy, its execution and implementation is a Clintonian liberal project. "The principle reason for the recent boom in NGOs," according to *The Economist,* "is that Western governments finance them. This is not a matter of charity but of privatization." In Africa and elsewhere Western governments routinely recruit NGOs to distribute aid and administer development projects. Indeed *The Economist* claims that governments rely to a greater and greater degree on "useful information" that NGOs can provide. By way of example they state: "the work of Global Witness is actually paid for by the British Foreign Office."

Supply and Demand

More profoundly NGOs can often be found in control of services formerly provided by Third World governments until debt and restructuring eliminated them. Caroline Fetscher has written of the situation in Bangladesh where up to 5,000 NGOs are involved in literacy programs. Alex Demirovic points out that due to their mistrust of Southern governments, Northern NGOs can become shadow bureaucracies parallel to Southern Nation State administrations. These NGOs "often work as public service contractors with headquarters in the large cities, far removed from the problems of the population, sturdily professional and apolitical. The agenda for the aid is, in fact, frequently determined by the self-inter-

James Davis

est of these organizations." As these relationships become more institutionalized the implications for democracy among the recipients, i.e. the poor of the Global South, are fairly clear.

If Bono's elite power is exclusively to do with the image then the NGO's can more powerfully claim to be the real fake. As Antonio Negri and Michael Hardt describe it, "these NGOs conduct just wars without arms, without violence, without borders. Like the Dominicans in the late medieval period and the Jesuits at the dawn of modernity, these groups strive to identify universal needs and defend human rights." In the new framework of legitimacy that Negri and Hardt describe as "Empire" (and which the Zapatistas, among others , recognize loosely as neoliberalism), "new articulations of the exercise of legitimate force" are demanded. The pattern is a familiar one with the shibboleth of morality wheeled out to underline the economics of war and intervention. As such, Negri and Hardt point out that NGOs, in this case Oxfam, Medicins Sans Frontieres and Amnesty International, are precursors and perpetuators of imperial intervention. Kosovo is the most recent example where liberals cheered the Luftwaffe's support as American ordnance fell on defenseless Serbs. And this after multiple fabrications announced by NATO and the CIA but dutifully reproduced, reported and spectacularised by the media.

To simplify with a metaphor, NGOs are to imperialism what artist bohemians are to urban gentrification. For NGOs authenticity is derived from their branding, or more accurately from the composite of their brand identity. As is the case with the more traditional corporate brands authenticity remains a holy grail. Nike and Benetton derive theirs from 'Blackness,' diversity and

> NGOs are to imperialism what artist bohemians are to urban gentrification.

the urban street credibility of their billion dollar illusions. NGOs generate their authenticity from compassion extraction activities. For them cultural otherness and the mediation of abject desperation is the foundation of moral authority. This is most obvious in the Fair Trade game, whereby NGOs import, distribute and sell crafts and produce from the South. "Buy a basket from a typical crafts importer and the peasant artisan receives a tiny fraction of what you pay. At the Global Exchange Fair Trade Craft Stores, you know the producer got her or his fair share, around 15-30% of the retail price." Like World Bank and IMF activities, the currency of fair trade is market rather than social relations.

As is the case with most valuable raw materials such extractions are located most often in the South. And like gold and diamonds, 'compassion' and 'authenticity' mined in the South are most profitably consumed in the North. And as with gold and diamonds the scarcity of compassion must be carefully managed owing to its natural abundance. The compassion market is notoriously inelastic as was evidenced by the 'compassion fatigue' crisis suffered by NGOs during the second Ethiopian famine of the 1980s. As brands go, the NGO sector has succeeded in accumulating that most scarce of resources, compassionate capital. Like Lady Diana's landmine campaign, their moral appeal is absolute.

Movement(s)...

Elsewhere in this collection the notion of prefiguration in praxis is discussed. It is relevant to any discussion of NGOs also. The movement against global capitalism is marked by political evolution from those movements that have gone before. In its style it owes a debt to the women's movement and its rejection of hierarchy and charismatic oratory, to the peace movement of the seventies in its mass nonviolent demeanor, to the European black bloc of the eighties in its tactical probing for the weaknesses of a jack booted foe and to the radical environmental movement for the joy with which it goes about its work and its emphasis on changing everyday life for the better. The radically democratic nature of the movement is its strongest suit. Perhaps this is a lesson that NGOs are incapable of learning if we consider that NGOs were granted a seat at the UN as consultants and fundraisers when the charter was written at the dawn of the post colonial era. There is a political difference between the movement described and the manner with which the majority of NGOs organize themselves, particularly those with the profile and organizational ability to seize the moment.

And Miners

Hierarchical in structure and often led by careerist NGO celebrities, the industry is degenerate in its industrial relations and, as is often the case with countercultural outfits, relies to an outrageous degree on volunteer labor. In this arena too NGOs find ways to profitably invest political rhetoric. They exploit their workers using the goodfight jargon just as sweatshops use motifs of 'familia' or nationalism to justify injustice or as IMF officers argue for particular environmental or labor abuses by reference to general growth rates and so on.

NGOs might indeed operate in the moral economy ignoring the dictates of the surplus value theory of labor. One can't accumulate compassion in this manner without exploiting workers. Along these lines Ralph Nader, Trojan corporation killer and the Elvis of reformism, has stated that the NGO business has no need of trade unions. Back in the eighties at *Multinational Monitor,* a magazine he owned, he expressed the opinion that workers at the magazine had no right to unionize. The editor, Tim Shorrock, was fired for attempting to organize. The following is extracted from an essay by Nick Mamatas published by the *Greenwich Village Gazzette* (New York).

"Public interest groups are like crusades, Nader explains, you can't have work rules, or 9 to 5." Workers should be treated equitably, using the resources the "crusade" has, but anyone in a public interest firm in Washington "can leave and double their income by going across the street." Shorrock, with his "union ploy," became an "adversary" according to Nader. "Anything that is commercial, is unionizable," but small public interest organizations "would go broke in a month," Nader says, if they paid union wages, offered union benefits and operated according to standard work rules, such as the eight-hour day.

No surprise then that the majority of NGOs and Unions are reluctant to embrace street demonstrations and risk the contagion of radical democracy infecting their workers and members. The crucial moment in Seattle came when

James Davis

Union leaders steered the rank and file away from sites where demonstrators confronted police and succeeded in derailing the meetings, a tactic employed once more by Canadian Trade Union leaders at the FTAA demonstrations in Quebec City in April, 2001.

While the street movement in Seattle drew together a wide range of issues into a generalized critique, many NGOs seem fixated with specialization. Salaried professionals rely on teams of researchers, media spinners, accountants, import/export consultants, tax lawyers and all the poorly paid but very committed staff one would expect from a professional operation. And incredibly they actually refer to these people, the majority of whom are motivated young idealists, as 'our staff'. Alex Demiroric: "The danger of yuppie-NGOs (a jet-set civil society) forming at the global level is not insignificant." This leadership of professional reformers acts as if in the belief that the head and the feet are separate. A morbidity pervades this division of labor where everyday is casual Friday.

In part because they organize as businesses in a manner determined by capitalism, this is all they can do. A brand will suffer in the market place if it lacks focus; the specialized niche is life or death. What is generalized is their moral appeal and that is packaged as pity, condescension, remorse and self-righteousness.

Shortly after Seattle, *The Economist* bemoaned that in France, where blockades were happening over fuel prices, politics was again being conducted in the streets. *The Economist* was remembering the derailment of the MAI, the ritual slaying of the WTO, the incineration of French plans to get rid of guaranteed pensions through general strikes in 1996 and 1997 and a litany of other 'setbacks' due to people power. They recalled the chaos of the 1960s when it was impossible to make 5 year business plans, when social movements in France and elsewhere were 'out of control' and the demands on capital were intolerable. *The Economist* was one of the first to identify the NGOs as potential allies in the war for globalization. Open any page of *Foreign Affairs,* read the output of the British Treasury Department, or even The World Bank's own literature and it will be found now as doctrine. Indeed on the World Bank's homepage NGOs appear in the 'partners' window alongside business and bond investors.

We are not without historical precedents, for it is the history of resistance and social movements which gives capitalism many of its great ideas. A look back at the civil rights movement and the manner in which it was co-opted and neutralized is indicative of the dangers the movement now faces. And few will need to be reminded of the serial sell-outs in the chilling history of trade unionism, usually by its own leadership. The trouble with trade unionism, remarked Winston Churchill at a cabinet meeting at the end of WWI, is that there is not enough of it—that is, of the sound patriotic kind at least.

A further trait of the contemporary movement is that it levels its demands against capital in isolation rather than against the state. Historically the state has mediated between the two, closeting its loyalty to employers behind a rhetorical or legalistic impartiality. But the state has shored up its own position via a host of institutional defenses, welfare and social work among them. In part globalization is the end of these as capital transcends its perceived need for the state brokered compromise. Privatization was the answer to which a question had to be found and simultaneously the discourse of entitlement was replaced by that of 'responsibility'. In abandoning any notion of social contract and by evacuating the space of 'public good', capital, via the state, has created a subtle symbiosis whereby charity is the new welfare and NGOs are the new social workers. Structural adjustment has achieved this in the South while Bush's state-sponsored religious volunteerism, combined with the philanthropic experimentalism of Bill Gates, Ted Turner and George Soros, are its latest expressions in the North. The market economy and the market society are indistinguishable...compassion in all things. "The international institutions, which clearly recognize the problem of internationally controlling the financial and capital markets...are also aware of the need for intermediary organizations. With NGOs they form complex political networks and negotiation systems. The result can be described as global governance."

The implications for the movement are predictable. Those who most loudly condemned the militants of Prague and Seattle are most likely to have their loyalty to the politics of the negotiating table rather than the street rewarded. Indeed the more sober among them speak of 'reforming' the institutions rather than their abolition. Like Bono's generosity in 'forgiving' debt to those who never borrowed, not to mention reparations, among the NGOs the language of forgiveness is abject. Thus can Kevin Danaher, co-founder of Global Exchange and prominent critic of the World Bank intone that "If we really care about the future of the planet, we must struggle to transform the World Bank." What we would transform it into is left unsaid.

The Last Bureaucrat

This posture, assumed by most of the leading NGO's concerned with trade in particular and globalization in general, belies a fascination they share with a gamut of capitalist functionaries throughout the West. Mainstream economics is in theory as imperialist as capitalism is in reality. It has in the last generation become a theology. Academically the discipline is contained within a system of imposed ignorance, its most interesting challenges are excluded as 'externalities' (famine, pollution) or more glaringly as 'market failures', "Land has no production cost, it is a free and unreproducable gift of Nature" proclaims a basic introductory textbook. War, the great engine of accumulation, is dismissed as outside its remit though without it there would be no property, or at least no destruction and regeneration of it. The contemporary economist is a number cruncher obsessing over the harmony of equations as the bodies pile up around him. Yet NGOs, particularly their intellectual elites, remain under the spell of professional economics, convinced that more sensible theories will prevail and that the World Bank needs to reorient itself towards 'micro loans' to better deliver the theology of the market to those as yet 'underdeveloped'.

James Davis

NGOs, however well intentioned many may be, are not a substitute for real social and political movements. Above all, neither capital, the state, nor the NGOs should be allowed dictate who the movements leaders are. It should be remembered that the Seattle victory was revised by many NGO and union leaders as the outcome of a great collaboration between them. This clearly overstates the case and purposely overlooks the tensions between them and the 'street warriors' who did the heavy lifting. But pragmatically many NGOs have valuable research and mobilizing resources and, like the media, any serious political or social movement cannot ignore its relationship with them. For the first time in 20 years real radical possibilities have opened up. Where once the committed had few options but a professional NGO track there is now the inkling of a truly global anticapitalist movement to work towards. Essentially the NGOs are a class of professional activists with whom the movement has a relationship. They are often strong critics of the excesses of capitalism and are willing to commit resources and considerable ability and talent to the creation of a just order. What is demanded of them will determine whether their political choices have to do with the movement's agenda or that of capital.

It can go either way. The following from Lori Wallach, a prominent researcher, writer and director of Public Citizen in Washington DC, in a *Foreign Policy* interview, illustrates the contours of this political divide. She described her work in Seattle; "[T]hese anarchist folks marched in there and started smashing things. And our people actually picked up the anarchists. Because we had with us longshoremen and steelworkers who, by their sheer bulk, were three or four times larger. So we had them just literally sort of, a teamster on either side, just pick up an anarchist. We'd walk him over to the cops and say, this boy just broke a window. He doesn't belong to us. We hate the WTO, so does he, maybe, but we don't break things. Please arrest him." This behavior is premised on a tactical assumption that reassuring capital is "getting more done."

Wallach's remarks underline a very important point. The conditions of negotiation between capital and the NGOs are the unilateral disarmament of the

movement's tactics. This is the only thing the NGOs have to offer neoliberalism; a special sort of police power and movement sabotage. In other words, the promise (articulated, indicated or simply understood) that the politics of the street will be replaced by the politics of 'heated' negotiation. But the potential exists for a genuinely radical movement to grow in opposition to capital itself, which has nothing to do with this sort of politics. The movement in the streets has made apparent capital's inherent irrationalism. In going on a new offensive without first seeing to it that a spurious opposition existed it has overplayed its hand and its vulnerability is exposed. It is now fighting a rearguard action to create one. NGO's, who couldn't get their calls returned even three years ago, can now write their own contracts and are privy, finally, to policy making at the highest levels. For Lori Wallach and her crowd it is almost like being a real cop.

The Meaning of Seattle

Noam Chomsky
Interviewed by David Barsamian
February 23, 2000

Let's talk about what occurred in Seattle in late November/early December around the WTO ministerial meeting. What meaning do you derive from what happened there?

I think it was a very significant event and potentially extremely important. It reflected a very broad feeling which has been pretty clear for years and has been growing and developing in intensity around a good part of the world. It is opposed to the corporate-led globalization that's been imposed under primarily U.S. leadership, but the other major industrial countries, too. It is harming a great many people, undermining sovereignty and democratic rights, and leading to plenty of resistance. What was interesting in Seattle was several things. First of all, the events reflected very extensive programs of education and organizing, and it shows what can be achieved by that. It wasn't just that people suddenly showed up. Secondly, the participation was extremely broad and varied. There were constituencies brought together that have rarely interconnected in the past. That was true internationally, Third World, indigenous, peasant, labor leaders and others. And here in the U.S., environmentalists, large labor participation and other groups, which had separate interests but a shared understanding. It's been pretty evident before. That's the same kind of coalition of forces that blocked the Multilateral Agreement on Investment a year earlier and that had strongly opposed other so-called agreements like NAFTA or the WTO agreements, which are not agreements, at least if the population counts. Most of the population has been opposed to them. It has reached a point of a kind of dramatic confrontation. Also it will presumably continue and I think could take very constructive forms.

Are there any lessons to be derived from Seattle?

One lesson is that education and organizing over a long term, carefully done, can really pay off. Another is that a substantial part of the domestic and global population, I would guess probably a majority of those thinking about the issues, range from being disturbed by contemporary developments to being strongly opposed to them, primarily to the sharp attack on democratic rights, on the freedom to make your own decisions and on the general subordination of all concerns to the specific interests, to the primacy of maximizing profit and domination by a very small sector of the world's population. Very small, in fact. Global inequality has reached unprecedented heights.

The United Nations Conference on Trade and Development meeting has been going on in Bangkok. Andrew Simms, writing in the Guardian Weekly *in mid-February, says that "UNCTAD, given the right power and resources, could help overcome failings in the international system" and it has "the confidence of developing countries." Any comments on that?*

That's a bit of an exaggeration. UNCTAD first of all is basically a research organization. It has no enforcement powers. It does reflect to some extent the interests of the so-called developing countries, the poorer countries. That's the reason why it's so marginalized. For example, there was very little reporting of the UNCTAD conference in the U.S. apart from the business press here and there. It has Third World, South participation. And when UNCTAD does reflect the concerns of the great majority of the world's people, it is generally ignored. One example with substantial contemporary repercussions is the UNCTAD initiative to stabilize commodity prices thirty years ago, so that poor peasant farmers would be able to survive. Agribusiness can handle a collapse in prices for a year; a poor farmer can't tell his kids to wait until next year to eat. The proposals conformed to policies routinely adopted in the rich countries, but were blocked by the rich, following the advice of "sound liberal economists," as political economist Susan Strange puts it—advice that is followed when it contributes to profit and power, ignored otherwise. One consequence is the shift from production of "legitimate crops" (coffee, etc.) to coca, marijuana, and opium, which are not subject to ruinous price fluctuations. The U.S. reaction is to impose even harsher punishments on the poor, abroad and at home, sharply intensifying next year if current proposals are implemented. It's not the only case. UNESCO was undermined for rather similar reasons. But to speak of "confidence of developing countries" would be overstating it. Have a look at Third World-based publications, say from the Third World Network in Malaysia. One of their important publications is *Third World Economics*. A recent issue has run several very critical reports of the UNCTAD conference because of its subordination to the agenda of the powerful. It's true that UNCTAD is more independent and more reflects the interests of the developing countries than, say, the WTO, which is run by the industrial states. So yes, it's different. But one shouldn't exaggerate.

The issue of inequality, not only in the U.S. but around the world, as you just mentioned, is certainly hard to ignore. Even the Financial Times *recently commented that "At the start of the nineteenth century, the ratio of real incomes per*

*head between the world's richest and poorest countries was three to one. By 1900,
it was ten to one. By the year 2000 it had risen to sixty to one."*

And that is extremely misleading. It vastly understates what's going on. The real
and striking difference is not the difference among countries but the difference
within the global population, which is a different measure. That's risen very
sharply, which means that within countries the divisions have sharply risen. I
think it's now gone from about something like 80 to 1 to about 120 to 1, just in
the last ten years or so. Those are rough figures. I'm not sure of the exact numbers. But it's risen very sharply. The top one percent of the population of the
world now probably has about the income of roughly the bottom sixty percent.
That's close to three billion people.

And these outcomes are not the law of some natural force.

Those are the results of very specific decisions, institutional arrangements, and
plans which can be expected to have these effects. And they have these effects.
There are principles of economics that tell you that over time things ought to
even out. That's true of some abstract models. The world is very different.

Thomas Friedman, writing in the New York Times, *called the demonstrators at
Seattle "a Noah's ark of flat-earth advocates."*

From his point of view that's probably correct. From the point of view of slave
owners, people opposed to slavery probably looked that way. If you want some
numbers, I just found some. The latest issue of Doug Henwood's invaluable *Left
Business Observer* gives the global facts. This is a recent estimate by a World
Bank economist. It actually only goes as far as 1993. In 1993, the richest one percent of the population had as much wealth as the bottom fifty-seven percent. So
that's 2.5 billion people. The ratio of average incomes from the world's top five
percent and the world's bottom five percent, that's the one that increased from 78
to 1 in 1988 to 114 to 1 in 1993, and probably considerably more since. The
inequality index, the Gini index, as it's called, has reached the highest levels on
record. That's world population. One might argue that this doesn't matter much
if everyone is gaining, even unequally. That is a terrible argument, but we don't
have to pay attention to it, because the premise is incorrect.

Going back to Friedman, from his point of view, it's correct. For the 1% of
the population that's he's thinking about and representing, the people who are
opposing this are flat-earthers. Why should anyone oppose the developments
that we've been describing?

*Would it be fair to say that in the actions in the streets in Seattle, mixed in with
the tear gas was also a whiff of democracy?*

I would take it to be. A functioning democracy is not supposed to happen in the
streets. It's supposed to happen in decision-making. This is a reflection of the
undermining of democracy and the popular reaction to it, not for the first time.
There's been a long struggle, over centuries, in fact, to try to extend the realm of

democratic freedoms, and it's won plenty of victories. A lot of them have been won exactly this way, not by gifts but by confrontation and struggle. If the popular reaction in this case takes a really organized, constructive form, it can undermine and reverse the highly undemocratic thrust of the international economic arrangements that are being foisted on the world. And they are very undemocratic. Naturally one thinks about the attack on domestic sovereignty, but most of the world is much worse. Over half the population of the world literally does not have even theoretical control over their own national economic policies. They're in receivership. Their economic policies are run by bureaucrats in Washington as a result of the so-called debt crisis, which is an ideological construction, not an economic one. That's over half the population of the world lacking even minimal sovereignty.

Why do you say the debt crisis is an ideological construction?

There is a debt, but who owes it and who's responsible for it is an ideological question, not an economic question. For example, there's a capitalist principle which nobody wants to pay any attention to, of course, which says that if I borrow money from you, let's say, I'm the borrower, so it's my responsibility to pay it back and you're the lender, so it's your risk if I don't pay it back. That's the capitalist principle. The borrower has the responsibility and the lender takes the risk. But nobody even conceives of that possibility. Suppose we were to follow that. Take, say, Indonesia, for example. Right now its economy is crushed by the fact that the debt is something like 140% of GDP. Trace that debt back. It turns out that the borrowers were something like a hundred to two hundred people around the military dictatorship that we supported and their cronies. The lenders were international banks. A lot of that debt has been by now socialized through the IMF, which means Northern taxpayers are responsible. What happened to the money? They enriched themselves. There was some capital export and some development. But the people who borrowed the money aren't held responsible for it. It's the people of Indonesia who have to pay it off. And that means living under crushing austerity programs, severe poverty and suffering. In fact it's a hopeless task to pay off the debt that they didn't borrow. What about the lenders? The lenders are protected from risk. That's one of the main functions of the IMF, to provide free risk insurance to people who lend and invest in risky loans. That's why they get high yields, because there's a lot of risk. They don't have to take the risk, because it's socialized. It's transferred in various ways to Northern taxpayers through the IMF and other devices, like Brady bonds. The whole system is one in which the borrowers are released from the responsibility. That's transferred to the impoverished mass of the population in their own countries. And the lenders are protected from risk. These are ideological choices, not economic ones. In fact, it even goes beyond that. There's a principle of international law which was devised by the U.S. over a hundred years ago when it "liberated" Cuba, which means conquered Cuba to prevent it from liberating itself from Spain in 1898. At that time, when the U.S. took over Cuba, it cancelled Cuba's debt to Spain on the quite reasonable grounds that that debt was invalid since it had been imposed on the people of Cuba without their consent, by force, under a power relationship. That principle was later recognized in international

The Battle of Seattle

You're *Pre*-Approved!

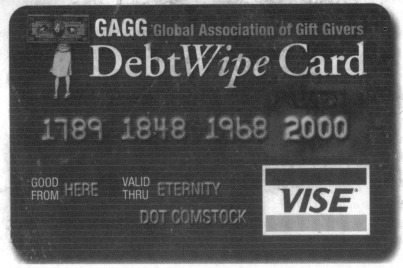

GAGG Global Association of Gift Givers

Debt*Wipe* Card

1789 1848 1968 2000

GOOD FROM HERE   VALID THRU ETERNITY

DOT COMSTOCK

VISE

Committee for a Full Enjoyment

law, again under U.S. initiative, as the principle of what's called "odious debt." Debt is not valid if it's essentially imposed by force. The Third World debt is odious debt. That's even been recognized by the U.S. representative at the IMF, Karin Lissakers, an international economist, who pointed out a couple of years ago that if we were to apply the principles of odious debt, most of the Third World debt would simply disappear. These are all ideological decisions. They're not economic facts. It is an economic fact that money was lent and somebody owes it, but who owes it and who takes the risk, those are power decisions, not economic facts.

To return briefly to the events at Seattle, Newsweek *had a cover story on December 13 called "The Battle of Seattle." They devoted some pages to the anti-WTO protests. There was a sidebar in one of the articles called "The New Anarchism." The five figures the sidebar mentioned as being somehow representative of this new anarchism are Rage Against the Machine and Chumbawamba. I don't suppose you know who they are.*

I know. I'm not that far out of it.

They're rock bands. The list continues with the writer John Zerzan and Theodore Kaczynski, the notorious Unabomber, and then MIT professor Noam Chomsky. How did you figure into that constellation? Did Newsweek *contact you?*

Sure. We had a long interview. (chuckles)

You're pulling my leg.

You'd have to ask them. I can sort of conjure up something that might have been going on in their editorial offices, but your guess is as good as mine. The term

Noam Chomsy inveiwed by David Barsamian

"anarchist" has always had a very weird meaning in elite circles. For example, there was a headline in the *Boston Globe* the other day in a small article saying something like "Anarchists Plan Protests at IMF Meeting in April." Who are the anarchists who are planning the protest? Ralph Nader's Public Citizen, labor organizations and others. There will be some people around who will call themselves anarchists, whatever that means. But from the elite point of view, you want to focus on something that you can denounce in some fashion as irrational. That's that analog to Thomas Friedman calling them flat-earthers.

Vivian Stromberg of Madre, the New York-based NGO, says there are lots of motions in the country but no movement.
I don't agree. For example, what happened in Seattle was certainly movement. Just a couple of days ago students were arrested in protests over failure of universities to adopt strong antisweatshop conditions that many student organizations are proposing. There are lots of other things going on which look like movement to me. While we're on the Seattle matter, in many ways what happened in Montreal a few weeks ago is even more dramatic.

That was the Biosafety Protocol meeting.

That wasn't much discussed here, because the main protesters were European. The issue that came up was clear and important. A kind of ambiguous compromise was reached, but the lineup was very sharp. The *New York Times* report stated it pretty accurately. The U.S. was virtually alone most of the time in the negotiations leading to the compromise. The U.S. was joined by a couple of other countries which would also expect to profit from biotechnology exports. But primarily the U.S. against most of the world over a very significant issue, the issue that's called the "precautionary principle." That means, is there a right for a country, for people to say, I don't want to be an experimental subject in some experiment you're carrying out? At the personal level, that is permissible. For example, if somebody comes into your office from the university biology department and says, You're going to be a subject in an experiment that I'm carrying out. I'm going to stick electrodes into your brain and measure this, that and the other thing, you're permitted to say, I'm sorry, I don't want to be a subject. They are not allowed to come back to you and say, You have to be, unless you can provide scientific evidence that this is going to harm you. They're not allowed to do that. But the U.S. is insisting on exactly that internationally. That's the precautionary principle. In the negotiations at Montreal, the U.S., which is the center of the big biotech industries, genetic engineering, and so on, was demanding that the issue be determined under WTO rules. According to those rules, the experimental subjects have to provide scientific evidence that it's going to harm them, or else the transcendent value of corporate rights prevails and they can do what they want. That's what Ed Herman calls "producer sovereignty." Europe and most of the rest of the world insisted on the precautionary principle, that is, the right of people to say, I don't want to be an experimental subject. I don't have scientific proof that it's going to harm me, but I don't want to be subjected to that. I want to wait until it's understood. That's a very clear indication of what's at stake, an attack on the rights of people to make their own decisions over things even as simple as whether you're going to be an experimental subject, let alone controlling your own resources or setting conditions on foreign investment or transferring your economy into the hands of foreign investment firms and banks. Those are the issues that are really at stake. It's a major assault against popular sovereignty in favor of concentration of power in the hands of a kind of state-corporate nexus, a few megacorporations and the few states that primarily cater to their interests. The issue in Montreal in many ways was sharper and clearer than it was in Seattle. It came out with great clarity.

Food safety, irradiation, and genetic engineering seem to touch a deep chord in people and also to cross traditional what's called left-right, liberal-conservative lines. For example, French farmers, who are fairly conservative, are up in arms around these issues.

It's been interesting to watch this. In the U.S. there's been relatively little discussion and concern about it. In Europe and India and Latin America and elsewhere, there's been great concern and a lot of very activist popular protest. The French farmers are one case. The same is true in England and elsewhere, quite extensively. There's a lot of concern about being forced to become experimental subjects for interventions in the food system, both in production and consumption, that have unknown consequences. That did cross the Atlantic in a way that I don't entirely understand. At some point last fall the concerns became manifested over here as well, to the extent that something quite unusual happened. Monsanto, the major corporation that's pushing biotechnology and genetically engineered crops, their stock started to fall notably. They had to make a public apology and at least theoretically, maybe in fact, cancel some of their more extreme projects, like terminator genes, genes that would make seeds infertile so that, say, poor farmers in India would have to keep purchasing Monsanto seeds and fertilizers at an exorbitant cost. That's quite unusual, for a corporation to be forced into that position. It reflected in part the enormous protests overseas, primarily Europe, which is what mattered because of their clout, but also a growing protest here.

On the other hand, we should also take account of the fact that in the U.S. it's essentially a class issue. Among richer, more educated sectors, there are tendencies which amount to protecting themselves from being experimental subjects, for example, buying high-priced organic food.

Do you think the food safety issue might be one around which the left can reach a broader constituency?

I don't see it as a particularly left issue. In fact, left issues are just popular issues. If the left means anything, it means it's concerned for the needs, welfare and rights of the general population. So the left ought to be the overwhelming majority of the population, and in some respects I think it is. There are other related matters that are very hard to keep in the background. They're coming to the fore all over the place, dramatically in the poorer countries again, but it's showing up here, too. Take, say, the price of pharmaceuticals. They are exorbitant. In the U.S. they're much higher than in other countries. Drugs in the U.S.

LIFE! NOT TRADE!

Human life is about
much more than trade –
"free" or "fair". It's time to overthrow the
Dictatorship of the Economy and get on with the
task of building a society based on *real* freedom.

ANTI BUSINESS CARD

Committee for a Full Enjoyment

are twenty-five percent higher than in Canada and probably twice as high as Italy. This is because of monopolistic practices that are strongly supported by the U.S. government and were built into the WTO rules—highly protectionist devices called intellectual property rights—so huge megacorporations that produce pharmaceuticals are allowed to stay off the market, and charge what amounts to monopoly prices for a long period. This is being very strongly resisted in Africa, in Thailand and elsewhere. In Africa, the spread of AIDS is extremely dangerous and may lead to a major health catastrophe. Here, when Clinton or Gore makes a speech, they talk about the need for Africans to change their behavior. Well, OK, maybe Africans should change their behavior. But the crucial element is our behavior of guaranteeing that the producers, mainly, though not entirely, U.S.-based, be able to charge prices so high that nobody can afford them. According to the latest reports, about six hundred thousand infants a year are having HIV transmitted to them from the mother, which means they'll probably die of AIDS. That's something that can be stopped by the use of drugs that would cost about a couple of dollars a day. But the drug companies will not permit them to be sold under what's called compulsory licensing, that is, allowing the countries to produce them themselves at a much cheaper rate than the drug companies charge under the monopolistic conditions. We're talking about huge numbers of people. There may soon be forty million orphans just from AIDS alone in Africa. Similar things are going on in Thailand. And they're protesting. They have their own pharmaceutical industries in Thailand and Africa, particularly trying to gain the right to produce generic drugs which would be far cheaper than the ones sold by the major pharmaceutical corporations. This is a major health crisis. There are tens of millions of people involved. The same is true in other domains: malaria, tuberculosis. There are preventable diseases that are killing huge numbers of people because the means of prevention are kept so expensive that people can't use them. That's not as much of a problem in the rich countries. Here there's a problem of getting the pharmaceutical companies to permit Medicare to provide prescriptions for the elderly. That's a problem, and it's a real one. But in the poor countries, and not so poor, like Thailand, for example, Africa, South Asia, we're talking about the deaths of tens of millions of people in a few years. Why do drug companies get this enormous protection and in effect monopolistic rights? They claim that they need it because of the costs of research and development. But that's mostly a scam. A substantial part of the costs of research and development is paid by the public. Up until the early 1990s, it was about fifty percent, now maybe it's forty percent. Those numbers much underestimate the actual public cost because they don't take into account the fundamental biology on which it's all based, and that's almost all publicly supported. Dean Baker, a very good economist who has studied this carefully, asked the obvious question. He said, OK, suppose the public pays all the costs, double the public cost, and then insists that the drug simply go on the market. His estimates are a colossal welfare saving from this. We're now talking about not abstract issues. We're talking about the lives and deaths of tens of millions of people just in the next few years.

Returning to the U.S., talk more about the student sweatshop movement. Is it different from earlier movements that you're familiar with?

It's different and similar. In some ways it's like the anti-apartheid movement, except in this case it's striking at the core of the relations of exploitation that are used to reach these incredible figures of inequality that we were talking about. It's very serious. It's another example of how different constituencies are working together. Much of this was initiated by Charlie Kernaghan of the National Labor Committee in New York and other groups within the labor movement. It's now become a significant student issue in many areas. Many student groups are pressing this very hard, so much so that the U.S. government had to, in order to counter it, initiate a kind of code. They brought together labor and student leaders to form some kind of government-sponsored coalition, which many student groups are opposing because they think it doesn't go anywhere near far enough. Those are the issues that are now very much contested. Last I heard, I don't know the details, there was a big demonstration in Wisconsin with students arrested.

Aren't the students asking the capitalists to be less mean?
They're not calling for a dismantling of the system of exploitation. Maybe they should be. What they're asking for is the kinds of labor rights that are theoretically guaranteed. If you look at the conventions of the International Labor Organization, the ILO, which is responsible for these things, they bar most of the practices, probably all of them, that the students are opposing. The U.S. does not adhere to those conventions. Last I looked, the U.S. had ratified hardly any of the ILO conventions. I think it had the worst record in the world outside of maybe Lithuania or El Salvador. Not that other countries live up to the conventions, but they have their name on them at least. The U.S. doesn't accept them on principle.

Comment on an African-American proverb that perhaps intersects with what we're talking about: "The master's tools will never be used to dismantle the master's house."

If this is intended to mean, don't try to improve conditions for suffering people, I don't agree. It's true that centralized power, whether in a corporation or a government, is not going to willingly commit suicide. But that doesn't mean you shouldn't chip away at it, for many reasons. For one thing, it benefits suffering people. That's something that always should be done, no matter what broader considerations are. But even from the point of view of dismantling the master's house, if people can learn what power they have when they work together, and if they can see dramatically at just what point they're going to be stopped, by force, perhaps, that teaches very valuable lessons in how to go on. The alternative to that is to sit in academic seminars and talk about how awful the system is.

Tell me what's happening on your campus, at MIT. Is there any organizing around the sweatshop movement?

Yes, and on a lot of issues. There are very active undergraduate social justice groups doing things all the time, more so than in quite a few years.

What accounts for that?

What accounts for it is the objective reality. It's the same feelings and understanding and perception that led people to the streets in Seattle. Take the U.S. The U.S. is not suffering like the Third World. In Latin America, after by now twenty years of so-called reforms, they haven't moved. The president of the World Bank has just reported that they're where they were twenty years ago. Even in economic growth. This is unheard of. The whole so-called developing world, I don't like the term, but it's the one that's used for the South, is pulling out of the 1990s with a slower rate of growth than in the 1970s. And welfare gaps are increasing enormously. That's in the rest of the world. In the U.S., there's also an unprecedented development. Economic growth, by all macro-economic measures, growth of the economy, productivity, capital investment, in the last twenty-five years has been relatively slow compared with the preceding twenty-five years. Many economists call it a "leaden age" as compared with the preceding golden age. But there has been growth, even though slower than before. However, it's accrued to a very small part of the population. For the majority of non-supervisory workers, which is the majority of the workforce, wages are maybe ten percent or more below what they were twenty-five years ago. That's absolute level. Relative, of course, much farther below. There has been productivity growth and economic growth during that period, but it is not going to the mass of the population. Median incomes, meaning half below, half above, are now barely getting back to what they were ten years ago, well below what they were ten and fifteen years before that. This is in a period of reasonably good economic growth in the last two or three years. They call it amazing, but the last two or three years has been about what it was in the fifties or sixties, which is high by historical standards. It's still left out most of the population. The international economic arrangements, the so-called free trade agreements, are basically designed to maintain that. They undergird what's called a "flexible labor market," meaning that people have no security. The growing worker insecurity that

Alan Greenspan once said was one of the major factors in the fairy-tale economy. If people are afraid, they don't have job security, they're just not going to ask for better conditions. If they have a fear of job transfer, which is one of the consequences of the mislabeled free trade agreements, and there's a flexible labor market, meaning you don't have security, people are not going to ask for better conditions and benefits.

The World Bank has been very clear about the matter. They recognize that labor market flexibility has acquired a bad name as a euphemism for pushing wages down and workers out. That's exactly what it does. It acquired that bad name for a good reason. That's what labor market flexibility is. They say it's essential for all regions of the world. It's the most important reform, I'm quoting from a World Bank development report. It calls for lifting constraints on labor mobility and on wage flexibility. What does that mean? It doesn't mean that workers should be free to go anywhere they want, say, Mexican workers come to New York. What it means is they can be kicked out of their jobs. They want to lift constraints on kicking people out of their jobs and on wage flexibility, which means flexibility down, not up. People are at some level aware of this. You can hide a lot under glorification of consumption and huge debt, but it's hard to hide the fact that people are working many more hours a week than they did twenty-five years ago just to keep incomes from stagnating or declining.

Oakley

Oakley

Seeds of a Movement

From Seattle to Washington and Beyond

Stanley Aronowitz

From the moment we stepped out of the Metro and began walking toward the demonstration I had a feeling that organizers' predictions of about ten thousand protesters were a little overstated. When we arrived at the Ellipse early on a hot April Saturday morning the area was sparsely filled and my heart sank. Is there a new movement being born or was the Seattle march in December 1999 a fluke, and whose success was made possible only by union members who were mainly interested in protecting their jobs? Getting closer to the epicenter of the event it became clear that the emblems of labor presence, banners, t-shirts and hats were largely missing.

With few exceptions the labor movement had not shown up to oppose the many insults visited on the planet and upon its populations by the IMF and the World Bank. Trade is one thing: what the WTO does to labor is crystal clear. It puts it in competition with itself on a world scale and unions, particularly in the manufacturing sector, are ready to fight against free trade that would export their jobs to low wage areas of the globe. But the complex activities of these international financial institutions are something else. Often their interventions damage the physical environment, reduce or obliterate the sovereignty of struggling nation-states and determine patterns of global investment, resulting in the expansion of low wage industries here, and starvation and joblessness there. These issues touch the hearts of rain forest defenders and tree huggers, students who morally condemn corporations which subject women and children to long hours and slave wages. But the attempt to broaden the struggle against capitalist globalization has not (yet) gripped American working men and women. Except for the embattled garment and other low wage workers, the direct connection between the shop and the new global economic and physical environment is simply not evident in the same way that the Mexican macquiladores or Chinese TV and computer factories are. In these instances plants in economically disadvantaged countries threaten the relatively high wages and benefits of workers in this country. What enrages union members is the Husky case where the company pulled up stakes in Ohio to escape $17 an hour union wages and set up shop in China to pay 25 cents. What was left at the Washington demonstration is a band of individuals, most of them inspired by the anti-WTO Seattle days, by anti-sweatshop sentiments, and by their intellectual grasp of how dangerous are these agencies. It was clear though, despite many union endorsements for the Washington rally, that, unlike Seattle, the event had inadequate organization and even fewer resources.

An hour later more people started streaming into the area and by early afternoon it was plain that the slim ranks had swelled, if not to ten thousand at least to respectability. Many quickly filled the spaces under the trees that surrounded the nearly unbearably hot open field where thousands strained to hear the steady stream of barely audible speakers recite the litany of IMF calamities. Announcing their attendance a small band of black, Asian and Latino marchers circled the periphery, as if to rebuke an earlier report, published in the *Wall Street Journal,* that this was to be virtually an all-white convocation. Their spirited rebuttal only highlighted the accuracy of the *Journal's* prediction. For there was little doubt that if the organizers had made a serious effort to attract racialized minorities to the event they had failed abysmally. But, of course they did not. The fact is the incipient movement, reflected in the crowd, was composed largely of an agglomeration of student Nike haters, environmentalists, the small but growing group of anarcho-ecologists, themselves split eight ways to Sunday, and old and new leftovers, almost all of whom were middleclass whites.

I had a moment of nostalgia for another spring day in Washington thirty-five years ago when an unprecedented twenty-five thousand people—mostly students—filled the same precincts to mount the first significant national protest against the Vietnam War. Far from suffering the absence of organized labor, that demonstration faced the almost united opposition of a prowar labor movement, liberal wing of the Democratic Party, and Cold War intellectuals. Like the earlier insistence of the militant wing of the civil rights movement that the regular, segregationist delegation of the Mississippi Democratic Party be unseated at the 1964 Atlantic City Democratic convention, the resolve of Students for a Democratic Society to set its face against the wheel of American foreign policy and its friends in the liberal establishment had been greeted with alarm by those allied to the Johnson administration's New Dealish domestic policies which, by the standard of the period, were considered very progressive. The war opponents persisted and, in time, put millions into the streets, forcing a sitting president out of office and changing the complexion of American politics. The images of that struggle flashed and then flickered. The two moments, then and now, were sufficiently different to suppress comparison. This new movement had to be taken on its own terms as well as in the context of the last two decades of retreat and regroupment, decades that witnessed the virtual disappearance of a political opposition worthy of the name in every developed capitalist nation.

In an ironic twist, we who made the insurgent politics of the 1960s—movements of black freedom, second wave feminism, students, the "new" public and service sector labor unions, the poor, the disabled, antiwar, and those associated with consumers—were helped as much as hindered by the politics of the Cold War. As long as the Soviet Union, despite its warts, remained an alternative, world capitalism's ability to roll back the great postwar compromise between labor and capital was severely restricted. The compromise, according to which, in return for political and ideological loyalty, capital agreed to a series of regulations and to social welfare programs, had weathered conservative Eisenhower and Nixon presidencies and the exigencies of full wartime mobilization which all but halted Johnson's own resolve to produce a New Deal for blacks. The social movements of the 1950s and 1960s operated well within the boundaries created by the global stalemate: through mass pressure—including civil disobedience—the black freedom movement and its allies held up to world scrutiny the tacit and overt state policies of black oppression which became intolerable even for the ruling elites (in the 1960s blacks actually narrowed the wage gap considerably and gained increased access to education, health care and other services); radicals prodded liberals in the feminist movement to take up the social and cultural, as well as the economic position of women and brazenly asked how the United States could maintain inequality with respect to abortion rights, opportunities for higher education, and for day care services when these were available in Communist countries; and after Caryl Chessman was executed in 1967, a movement for prison reform, in the first place against the death penalty, made unprecedented strides. Berkeley students demanded that their education be something different from what their leader, Mario Savio, termed a knowledge factory. Even the Reagan administration, which ruthlessly fired eleven thousand air traffic controllers for striking against the government and did everything it could to weaken and to devalue all manner of public goods, was unable to abolish welfare and to privatize social security, a hesitance which led David Stockman to resign in disgust.

The collapse of the Soviet Union and the transformation of China into a state capitalist society unquestionably changed the terms of global political engagement. Driven by neoliberal economic ideology which proclaimed the "free market" the best guarantee of prosperity for all, the IMF, the World Bank, and a gaggle of consultants trained in the Milton Friedman school of economic policy flooded both the former Communist countries and the Third World. They counseled governments to dismantle their state-run welfare programs, tear down tariff barriers, and open their markets to Coca Cola and other consumer products. In order to minimize the political turmoil that might result from such policies they were advised to build their police and military forces, even at the cost of increasing their already bloated debt to Western banks. Beneath the advice was the news that World Bank loans to pay for reconstruction and the huge debt already accumulated would be contingent upon slashing budgets, removing state regulation of investment and opening the veins of their natural and human resources to international capitalist exploitation. All in the name of *development*. To an eerie silence, in the United States a Democratic President signed the Welfare Reform Act and condemned millions to work at minimum wages on penalty of losing their meager public allowances. And, falsely warning that funds would soon dry up without "reform," heeding their Wall Street patrons, conservatives once more beat the drum for schemes to allow holders of social security accounts to invest all or part of their savings in the skittish stock market.

When a reluctant Bill Clinton launched his presidency in 1993 by backing the North Atlantic Free Trade Agreement and driving it through a Democratic

Congress it was apparent to many, including a mostly somnolent, but suddenly partially revived AFL-CIO, that globalism was now more than slogan; it had become the basis for a major turn in American foreign economic policy. The United States and its network of Western European partners were, through the governing boards of newly strengthened international trade and financial organizations, forcing into existence a New World Order. National sovereignty was a thing of the past for many struggling countries of the South and of the East. The national context for collective bargaining and for environmental legislation was seriously eroded by the removal of production industries from the advanced industrial societies to low wage regions, especially Asia, and by IMF sanction for the wholesale destruction of ecosystems in raw material rich regions of Latin America and Africa. For many activists the nation-state was regarded as no more than one among many sources of contestation. Recognizing that power had been massively displaced to new institutions constructed in the service of a host of recently created transnational corporations, in the 1990s activists began a fervent search for new targets and for new levers.

Prior to the Seattle demonstrations, environmentalists and other Non-Governmental Organizations eagerly attended a series of mostly UN hosted summits in which the major powers solemnly pledged a new course and the IMF and World Bank echoed these false promises of substantial concessions to the NGOs. By the middle of that decade it was apparent that some once militant groups such as the Sierra Club had entered an alliance with the "reformed" transnationals and the United States government. Others were not so convinced and began to focus on trade policy, one of the main arenas for the free marketeers.

Seattle was a miscalculation for the Empire on more than one count. When a coalition emerged to protest a major meeting of the World Trade Organization, not a few unions were among the endorsers, but the federal and the local governments really did not expect that more than the usual suspects would show up. After all, John Sweeney, the AFL-CIO president, was tied by the hip to Gore's presidential campaign and did not relish the prospect of the embarrassment from massive trade union participation in the protest. Yet the Steelworkers, which accused the WTO of encouraging dumping low-priced foreign steel on the domestic market, and UNITE, the union of garment, textile and shoe workers, showed uncharacteristic independence when they boldly declared their full support of the event. Sweeney had to be cajoled and ultimately dragged to condemn the administration's trade policy and eventually to support the march and rally. Nor did the authorities anticipate the West Coast Longshore Workers Union, which closed all Pacific coast ports for a day. And the authorities surely did not prepare for the more than thirty thousand demonstrators outside of Labor's ranks who showed up to join more than twenty thousand union members. Among these were a relatively large contingent of proponents of direct action and civil disobedience who, upon entry into the city, promptly overwhelmed the local police and together with other demonstrators, effectively shut the city down. By the end of the days of protest Seattle's mayor had egg on his face. Politically shy of clamping down on protesters in the relatively liberal city, he was forced at the eleventh hour by the Feds to come out swinging. Conservatives condemned him for too little and too late and the labor and liberal groups yelled police brutality.

The Seattle debacle was a wake up call to Washington law enforcement officials. They would not be caught napping. Washington Police chief Charles Ramsey hired the former FBI official charged with containing and otherwise breaking up the 1960s demonstrations. The former FBI official had handled the obstreperous crowd at the 1968 Democratic convention. Shortly before April 15 he told an interviewer that Washington authorities would take a zero-tolerance policy, meaning they would crack down hard on disobedient demonstrators. As we marched down Constitution Avenue past the IMF and World Bank headquarters it was hard to miss the presence of hundreds of cops assigned to the peaceful activities. On a pretext of health and safety hazards the authorities had already shown their hand by shutting down the hastily erected headquarters of the anti-IMF/World Bank coalition. Not visible were hundreds more police and other government security authorities assigned to break the extralegal activities of demonstrators who were attempting to block the streets leading to the IMF and World Bank headquarters. Hundreds of direct actionists were beaten and arrested in the side streets away from the TV cameras and from public view. Weeks later more than one hundred of them were still in jail.

As the boisterous demonstrators shouted and sang their demands, one could hear a note that almost never passed the lips of earlier movements. To be sure there was that elliptical enunciation by SDS president Paul Potter at the 1965 antiwar rally of the "system" but here on the banners it was named: capitalism. Instead of emanating from tired leftist sects, these flags were hoisted by sixteen- eighteen- and twenty-year-olds. And then the scales fell from my eyes. I was in the midst of a parade of young people and with the exception of some who were there, literally in wheelchairs, I was among the oldest participants in the event. This was no Socialist Scholars Conference where, at times, perhaps half the attendees were over fifty. This was a march led and dominated by people well under thirty. The new movement against global capitalism was a youth movement.

For that reason there was a welcome absence of the signs of the old left. Sure they sold their papers and stuck out in the crowd. But they were not the driving force of the movement. The first SDS president, Al Haber, now more than sixty, strode alongside me with eyes shining and a big grin almost dwarfing his huge gray beard. He said, "maybe it's starting again." I nodded my agreement, hoping against hope that what we were witnessing was the energy of a generation rather than a raggle taggle group of inveterate antis. We knew a fair number of participants but could not have known the veterans of antisweatshop campaigns who succeeded in persuading their university administrations to join workers rights coalitions, the brigades of anarchist youth in their black hats and armbands, and the greens of many stripes who were fighting to preserve wildlife and clean water. As I came away from that day, I was half convinced that, finally, a new breed of radicals was emerging and that it had a fair chance to spread to a generational movement. I had seen high school as well as college students and it reminded me of my own teen activist days.

On Monday after the march, writers for the *Legal Times* reported that the police were taking a hard line against the protesters: "The DC police, armored and with visors down, marched in formation toward the barricade separating them from 500 protestors clustered at the intersection of 20th street and

Stanely Aronowitz

Pennsylvania Avenue on Monday morning. As they marched, the officers slapped their batons against their shinguards in rhythm." They showered pepper spray at the protesters who, according to the reporters "recoiled in agony their eyes swollen and closed. Other protesters surrounded them, rinsing their eyes with bottled water...Meanwhile the crowd chanted 'Sit Down, Sit Down,' and more than a hundred protesters [did] so settling down in the middle of Pennsylvania Avenue. It worked: the spraying stopped. The atmosphere lightened."

Having said all this, it's still not a genuine social movement. I returned from D.C. to an email from L A Kaufman, a former editor of *Socialist Review,* whose newsletter extolled the network that provided the sinews of organization and the larger forces that are straining to forge a new alliance against global capitalism. She praised their lack of ideologies and programs and urged her online readers to concentrate on direct action tactics. While I would not want to see the incipient alliance adopt a sterile ideological framework of, say, socialism in its current permutations, I would want to see a vigorous debate over *ideas*. If anticapitalism is the leading edge, what are the alternatives? Is resistance enough to persuade more than an elite of semiprofessional organizers to stay the course of opposition? Or does the movement need a rich address to the cultural, educational, and social dimensions of life? Do we need to consider running candidates as one tactic without sinking into electoralism? Or is direct action the bottom line against which all else is mere tinkering?

In a time when the imagination is stultified and rechanneled into the dead end of practical reform, rechanneled by the pervasive pessimism that has overcome those still encapsulated in the prisonhouse of defeat, what we need now is a healthy dose of utopian thought. Socialism carries too much baggage, not only that of the discredited Communist version but also the severely compromised social-democratic variant. Socialism equals the welfare state and perhaps anarchism—the endgame of any genuine radical movement—and ignores the mediations. Yet, somewhere between is the beginning of a solution. For what we have learned in the last decade is we have little or no wiggle room, leading some to conclude that all that remains is direct confrontation with Empire and with capital. Capital and its supplicants provide little space for compromise because the forces of the opposition are still incipient. Does this justify all-out confrontation? Clearly many who made the alliance that produced Seattle and Washington—and not only the trade unions—are still caught in the logic of incremental reform. They believe the nation-state still has enough juice to yield concessions. So the problem is to think and debate the alternatives, to experiment with reform even if it yields very little or nothing, and to craft a new politics of internationalism that takes into account the still potent force of national states and their identities. The hardest work is thinking.

Together with the Right

Against Globalization?

Oakley

"Millenium Round" of the WTO Under Fire From Both the Left and Right

Alain Kessi
Jungle World, *November 1999*

A whole range of activities are planned around the Third Annual Ministerial Conference of the WTO by radical left and progressive grassroots groups, NGOs, and trade unions: from street theater and actions of civil disobedience all the way to large demonstrations. Kept at a distance by the aforementioned organizers, but nevertheless quite present in the weeks leading up to the protests, are extreme-right Republicans as well as conservative environmnetal organizations with essentialist lines of argument like the Sierra Club. While the Republicans demand—just like the radical left—that the US government leave the WTO, the Sierra Club wants—like the established leftist NGOs—that "civil society," meaning themselves, be given a place in the decision-making process of the WTO.

The blurring of the difference between left-wing and right-wing approaches is especially visible in Seattle. The city council has declared a Multilateral Agreement on Investment-free zone on the city territory. The symbolic antiglobalization measure was proposed by Brian Derdowski, Republican member of the King County council, where another such zone has been implemented.[1]

On a US-wide level John Talbott, spokesperson for the Reform Party, does not see much difference between Ralph Nader on the left and Pat Buchanan on the right when they talk about globalization, and proposes that a new party be created that is neither right nor left, but created to represent the hard-working average American. In this he closes his eyes to Pat Buchanan's racist, sexist, and homophobic attitude. The latter's right-wind "producerist"[2] populism refers to a hard-working productive middle class and working class being squeezed from above and below by "lazy social parasites."[3]

What has gone awry, if one of the greatest leftist mobilizations of the past years—the one against "free" trade, against "globalization," against "transnational corporations" and especially against the MAI—is so attractive for right-wing conservative groups?

In June 1999 the Dutch antiracist group De Fabel van de Illegaal, whose work had greatly contributed to building a strong movement against the MAI, decided to leave the campaigns against "free trade." "After taking a closer look we concluded that to take 'free trade' as a primary target is not a logical choice based on a radical Left analysis, but instead comes more from a New Right analysis," the group explained in an open letter in September 1999. A year before that, in October 1998, they published a discussion paper: "With 'New Right' against Globalization?"[4] They followed it up with a series of articles dealing with the weaknesses of the discourse on "globalization" and "free trade" as well as with people serving as intermediaries between left-wing and right-wing activists and groups.

In his analysis of the crisis of antiracism, Pierre-André Taguieff describes the appropriation of leftist discourses by the neoracists as retorsion (not in the sense of revenge, but in a slightly less common French meaning of the use of an argument against its author).[5] This raises the question of when a leftist discourse is open to retorsion. Or the other way around: How would a discourse have to be structured so that it would not serve right-wing propaganda. I would like to take a look at five characteristics which make discourses suitable for retorsion: a simplistic analysis of capitalism linked to an uncritical attitude towards the national (social) state, emotionalization, a conspiracy theorist approach, and speech of modernity destroying "nature."

The discourse on globalization fits so well into right-wing racist rhetoric because it blames an international capital not tied to a geographical location for the economic and social difficulties. This simplistic analysis overlooks the role of local capital in the process of accumulation and exploitation and thus allows the demand to protect the latter against the international financial capital, which is artificially separated from the "productive capital." Karl A. Schachtschneider, who together with others has filed a court action against the Monetary Union with the Federal Constitutional Court of Germany in Karlsruhe, warns in the far-right newspaper *Junge Freiheit:* "We will be pushed further into globalization. This will serve as the big excuse for the social tensions. We have to compete with slave labor."[6]

Those who, like parts of the anti-MAI campaign, or like those Trotskyist and other old leftist theoreticians writing in *Le Monde Diplomatique,* defend the social state are especially prone to national-chauvinist retorsion. Since they describe the object of their desire as outside history and independent from colonialism and the conditions of the Keynesian era, they do not seem to notice that the nation-state by no means withers away with deregulation. They also close their eyes to the fact that it is national state governments who drive the deregulation ahead—and hope thereby to create an advantage for their respective nation-state.[7]

The imperialist nation-state serves as a door-opener for corporations as governments exert diplomatic and military pressure on dependent governments. Representatives of the large US corporations and the US diplomacy for instance work hand in hand in developing and securing the access to new investment zones. In this field of interconnections the efforts of some US corporations serve other US corporations as well. In order to do justice to this interconnectedness between corporation and "their" government, critical observers have in the past few years come to replace the delocalized term of multinational corporation with transnational corporation, which is rooted in one country and extends its activities from there beyond the state boundaries (transnationally).

The discourse on globalization easily fits in conspiracy theories. These already appear in the cliché of the disinterest in politics on the level of the nation-state—"Those guys in Berne/Berlin/Vienna do what they want anyway." Beyond the boundaries of the nation-state, as the distance to the relevant decision-making bodies becomes greater, the propensity to see conspiracies really breaks out.

It is not any longer the processes of production and of capital accumulation that are at the center of the attention, but clubs of influential men (and some women) who negotiate among themselves the future of the world behind closed doors. The outrage about the initially secret negotiations at the OECD played an essential role in the mobilization against the MAI. Since in this reading the actors of "globalization" are so powerful and their business so mysterious, it is hardly possible to oppose any resistance to them. Thus the work of the conspiracy theorists limits itself to the missionary "enlightment" about the dangers of the "New World Order" (a term that finds itself reified in the abbreviation NWO used on web sites drawn to conspiracy theories[8]), the Bilderberg meetings[9] or the World Economic Forum[10].

A substantial part of even the leftist variants of the discourse on "globalization" work through emotionalizing—calling upon fears about the threat to one's livelihood represented by "multinational corporations." This is very pronounced in the struggles against Monsanto and other gene technological corporations, for instance. Such emotionalizing distracts from societal analyses and makes people receptive to other emotionalized discourses—including those from the right-wing.

In parts of the ecological left the perceived threat to their livelihoods is not seen so much as a power relation between social groups, but as the destruction of "Mother Earth" by a "modern world" gone astray. Traditionally leftist ideas about self-management and autonomy get mixed with discourses on regionalism which tend towards racism, and leftist criticism of technology receives support from essentialist and fascistic discourses about living in harmony with "nature," "according to the natural social laws of Gaia" (to quote Edward Goldsmith[11], the founder and chief editor of the *Ecologist,* a newspaper that is widely read internationally, also by leftists).

Retorsion can, if we take those criteria into account, be made much more difficult. In the preparations for the Innercity Action Week in Germany in June 1997, many activists acquired the requisite know-how for analyses of the world market, of the competition between economic locations, and the myths of globalization which would not so easily yield to retorsion. The close look at local consequences of global processes, the analysis well-rooted in the material, and especially the connection made with a critical assessment of "public space" including the mechanisms of its racist regulation, are hard to integrate into a right-wing discourse.

During the preparations for the protests in Seattle, right-left overlaps were repeatedly brought up. One of the grassroots networks involved, Peoples' Global

Action[12], decided at its second conference in Bangalore, India, in August to direct its struggle no longer against "free" trade, but against capitalism. But the preparations for Seattle also made it clear that for a massive mobilization, a broad alliance was possible and desirable. The more radical groups and activists seem to have succeeded in the time before the actions to set forth their criticism of attitudes prone to retorsion to a wider audience. Especially the caravans inspired by the PGA[13], with their numerous stops, actions, and events on the way to Seattle offer plenty of opportunities to approach people who have not so far been internationally networked, and to build up a reliable network in the US also.

1. Sam Howe Verhovek, "Seattle, Triumph and Protest," *New York Times,* 13 October 1999. http://www.corpwatch.org/5-seattle.html.

2. Geov Parrish, "Shutting down Seattle," *Seattle Weekly,* 19-25 August 1999. http://www.seattleweekly.com/features/9933/features-parrish.html.

3. For a critical description, see: http://www.publiceye.org/pra/tooclose/producerism.html.

4. Berlet, Chip, "Beware Right Wing antiglobalism," Political Research Associates, October 1999. http://www.corpwatch.com/5-antiglobal.html.

5. This and other articles about right-wing influences on leftist campaigns can be found on http://www.savanne.ch/right-left.html.

6. Taguieff, Pierre-André, "Die ideologischen Metamorphosen des Rassismus und die Krise des Antirassismus" ("The Ideological Metamorphoses of Racism and the Crisis of Antiracism"); Bielefeld, Uli ed., *Das Eigene und das Fremde: Neuer Rassismus in der alten Welt?* (*The Self and the Other: New Racism in the Old World?*), Hamburg 1991, pp. 221-268. See also Schönberger, Klaus, "Überlegungen zur Retorsion der Sozialen Frage" ("Reflections on the Retorsion of the Social Question"), AZ-Seminar in Pesina (Aug. 6–13 '97); as well as Terkessidis, Mark, *Kulturkampf: Volk, Nation, der Westen und die Neue Rechte,* (*Kulturkampf: People, Nation, the West and the New Right*), Köln 1995, pp. 67 ft.

7. Stein, Dieter, "Es geht um die Freiheit der Völker: Die Euro-Klage" ("This Is About the Freedom of the Peoples: The Euro Court Action"), Karl A. Schachtschneider, "zum juristischen Kampf gegen die Währungsunion" (About the Juridical Struggle Against the Monetary Union), *Junge Freiheit,* April '98. See also *Jungle World* '98, issues 4, 5 and 14.

8. For a rebuttal of the myth of the state that abolishes itself through the MAI negotiations, see Peter Decker, "Verkehrte Aufregung über das MAI-Die Staaten verschärfen ihre Standortkonkurrenz ... und Linke sorgen sich um das Überleben des Nationalstaates" (False Exasperation About the MAI—The States Increase Their Competition Between Economic Locations ... and the Left Are Worried About the Survival of the Nation-State), *Junge Welt,* April '98, p. 29. http://www.jungewelt.de/1998/04-29/014.htm. More generally on the changed role of a still strong nation-state, Joachim Hirsch, "Vom Sicherheitsstaat zum nationalen Wettbewerbsstaat" (From the Security State to the National Competition State), ID-Verlag, Berlin 1998.

9 Examples abound, see for instance http://www.truthinmedia.org/.

10 A potpourri containing partly probably historical descriptions, partly imaginative conspiracy theories can be found on http://www.bilderberg.org. The entire world elite is said to meet annually in the Bilderberg group in order to decide on the future of humanity.

11 See the official web pages of the World Economic Forum on http://www.weforum.org/. Besides the annual meetings in Davos, a number of regional meetings take place, like the one about Eastern Europe (in Salzburg, Austria) or about Southeast Asia (Beijing and Shanghai).

12 Krebbers, Eric (De Fabel van de Illegaal): Goldsmith and his Gaian hierarchy, http://www.savanne.ch/right-left-materials/gaian-hierarchy.html. Gaia is the personified Earth in the Greek mythology (Theogony according to Hesiodos) and serves as a symbol to conservative environmental movements.

13 See http://www.agp.org.

Seattle '99

Wedding Party of the Left and the Right?

Eric Krebbers and Merijn Schoenmaker
(De Fabel van de Illegaal)
Some editing of the English translation by Alain Kessi

At the end of November the members of the World Trade Organisation will discuss their new Millennium Round in Seattle. The North American city will see a whole series of demonstrations, actions, and discussion meetings. By now a very diverse mixture of activists, lobbyists, and politicians are gathering under the vague banner of the antiglobalisation movement. Both the left and the right are joining and seem to have put their quarrels aside.

"A historic change is under way at the very heart of the globalisation process: millions of people are mobilising. Tens of thousands of them will be in Seattle,"[1] says lobbyist Susan George. "The fight against the WTO and all it stands for is in my view the main one. There is even a chance of winning this fight."[2] George is one of the foremost European lobbyists against "globalisation".

Many lobbyists seem to somewhat overrate the movement. "Seattle will be the protest of the century," some of her colleagues say, without much knowledge of history. "The bosses are scared," others add. But who are they supposed to be scared of? The left has not been a very strong force since the fall of the Berlin Wall, and it hardly exists nowadays. That's why the lobbyists are no longer exclusively looking to their left. They have started to actively build a new worldwide movement in which not only left-leaning people, but also conservatives, nationalists, and even the New Right must be able to feel at home. The extremely unclear concept of "globalisation" comes in handy. Political activists of all creeds can project their own problems on it.

George and some sixty other lobbyists, researchers and opinion leaders and their NGOs are members of the International Forum on Globalisation, an elite think tank. They organise a congress in Seattle and never tire of repeating that they expect some twenty-four hundred participants. IFG members often participate at meetings all around the world. They are the main driving force behind the campaigns against "globalisation," and they initiated the actions against both the MAI and the WTO.

They want to bring the Left and the Right together in one big movement, and they seem to be successful at it. Therefore the IFG lobbyists cherish their somewhat progressive image and at the same time try to remain acceptable for the Right. But after reading their articles and books it becomes very clear: the IFG is politically right wing and very conservative.

By criticising "globalisation" and multinationals they try to use the remaining left-wing activists to further their own conservative goals, and also try to influence them ideologically. Therefore the IFG are a danger to the already vulnerable left.

In the Netherlands, a lot of left-wing activists are also enthusiastically participating every time the IFG members initiate a new campaign. They are also organising actions at the end of November, taking part in the worldwide coordinated protests. In the beginning of this year the Dutch organisation De Fabel van de Illegaal, together with some other groups, was still actively asking organisations to sign the NGO declaration on the WTO, which was written by some IFG members. When the ideas of the IFG became clearer to them, De Fabel decided to stop, although other groups continued.

French Culture in Danger

Seattle prepares for the reception of activists from many countries. Peoples' Global Action this time organises two action caravans to the WTO meeting. One across the US, includes activists from Chiapas, Mexico, and another one from Canada, ending at the elite IFG meeting. It is a strange choice, for the PGA is known as a left-wing grassroots movement. Also expected in Seattle are eco-activists, union members, steelworkers, lorry drivers, farmers, fisherfolk, postal workers, women's rights activists, artists, students, gay and lesbian activists, and pacifists. Only a small minority will want to get rid of capitalism altogether. The rest will rather aim at an international regulation of "the economy" or will opt for a nationalist future.

The French farmer and leader of the Confederation Paysanne, José Bové, no doubt belongs to the nationalist category. The farmers of the CP are angry with the US government, which doubled the import tariffs on French chees, in retaliation for the decision of the EU to put a ban on meat with hormones coming from the US. The farmers immediately started a dynamic campaign against McDonald's, which is, after all, an American multinational.

The angry farmers organised many actions, and even broke down a McDonald's restaurant in Millau. Last June farmers from India, arriving with the PGA action caravan, came to help a bit. At home they also have a tradition of attacking American companies. The French farmers also disturbed an American film festival because they are very much worried about their own French culture. Bové got arrested but was released shortly after. He sent his regards to the French premier and president for their support and received a ticket to Seattle from the ministry of agriculture to defend the French interests there. Besides the French Communist Party and the Front National, some Dutch antiglobalisation activists also reacted very positively to the farmers' actions.

They called for solidarity with Bové.[3]

Supporting Working Families

"The Seattle summit will be a historic confrontation between civil society and corporate rule," says Mike Dolan. He works for the American consumer watchdog group Public Citizen founded by Ralph Nader. Public Citizen is connected to the IFG and initiated the campaign against the MAI treaty. Dolan now acts as the great coordinator and spokesman of the countermovement in Seattle. Not everyone seems to be happy with him, but little can be done about his presence. He sits in the middle of the web, like a spider. On the one hand Dolan supports the American PGA caravan with several thousand dollars; on the other he speaks up for the extreme right Pat Buchanan, now a candidate for the American presidency, representing the Reform Party. "Whatever else you say about Pat Buchanan, he will be the only candidate in the 2000 presidential sweepstakes who will passionately and unconditionally defend the legitimate expectations of working families in the global economy,"[4] Dolan writes. Indeed, Buchanan supports American workers, as long as they are conservative and obedient and not unemployed, black, gay, female, lesbian or Jewish. He's also not particularly fond of left-wing workers. Buchanan on Argentina: "With military and police and freelance operators, between six thousand and one hundred fifty thousand leftists disappeared. Brutal: yes; also successful. Today peace reigns in Argentina; security has been restored."[5]

Closed Eyes

Former Republican big shot Buchanan is known for his sharp attacks on international trade treaties like GATT, NAFTA, MAI, and now the WTO. "Traditional antagonists as politically far apart as Ralph Nader and Pat Buchanan are finding some common ground on trade issues,"[6] says IFG member Mark Ritchie. He is also director of the American Institute for Agriculture and Trade Policy, which supports small farmers. Reform Party spokesman in New Hampshire John Talbott agrees with Ritchie. "If you close your eyes, it is difficult to hear much of a difference between Ralph Nader on the left and Pat Buchanan on the right when they talk about the devastating effect of free international trade on the American worker and a desire to clean big money and special interests out of Washington."[7] According to Buchanan this big capital is mainly in the hands of "the Jews." He presents himself as "the only leader in this country who is not afraid of fighting against the Jewish lobby."[8] Buchanan calls Hitler "an individual of great courage" and doubts whether the holocaust really was that big an event.[9] But "Jewish capital" isn't the most important reason why Buchanan wants to be a candidate for the presidency. No, in the first place he wants to end "illegal immigration," that is, according to Buchanan, "helping fuel the cultural breakdown of our nation."[10]

The populist Buchanan is probably the foremost representative of the extreme right in the US. His constituency consists of Christian fundamentalists, militia members, and neoNazis. These millions of people might explain Dolan's flirt with Buchanan. Together with his enthusiastic commentary Dolan sent around a newspaper article in which Buchanan openly says: "American workers and people first."[11] But Buchanan is not alone with that opinion. Also the big right-wing trade union AFL-CIO wants to make "the rights and interests of US workers a priority."[12] The union also mobilises their rank and file for the demonstrations in Seattle.

The Government Is Not the Enemy

When Dolan's work and ideas were criticised from the grassroots level, the coordinator of the American PGA caravan immediately took his side. "Let's work together when we can, work in parallel when we must, but never work against each other when our goal is the elimination of the WTO and its corporate benefactors."[13]

While organising, Dolan keeps repeating his mantra: "Remember, for us, the enemy isn't these governments that comprise the WTO. The enemy is the transnational corporate, free trade lobby."[14] Consequently Dolan can perfectly work together with the right-wing Republican council member Derdowski, who earlier initiated plans for a Seattle MAI free zone. Also according to Derdowski the discussion around the WTO transcends the old borders between the left and the right. "The issue for conservatives is the sovereignty of America, the Constitution. State and local authority are in danger of being eroded through international treaties ceding authority to foreign regulatory bodies."[15] Together with the Republicans Dolan organises a demonstration in Seattle.

On a meeting they brainstormed on how to get the conservative inhabitants of the affluent districts of Seattle to also take to the streets. They decided to put IFG member David Korten on the task. They assumed this former businessman would easily connect to the rich.[16] Shortly after, Korten showed up at the grassroots level. He acted as the most important guest lecturer at a strategy meeting on nonviolent direct action. Korten would very much like to return to the '50's, when the economy was, according to him, still local and capitalism was not yet "perverted." His second hang-up is neo-Malthusian. He wants to reduce the world population from six to one billion. How? That he has, wisely, not revealed yet.[17]

Crucial Battles

Susan George also believes that "state sovereignty" is "under threat."[18] Therefore she wants us to strive for the "greatest possible unity."[19] The need for that also became clear to George in the US fight against fast track, a special presidential authority to push through trade treaties. "The anti-NAFTA and anti-WTO forces of the left defeated fast-track authority for the president only with the help of the far right. It was still a good thing to defeat fast track."[20] Ritchie, her colleague at the IFG, also has a good deal of experience in working together with the extreme right. "Aside from Nader and Buchanan, the anti-GATT and NAFTA trade alliance include a wide spectrum of what would have previously been called left and right elements. This diversity of views and constituencies gave the campaigns much of their strength."[21]

De Fabel van de Illegaal, on the other hand, fights the coming together of the left and the right. Whoever starts working with the right automatically drops migrants, women, and gays as potential allies, for they are always under attack from the right. The last couple of months De Fabel have heavily criticised collaborations with the right. Articles have been written on the ideas and activities of the New Right ideologist Goldsmith, who is also an important IFG member and sponsor of the think tank.[22] George got very angry about the criticism. De Fabel was splitting up the movement, she wrote. And because of that "we" would lose the "crucial battles" that "will be fought" in Seattle.[23]

1. George, Susan, "Seattle Prepares for Battle," *Le Monde Diplomatique,* Nov. '99.

2. George, Susan, "Letter to De Fabel van de illegal," 21 Sept. '99.

3. Stad, Kees, "Dolle toestanden in Frankrijk," 7 Sept. '99.

4. Dolan, Michael, e-mail, 2 Mar, '99.

5. Berlet, Chip and Margaret Quigley, "The right wing revolt against the modern age," *The Public Eye,* Vol. VI, No. 1, Dec. '92.

6. Ritchie, Mark, "Cross-border organizing," *The Case Against the Global Economy and for a Turn Towards the Local,* Jerry Mander and Edward Goldsmith, eds., 1996.

7. Berlet, Chip, "Right wing populism/Reform Party" *Public Eye* Homepage, 11 July, '99.

8. Lanting, Bert, "Kritiek op Buchanans kijk op nazi-Duitsland," *De Volkskrant,* 25 Sept. '99.

9. "Pat Buchanan in his own words," *Fair Report,* 26 Feb. '99

10. Zeskind, Leonard, "Free Trade and Foul," *Searchlight,* Oct. '99.

11. Walsh, Edward, "Buchanan dumps on Clinton steel policy," *Washington Post,* 2 Mar.'99.

12. Gilroy, Tom, "Gephardt calls for a seat at the table for labor, environmentalists in WTO-talks," *Washington Post,* 13 Oct. '99.

13. Morrill, Michael, e-mail, 13 Oct. '99.

14. Postman, David, "Protesters busily practice for WTO meeting," *Seattle Times,* 10 Sept. '99.

15. Parrish, Geov, "Shutting down Seattle," *Seattle Weekly,* 19 Aug. '99.

16. Cooper, Helene, "Globalization foes plan to protest WTO's Seattle round trade talks," *Wall Street Journal,* 16 July '99.

17. Henwood, Doug, "Antiglobalization," *Left Business Observer* No. 71, Jan. '96.

18. George, Susan, "State sovereignty under threat-globalising designs of the WTO," *Le Monde Diplomatique,* Jul. '99.

19. George, Susan, "Letter to De Fabel van de illegal," 21 Sept. '99.

20. George, Susan, e-mail, 17 Sept.'99.

21. Ritchie, Mark, "Cross-border organizing," *The Case Against the Global Economy and for a Turn Towards the Local,* Jerry Mander and Edward Goldsmith, eds., 1996.

22. Krebbers, Eric, "Millionaire Goldsmith supports the Left and the Extreme Right" and "Goldsmith and his Gaian hierarchy," *De Fabel van de Illegaal,* No. 36, Sept. '99.

23. George, Susan, "Letter to De Fabel van de illegal," 21 Sept. '99

Eric Krebbers and Merijn Schoenmaker

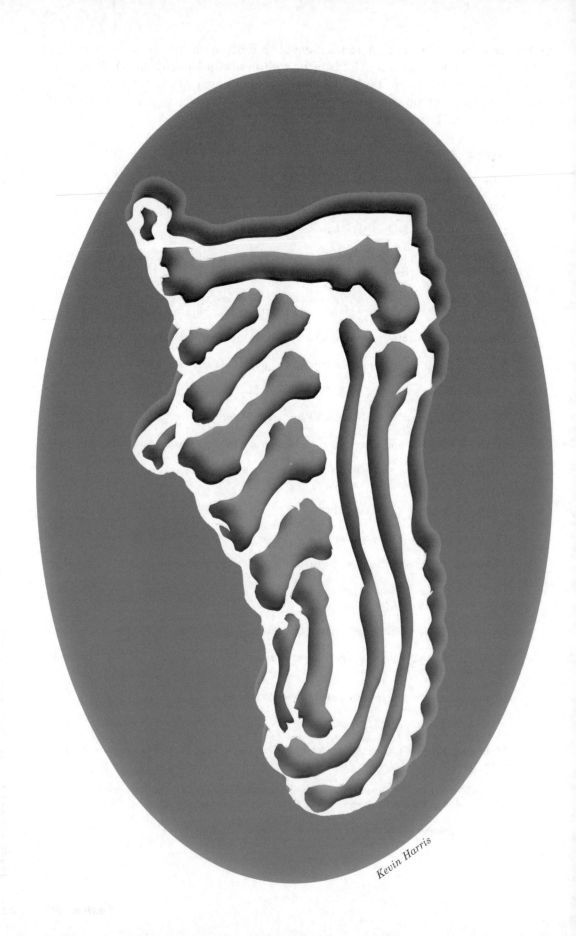

Kevin Harris

The Showdown Before Seattle

Race, Class, and the Framing of a Movement

Kristine Wong

From October 1997 to August 2000, I worked as the community organizer for the Community Coalition for Environmental Justice (CCEJ). Seattle-based and people of color–led, CCEJ waged local battles that furthered the global struggle for environmental justice. One of our most successful efforts was our Stop the Burning! Campaign. In 1998, the campaign successfully pressured the local Veterans' Administration hospital to shut down a medical waste incinerator that was releasing dioxin into the Beacon Hill neighborhood, an area where the majority of the residents were low income and people of color. CCEJ's Stop the Burning! Campaign organized Seattle residents against a global problem—the incineration of medical waste, which produces dioxin, one of the most toxic chemicals known. Dioxin migrates across countries, continents, and cultures, poisoning our bodies, food supply, and environment. Incinerators all over the world are operated by transnational corporations (TNCs), primarily located in low income communities and communities of color. These facilities have also been supported by international institutions such as the World Bank, which has promoted hospitals that incinerate their waste, rather than use safer disposal methods. Consequently, our local victory had global impact.

By the end of Summer 1999, organizing against the WTO Ministerial Meeting was accelerating. The mobilization provided an opportunity for collaboration among local activists, and to build an inclusive movement that linked the struggle at a local and on a global level. My concern was that the great majority of anti-WTO forces were not addressing the connections between WTO policies and the daily lives of the working class and communities of color, much less recognizing or including grassroots groups as an integral part of their leadership.

Whether or not the protests succeeded in shutting down the WTO, local campaigns like CCEJ would still exist. To be a genuine victory, the protests would have to broaden and unite existing grassroots movements, not recreate the oppressive structures they attempt to replace. A successful shutdown of the WTO

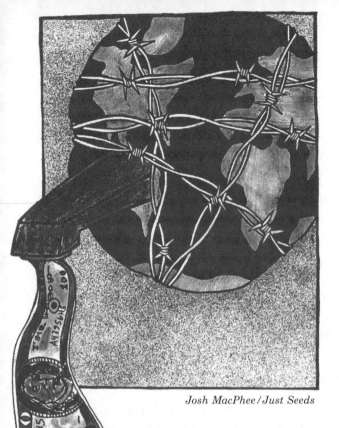

Josh MacPhee / Just Seeds

would be an incredible victory for low income communities and communities of color around the world, especially for countries in the Global South. However, it would limit the potential of such a movement if those most affected by globalization were unrepresented.

Riding on the golden waves of Seattle, activists have flocked from one protest to the next, hoping to pressure international institutions like the World Bank and IMF, and the U.S. Presidential Election Conventions to reconsider their financial ties to TNCs. At all these events, protesters of color have been outnumbered by whites.

Since Seattle, there has been a dialogue about the role people of color play in this movement. In this essay, I write about how people of color have been marginalized in the antiglobalization movement due to their absence in the movement's leadership and practice, and how the media has compounded this problem.

Elite Supergroups:
Framing "Fair Trade, Not Free Trade" for the Masses

While the marginalization of people of color in the antiglobalization movement can be attributed to a number of factors, the manner in which the elite "supergroup" leadership articulated and marketed the "fair trade, not free trade" demand is one of the main reasons. While smaller groups are the backbone of the movement, it was financial and political muscle that put Public Citizen, organized labor, and The Sierra Club in some of the key positions of power, influence, and recognition in the months leading up to the WTO.

After the WTO announced that Seattle would be the site of its Millennium Round Ministerial, Public Citizen, a well-established, non-governmental organization (NGO) based in Washington, D.C., set up an office downtown for their anti-WTO organizing arm, called People for Fair Trade (PfFT). Though the operations were lean in Seattle, it had a full time staff working on trade issues through Public Citizen's Global Trade Watch program in DC. Moreover, PfFT's Seattle staff alone was larger than that of most other grassroots organizing groups in Seattle, including CCEJ, and employed mostly whites within their ranks.

In the fall of '99, I attended an educational presentation sponsored by PfFT about the WTO. The meeting was held in Rainier Valley, one of the largest communities of color in Seattle. As soon as I entered the room, it was clear that, despite the demographics of the neighborhood, the atmosphere was not inviting to a variety of races and ethnicities. Hand-painted cardboard cut-outs depicting a sea turtle, a loaf of bread, and a tree were propped against the wall. Seats were arranged lecture-style, facing a blackboard.

The presentation was devoid of anything that could resonate with most working class people of color, focusing on three cases showing how the WTO had the unprecedented power to rule against countries' ability to make their own laws. This was illustrated by three WTO rulings. The first ruling sacrificed a sea turtle protection law for the shrimp fishing industry, while the second forbade the United States from enforcing its own gasoline quality laws. The third had to do with food quality—prohibition of banning hormone injected beef in the European Union.

A few other people of color were present at the Rainier Valley event—I watched their reactions closely. A middle-aged African American woman and a Latina with two young children stared at the presenters blankly. The presentation favored passive learning through listening rather than active learning through educational exercises and activities that draw upon the interest and experience of the participants. For entertainment, two young white women with facial piercings and matted hair earnestly led the attendees in a folk song against free trade accompanied by an instrument resembling a ukulele. The women said they were going on a national tour to spread the message of why people should take action against the WTO. Both women of color politely gathered up their belongings and left the room.

BAYAN, an international Filipino organization, was also at the event. They were convening a People's Assembly in late November, consisting of delegates from the Global South opposed to WTO policies. Their lead organizer in Seattle, Ace Saturay, had a few minutes to speak at the end of the meeting. Yet by that time, almost all of the other people of color had left. After the event I approached one of the presenters with my concern about the style and content of the presentation. She mentioned that a curriculum addressing globalization and its impact on health care was being developed. While she was open to my suggestions, she did not address my concern.

People for Fair Trade's presentation was a replica of an educational brochure about the WTO, published by the Working Group on the WTO. Titled "A Citizen's Guide to the World Trade Organization," the brochure was one of the first and most widely distributed publications, and played a key role in articulating the issues around the WTO to the activist public, as well as to the mainstream media. An analysis of its content easily illustrates how the antiglobalization movement has not engaged people of color.

The brochure addressed democracy but did not use language or content applicable to many people of color, beginning with its very title. Many people of color are immigrants or refugees, and not all are "citizens." The most pressing issues for the majority of the world's people go beyond consumerism: access to a living wage, privatization of traditionally public sector services, disproportionate exposure to toxic pollutants, police brutality, and the rise of the prison-industrial complex. The brochure referred to none of these. Instead, they were labeled as "environmental" and "health" issues, even though the gasoline and beef cases were environmental health issues.

While choosing to describe the issues as "environment," "health," and "labor" rather than the complex "public health and environmental justice" may appear to be splitting hairs, the simplification had its consequences. As a result, people of color–led grassroots groups in the environmental justice movement, such as CCEJ, whose work was already challenging the root causes of globalization, were not viewed as key players who should have been included in the public discourse about globalization's effect on "environmental" issues. While the International Forum on Globalization's "Invisible Government" report, and the Earth Justice Legal Defense Fund's "Trading Away Public Health" more accurately described the WTO as having an impact on public health issues, they also neglected to term them as environmental justice issues.

Environment and Health Day: Dioxin or Sea Turtles?

Around October, I heard that the organizers of the protest were planning a different theme for each of the five days of the ministerial. The first day, Monday, November 29, was to be "Environment and Health Day." I contacted the main coordinators for that day, senior staff at the Public Citizen and the Sierra Club, to talk to them about including a section about dioxin in the day's events. My intention was to make sure that a race, class, environmental health, and justice analysis would be included in the day's proceedings. My experience is a perfect example of the power dynamic that white groups have wielded over smaller, community-based people of color groups in the antiglobalization movement.

While I did not receive a return call from the Sierra Club, I did get a response from the staffperson at Public Citizen. She acknowledged that race and class dimensions were of concern, informing me that people of color would be represented in the day's events. She said I could participate in the planning group for Environment and Health Day, and that she would add me to the email list of organizers. This never happened. When I realized that she was not including me in the group, I decided to plan a separate environmental justice event about dioxin that would illustrate how local environmental justice struggles are connected with global ones. All I needed was to find a space downtown to hold the event. However, after contacting United Methodist Church, one of the few non-business spaces downtown open to renting space for anti-WTO events, I found that Public Citizen had already rented it for the day. This left me with no choice but to again ask Public Citizen if I could reserve some part of the facility for about one-two hours, so that the dioxin event could take place. The fact that I had to ask a Washington, D.C.-based group for permission to get access to space to educate others about local struggles in my own city of residence was ironic and disturbing.

When I asked the Public Citizen staffperson for access to the space, I informed her of my plans for the dioxin event. She let me know that she could not give me an answer, as plans for Environment and Health Day had not been finalized. About a month later, she contacted me to let me know that the planning group had decided to hold a march featuring protesters dressed as sea turtles for the day. The group's decision was exactly what I had feared. The sea turtle march was the day's main public event. A march full of sea turtles would send out an extremely limited message to the public—that the WTO hurt endangered species and the environment, but not the health and welfare of people around the world. I could picture the media images already—turtle-protesters splashed in newspapers and magazines all over the world, permanently branding the WTO in people's minds as just another environmental issue.

The Public Citizen staffperson added that she knew people who could explain to me the connections between CCEJ's local struggle and the policies of the WTO. I found this to be extremely condescending and insulting, as the scope of the event I was planning should have indicated to her that I was aware of the connections between local and global environmental justice. Soon after, an organizational ally asked the Public Citizen staffperson via email to include CCEJ in the planning committee, a completely unsolicited request. The staffperson replied that I had been included in the planning for Environment and Health Day.

Exclusionary Images:
The Sierra Club and the American Revolution

The Sierra Club's anti-WTO materials defined fair trade with exclusionary imagery. A postcard by the Club's Seattle chapter clearly targeted mainstream white environmentalists. "We can make trade clean, green, and fair," it proclaimed. Calling for "Clean air standards, Food safeguards, and Wildlife protections," against a blue and green background, it featured three colonial-era men marching defiantly, one brandishing an American flag. At the bottom of the postcard ran the slogan "No globalization without representation." The Sierra Club's intent was for the trio to be viewed as American revolutionaries on their way to the Boston Tea Party, protesting taxation without representation. Rather than choosing an image that reflected the global implications of the issue, the Sierra Club chose a nationalistic approach that glorified the American Revolution. An African-American friend remarked to me that the picture reminded her of the days of slavery.

Fortunately, not all of the local events excluded people of color. Teach-ins organized by BAYAN, the People's Assembly, and Seattle Central Community College students provided a few opportunities for participants to learn about the connections between local and global issues. Coordinated by Lydia Cabasco, student organizers of color gave presentations in local high schools. At the Seattle Central teach-in, I gave my local-global dioxin, environmental justice, and global waste trade presentation. Yalonda Sindé, of CCEJ, gave a presentation about how corporate globalization both causes and perpetuates poverty. The International Forum on Globalization's Seattle teach-in on November 26 and 27 featured a selection of well-known speakers from across the Global South, while Seattle's Workers Voices' Coalition and the Northwest Labor and Employment Law Office (LELO) sponsored events and a December 4 workers' conference focused on immigration, women, and the global economy.

Seattle and D.C. Media Spin
Manufacturing White Identities; People of Color Ignored

Part I: Seattle

Despite wholehearted efforts by people of color to get the word out to the community and the media about the way local issues are affected by globalization, the supergroups' agenda prevailed. The media fashioned these groups into an activist family of identities: fair trader/anti-corporate crusader, labor loyalist, and environmentalist. These identities were prized by the mainstream media for providing the official advocacy position of the protesters. Their "newfound" alliance was neatly packaged in the nickname of "Teamsters and Turtles," a sound bite that described labor and environmentalists "together, at last." On the other hand, the Direct Action Network and the great majority of peaceful young protesters were portrayed as rebellious and irresponsible. They were good for action-packed photo opportunities with shock value—white youth with matted hair and piercings that either ravaged downtown stores, occupied the streets in droves to make political statements, or were hauled off to jail in handcuffs.

While the media's fixation on "Teamsters and Turtles" and white youth was easily digestible by the public, it completely eclipsed the problems of the people most affected by globalization. Similarly, media promotion of white activists gave power to these groups to define the antiglobalization movement: who are the experts, what are the issues, and where will it head next.

Worst of all, the media completely ignored the participation of people of color in the protest. The People's Assembly march of international delegates and local activists of color marched from Seattle's International District to 4th and Pine Streets downtown. There it converged with the student march coming from Seattle Central Community College, and the labor march coming from Memorial Stadium. CCEJ organized an environmental justice contingent as part of the march, and marched alongside representatives from the Southwest Network For Environmental and Economic Justice, and later with the Indigenous Environmental Network. At 4th and Pine, the People's Assembly held a participatory rally, among the most powerful images of the week, that welcomed any protester to take their turn addressing the crowd. The result was an exhilarating, electrifying mix of everyday people with an international perspective, mostly women of color, who spoke from their hearts on the impact of globalization. Their words, full of raw energy, vision, and power, never reached the ears of the larger public. As noted by Yalonda Sindé, who monitored television media during the week, the coverage of people of color was largely reduced to images of African American youth looting stores whose windows had already been broken during the November 30 march.

The domination of "Teamsters and Turtles" and white youth in the media was no surprise. True to form, the corporate media followed the lead of the "supergroups" and presented the issues in safe, clichéd terms. Just as I had predicted, the sea turtles hit the pages of the *Seattle Post Intelligencer* on Tuesday, November 30, were splashed across a two-page photo spread in *Newsweek*'s "Battle of Seattle" issue, and were placed atop a *New York Times* op-ed about the protests. "Teamsters and Turtles" and young white demonstrators became the

Josh MacPhee/Just Seeds

universal symbols of the antiglobalization movement, rather than the numerous communities around the world who have resisted globalization.

Part II: Washington, D.C.

The next major protest that I took part in was "A16"— a protest against the World Bank and IMF in Washington, D.C. As in Seattle, I was also a print journalist with the Independent Media Center (IMC). Connecting with and interviewing activists of color in the streets, I found them to be well-informed, committed, and inspiring. They had traveled from all around the United States and all over the world to be a part of the protests, and hailed from different generations, faiths, sexual orientations, and economic backgrounds. They spoke passionately about how the policies of the World Bank and IMF were responsible for gentrification, sweatshop labor, environmental racism, the global trafficking of women, poor access to HIV/AIDS treatment, police brutality and racial profiling, and the rise in the prison-industrial complex at the cost of education.

Another priority of mine was to seek out local organizers and events that made the connection between the policies of the World Bank and IMF and the current state of affairs in the low income, communities of color in Washington, D.C. In the Columbia Heights neighborhood, I attended an antigentrification rally that stopped at several apartment complexes. At each stop, black, Asian/Pacific Islander, and Latino immigrant residents who were being evicted came outside to tell the crowd the unjust circumstances of their displacement. Many of these residents tied their situation to those around the world who have also been displaced from their homes by World Bank and IMF-funded development projects.

Just as in Seattle, I found nothing of these experiences in the mainstream media accounts of the A16 protests. With labor withdrawing their support from the D.C. protests, and sea turtles nowhere to be found, the *Washington Post* focused on pierced, alternative-looking white youth as the new American revolu-

Kristine Wong

tionary icon, showcasing them as the main participants engaging in this social movement. Although people of color did not constitute a majority of the protesters, this does not mean their presence was not worth mentioning. Ignoring their presence rendered their participation invisible to mainstream society. This dynamic seriously impacts the relationship of people of color with this growing social movement.

The media's elimination of people of color from coverage of the Seattle and D.C. protests created a public perception that these people had not participated. The media then used this representation to criticize white activists for expressing anger toward policies that do not (as the corporate pundits see it) directly affect them. In their view, if a critical mass of people who were most affected by globalization weren't out in the streets protesting the event, then how valid could the concerns be?

What the media ignored was that the numbers of protesters of color present were not necessarily indicative of popular opinion in those communities. Several factors influenced the numbers of people of color at these protests. Due to the cost of travel and accommodation, as well as the luxury needed to take time off work and family responsibilities, it was less likely that working class people of color would have been able to come. Secondly, in light of widespread brutality to people of color by police and in the prison system, especially African Americans, it was clear that protesters of color risking arrest was an entirely different prospect than those in the Direct Action Network (DAN) with white skin privilege. Additionally, many immigrants of color who were not legal residents were not in any position to risk arrest. Others may have been discouraged from protesting, whether it be through painful memories of the way protesters were treated by the political regimes of their home countries, or through the stories of family members who had witnessed or experienced violent repression of those who spoke out against unjust policies.

Finally, media coverage may have affected the way people of color perceived the globalization issue due to its focus on the protesters and not on the real issues at hand, much less the local-global connections. Predictably, this only exacerbated the racial imbalance by sending out messages to people of color that the WTO, the World Bank, and the IMF had nothing to do with their lives.

Whose Independent Media?

In the months preceding the WTO Ministerial Meeting, the IMC in Seattle was founded to give the underrepresented greater access to the media during the protests. The IMC was a work and resource space for independent media, and a website where anyone could contribute up-to-the-minute audio, video, or print news on the webcast. The IMC's print team produced a daily paper for distribution on the streets of Seattle, titled the *Blind Spot*. While the IMC has stimulated a grassroots independent media movement and challenged the corporate media, it has difficulties in determining how it can work with local community-based organizations and the ethnic media.

During the WTO and D.C. protests, I doubled as a print journalist for the *Blind Spot*. As a local activist who knew a few other locals in the space, I was able to find out what the writing, editing, and printing processes were, even though I had to push my way through various channels to get that information.

However, had I been a person of color from out of town, it would have been more difficult to determine how to get involved. The atmosphere was chaotic and not very welcoming to people of color, as there were so few around. Although a workspace had been set aside for people of color, I was not aware of it at the time.

Evaluative meetings between the Seattle IMC and local activists of color took place in the winter and spring following the WTO. While I was unable to attend all the meetings, I took part in some, letting others know that the IMC needed to meet with local community groups and the ethnic media before determining their place in the Seattle landscape. Others had recommended antiracism training. While a good group of IMC staff, co-founders, and activists were committed to moving in the direction of these recommendations, the overall membership was divided on how best to proceed.

After the WTO protests, activists in D.C. began to organize an IMC for A16. As a print reporter, I focused on stories about people of color that made the local connections to globalization, writing a story for the *Blind Spot* about the Columbia Heights evictions/antigentrification rally on April 15 and turning it in that night. Earlier, I also sent them my interview with a Malaysian-born activist from JustACT, the San Francisco-based group who had brought a number of youth activists of color to the protest. The interview had an international perspective about the repression of Asian/Pacific Islander student activists and linked U.S. youth of color's struggle against police brutality and the prison system with globalization and privatization.

At the editorial meeting that night, I was told that both pieces were slated to be published the next day, the April 16 edition of the *Blind Spot*. On that day, I marched with the People's Assembly, this time as a reporter as well as an activist. To meet the *Blind Spot* deadline, I headed back to the IMC later that afternoon.

While I was writing my story, the *Blind Spot* arrived. Neither of my pieces had been published. Reading the issue, I found the content to be problematic. It was closer to the mainstream media than to the voice of the underrepresented. None of the articles provided perspectives outside those centered around white protesters and their efforts to represent people of color struggles. For example, instead of printing an article focused on the evictions rally in Columbia Heights, editors of the *Blind Spot* chose to include an article about a group of squatters that took over a house as their way of protesting on behalf of the residents being evicted. The story that should have gotten printed was the Columbia Heights rally that covered affected residents who were speaking out for themselves.

The content that did involve stories mentioning the struggles of people of color failed as substantive analyses of the issues. Rather, it appeared to have been placed there for token value. Someone without much exposure to these issues might look at the April 16 issue and think that it covered a diverse range of perspectives, simply because the code words "race," "Mumia Abu-Jamal," and "class" appeared in the stories. The lack of analysis could have been avoided had people of color with an understanding of and experience with these issues been part of the editorial team.

However, while the IMCs have challenges ahead of them regarding people of color issues, they have succeeded where the mainstream media have failed, giving the world first-person, unedited coverage of what really happened on the

Kristine Wong

streets of Seattle. They should be commended for that, and for creating a world-wide movement of IMCs, one of the lasting contributions of the WTO protests.

Recommendations and Conclusion

While people of color in the Global South have been fighting against globalization for decades, the WTO protests have given the spotlight to the post-Seattle antiglobalization movement. In contrast to movements in the Global South, the post-Seattle movement has spawned a new group of activist nomads, involving thousands protesting international trade and lending policies at events all over the world. Ironically, these event-based convergences that have built the post-Seattle movement are the very same events that have dissipated it, by encouraging activists to protest so globally that many forget the importance of acting locally. A year later, the movement has reached a turning point in its evolution. If it is to survive, it must look to people of color–led groups fighting globalization on a local level to build its own leadership, foundation, and direction.

Looking to these groups for leadership and direction means acknowledging the disproportionate effects of globalization on low income communities and communities of color, especially in the Global South, and how people of color–led movements have fought back. This means acknowledging grassroots community organizations that are the movements' backbone and giving them the space to frame globalization in a way that resonates with the daily lives of low income communities and communities of color around the world.

However, while this is an approach that will build the movement, it will fail unless the Northern, mostly white leadership is committed to using its power and resources to make this vision become a reality. True sharing of leadership would require elites to sacrifice some of their organizations' power and funding. While seemingly unrealistic, this is what is necessary if the movement is to mature and develop into one that can build a truly globalized movement for social justice.

The media has an integral role in the future direction of the movement. Media images, whether they are mainstream or independent, need to go beyond the protests and focus on the real issues of corporate-led globalization. The images must include people of color in the struggle, draw from multiple sources, and dispel stereotypes. Likewise, the IMCs must find a place in the community through collaborating with grassroots groups and the ethnic media to determine what their role will be.

I look forward to an antiglobalization movement that is collective in scope, where people of color and community-based organizations are recognized in the fight against globalization.

A community resource guide on environmental justice is available from the Community Coalition for Environmental Justice. Write to: CCEJ, 105 14th Avenue, Suite 2C, Seattle, WA 98122, (206) 720.0285, http://www.ccej.org

Spark, Fire, and Burning Coals:
An Organizer's History of Seattle

Stephanie Guilloud

N30: Fifty thousand people from across the country and the world flood downtown Seattle to protest the oppressive policies of the World Trade Organization. Police attack protesters, triggering a "riot."
D1: Over six hundred people are violently arrested by the riot armies.
D2: The Direct Action Network Tactical Team asks our affinity group, the Small Town Sleazy Cowboy (and Lady) Puppet Rodeo Association, to lead a lockdown at the King County Jail. We agree.

A friend and I leave a restaurant on Thursday, December 2 with two laminated menus tucked in our jackets. We scurry into an alley and cut stencils into them: "Liberation" and "No WTO." We spraypaint squares of white cloth with our stencils and pin them to our backs so we can identify each other. We leave Capitol Hill to meet up with the march to the farmer's rally at Pike Place.

After the rally at Pike Place and another at Weyerhauser, we make our way to the jail. The cops have no idea what we are doing. They think we're going to take I-5, and they get all riled up. We politely turn a corner and move down the hill to the doors of the jail. Ten to fifteen of us block the doors with our bodies. Hundreds join us and we sit for hours. Others circle the entire jail, arms linked. Some actions don't get planned ahead of time. But in Seattle they all worked.

My affinity group was five people—three women and two transgendered folks—I trust and love. We established ourselves in October of '99 after many meetings, trainings, and conferences about the WTO. We were all loosely affiliated with the Direct Action Network and worked with the Spokescouncil, a nightly meeting of representatives from all the affinity groups involved. The group met together in the Convergence Center, an abandoned nightclub at 420 Denny Way, a street steeply sloping downtown from Capitol Hill. We held trainings, meetings and fed hundreds of activists in the days before N30.

We built our cluster of affinity groups to over one hundred fifty people. They came from California, Lewis and Clark College in Portland, and Prescott, Arizona. On November 30, we successfully blocked two intersections. We painted a huge street mural in our intersection to express our outrage at the WTO's corporate agenda. In the streets, we relied on trust and consensus to make quick decisions about how to respond to tear gas and where to move next. Our process embodied the nonhierarchical vision we were working to realize.

Organizing to Shut It Down

The Third Ministerial meeting of the World Trade Organization provided an unprecedented occasion for diverse movements to converge in opposition to corporate globalization. Each sector—the police, the WTO delegates, the direct action affinity groups, the labor unions, and the people of Seattle—planned for the week separately and with very little overlap. We met in the streets without knowing what to expect. All of us walked away changed.

The labor movement—represented by but not isolated to the AFL-CIO—decided in late summer to participate with a reform position: "If the WTO doesn't work for working families, it doesn't work," hailed the union's signs. Positions on the WTO traversed the spectrum from reformist to radical whether you talked to AFL leadership, local labor councils, or rank-and-file membership.

Progressive organizations like Ralph Nader's Public Citizen began organizing early and built on their successful campaign to expose and defeat the Multilateral Agreement on Investment. The MAI was a corporate bill of rights drafted by the elite representatives of the Organization for Economic Cooperation and Development to allow corporate entities to sue nation-states for imposing restrictions on trade. The progressive groups and liberal Non-Governmental Organizations demanded the reform of environmental and labor laws.

The international contingent, like the Seattle-based Filipino group Sentanaryo-Bayan, took a strong anti-imperialistic stance against the WTO and organized a broad base to participate. "After a year of preparations, delegates from various organizations, citizens' movements, and NGOs from twelve countries participated in discussions and shared their experiences on how the globalization policy on free trade affects them," reported Ace Saturay, an organizer of the People's Assembly. The People's Assembly held conferences and rallies opposing the WTO.

The Direct Action Network (Against Corporate Globalization) galvanized the already existing radical dissent. It included the action-oriented politics of groups like People's Global Action, Earth First!, Ruckus Society, Rainforest Action Network, Art & Revolution, and small community groups. From the first meetings to the final hours, DAN never compromised its goal of shutting down the WTO through direct action.

This article concentrates on the Direct Action Network tactics and history. A&R organizers began talking about strategy and tactics in the summer of '99. David Solnit and Sonja Sivesind, two organizers in A&R, began to initiate a conversation among other West Coast organizers, including myself, in late spring. By the time the WTO announced that Seattle would host the Third Ministerial, a powerful core of organizers was committed to a mass action in Seattle.

This working group held organizing meetings over conference calls throughout the summer of '99. Each of us—located in Seattle, Olympia, Portland, Vancouver, BC, San Francisco, and Santa Cruz—organized meetings in our communities. Olympia students and community members got fired up.

Over sixty people met on July 24 in Seattle to discuss direct action possibilities. The conference call organizers created a broadsheet describing the WTO and providing guidelines for how to create nonviolent direct action affinity groups. The broadsheet was printed in the *Earth First! Journal,* reaching over nine thousand people. We printed more than fifty thousand more and distributed them across the country. This four page tabloid and rave-style postcards announcing "a festival of resistance" served as our main propaganda.

Who were the organizers and who were we calling out? The organizers were predominantly white, mostly, but not all, young and fairly experienced radicals. Our ranks included the environmental direct action crowd, activists from the prison movement, international solidarity and anarchist movements. Our constituency reflected these networks.

Through a number of difficult meetings, DAN adopted its name and David Solnit's proposal for four action guidelines. The guidelines were not philosophical or ideological guidelines; they were intended as reassurance to groups we wanted to work with. We understood that they would alienate others.

The guidelines were: No weapons; No violence, physical or verbal; No drugs or alcohol; and No property destruction. This last guideline would later be hotly disputed.

Maegan Willan, an Olympia organizer, wrote about the adoption of these guidelines:

> I remember being annoyed and confused by the people who questioned the property destruction element of these guidelines at that meeting (that was the only part questioned)... I had never thought about property destruction and whether or not it was violent. I never had to really question how far I would go to protect myself from a cop. I didn't concern myself with the implication of 15 people creating guidelines that 50,000 people were supposed to follow... My closedness was shaped by the privileged position I hold as a white North-American woman coming from an upper middle class family, living in a place like Olympia... [Afterwards] I felt so sheepish and sad about being one of the fifteen people at that meeting in August who decided 'the rules.' How arrogant we were to think we had the right to determine what was going to happen in the streets. No one has the right to 'police' the movement when we are fighting for self-determination.

The major organizing events of the fall were the Roadshow and the Action Convergence. The Roadshow was a band of puppeteers and theater folk staging performances and trainings up and down the West Coast. It trained many in nonviolent direct action tactics, affinity group formation, and dance/street theater skills, and urged people to attend the two week convergence in Seattle directly preceding the Ministerial.

Time began to be a significant pressure in the DAN meetings, which were still alternating between Olympia and Seattle. In October, time was pressing; it was hard to bring up outreach ideas or question the racial diversity of a group poised for action but lacking structure. At a meeting in Olympia the conversation turned to diversity, or the complete lack thereof, and our organizing efforts. Some claimed that people of color weren't interested in direct action or radical ideas, and we shouldn't waste our energy. A white person responded that white people by no means developed nonviolent direct action tactics or radical thought. The meeting was tense and unpleasant, and after it a number of organizers didn't return. When "outreach" (the only means of diversifying we discussed) was brought up again, someone suggested that "everybody call one person of color and invite them to the group." Rage and hard words met this tokenizing proposal.

I would've been interested in redirecting our organizing efforts or looking outside our group to try to work with and support people of color already organizing against the WTO. Instead we spent time playing damage control to racist comments, attitudes, and declarations. We were realizing that we mirrored oppressive tendencies of the system we were trying to resist.

Olympia DAN organized an anti-oppression training in response to the confusion and hurt. Many people showed up, but institutional racism and domination can't be dissolved in a two hour training. After the training many Olympia organizers realized that we were working with a group of people who were not committed to dismantling racism, sexism, classism, homophobia, and other oppressions. We were not building a long-term resistance movement: we were mobilizing for a protest.

We made a final push to November 30.

Strengths and Weaknesses in Seattle Direct Action Organizing

Strengths of the direct action organizing done in Seattle include the affinity group structure, consensus process, innovative popular education techniques, the consistency of a radical critique of the WTO and capitalism, and the protesters' high level of understanding of the issues at stake. Weaknesses include the limited base of people that we mobilized rather than creating community bases, the invisible hierarchy that emerged in the organizing, and the lack of an anti-oppressive vision.

The affinity group structure remains one of the strongest organizing tools to re-emerge in Seattle. Small groups acted autonomously to create and execute direct actions all week. The principle of autonomy reflected our greater vision of participatory democracy. The decentralized actions eliminated dictating leaders and reflected collective work. The affinity group structure kept security tight and allowed the Spokescouncil to make big decisions. Afterwards a friend told me, and her instinct rings true, "Everybody walked away from Seattle feeling like they did it."

Consensus is a method of decision making that requires all participants to consent to the decision before moving on. The principle of consensus encourages placing value on every voice: no single person or entity at the head. It is difficult to do well with hundreds of people, but practice is necessary to identify problems and improve. The street actions were some of the hardest times we worked with consensus. Coming to consensus with over one hundred fifty people in wet, scary, and threatening conditions on the street was a huge success for the model of democracy we are working to create.

The internalized education techniques the Direct Action Network utilized prepared people for successful actions. Trainers provided information through role-playing scenarios. Trainings were held on nonviolent direct action, medical support, puppet building, theater skills, legal rights, spoken word, music and dance, and direct action tactics like banner drops or body blockades. These trainings strengthened the level of participants' abilities to act and react in the street.

As far as weaknesses, I have mentioned a limited base. By drawing on already existing radical populations, we were able to amass numbers, but we did not expand a base for a movement. The folks doing direct action in the street were mostly white and young and carried privilege. We carried the privilege of mobility (able to leave jobs or school and get to Seattle) and white skin—which protected us from lead bullets, not rubber ones. Most of us also carried the privilege of leaving Seattle once it was all over. The direct action contingent did not take the time to acknowledge who we were or what our actions would mean for the local communities. Lydia Cabasco, a Filipina organizer for the Workers' Voices Coalition and the No WTO Student Outreach Committee, said, "In terms of the Direct Action Network, they started thinking fairly late about how direct action would impact people of color and communities of color in Seattle. If they wanted to get people involved, risking arrest and police confrontation is a real concern for brown people." The Network's limited base contributed to the lack of process around central issues. We did not identify ourselves or clarify our goals adequately. That silence alienated many groups and people from working with us.

Nearly all our organizing was under crisis conditions. This caused weak links before, during, and after the actions. The week of November 30–December 3 demanded quick, well-timed decisions and fast action. The problem was we had been operating that way for months. We were all walking zombies. It was not sustainable at all, impacting consensus process, precluding the development of allies from outside groups, and completely draining the individuals involved in the group. Many of us dropped away from DAN after Seattle because of these issues.

An inevitable problem that occurs during crisis organizing is leader-dominant decision making. An invisible hierarchy emerged throughout the last few weeks of organizing. It could be argued that hierarchies based on gender, race, age, and experience existed all along. Experienced folks and those directly tied to money sources separated themselves from the Spokescouncil and concentrated on tactics and strategy. Local organizers were caught in the middle of these informal groups. I felt my work was undermined by 'ringers' that flew in from all over and didn't manage to introduce themselves before they began running the show. Jennica Born, an Olympia organizer, was asked days before the action to participate in one of the closed meetings. He decided to participate with his affinity group rather than work with that team. He later reflected:

> As developments grew in the direct action organizing against the WTO we watched and participated as an invisible hierarchy was constructed. The initial conference calls (of the Direct Action Network) which made decisions on outreach materials and action guidelines with no input from local organizations or

activists, are primary examples of this. These hierarchies continued into the protests themselves, where tactical teams and strategy circles were formed in closed rooms and without the consent of most protest participants.

Clear process and secure planning during a mass-action is difficult and maybe impossible, but the hierarchies and secret meetings revealed weak areas that need to be discussed and clarified as we move forward.

The Sleazy Cowboys wrote an open letter in December discussing many of these weaknesses, especially the lack of acknowledgment around racial dynamics. Our call for evaluation was met with assertions from key organizers about the urgency to build on the Seattle momentum. Carolyn Cooley was told that "DAN is a brand-name with a high market value" and that we would fall apart if we tried to address internal problems. She said, "People seemed to stop listening as soon as they heard the words 'race' and 'oppression.' They gave us a 'yeah, yeah, yeah—we've heard it all before' response. Although we had played critical roles in organizing, we wondered if our affinity group, made up of trannies and queer women, was easy to dismiss as oversensitive and process-prone females wanting to drag everyone into hashing over things like identity and power." DAN organizers pushed forward despite the lack of evaluation.

After weeks of crossing post-WTO networks and organizing efforts off the agenda, people began talking about how to keep the momentum from Seattle rising. Eyes turned to the International Monetary Fund/World Bank meeting in Washington, D.C. Focus moved away from strengthening the community organizations that formed in response to the WTO. Evaluation efforts were dismissed and ignored. I could see little effort to track the development of the WTO or how the protests had affected this massive institution. Instead of reevaluating the actual role of DAN and perhaps the necessity to create a new organization, I watched people ride the wave, and I closed my eyes with gritted teeth anticipating the crash. In Olympia it came quickly. We faced the racism in our organization earlier than the other groups and showed deeper wounds from the whole thing. We did not have a community base, and we did not have a vision of our purpose or identity. We fell apart.

Though some groups dissolved and others were building the Continental DAN Spokescouncil, individuals worked in different ways to organize around the same issues. People who were inspired in Seattle created teach-ins and workshops on police brutality, mass action organizing, and WTO education. Many Olympia activists worked with the locked out Kaiser Steelworkers to plan a direct action that connected to the company's environmental destruction. I continued to work on efforts to document, process, and evaluate the events that changed all of our lives. I worked on *Voices from the WTO*—an anthology of first hand accounts, poetry, essays, and stories from people who participated in the protests. I organized a follow-up conference in April 2000 to discuss the WTO and the IMF and how to strengthen the community alliances that were formed by the solidarity in the streets. People were excited to reunite and continue looking forward, but the same limitations stared at us from all directions. Where and who is the local base? How do we act locally to resist these global institutions? What if we don't have the money to get to DC or Philly or LA? What can we do here, and who do we do it with?

The significance of Seattle is hard to gauge only a year after the protests. I argue for a critical look at our goals and our tools to realize them: strengthen affinity groups, identify and work with our local communities, challenge each other on our racism and privilege, and continue popular education workshops on capitalist globalization and direct action tactics.

In this work, the spirit of Seattle should guide us, but with a realistic understanding of what it was and what it lacked.

THE MOVEMENT SO FAR

part IV

SPRING 2000

WHAT'S IT ABOUT?

WORLD BANK & I.M.F. ARE FINANCIAL INSTITUTIONS CLAIMING MOST COUNTRIES AS MEMBERS.

BUT THOSE STATES WHICH CONTRIBUTE THE MOST MONEY HAVE THE LOUDEST VOICE.

20% OF THE MONEY THE U.S. PUTS IN COMES DIRECTLY FROM TAXES. 80% COMES FROM PENSION FUNDS.

BANKS, UNIONS COLLEGES (MAYBE YOURS) EITHER WAY, U-PAY-4-IT!

WORLD BANK I.M.F.

IN THE 1970s THE WORLD BANK GAVE BIG LOANS

TO POOR COUNTRIES.

LOANS OFTEN PAID FOR DAMS, ROADS, HUGE PROJECTS

THAT HURT THE ENVIRONMENT.

MONEY WENT TO THE ELITE,

NOT THE PEOPLE.

SOON THESE IMPOVERISHED COUNTRIES WERE HOPELESS-LY IN DEBT TO THE WORLD BANK!

THEIR ONLY HOPE, NEW LOANS TO COVER THE DEBTS. BUT TO GET

NEW LOANS THEY HAD TO AGREE TO STRUCTURAL ADJUSTMENT.

STRUCTURAL ADJUSTMENT IS WHEN A COUNTRY AGREES TO MAKE CHANGES IN ITS

ECONOMY THAT FAVOR MULTI-NATIONAL CORPORATIONS.

THEY MUST CUT FOOD PROGRAMS FOR THE POOR.

THEY MUST RAISE INTEREST RATES MAKING IT HARD FOR LOCALS TO BUY HOMES OR START BUSINESSES

THEY MUST LIMIT ACCESS TO PUBLIC EDUCATION.

THEY MUST SMASH UNIONS,

SELL STATE OWNED INDUSTRY AND NATURAL RESOURCES

FINALLY GLOBAL BUSINESS

TO MULTI-NATIONAL CORPORATIONS

COMES IN TO EXPLOIT THE CHEAP LABOR.

SOUND FAMILIAR? IT SHOULD! STRUCTURAL ADJUSTMENT IS BASED ON THE ECONOMIC POLICIES THAT RONALD REAGAN TRIED IN THE UNITED STATES IN THE 1980s.

OUR SOCIAL PROGRAMS HAVE BEEN CUT IN THE NAME OF

PAYING THE NATIONAL DEBT.

STRUCTURAL ADJUSTMENT HAS LED PEOPLE ALL OVER THE WORLD TO RIOT

TIME TO SMASH THE WORLD BANK I.M.F.

by Seth Tobocman

Kevin Harris

Where Was the Color at A16?

Colin Rajah
ColorLines, *Fall 2000*

Last year's World Trade Organization shutdown in Seattle was a historic moment for the growing U.S. movement against corporate globalization. However, the Seattle actions, dazzling as they were, also cast a spotlight on serious issues of race within that movement.

After Seattle, the movement set its sights on mobilizing for the annual Spring meetings of the World Bank and International Monetary Fund in Washington, D.C. Known as A16, these actions were also hugely successful. Although they did not completely shut down the meetings, the actions mobilized some 20,000 participants, gathered major national and international attention, and sustained the momentum of the anti-corporate globalization movement.

Yet the whiteness of the movement remained a thorny issue at A16. While Seattle is a relatively white location, D.C. promised a far better opportunity to mobilize people of color: its majority African-American population has a long history of international action and other large East Coast populations of color are nearby.

Indeed, a significant number of people of color participated in the D.C. actions, as they had in Seattle. Still, A16 was probably proportionately even whiter—and, since labor departed early—younger than the WTO protests. "A16 was indeed a sea of white," comments Eric Tang of Third World Within of New York City.

After the racial critique emerged in Seattle and was substantially analyzed by Elizabeth "Betita" Martinez's widely circulated *ColorLines* article, "Where Was the Color in Seattle?," various attempts were made to mobilize people of color to D.C. The Mobilization for Global Justice, the central initiating and organizing coalition for A16, hired Asantewaa Nkrumah-Ture, specifically to do outreach to black communities in D.C.

"The outreach we did was never 'affirmative action.' We answered questions, provided information, and asked for participation. To that extent, we did a very good job and we planted seeds that will bear fruit in the future," Nkrumah-Ture says.

Paternalistic Greetings

Nonetheless, the D.C. mobilization of color was thin. Damu Smith, coordinator of the National Black Environmental and Economic Justice Coordinating Committee and a veteran D.C. international solidarity activist, says that he "was only approached to pass on contacts." Given the meager interest in issues affecting people of color shown by A16 leaders, "I could not drop my ongoing campaigns and plunge myself into A16. Black and Latino leaders were not even asked to speak at the main events, let alone to really help lead the actions."

Luis Sanchez from Youth Organizing Communities and Los Angeles Direct Action Network (DAN-LA) describes the weak understanding of some white activists of how to create multi-racial solidarity. "If you go to a DAN meeting and ask, 'Why aren't there people of color here?' they just say, 'We should recruit more,' and that's it."

Eric Tang recounts how the Third World Within contingent was constantly greeted with white paternalism. "The best they could say was 'Yes! This is what democracy looks like!' Given how white-dominated the scene was, this was deeply insulting to all of us, as if the Third World people in our group were some sort of mere add-on to a struggle being waged by radical white college kids and the environmental movement."

The JustAct youth delegation and TWW were among the larger organized groups of color at A16. The JustAct delegation included groups from around the country, such as Youth Organizing Communities of Southern California, Student Liberation Action Movement from New York, the Brown Collective of Seattle, the Next Movement of Boston, and the School of Unity and Liberation and Students for Justice of the San Francisco/San Jose area. The TWW contingent was from New York City and included people from the Audre Lourde Center, the Committee Against Anti-Asian Violence, the National Congress for Puerto Rican Rights, Youth Force, the New York Metro Black Radical Congress, and others.

A Rallying Point

Both JustAct and TWW's organizing efforts began with people already active within their own communities who led their respective mobilizations. From there, both organizations invested time, energy, and resources to develop an analysis and organizing workshops that were relevant to communities of color. They also made sure that their respective delegations were provided with resources to get to D.C. and housed adequately.

Once in D.C., Mark Rand of JustAct says, "We tried to create space for leadership of communities of color to be exercised within the larger mobilizations." Organizers Jia Ching Chen and Edget Betru convinced St. James Church in D.C. to house 70 youth of color, and to allow the church building to be used as a meeting place, staging area, and strategizing center throughout A16. Hop Hopkins of the Brown Collective says, "You know, in Seattle, the biggest thing was, 'Where are the other people of color?' Here in D.C., we all know we're right here in the basement of this church. Democracy is what we're doing right here."

Emory Smith of the Nhia Project believes that people of color in D.C. "were able

Eric Drooker

to make a statement to America, to the world, that youth of color are concerned about how globalization is happening."

The welcoming atmosphere at St. James Church was absent elsewhere. Irene Tung, a member of the Young Communist League who helped organize a Brown University contingent to D.C. says, "There was definitely an insider's culture at A16, especially at the convergence spaces. There was a vocabulary and behavior, an assumed cultural commonality, that was somewhat eerie. It seems that the ideals of absence of leadership and 'facilitated chaos'—as they say— function best in a homogenous group."

While this movement continues to grow and mobilize this summer for actions at the Democratic and Republican conventions in Los Angeles and Philadelphia, the racial divide needs to be addressed appropriately if the movement is to have legitimacy and broad, lasting impact. Kim Fellner of the National Organizers Alliance argues that, "At this point, there is a need to reorganize power and control in the movement. To say 'Come in and be included' is different than 'We're turning over co-ownership of this organization.' I think the attitude of ownership instead of mere inclusion is critical."

Denise Gaberman of Paper Tiger TV adds that DAN and other organizations could learn from "talking with" rather than "talking to" people of color. "Why is DAN not asking older people of color for knowledge and experience?" Eric Tang agrees. "The generation of activists of color who participated in the anti-imperialist struggles during the 1960s and 1970s could provide a key link

Colin Rajah

between the past and the present."

Luis Sanchez suggests that this responsibility works both ways. "As people of color, we also have to bring these issues back to our communities. It's not just how white organizers deal with us, but at the same time, internally how we deal with educating our own people." Similarly, Tang says, "Raising criticism from the sidelines doesn't get us anywhere. We have to take this work upon ourselves."

Sadiqa Yancey of the Next Movement argues, "We need to recognize that this is affecting us. We need to recognize that we're not an island in the cities, in the U.S. These types of things are happening to people all across the world and it's unbelievable what they're doing to our people."

Mayday Diary

Jay Griffiths
London Review of Books, *June 2000*

Now that the commotion caused by the anti-capitalist demo on Mayday has died down, it's possible to judge the effect it has had on the future of the 'green' protest movement in this country. I have written about the movement for five years—about the Newbury bypass protest, the Fairmile tunnellers, the street parties. At the start, it was characterised by courage, cheek, idealism and wit. But now a battle is being waged within Reclaim the Streets and other groups over the use of violence at protests, and the belligerent minority isn't interested in these virtues. I have always been—and still am—deeply sympathetic to its aims, but it seems to me that the protest movement is betraying itself, its own best beliefs and its own spirit. This is not the end of modern protest. Not even the beginning of the end. But it is the sad end of the beginning.

The Mayday protest began in Hyde Park with a 'Critical Mass' bike ride. The first cyclist and the first copper on the scene were having an amiable chat. "Yes, we've gone too far with car culture," the officer says. The cyclist gives him a copy of *Evading Standards,* one of two spoof newspapers produced for the day. A 'pagan' samba band arrives, accompanied by people wearing green and gold body paint and masks of ferns, ivy and straw. One woman dressed as an angel gives out 'miniature gardens'—McDonald's cartons filled with grass or cress. People bring bales of hay and biketrailers of cabbage—for once Hyde Park smells like a park rather than a traffic jam. Then the black bloc arrives. They march en masse: black clothes, masks, hoods and balaclavas, like a cloud hiding the sun.

All day, there's the swarming sound of police helicopters: you feel buzzing in your head, while the drumming of the samba band makes the ground vibrate. Parliament Square is overrun with banners: "Global Capitalism Is Not Very Nice", "The Worms Turn." Wheelbarrows trundle, and someone decorated with sunflowers plays a watering-can as a musical intrument. The guerrilla gardening begins and the square is symbolically transformed as supposedly common land is reclaimed. Police guard the Houses of Parliament, fearing protesters may try to get 'inside', but they wouldn't bother.

Chard and rhubarb are planted, with rosemary, lemon balm and hemp. A maypole is put up with a garland of flowers at the top and children hop round it. Someone sand-sculpts a huge-breasted Gaia opposite Big Ben and another makes a six foot-long penis with pubic hair of straw. The statues are decorated. Lord Derby has a spliff in his hand. Jan Smuts is wearing a cycling mask. Churchill has his famous grass mohican and 'murderer' painted on the plinth by the Revolutionary Communist Unionists of Turkey.

RTS, the main orgaization behind the protest, began holding 'stop the streets' parties in 1995. These actions, held first in London, then around the country and around the world, were intended as a form of political street theatre—roads were filled with stilt-walkers, balloons, sound systems and sandpits. Influenced by the Situationists, RTS planned to start sudden and subversive political actions and then to say with a shrug: "It's out of our hands now; the rest is up to you." After the 'Stop the City' protest held on 18 June last year ('J18' as it is usually known), which began as a carnival and ended up as a full-on riot, some associated with RTS felt that the movement had come of age; others thought it was a disaster, alienating a huge number of potential supporters.

The overture to J18 was the ritual trashing of a McDonald's. Then the London International Financial Futures Exchange was stormed, targeted as an embodiment of the globalisation process and the power of capital. Elsewhere in the city, water released from a hydrant erupted in a 40-foot fountain; people sang and danced in the water of the walled-up Walbrook River. The rivers and streams of London, RTS supporters pointed out, are also 'commons': they were once freely accessible for swimming, drinking and fishing, but were then effectively stolen from commoners, first by pollution from factories, later by the enclosure of the rivers by private developers. The Walbrook used regularly to well up and flood the vaults of the Bank of England. On J18, for perhaps the first time in five hundred years, it bubbled up into the sun.

I was halfway up the escalators in the LIFFE building when I was showered by broken glass, as the man above me and the man below smashed every pane they could reach. I was scared. This violence, its defenders would argue, was targeted against a specific institution and designed to draw attention to other acts of violence, the ones we don't see: the systematic 'legal' seizures of land by logging and mining companies; the 'legitimate' forced homelessness of thousands on thousands of people in order to build a dam in Laos; the 'lawful' invasion of U'wa land in Colombia to steal the oil which the U'wa people believe is best left in the earth, as a result of which they have threatened to commit collective suicide.

In April this year, *Time Out* listed the hundred most influential people in London. At number 11 was 'Pete the Anarchist' who "lives in a squat in East London, can muster an army of thousands and organised...J18...which brought the City to a standstill. The anarchists will next flex their muscles on Mayday."

"Anti-City mob plans fresh riot," ran a headline in the *Sunday Telegraph*. Well, here's the 'planning.' RTS meets every Tuesday evening in the back room of a dismal pub behind Euston Station. The front bar is taken over by the Alcohol Liberation Front. In the back room, which is reached by walking through the toilets, the guerrilla gardening is being planned. Dan reads out a 'tatt list': "we need live willow for coppicing, and loads of soil; we need beach balls, performance artists, permaculture specialists and a parachute." There's a hopeful proposal to float a maypole down the Thames. Several people want an 'open mike,' an impromptu 'People's Parliament.' About forty people attend the RTS meetings, the majority of them men. They include environmentalists, social justice campaigners, socialists and anarchists. There are three rather stiff rules: no smoking, no interrupting, no journalists. There's also a language of gestures effective for group communication: hands rolling round each other means 'wrap it up—you've made your point'; hands rapidly waved equals 'strong agreement'; fingers making a P shape signals a proposal, and T stands for a technical point.

Writers and designers put together a spoof newspaper called *Maybe,* based on the free *Metro*. The aim is "to create an inspirational revolutionary piece of our own print media," and this paper is one example of a growing DIY media movement. This group does not admire the mainstream media which, it says, are in the hands of the state and corporations. (Consider, for instance, the BBC's invitation to the chairman of BP Amoco to give a Reith Lecture.) Its opposition to the media gives RTS a headache, however. By not talking to the press it grants journalists "licence to print lies." One protester, Steve, comes to a meeting fresh from court, where the Vestey heir, Mark Brown (accused but found not guilty of organising J18) is on trial. "The press, they were scum today; they were parasites." Outside the court, he says, RTS activists and the press were involved in a scuffle: "One cameraman got his camera smashed." (Sarcastic murmurs of "shame.") Steve adds with (understandable) relish that one of the witnesses for the prosecution, Keiran Sharpe (the head of the police investigation into J18), told the court that a *Sunday Times* article which had claimed that RTS used gas canisters and stun guns was "pure fabrication."

The group is riven with contradictions. It seeks equality but is, by its own admission, warped by machismo. Hating religion, it has a fundamentalist streak, and speaks of a radiant future in the way evangelicals speak of heaven. Arguing for tolerance, it sometimes—for the sake of ideological purity—derides opinions barely half an inch from its own. It preaches diversity but can practise a narrow monoculture of thought. It is both capricious and obsessed with orthodoxy.

At the final meeting before Mayday, things look grim. Two van-loads of police are outside, and a police cameraman films everyone who enters. Being filmed against your will leaves you ill at ease. To go in, you have to run a gauntlet of four officers. I ask one of them why they're here. "We're overpolicing. Zero tolerance. It's Big Brother." He looks at me with something like hatred. The previous day, the police turned up outside a flat and filmed people arriving for an RTS permaculture meeting; people going to the prop-making workshop were stopped and searched.

The most heated quarrels at the meeting are about violence. The *Maybe* collective want to print a statement calling for the action to be peaceful; a minority disagree. The traditional RTS line is that violence is "neither condoned nor condemned." But not to condemn seems to me to condone. The vast majority in RTS believe, as I do, in peaceful direct action; a small and vocal minority support violence against property. (No one condones violence against people, though violence against property inevitably leads to violence against the police.) An aggressive minority can create an aggressive atmosphere; those who favour peaceful means are heckled. To strengthen the argument for peaceful protest, a group has recently been formed called 'Reclaim the Satyagraha,' after Gandhi's policy of passive resistance.

The direct action movement (starting with the anti-roads movement) was one of Britain's most successful exports in the 1990s. RTS sent 'delegates' to the US last summer to prepare for the 'Battle of Seattle.' The tactics of American protest movement—or part of it—seem to be diverging, however. In the US there is an attempt to engage with the public, via the press, and the movement has been able to form broad coalitions (such as the Direct Action Network at Seattle) by asking all activists to agree to a strategy of nonviolence. British direct action appears to be moving the other way: despising the press and therefore ignoring the public, while becoming more open to those who espouse violence. As a result, public support for the movement is rocketing in the States and withering in Britain.

At Seattle, black blocks of anarchists smashed the shopfronts which were not protected by the police. One unsigned leaflet doing the rounds at an RTS meeting in April proposed that anarchists do the same on Mayday. In Seattle, it explains, "the police were completely occupied" so "the black block had a virtually free rein" in the city. There is no doubt, it says, that Parliament Square will be "swamped with cops" so "imagine how police-free the rest of the city could be." In effect, this undermines the guerrilla gardening by implying it could be used as a decoy (though the leaflet's author says he was actually trying to keep the black block away from Trafalgar Square). A number of those at the meeting are worried about violence on the part of the police, who want a "rematch after J18." Some suggest that, because of the trouble last time, many peaceful demonstrators will stay away while the army of the disaffected will come precisely because they want a ruck. An RTS supporter who works with the police outside London conjures a mirror image: "all those volunteering for duty on Mayday are the young and thuggish ones, which is really pissing off the older and nicer ones who think the young ones just want a scuffle."

Some speakers take the view that the Government wouldn't mind a bit of violence on Mayday—the Prevention of Terrorism Bill, which effectively criminalises political dissent, will be passed with much less fuss if protesters are seen to be violent. If the Bill becomes law, the threat of violence against property "for the purpose of advancing a political, religious or ideological cause" will constitute an act of terrorism. In other words, Greenpeace's actions in pulling up GM crops, though supported by 80 per cent of the British public, mean that it could be charged with terrorism. The law makes it an offense to support—even just with words—any political movement abroad which may 'endanger life by damaging property': supporting the ANC would, under the legislation now proposed, have been illegal; support for Ogoni activists in Nigeria or Kurds in Iraq or Turkey could become illegal. At the first RTS meeting I went to, someone asked me: 'So you don't mind being labelled a terrorist, then?' (Clause 18 of the Bill states that it is an offense, punishable by up to five years in prison, not to pass on any information about 'terrorist' activity discovered while acting in a professional capacity.)

Meanwhile, back in Parliament Square, there's a wooden woodcock on a pole. What does it mean? "It's a decoy," grins the polebearer with a wink. It's funny, superficially, in a cops-and-robbers way. In another way, it isn't funny at all. The masked, scarved-up black bloc moves down Whitehall. There are police and press cameras everywhere; three cameramen are beaten up by protesters. One or two of the CCTV cameras have been neutralised, covered with RTS stickers. Protesters hate cameras: CCTV represents the "overhead" powers using "surveillance"—"keeping watch from above." "Don't spectate, participate" is a key RTS motto.

The carnival atmosphere is on the turn: the masks of ivy and ferns are rare in the crowd; the masks of the black block are beginning to prevail. Masks are central to carnival, offering the liberation of anonymity. At the M41 street party a gigantic stilt-walker wearing a ballgown and playing the bagpipes was masking a Kanga drill under her voluminous skirts. It was being used to dig up the tarmac and plant a symbolic tree. Here, though, the masks are used to very different effect; black hoods and balaclavas are the uniform of the militia mentality.

The crowd moves past the gates of Downing Street and the Cenotaph, which—to the consternation of some RTS activists—is daubed and used as a urinal. Then on to a McDonald's. To general astonishment, it is unprotected; there it stands, a red (and yellow) rag to an anti-capitalist bull. There is barely a pause before someone chucks the first rock and everyone piles in: windows are smashed, chairs flung out, golden arches attacked. You could have predicted this after J18: it's something of a tradition. McDonald's and the police must have seen this coming. Missiles thrown at the police hit press and protesters. With 5,500 officers on the streets, and another 9,000 on standby, the police seal off Parliament Square and Trafalgar Square. Some demonstrators are trapped in Trafalgar Square for three hours, but the Parliament Square crowd are luckier, moving off en masse to Kennington Park. A group of protesters smashes a souvenir shop, a stationers, a mobile phone shop and several parked cars.

Kennington Park at the end of Mayday: a game of protester-football on one side and a line of riot police on horseback on the other. Meanwhile on the street outside, riot police pointlessly charge at the park railings. Behind the railings, protesters pointlessly chuck bottles and stones at the police. For a moment I think I'm going to get hit. A rock whizzes past and splinters on the ground by my feet. A protester walks by eating a bag of chips; a missile scores a direct hit on the chips and they explode out of his hands. A young girl in pagan robes with streams of long brown hair and a sash saying "PEACE" walks out into no-man's-land, and the rain of missiles slows. A glam-puss in pink steps out, faces the protesters and pulls up her blouse. All missiles cease. Only breasts can do that.

While the lovers and the football players enjoy themselves, the aimless ritual of police versus protesters continues. Who is there, ripping up tarmac and trees from the park, masked but recognisable? Activists from Earth First!—a body dedicated to protecting the environment—are chucking rocks at the police "for fun" (their words). And who else is there, shoulder to shoulder with the black bloc, throwing rocks at the police? The National Front.

All in all, a few nihilists wreck a few shops and a few cars. The media predictably overreacts. The *Express*'s headline is "May Day mayhem: Terror on the Streets." A *Telegraph* editorial complains that "some of those who perpetrated the worst violence were not even British subjects." The *Daily Sport* talks of "foreign rioters bussed in to wreck Britain." The *Daily Mail* claims that one "furious magistrate" discovered that nine of the thirteen men he remanded into custody were born abroad. In all the reports, violence is privileged, as ever. Five days after Mayday, 30,000 took part in a rally for the legalisation of cannabis: there was no violence and no press coverage.

At road protests over the past five years, activists have sought local support and won national backing. "We shall fight them in the beeches" read one banner unfurled from the treetops, and some war veterans gave their campaign medals to the tree protesters of Newbury in the belief that they were fighting for the same things. The characteristics the war veterans saw in the road protesters—many of whom, incidentally, had been in the Army themselves—are still present in the protest movement: a love of freedom and an identification with the underdog. Some of the people from Newbury who received campaign medals were on the RTS protest, but it also involved people who were more interested in violence than principle—a split which has, I suppose, emerged in many protest movements. During yet another quarrel about violence at one RTS meeting Rebecca intervened: "Let's stop arguing about that," she said. "Let's talk about guerrilla gardening, that's what this whole action is about." A sly voice cut in: "Oh no, it's not." The RTS let an atmosphere develop in which violence was surreptitiously encouraged and then refused to condemn that violence. Nobody had to take responsibility for it.

On Mayday, I recognise one of the famous tunnellers, once a green idealist, fantastically chirpy and eager to talk to anyone who would listen. Now, all in black, hooded and scarved-up, she seems to recognise me, but she definitely doesn't want to talk.

The Battle of Philadelphia

David Lindorff
In These Times, *September 4, 2000*

The "Battle of Philadelphia" got off to a much tamer start than the confrontations between demonstrators and police in Seattle last November and in
Washington in April, but it was clear from the beginning that things would get
nasty. And by August 1, midway through a week of planned protests, they did.

Police had been generally easy-going during earlier demonstrations over
the weekend. But on July 31, when the Kensington Welfare Rights Union led a
non-permitted march of several thousand people down the length of South Broad
Street to the First Union Center, the site of the GOP convention, the mood was
clearly different. And by the next day's demonstrations, things had become
downright confrontational. As opponents of the death penalty and supporters of
Pennsylvania Death Row inmate Mumia Abu-Jamal took to the streets that day
trying to block the flow of traffic between the downtown hotel area and the South
Philadelphia site of the convention, the police were out in force, and they weren't
smiling.

Thousands of demonstrators, some coordinated through a loose network of
observers equipped with cell phones, adopted hit-and-run tactics throughout the
afternoon and evening, blocking intersections with their bodies. The heavily
armed police, their numbers bolstered by reinforcements from the state police,
highway patrol and national parks police force, responded with shows of force.
They pushed demonstrators off the street, pressing forward behind teams of bike
cops.

Relations between police and the minority community are strained in this
racially segregated city, especially over the case of Abu-Jamal. On Death Row
since 1982 when he was convicted of murdering Daniel Faulkner, a white police
officer, this African-American journalist and former Black Panther awaits the
decision of a federal judge on whether to hold a hearing to consider his habeas
corpus appeal for a new trial. The Pennsylvania Fraternal Order of Police has
been actively lobbying for years for Abu-Jamal's death, and for many

Philadelphia officers the issue is personal. On the other side, a broad coalition of activists, black and white, has been working for years to keep Abu-Jamal's case in the international spotlight.

Given this background, the sense of confrontation at the August 1 demonstration was palpable, as when two bicycle cops angrily shoved their way through a crowd burning an American flag on the street and doused the flames with their bottles of spring water. For the most part, the police exercised restraint during arrests, as dozens of street-blocking demonstrators locked arms and went limp, waiting to be arrested and dragged to waiting sheriff's busses. Nearly 300 people were arrested.

But sometimes that restraint collapsed, as when two cops grabbed one young demonstrator who was arguing with a police officer on horseback during a sweep of one intersection. The demonstrator, who was standing on the curb where he was not obstructing traffic or violating an order to disperse, was yanked into the street and thrown face down onto the pavement, where five police officers jumped on him, wrenching his arms behind his back while his head was pressed into the macadam by one officer's knee. His face bloodied, he was led off to a wagon, while other protesters witnessing the incident shouted, "He didn't do anything!" Meanwhile, the police suffered casualties of their own, with several needing medical treatment for injuries, and some thirty police cruisers exhibiting spray paint damage, smashed windshields and slashed tires.

The Philadelphia District Attorney's office has been asking for and getting extremely high bail set for leading activists, and the court system has been dragging its feet on processing and releasing the over 400 people arrested during the demonstrations. Kate Sorensen of Philadelphia Direct Action Group has had bail set at $1 million, as has John Sellers of the Ruckus Society, in what local activists are saying is a clear example of preventative detention. Meanwhile, Police Chief John Timoney is calling for a U.S. Justice Department investigation to prosecute activists under RICO anti-racketeering laws.

Bail for some other protesters, particularly those who are protesting their arrests by refusing to provide their names or addresses, is reportedly being set at between $15,000 and $450,000. "To my knowledge, bail has never been set so high for misdemeanor charges in the history of this country," say Ron McGuire, an attorney working with R2K Legal. "I consider this a civil rights catastrophe of the first order."

Earlier on August 1, the police had gone to a warehouse rented by activists in West Philadelphia for use as a workshop to construct protest banners and puppets. After surrounding the building, the police demanded entry, claiming they had received reports of weapons inside. There was a temporary stand-off as the 70 or so activists inside refused to unlock the doors, and the nearly 100 police outside waited for the department to obtain a search warrant from a local judge.

Once armed with the search warrant, the police entered the building, arresting most of those inside. They claimed to find PVC piping and chains like those used by demonstrators to link their arms and make removal from intersections more difficult, but there were reportedly no signs of the alleged weapons used to justify the raid. Two city councilmen who raced to the scene denounced the police raid, which was similar to an effort before the start of the convention to use fire-code violation claims to shut down demonstration headquarters (a tactic also used to disrupt the April protests in Washington). Stefan Presser, legal director of the Philadelphia chapter of the ACLU, announced plans to file a civil rights lawsuit against the city for the police raid on the puppet-makers, which he said was a clear case of harassment of legitimate protesters.

Philadelphia authorities went to great lengths to try to minimize public disorder and protest during the GOP convention. This was seen as a great opportunity for the city, just recovering from a brush with bankruptcy, to show itself off to other potential convention hosts. Until the last minute, municipal authorities were denying march and rally permits to any organization, and were trying to force all protesters to confine their activities to a small fenced-in park out of sight of the convention center.

Nearly all major protest groups rejected this plan to confine their activities to a small "protest pit," and several, including Unity 2000, the main protest coalition, had threatened to sue, with backing from the ACLU. Unity 2000 eventually was granted a permit for a march on July 30, the eve of the convention. The event went smoothly, with some 10,000 marchers, most in a festive mood, moving under a bright sun along the broad boulevard past the city's museum row. The entire way, the march was lined with riot-ready police, but the mood that day was mellow even among the cops, and there were few incidents.

The following day, however, was more tense, as several thousand activists assembled without a permit for the KWRU march. As their numbers swelled and would-be marchers spilled into the street around City Hall, police kept pressing them back toward the sidewalk and insisting there would be no march. Then, in a brilliant tactical move, the organizers suddenly pulled a rope across the street, blocking all traffic, and an advance contingent of small children and disabled people in wheelchairs swept into the suddenly cleared intersection. The police, faced with the option of attacking the kids and the handicapped or of falling back, and under the glare of television klieg lights, decided to retreat. Other marchers fell into line, and the nonpermitted march was underway.

At several points along the route, police tried to stop the marchers or turn them away from Broad Street, the city's main north-south artery. But having backed down the first time, they were unable to stop the marchers' forward momentum. The march continued for the length of the street to the convention center, where police finally succeeded in turning the line into the FDR Center— the designated protest area for the convention. "This was a big victory," crowed Jonathan Blazes, legal adviser to KWRU. "We didn't know what to expect. The city didn't want this march—which is to call attention to the plight of the city's and the nation's poor and homeless—to happen, and we were able to make it happen. The police saw the number of people involved, and they finally made the sensible decision to allow it."

The reaction of locals to the escalating demonstrations was mixed, with commuters caught in the traffic tie-ups expressing anger and frustration at the demonstrators, while many pedestrian bystanders offered support. The local and national media were out in force to cover the protests—sometimes reporters, camera crews and photographers outnumbered protesters—but the tone of the reporting was decidedly pro-police.

This bias was particularly evident at local CBS affiliate WKYW Channel 3, which bragged about being first with the reports of the street battles between

David Lindorff

police and demonstrators on August 1. The news report that evening focused entirely on injuries to police and damage to police equipment. Police officials were interviewed, but no demonstrators were asked to explain their issues or actions. The one segment showing a protester being arrested, which was accompanied by visuals of the arrest taken from a helicopter, actually showed the demonstrator shouting at a policeman before he was grabbed by two other cops. "He was shaking his finger at a mounted policeman," the anchor intoned gravely, failing to comment that such an action is hardly a crime.

It remains to be seen what impact these rallies, marches and more militant protest actions in Philadelphia will have. The number of demonstrators was considerably smaller than at the earlier protests in Seattle and Washington, D.C. The biggest protest this time was the Unity 2000 march, which probably had no more than 10,000 participants (even though rally organizers put the total at under 25,000). Unlike the WTO in Seattle or the World Bank and IMF in D.C., both clear targets of protest, the focus in Philadelphia was not so obvious. Unity 2000 organizers stressed early on that theirs was not an anti-Republican demonstration, but rather was aimed at a broad range of issues, from arms spending and government corruption to environmental protection and workers rights. Thus it was little surprise that not far from a contingent of marchers from the Socialist Workers Party was a group of veterans from the defeated South Vietnamese Army.

If the protests in Philadelphia showed anything, it was that even with considerable advance planning, aggressive surveillance, overwhelming numbers and the arrest of more than 400 protesters, the police cannot expect to keep traffic flowing in the face of dedicated demonstrators willing to face arrest.

Throwing Away the Key

David Lindorff
In These Times, *September 18, 2000*
(updated by the author January 2001)

Police may have shown some restraint during several days of increasingly confrontational protests at the Republican National Convention, but the birthplace of American democracy has been looking increasingly authoritarian and hostile to the Bill of Rights.

At the urging of both Police Chief John Timoney and newly elected Mayor John Street, a former black activist turned establishment pol, city prosecutors sought and obtained bail as high as $1 million for people who they claimed were protest leaders, though the charges were mostly misdemeanors, not felonies. Timoney has been calling for federal prosecutors to file federal racketeering charges against the leaders of groups like the Ruckus Society, on the grounds that they were allegedly engaged in an interstate conspiracy to cause disruption and criminal mischief.

But if there was any interstate conspiracy, activists say it was among officials trying to prevent protesters in Philadelphia from getting to Los Angeles in time for the Democratic Convention two weeks later. Indeed, there appeared to be a deliberate slowing of the arraignment process in Philadelphia, leaving several hundred arrested protesters to languish in city jails and police lock-ups until well past the end of the Republican Convention and in some cases right into the start of the new Bush administration in 2001.

Official conspiracy or not, the police strategy during the protests was clearly to go after the protest leaders, who were reportedly followed by undercover officers and grabbed off the street when they talked on cellular phones, which were then declared devices of a criminal conspiracy. In a particularly egregious example, on August 1 police arrested seventy people at a warehouse where protest puppets were being made. At the time, police claimed they had received reports of weapons being stored at the site; despite a thorough search of the building, none were found. The arrests went ahead anyway, along with the destruction and confiscation of the puppets.

A team of activist lawyers called the R2K network, which includes members of the Philadelphia chapter of the National Lawyers Guild, has been representing many of those arrested. In a statement, the guild said: "The response of the city and courts of Philadelphia to protests seems a blatant attempt to silence dissent and seriously curtail First, Fifth and Eighth Amendment rights." By January 2001 all the cases against the puppeteers had been dismissed by the courts for lack of evidence, as were most of the other arrests made during the convention period, only a few ever went to trial.

While dozens of arrested demonstrators have deliberately made trouble in jail by refusing to provide their names and addresses (and in some cases have removed all of their clothes to make identification from surveillance photos more difficult), released prisoners have also charged that police and jailers have brutalized some prisoners and denied others access to lawyers. "I saw one man hogtied and dragged down the cell block," says Dan Murphy, twenty-six, who spent seven days in jail after being arrested on August 1 and charged with obstruction of traffic and disorderly conduct. "I also saw a hunger striker who passed out and was twitching on the floor, and they left him without treatment for an hour and a half. Then he was just given smelling salts. I also saw a lot of people with injuries—black eyes, cuts, welts."

By August 7, a week after arrests began, some judges were reducing the high bail against protest leaders to more reasonable levels. After prosecutors conceded that Terrence McGuckin, a Philadelphia community organizer who police had claimed was a leader of the protest actions, was not facing any charges for violent actions, a judge reduced his bail from $500,000 to $100,000, allowing him to get out of jail with the posting of a $10,000 bond.

By August 14, all those arrested during the convention protests reportedly had been arraigned, and most already had been released on bail. The 20 people who remained in jail—all hard-core activists who had refused to divulge their names—were finally released on August 17. In a remarkable show of solidarity, so far none of the hundreds of arrested protesters has copped a guilty plea and accepted a fine. "Everyone so far plans to go to trial and to demand a trial by jury," says Cris Hermes of R2K. "That should sure tie up the court system."

The harsh actions of police and prosecutors have led to some discord in the progressive legal community, with some R2K lawyers criticizing the Philadelphia chapter of the American Civil Liberties Union. ACLU legal director Stefan Pressler was initially outspoken in his praise of the police for their handling of the protests, saying as late as August 7 that they had shown "enormous restraint" and "smart tactics" and arguing that reports of jail abuses were "highly unlikely."

But by the end of the week following the convention, after mounting evidence of jailhouse abuses, the ACLU joined the Lawyers Guild and the R2K legal collective to prepare to file lawsuits against the city. Plans are to bring charges for civil rights violations in the arrest of the puppet makers, police brutality during the arrest and detention of demonstrators, and harassment for the arrest of clearly identified medics.

Prague 2000: The People's Battle

Boris Kagarlitsky

- *Do not wear your Annual Meetings ID badge in public.*
- *Be prepared to display your Annual Meetings ID badge at police check points or when entering the Prague Conference Centre (PCC), and wear it at all times in the PCC and at official Annual Meetings events.*
- *Do not take taxis on the street—ask the hotel or restaurant to call one for you.*
- *Avoid demonstration sites*
- *Leave in the opposite direction if one is encountered.*
- *Do not engage in debates with demonstrators*
- *Take leaflets or brochures without comment.*
- *If obstructed by demonstrators, do not try to force your way through, seek help from the nearest police officer.*
- *You are advised not to display jewelry, or wear ostentatious clothing such as furs.*

—From a memorandum to participants in the meeting of the World Bank and the International Monetary Fund.

September 20 Ordinary Prague citizens have been issued instructions that recall warnings of a nuclear attack. The police have put leaflets in people's letter-boxes appealing to everyone not to go out onto the street, and if possible, to leave the city altogether for the period of the summit. School holidays have been extended. Meanwhile, radical left groups have attached posters to the walls of buildings, calling on Prague residents to come into the streets, and in this way to express their disagreement with the people who are "violating our social rights and freedoms."

The truth is that in Prague, an opponent of the IMF and a critic of capitalism who decides to join in the demonstrations faces an unexpected problem— there are too many demonstrations and other actions. Each group has come up

Tim Russo

with its own initiative. Left intellectuals have refused to go to communist meetings, and non-government organizations have vied with one another. The antifascists for the most part have held independent actions, without informing anyone else. The humanists have been unwilling to collaborate with anyone either.

September 21 The more established NGOs are conducting their seminars under the aegis of the group Bankwatch, which, as its name indicates, monitors the actions of the international banks. Some of the participants in these deliberations are turning up in ties. People constantly stress their professionalism, and call for discussions with the heads of the IMF and the World Bank. More radical groups have united around the Initiative Against Economic Globalisation. Here the atmosphere is quite different, with men in torn jeans and women with tattoos. Each group regards the other ironically.

Nevertheless, they stress: we have common goals, and we are not going to quarrel. There are reports that in response to the actions of the left and of the "informals," a demonstration has been called by the ultra-right. Quite spontaneously, a new dominant idea is beginning to take hold of the left-wing youth, an idea formulated in the simple slogan "Beat up the skinheads!"

Putting this into practice would not be particularly hard, considering the huge numerical superiority of the left, strengthened by reinforcements in the form of German anarchists, for whom the week would be wasted if there were no fights with fascists. Fortunately, the police have kept the demonstrations of the left and of the nationalists far enough apart to avoid street fighting. A few fascists have nevertheless been beaten up.

September 22 Afternoon: We are received by World Bank director James Wolfensohn. He reminds me of Gorbachev. The same goodwill, the same desire for dialogue, and the same helplessness when it comes to the practical question of carrying out reforms.

The Battle of Seattle

Even his nickname—Wolfie—is similar. A wonderful man, no doubt, with whom to go to the opera or dine.

Wolfie reassures the representatives of civil society, and tries to justify himself. As proof of the changed character of the bank, he cites what seems to him to be a very convincing figure. Earlier, the bank had two employees working on the problems of civil society: now there are several dozen. New departments and new posts have been created.

The news of a massive growth in the bureaucracy fails to arouse the representatives of civil society. "Give us a chance," Wolfensohn repeats. I begin to feel sorry for him.

Everyday political life was terribly like that in Moscow in the late 1980s. Informal organisations, perestroika. . . The same stormy meetings, the queues for the microphone, the cacophony of demands behind which lies a general discontent, understood and formulated in different ways, with the way life is organised. And the same helpless promises from the authorities, who already understand that carrying on as before is impossible, but who cannot manage anything new. The international financial institutions are just as unreformed as the Soviet bureaucracy. And just like the Soviet party system when it felt the challenge of the times and of society, they are trying somehow or other to reform themselves. Everyone knows how perestroika ended in the Soviet Union. It is quite possible that for the IMF and the World Bank, the consequences of reform will be just as dismal. And even fewer people will regret this than mourn for the USSR.

September 23 09:00: I am travelling across the city by tram. At 11 o'clock president Havel is to lead a discussion in the castle between participants in the movement and the heads of the IMF. The city is still almost empty. But sometimes groups of young people are to be seen on the streets, their appearance leaving not the slightest doubt as to why they are here. T-shirts with pictures of Che Guevara, and threadbare jeans. Closer to the centre of town, little herds of confused tourists are visible. Making their way through the streets are cavalcades of Audi cars, protected by police cars with flashing lights; inside the Audis are the conference delegates. Meanwhile, the police are taking up their positions. Helicopters circle over the city. Blue uniforms are everywhere. On the flanks of many of the uniforms I notice sickeningly familiar canvas bags containing gas masks, the same as used to be given to us in school during elementary military training exercises. The gas masks have evidently not been used since 1989. The thought strikes me: they are firing off "cherry" gas. It feels as though a war is about to break out.

The sun has emerged, the embellishments on the medieval spires have begun to shine, and the Charles Bridge lies revealed in all its loveliness. Prague during these days is so beautiful you feel like crying.

I ask a middle-aged policeman the way. He starts speaking Russian cheerfully enough, but immediately apologises. He doesn't know a short route to the castle. He and the other police standing there have been brought in from Moravia. Police have been brought from the whole country, and the armed forces have been put on alert.

I am now in the castle. There is an unexpected call on my mobile phone; my wife in Moscow is worried. I explain that there is no reason to be concerned. In my pocket I have a card identifying me as a participant in the meeting of the IMF and the World Bank, together with an invitation from Havel. On the cover of my passport the police have stuck a special hologram affirming my loyalty. None of this strikes her as especially convincing. "They don't hit you in the passport, they hit you in the face."

The meeting with Havel recalls the last talks before the outbreak of armed hostilities. The sides are still meeting for negotiations, although the troops are already taking up their positions.

We go up to the castle. There are numerous stops for document checks, and for checks with metal detectors. Soldiers of the presidential guard are in booths, standing just as in London, only their bearing isn't as erect, their uniforms don't fit especially well, and to judge by everything, they're not particularly well fed. In a medieval hall built for ball games, about a hundred representatives of NGOs are assembling, together with a similar number of functionaries of international financial organizations. And television cameras, television cameras...

Now Havel arrives. In front of the podium, a small military band has appeared. Guards in red uniforms start playing something like the overture to a Viennese operetta, but an unshaven saxophonist strikes up as well. For several minutes the theme of power and the theme of discontent alternate, but then the guards and the dissident saxophonist begin to play in unison, and all the instruments merge into an optimistic coda. This is evidently meant to reflect Havel's idea of the reconciliation of the authorities and the dissidents.

The reconciliation does not happen.

The first address is from Katarina Lizhkova, speaking in the name of the demonstrators gathering on the streets. A striking young woman from Brno, she speaks impeccable English. "There will not be any dialogue. You talk about dialogue, but the police have already prepared water cannon and tear gas. Thousands of people have been illegally held up at the border, and here in Prague thousands more are being subjected to police persecution simply because they want to exercise their legal right to protest. But we will not stop until the anti-democratic institutions of the financial oligarchy are abolished." The left side of the hall applauds, while the right maintains a gloomy silence.

Walden Bello, one of the movement's most popular ideologues, takes the microphone. "The international financial institutions are a danger. They aren't answerable to anyone. Don't believe what they say. They talk of fighting against corruption, but they supported Yeltsin in Russia! They talk about democracy, but they gave money to the dictator Suharto in Indonesia.

"Now that you've lost your authority, you start talking about social justice. But the words and the deeds part company. If you want changes, then cancel the debts of Russia, cancel the debts of Indonesia. You've made your loans conditional on policies that have brought these countries to ruin and collapse. The programs that are being implemented under the dictates of the IMF almost invariably fail. What right do you now have to demand this money back?" The leftists applaud, while the rightists keep silent.

Trevor Manuel, a one-time communist and revolutionary, and now South African finance minister, objects to Bello: "Without the international financial institutions, things would be even worse for poor countries." The right-wingers applaud. Someone among the leftists mutters: "Traitor!"

In the hall the atmosphere of confrontation is even stronger than on the street. Encountering a hostile audience, Wolfie has become completely self-effacing. Crushed, he hangs his head, again trying to justify himself. By contrast, new IMF director Koler holds forth aggressively. "I have spoken with Third World leaders, and they have had a mass of questions, but no one has demanded that the fund be dissolved. On the contrary, they want to work with us!" "You mean they want to thieve together," mutters the British journalist Alex Kallinikos, who is sitting next to me.

George Soros takes the stand, and unexpectedly, begins to expound the general positions of Marxism on the nature of the capitalist system. Then, just as unexpectedly, he declares:

"So long as the rules are as they are, we are going to play by these rules. You should not expect anything else from us financiers. I don't want to lose."

He finishes up with an appeal for reform of the system, while there is still time.

Bello once again flings himself on Koler. "Why are you unwilling to reorganise the administration of the IMF? The structure is completely undemocratic. Where are your promised reforms?" Koler replies that the fund is making efforts, and is improving its work.

"That's not a reply," Bello shouts. "I asked a concrete question. You are simply not willing to reorganise the system of administration! So what is there for us to discuss with you?"

Havel thanks all the participants in the dialogue. The two sides go their separate ways.

14:00: The first demonstrations begin. We go to look at the communists. There are not especially many people, and the speeches are dull. Surrounding the platform is a solid bank of grey heads.

Further along, young Trotskyists, anarchists, Greeks and Kurds are gathering and talking. I discover two American students from Madison. A year and a half ago I delivered a lecture to them. What are they doing at a communist meeting? "This is a warm-up. Like a bad rock group before a good concert. You have to start with something."

September 24 14:00: A seminar on problems of globalisation, conducted by the IAEG. The hall is full of a polyglot crowd. The only ones missing are Russians—no "suspicious elements" have been granted visas. The average age in the auditorium is about 25. Someone has come with a baby. People laugh, applaud, come out to the microphone and make wordy declarations. The chairperson grows nervous. "Let's have fewer declarations and more discussion. We have to show the gentlemen from the establishment an example of real democracy!"

A small group of young women from Latvia have come, and sit in a corner on the floor. They chew gum, speaking a mixture of Russian and Latvian, and enthusiastically applaud the speeches on the tyranny of the transnational corporations. Various Americans arrive late; they are coming directly from the airport, some with rucksacks and bags. They exchange remarks—who was allowed in, who was taken from the plane. It turns out that the FBI gave the Czech authorities "blacklists" of citizens of its own country who, it recommended, should not be allowed to get to Prague.

The word *nevyezdnye*—in Soviet times, people denied the right to travel abroad—flashes through my head.

A report arrives saying that a further thousand or so people have been held up at the border by the Czech authorities. Bello interrupts his speech; he is backed up by Kallinikos: "Eleven years ago in Prague, the people came out onto the streets demanding freedom of movement, and at that time President Havel was on our side. Now his police are illegally closing the border!"

It is announced that a spontaneous demonstration against the illegal actions of the police is under way at the Interior Ministry. But the protesters are few: two hundred at most. The chairperson of the meeting appeals to everyone who has nothing else to do to join the picket line. With a clatter of chairs, people from the back rows get up and head for the exit. Fortunately, I have already delivered my speech.

On the border, it is obvious, total confusion reigns. Some people are being held up, while whole columns of others are getting through without the slightest hindrance. The border guards are searching each car thoroughly, rummaging in suitcases and leafing through printed material.

Queues have appeared, and the honest burgers have got stuck in them. Meanwhile, the demonstrations are continuing. Today about two thousand people form a living chain in support of Jubilee 2000, a movement demanding the writing off of the debts of the Third World and the former communist countries. A similar number of people gather for a meeting of the Humanist Alliance. The main events, however, are expected on Tuesday, when a protest march is due to take place. Reports come through that the march has been partially banned. Some districts of the city are closed to the demonstrators. Lawyers for the protesters argue that the ban is illegal. But this is no longer the main thing. The general mood has taken on a definite shape: we know that we will go there anyway, and that no one will stop us.

Walden Bello is like Lenin in October. Since the demonstrations in Seattle, he has been transformed from an academic into a real leader. Now he is on the platform. "Everything is decided on the streets! All available resources must be mobilised. We need living strength, you understand, everything depends on living strength! We need bodies!"

"Living strength" continues to arrive. Everywhere there are groups of young people, speaking in every imaginable language from Hungarian to Basque. The language of international communication is, of course, the same as among the bankers—English. Alongside the Lidensky Bridge is the Convergence Centre, the organisational headquarters for the march and the workshop where placards and effigies are made. Here as well, instruction sessions are held, maps of Prague are distributed, and suggestions are made as to where people should go in order to find places to stay. This is important, since the youth hostels are full to bursting. People are told how to give first aid to the wounded, and what to do if they are affected by tear gas. When the work ends an improvised concert begins. Along with the activists, rock groups are arriving, and street theatre troupes from throughout Europe. Elsewhere, a "Festival of Resistance" is also underway. Here about a dozen groups from the Czech Republic, Holland, Britain and Italy are playing.

Dusk has already fallen, and people are still coming, in jeans and carrying rucksacks. Some are carrying placards. A group of young Germans are seated directly on the grass next to the tram stop, and are discussing something. The Swedes have already held an instruction session. There were several hundred of them, and they were discussing how to act in the case of a clash with police, how to act if arrested, and where to phone in Stockholm, since every third one of them has a mobile telephone. One woman is returning to Sweden; on Tuesday she will have to spend the whole day at home by the telephone.

The tension is growing. The feeling is like before a battle. Everyone is waiting for reinforcements. News reaches the "Standart" and the Convergence Centre: three hundred Austrians are already on the way, and will arrive tomorrow. It is unclear where the Hungarians are; they are expected any minute. The Slovaks have already arrived, but fewer of them than were expected. The Spaniards and Greeks are due to come on special trains.

The advance guard of the Italian contingent appears on the Charles Bridge. More than a thousand of them have come. Four people were not admitted. The rest sat at the border for several hours, demanding that their comrades be admitted, before deciding in the end to carry on to Prague. Now the most active of them, a hundred or so people, are sitting directly on the Charles Bridge, singing "Bandiera Rossa" and partisan songs from the Second World War. On the bridge, activists of the protest movement are mingling with people in respectable suits who have come for the IMF meeting. Everyone wants to feast their eyes on Prague.

September 25 In the Standart, the seminars and discussions are continuing. The World Bank and the IMF are also holding their meetings in the Congress Centre. The two sides, of course, are behaving quite differently; the officials of the World Bank are still trying to justify themselves, meeting with representatives of the non-government organisations, promising to investigate matters and to put them in order. The IMF ignores the protests. Larry Sommers, the US treasury chief, has already warned the heads of the World Bank that he will not permit any serious concessions to the developing countries or to critics of the system.

By Monday evening, around 8,000 activists from various countries are in Prague. Most of the Czechs are coming from Brno; they appear at the last moment. The police are preparing to meet the demonstrators on the bridge that leads to Visegrad, where the Conference Centre is located. In the neighbourhoods nearby, residents are being asked to remove their cars from the streets. The ambulances and hospitals are preparing to receive casualties. The schools have already been shut for a week. In all, 11,000 police and riot troops have been mobilised. Around 12-15,000 demonstrators are expected.

In the Convergence Centre, a battle plan is worked out. When the demonstrators approach the bridge, they will split into three columns. One will go onto the bridge, while the two others will try to outflank the police on the sides. One of the Britons observes that for such a manoeuvre, you cannot do without cavalry.

The column going onto the bridge is not supposed to get into a fight with the police; its job is only to stand and chant slogans. The Italians advance; this deci-

Boris Kagarlitsky

sion does not suit them. "We're going to force our way across the bridge," they declare. "We're not here to pay compliments to the police." The Italians were not in Seattle (save the four detained at the border) and they want to show what they're capable of. A few French people of the older generation share their experience, explaining how in Paris in 1968 they built barricades. There is just one question: in those days demonstrators had cobblestones to use for these purposes, but what are you supposed to do with asphalt?

The leaders of the groups are given maps of the city with the traffic routes marked on them. On the reverse side, a brief plan of action is printed in several languages. The proposal is that irrespective of the outcome of the fight at Visegrad, in the evening the protesters will blockade the opera, where the bankers and bureaucrats will be assembling. First the protesters will try to stop them getting into the hall, and if they do get in, then not to let them out again until morning. Other groups go to the expensive hotels where the delegates have installed themselves, and will keep up a barrage of noise the whole night. Around a dozen rock groups and bands will take part in the action.

Sleepless nights are nothing new for the protesters. I see Martin Brabec, one of the ideologues of the IAEG. He looks totally exhausted, but happy. "Martin, do you ever sleep?" "About three hours a night."

There is to be a meeting at 9 o'clock. After the meeting, at 11 o'clock, the march on Visegrad will begin.

September 26 08:00: At the entrance to the metro there are police patrols. Over the radio comes the announcement that Visegrad metro station is closed.

08:30: I have breakfast with Petr Uhl, an old friend from the dissident movement of the '80s. Petr himself is not going to the demonstration, but his daughter has already set off for Peace Square, where the participants are assembling. His apartment in the centre of Prague is like the yard of an inn. Staying with him have been members of the French movement ATTAC, which calls for new rules for international finance and for the defense of debtor countries. Last night Petr was host to a group of German teenagers—their hair green, rings in their noses, ears and lips. Catherine Samary, who teaches economics in Paris, laments: "In one night, these kids ate everything in the fridge!"

09:00: We are on Peace Square. The area where the protesters are gathering in front of a church is like a Tower of Babel. About ten thousand people are speaking all the languages of Europe at once. Turks, Greeks, Kurds, Spaniards and Basques are standing next to one another. A huge balloon, symbolising the IMF, rolls over the crowd, and everyone can push it. Among the crowd are comic effigies and revolutionary placards. From time to time new columns arrive, often accompanied by small bands or musical groups. Here there are Scandinavians, and behind them, Britons and Spaniards. In the back rows are a dozen Dutch people in white coats painted with pictures of a huge tomato—the symbol of the Socialist Party. Trade union activists from northern Europe carry their banners, looking like the icons carried in old-time church processions. The Italian column, with its banners unfurled, surges onto the square. Heading the column is a minibus, and behind it are members of the Ya Basta! movement, which has already distinguished itself by breaking up several international gatherings. The Italians have a menacing air. All of them are wearing helmets, are carrying shields, and are dressed in white coats of the type worn by chemical clean-up squads. Some are wearing homemade body armour of fibreglass or cardboard. And of course, there are protective masks, in some cases gas masks. The people on the square applaud them.

11:00: The action gets under way. On the plan, the three columns are marked in different colours—blue, yellow and pink. The strangest of the columns is the pink one. Here there are very few political placards, and party banners or ideological symbols are totally absent. Many participants are dressed in pink, and have even painted their faces pink. In place of banners, there are pink balloons. In the middle of the column is a pink cardboard tank, with flowers sticking out of its make-believe guns.

On the recommendations of the police, the shops and cafes along the route to be taken by the column are closed. I recall a line from the poet Blok: "Fasten the shutters, now there is going to be looting!" For a while I march with the pink column, but then I decide to join the yellow column, which has the menacing-looking Italians at its head. In the yellow column are around three hundred Hungarians, French, Americans and Turks. From time to time someone encounters a friend, and rushes to embrace them. We swap stories with Hungarian friends, and hear the latest news from New York. Here there are more journalists than anyone else. They are following the Italians, not concealing the fact that they are hoping to see and to photograph clashes with the police. I have other motives: I prefer the yellow column because here it is obviously safer. No surprises are expected, and no one will attack us until the approach to the bridge. In the two other columns it is still not clear what might happen.

The final turning before the bridge: the column stops. From a loudspeaker on the Italian minibus there are orders and instructions; the main thing is not to do anything without coordinating it with the organisers. The orders are given in Italian, then repeated in English, Spanish, Czech and French. Drums begin beating. A group of people in blue protective jackets appears, wearing armbands with the red cross. Many demonstrators don gasmasks. Someone communicates with the other columns over a mobile phone, trying to work out what is happening with them. We approach the bridge.

The bridge has been blockaded by the police in a highly effective fashion. Behind metal barriers stands a front rank of police, all in body armour, with shields and clubs. The most modern equipment has been got ready especially for this encounter, to the order of American specialists. The feeling arises that what we are faced with is perhaps a troop of medieval samurai warriors, perhaps several dozen Darth Vaders.

Behind the backs of the first rank of police, there are armoured personnel carriers! The bridge is totally blocked, but to judge from everything, not even armoured vehicles seemed to the police commanders to be enough. Behind the APCs, along the whole length of the bridge, police cars, trucks and minibuses are parked bumper-to-bumper. There is no possibility of getting through here, but neither are the police going to attack.

Boris Kagarlitsky

On the bridge, the police feel confident, but who knows what might happen if they have to fight these fearsome Italians on the streets? Both sides push and shove one another a little with their shields, but do not shift from their positions. An order to disperse immediately is read out to the demonstrators in Czech and English, but no one moves. The police try shooting off a little tear gas, but this does not make the slightest impression on the protesters. The gas quickly dissipates. From behind the backs of the Italians, young Czechs taunt the police, reminding them that not even the Communists used APCs against unarmed demonstrators. Instructions come from the minibus: everyone who does not have a gasmask is to go to the rear of the column, but not to leave the vicinity. If there is a clash, it is important for the front ranks to have a rear guard.

The standoff continues. The journalists are getting bored. Behind the column, the demonstrators have set up a field kitchen, where they give a bowl of soup and an apple to all who want them. Everyone can decide for themselves whether to pay or not. I pay 20 kronas, but the soup isn't worth that much. . . .

14:20: The standoff at the bridge continues. The demonstrators are bored, and the police in their armour are getting hot in the sunshine. Meanwhile, a real battle is under way further north. It seems that someone from the blue column has started throwing rocks at the police. Other people speak of a truck being driven at full speed into a crowd of demonstrators. They also speak of police provocateurs (the next day I see four of them, still dressed like anarchists, returning to police headquarters). One way or another, a real battle has broken out. Shots can be heard occasionally, through the screeching of sirens and the clattering of helicopters. From time to time, ambulances drive past. There are wounded on both sides. The police are using tear gas, and from time to time are firing their weapons simply in order to frighten people. The demonstrators are building barricades, have burnt several cars, and are throwing stones. The Poles and Germans throw themselves into the fight with particular fury. A number of anarchists prepare Molotov cocktails. Later, it would emerge that they even managed to set fire to a police APC, but that the flames were promptly extinguished. The police drive the blues out of one street, but regrouping, they immediately appear on another.

The yellow column does not move. Several young Englishmen approach me; from the look of it, they are students. They complain that they are wasting their time here. Obviously, they too would rather be fighting the police. For some reason I recall a phrase from *War and Peace*: "Prince Andrey's regiment was in reserve."

I attach myself to a group of French protesters; here, the people are older, and the conversations are more interesting. Olga, an ATTAC staff member, explains to me that she has never joined a political party, and that ATTAC is something quite different—a real movement, radical but not sectarian. Two more French people from a "contact group" appear unexpectedly. The pink column has managed to reach the Congress Centre along a side street, and has blocked the exits, but there are not enough people, and reinforcements are urgently needed. The French group moves off, and I follow them.

It has been discovered that the police barriers are not so difficult to break through. We go down under the bridge by footpaths, cross a street—and there we are at the Congress Centre! The police observe with amazement how our detachment has appeared behind their barricades. A helicopter flies above.

The exits from the Congress Centre are blockaded by groups of a few dozen people. They sit directly on the pavement, singing and chanting slogans. Street theatre troupes perform in the "no man's land" between the police and demonstrators. Here there are French, Israelis, and a mixed group from Eastern Europe. People exchange news. It turns out that a Belarussian detachment has formed here spontaneously. The Belarussian students doing courses in Prague have turned out for the demonstrations to a man and woman.

The Czechs sing some doleful song, and along the police barriers the French stretch out ribbons like those that are used to mark danger zones on a building site. The police are no longer blockading the demonstrators; rather, they are themselves blockaded. A number of bankers in dark suits, who have gathered to the accompaniment of shouts and whistles, pass through to the Congress Centre. One of the organisers of the column, a huge young Austrian with long hair, comes running up. He shouts: "Why did you let them through? Have you forgotten why we're here?" Now, men in expensive suits are no longer allowed through. Journalists in jeans pass through without impediment, as does an ambulance. So too do several local residents whose doors are beyond the police barrier. From beyond the barriers, another group of men in ties and expensive suits appears. The demonstrators link arms and block their path. The police start beating demonstrators, and a melée breaks out. The crowd screams: "Shame!" "Down with the IMF!" The bankers run back in fright. A few minutes later some very important gentleman emerges from the Conference Centre. A number of police immediately rush to clear a way for him with their clubs. The police have almost broken through, but at that moment, from around the corner there appears a new group of demonstrators. They are singing something as they march, and have raised pink balloons. Despite the group's thoroughly peaceful appearance, the police hide behind their shields, and begin retreating. The banker flees. Singing all the while, the demonstrators carry on marching.

16:30: A column of around a thousand people marches around the hill, following exactly the same route as a French group shortly before. Once again there are shouts, the beating of drums, and singing. At the end of the column, a group of very youthful Britons in ski masks is assembled around their banner—a smiling green skull on a black background. We are already next to the bridge. Where the police had earlier drawn up their lines, overturned barriers are lying. The police are retreating up the path toward the Congress Centre. These are ordinary police, without helmets, shields or armour. They are clearly not anxious for a fight.

Pursuing the police, the demonstrators charge up the hill. Everything recalls the storming of a medieval castle. The police on the hill draw up their ranks and throw themselves into the attack, but from down below comes a hail of stones. These are from the Britons. The police turn and run. With shouts of "Hurrah!" and "Down with the IMF!," several dozen people rush onward and upward. They have now reached the gallery on the ground floor of the Congress Centre. Others, forming ranks, begin moving up the path that by this time has been cleared of the enemy. Over the building, as a sign of victory, soars a pink balloon. A placard reading "Stop the IMF!" is attached to the balcony of the Congress Centre. To help the assault force, reinforcements—Italians, Britons and Dutch—come down from the direction of the bridge. To block the way of police vehicles, they build a barricade of overturned rubbish containers and police barriers. There is the sound of drums, whistles and rattles. Beneath the walls of the Congress Centre, young women in pink gas masks are dancing. The upper balconies are full of people watching the assault, some in horror and others in curiosity.

I realise that the battle has been won.

The Congress Centre is not taken by storm today, but this has not been part of the plans of the demonstrators. The riot police who rush to the scene clear the balcony and the entrances to the building, and then release tear gas. The gas disperses quickly, without causing much harm to the attackers, but a certain amount of it drifts up and penetrates the building of the Congress Centre, causing discomfort to the delegates and officials. After this, the demonstrators retreat in organised fashion to nearby streets, and continue the siege.

By five o'clock, the spirit of the defenders has been broken once and for all. The blockade has succeeded. For two and a half hours not a single car, and not a single bus, has been able to leave the besieged building. The police have had to evacuate particularly important people by helicopter. The rest, after somehow or other managing to break out of the building, reach their hotels by evening, using public transport. Half of the stations of the Prague metro, however, are not working. The delegates to the summit try to force their way onto crowded trams, elbowing Prague residents aside. The residents hit back. Wolfensohn too is forced to travel by metro, evidently for the first time in his life.

On the tactical level, the battle went brilliantly. The American instructors who trained the Czech police were expecting a repeat of Seattle, where the demonstrators first blockaded the hotels, and then tried to march along the main street in a single large crowd. The organisers of the Prague protest decided to do everything differently, and although the police undoubtedly knew of the plans of action, they could not understand them. In Seattle, the demonstrators had tried to stop the delegates from getting into the conference hall. In Prague, they did not let the delegates out, and this proved even more effective. Secondly, the demonstrators, in the best traditions of the military arts, carried out the tactical manoeuvre of dispersing their forces. While the main brunt of the special police attacks was diverted onto the blues, and while the yellows blocked the bridge and disrupted traffic movements, the pinks were able to make it through to the building by breaking up into small detachments. Once there, they regrouped, and the circle was closed. Each column had its own national and political peculiarities. The people who were mainly looking for a fight finished up in the blue column. In the yellow column were the most disciplined and organised elements; this was where most of the members of left political groups were to be found. The Italians looked extremely threatening, but when they clashed with police, would break off the engagement relatively quickly. On the bridge, however, they made the necessary impression on the enemy.

What happened at the bridge was not a pointless waste of time. To use military terminology, this was a "demonstration." The APCs, trucks, large numbers of police cars, and riot squad units were kept there as though paralysed. By five o'clock the yellow column had marched off in a body to the opera house, but the police themselves could no longer unblock the bridge, which remained closed to traffic. The pinks seemed the most inoffensive and even absurd, but behind this absurdity were cunning and persistence. It was no accident that the dominant forces here were the Czechs and British. It was they who decided what the day's outcome would be.

18:00: The Opera House. Several thousand people surround the Opera on all sides, blocking the entrances. There are no police anywhere, and groups of demonstrators roam about the centre of the city unhindered. On many streets, traffic is closed off. The demonstrators stop a Mercedes full of "new Russians," whom they have taken for conference delegates. At first, they want to overturn the car, but on hearing that the owners are "mere businessmen," they leave them be.

At the Opera, an impromptu meeting is under way. Speakers are addressing the crowd over a megaphone, in several languages. Sometimes there is translation, sometimes not. "The Prague Spring of 1968 was the beginning of the end for Soviet totalitarianism. Prague in 2000 is the beginning of the end for the dictatorship of the international financial oligarchy!" The crowd chants a new slogan: "Prague, Seattle, continue the battle!"

It is announced that the operatic performance scheduled for the summit delegates has been cancelled. The crowd applauds, and one of the speakers suggests organising "our own alternative opera." The Britons and Americans break into "We shall Overcome!" On the balcony of the opera house, the Austrian Erich Probsting appears. "Today Prague has belonged to us. We have won a victory over global capitalism. We have united people from Eastern and Western Europe, people from north and south. We are forcing them to respect our rights. We want to decide our fate for ourselves! Tomorrow we shall go out onto the streets again, to show that the struggle is continuing!"

22:30: Wenceslas Square. While we are sitting in a pizza shop discussing the day's events, a new fight breaks out a few dozen metres away. A group of Germans and Poles are sacking a McDonald's outlet. These restaurants are favourite targets of all the protest actions. Anticipating trouble, the managers of the restaurant have put safety glass in the windows, but this merely excites the young radicals further. They use police barriers as rams. When we go out onto the square, there is no longer a McDonald's. The windows are broken, and the sign has been smashed. Over the square hangs the sharp smell of tear gas. People are having their photographs taken against a backdrop of shattered glass.

Police and demonstrators mingle chaotically on the square. No one understands anything, or controls anything. A bus appears, full of participants in the summit. Its safety glass windows have been cracked by stones, and the windscreen is smeared with something white. The faces of the passengers display terror. The crowd hisses and whoops. Police appear in body armour, with dogs. The dogs are extremely savage, so savage that they start attacking one another. They are taken away.

By the end of the day, the police are starting to behave far more viciously, not only against people who are using violence, but also against peaceful demon-

Boris Kagarlitsky

strators. The blockade on the Congress Centre has somehow been broken, and many of the protesters have been beaten and arrested. The total number of those detained is more than four hundred; of these, about a hundred are foreigners, and the rest Czechs. More than sixty people have been injured on both sides. The Convergence Centre has been seized by the police. Before the demonstration began, the participants were given a map with the telephone number of a lawyer who could be called in case of arrest, as well as the telephone numbers of the fire and ambulance services. The law notwithstanding, the detainees have not been given the right to contact a lawyer. The Czechs are having a particularly bad time. The foreigners, as a rule, are being deported from the country within a few hours. The other detainees are being taken to Plzen, where they are beaten, are denied anything to eat or drink, and are prevented from sleeping.

22:30: The press centre of the IAEG. Work is going ahead on collecting information. The press centre's telephone line was cut off several days ago, but mobile phones are still working. While we are making our inquiries about the day's events, an uproar resounds from the entrance. With a crash, a metal grille closes in front of the door. The neo-Nazis are attacking the press centre. I realise to my horror that the building does not have an emergency exit. The attack, however, is beaten off. The episode has lasted no more than three or four minutes.

23:00: The Charles Bridge. Several dozen weary young people have gathered beneath the statues, and are eating ice cream. Several of them have torn clothes and bruised faces. All are indescribably happy.

September 27 The events of the previous day have provoked differences within the movement. Many American intellectuals are shocked by what has happened. Chelsea, the American press-secretary of the IAEG, is almost crying. "We aren't violent people, we're peaceful, all this is terrible." The German press-secretary Stefan takes a quite different attitude: the violence was inevitable. The police tactics were all aimed at ruling out any possibility of a successful nonviolent action. Those who wanted violence most of all were the press. "If there hadn't been barricades and broken windows, they wouldn't have shown anything at all. The police intended to disperse us from the very first. In West Berlin, clashes like this are commonplace. So what's all the discussion about?"

The demonstrations are continuing in various places, and from time to time they are broken up. The main demand is for the release of the detainees, but the number in custody is constantly growing. On Peace Square, most of those who have assembled are Czechs and Germans. Riot police are dragging a young Czech activist along the ground. The crowd screams "Fascists!"

18:00: Young people are walking about the Old Place with placards declaring: "I am an activist too—arrest me!" A jazz band is playing beneath the medieval clock, and the crowd chants, "The IMF must go!" Demonstrators go onto the Charles Bridge. On the other side of the bridge, police in body armour are drawn up. "There's a McDonalds there, and they're scared we're going to storm it," explains an Australian journalist working for an environmental organisation.

People question one another on the details of what happened on the previous day, who marched in which column. Maksim, a Ukrainian television journalist, tries to obtain an interview from the young Portuguese woman who we thought at first was British because of her impeccable London accent. She and a few friends bought tickets to Prague just three days ago, setting off, as she puts it, "to war." She laments that there are almost no Portuguese present. "We're so unorganised!" Maksim suggests that she repeat this on camera, but she refuses and makes off, declaring "I hate the television!"

22:30: A bar in Old Place. I drink beer with Maksim, one of his colleagues, and a number of activists from Germany. The Ukrainians have just completed a direct broadcast in which Maksim was asked to comment on a rumour that the IMF meeting would be cut short. We phone colleagues from the BBC, who confirm it. Yes, the summit will end a day ahead of schedule, and there will be no concluding press conference. The reasons are not announced. The triumphant closing ceremony has been cancelled; in the press release something vague is said to the effect that all the speeches by the participants have been unexpectedly short. There are also some general comments about the uprising in Prague.

We order another round of beer. At the neighbouring tables, British and Dutch protesters shout with joy and embrace one another.

"What the hell," says one of the German women. "It turned out to be so easy!"

Infernal Pain In Prague

pol potlatch as told to fran harris and paul hawkin

The Infernal Noise Brigade is an insurrectionary drum corps and performance unit with a primary drive towards street action. They travelled to Prague to provide the soundtrack for popular rage against the World Bank and the International Monetary Fund. Formed for the N30 WTO protest and based in Seattle, the INB is a mélange of black and green uniforms, twirling batons, rifles, fire chains, snares bass drums and metal percussion. They have been seen marching with gas masks through clouds of tear gas and backlit by flaming barricades. Gigs have included San Francisco's and Portland's May Days of 2000 and 2001 respectively, the Black Rock Desert Burning Man Festival and several rowdy street events.

After the crazy day of S26, with anticapitalist activists contesting control of our global future, state forces attacked with violent rage as night fell. The vengeful state apparatus consumed over 800 activists, citizens, and ethnic minorities. Two INB members were unfortunate enough to be counted among these numbers. The following is an account by bass drummer, pol potlatch. Notably, pol was one of a handful of brown activists in Prague for the convergence.

Everyone in the marching band was exhausted from having played all day. We split into groups so everyone could do what they wanted. I went off with two other members of the INB to get something to eat and try to meet up with other activists.

There is an amazingly large and aggressive police presence. They're shooting off so many concussion grenades that the sky overhead is lighting up. Everyone on the streets is being corralled and hauled to jail. We're thinking, "Wow. Things are really getting crazy here all of a sudden."

We try to pretend that we have nothing to do with the protests to get past the police lines. Soon a crowd comes running towards us. Someone is yelling, "Oh my god, run away. It's the fascists." People grab and drag us to get us moving.

Our majorette starts yelling that a man is getting the shit beat out of him by a gang of thugs. I turn around, see that no one is chasing us, and so I yell,

"Hey stop running." As we look back a man emerges from the shadows covered in blood. His fingers are broken and shattered, sticking in wrong directions. He's dazed and disoriented. The crowd has dispersed by now. We are trying to help this guy get home.

Every direction we go in, people yell, "You can't go down this street; the fascists are coming." We're getting hemmed in to a smaller and smaller area. Gangs of thugs are running through the streets of Prague armed with medieval weaponry: maces and clubs, long stakes and halberds. The police allow and encourage them to attack anyone who looks like an anarchist. Over the next couple of days we also find out that they were encouraged to attack gypsies, Jews and anyone who was brown-skinned.

All of sudden a tram pulls up in front of us. This Irish guy comes up from behind and pushes the four of us onto it. He yells, "Get the fuck on the tram! The fascists are right behind you. We've got to get out of here." On the tram he says, "Okay. Don't say anything. We don't know who is on this tram or who might turn us in." Then he asks us, "Where do you need to be? I can help you get home." We decide on the spot we can trust this guy. We tell him where we need to be and he tells us how to get there. But we misunderstand his directions and end up in a big, dark intersection where we don't want to be.

Police are driving all around us. Our majorette has giant, silver serpents climbing out of her hair. Her lover, an INB support person, has facial piercings and is wearing a lot of anarchist paraphernalia. I am black. We obviously stand out to them.

As I'm looking at my map trying to get back to base ("Commie Bloc") someone yells, "Oh my god! They're right behind you! Look out! Run!" Before I can even turn something hits me in the head and in the back, in the head again, and in my arms.

Ninja-garbed soldiers are screaming at me in Czech and pummeling me with sticks. I'm thrown on the ground, punched and kicked, and hogtied. They pull a hood over my head. I receive a very intense beating. I blackout repeatedly.

I guess my legs are unbound at some point because I'm standing though I'm still handcuffed. I'm being held up by a billyclub. The military police remove the hood. I don't see my people anywhere. I think, 'Good they got away. . .boy, I guess I'm fucked.'

Two of the military police that have been working me over turn me around. I see one of my companions, the majorette, across the street, handcuffed as well. She already had a broken arm, which was in a cast. The police refrained from beating her. I don't see her lover which I hope means he got away so that the rest of the Brigade can find out what happened to us.

Police are everywhere. I'm on the verge of blacking out and I'm trying not to hyperventilate. The soldiers drag me across the street and stand me up next to my friend. I try to talk to her. A soldier presses a club into my throat and barks, "Shut up! Shut up!"

We demand an English-speaking lawyer and state clearly that we are not to be separated. I also tell them I'm going to faint and need to throw up. As I start to fall over a cop throws me against the wall and shouts that I'm not allowed to faint. A bunch of British kids had come out of a bar and were watching me get brutalized. The police arrest them for watching.

Police cars arrive to take us away. The police try to separate my bandmate and me. I yell at them and demand that my companion and I be taken in together. They throw me in the back of a car with a bunch of white boxes full of donuts and pastries. As the car tries to drive off, one of the soldiers who had been working me over whacks the hood of the car to stop it. In a strange lapse into humanity, he opens the back door and gently seats my friend next to me. He slams the door and yells in English, "Go! Get out of here!"

As we fly though the city we see people being stomped everywhere. State police, military police, riot cops, Special Forces are on a rampage. I think that the driver is showing us these scenes intentionally.

We are taken to a torture chamber/detention center in the heart of the city. It is the place where state enemies, Jews, gypsies and politicos were tormented before the revolution. Now it's a jail. As we are dragged into the station a cop throws me down the stairs; the driver of the car catches me and tells the other officer to stop.

In the processing area detainees are spread around the room with cops pressing their faces against the concrete. They are all handcuffed and some have their feet cuffed as well. The police are jamming billyclubs into the spines and kidneys of the arrestees and bouncing their faces off walls. They are kneeing the males in the nuts. And for their amusement, they're intimating raping the women by rhythmically stabbing their billyclubs at them from behind. I turn to see them doing this to my friend. My face is slammed against the wall. The sexually assaulting officer is female.

I see one of the British kids who is on the streets when we were arrested. He had been a loudmouth then and he was a loudmouth now. A cop smashes his face into the concrete. He staggers back with blood flowing from his mouth and nose. He quips, "Thank you, sir. May I have another?" The cop bashes his head into the wall several more times. The Brit's eyes roll into the back of his head. "You think you're a tough guy now? Wait'll I get these handcuffs off...," he taunts the cop.

For processing they dig through our pockets, take our IDs and all our belongings. We're led into a room with two giant cages on either side. Each cage is divided into four cells. The one to our left is full: three cells of men; one of women. The cage to our right holds a gang of Czech fascists; they sport shaved heads, black flight jackets and swastika tattoos, and are yelling obscenities at the women in the cage across from them. The guards line us up, put little numbers on us and photograph us. I'm put in a cell with the men; my friend is put in a cell with the women. The cops are really nice to the fascists; smiling brightly at them like, "Hi! How's it going?" All the cops are white; the Czech Republic is a white country. Some of the cops and Nazis know each other by name.

The cops bring the skinheads hot chocolate and let them go to the bathroom whenever they ask. When the cops walk past our cages they yell and scream at us, jab sticks through the bars and threaten to come in and beat us more. They refuse to give us water.

The police start to release the fascists. The cops tell us they can't process us because we are foreigners and we must wait for the Special Police. We are incensed by our treatment, but people are maintaining beautiful spirits.

The cell is stuffed. We take turns sitting and standing. The people who are really fucked up lie beneath the benches. The police come by with photographs looking for specific individuals. We hide them with our bodies.

The guards refuse to bring us food and are recalcitrant in taking us to the bathrooms. The women start to chat them up the, trying to make friends so we can get food and water. A small collection of stashed money is quietly passed to a sympathetic guard. What comes back is the best apple I ever tasted, the most refreshing water and herbal tea I've ever drank. We get a pack of smokes as well.

Every now and then people are taken out of their cages. Some are beaten. I hear that a group of women are taken into a back room and are forced to do exercises in their underwear. I'm taken out and a statement is extracted from me. I lie outrageously. After being photographed I am returned to the cage, though some folks never return. At some point—I have no idea if it is day or night—the Greek ambassador comes and takes all the Greek activists with him. He pays off the cops. I think that is brilliant.

I'm fainting continuously. I remember the sun coming up at some point. The Special Police arrive and begin moving people in large numbers to a different holding center. My friend the majorette and I are reunited. We are pulled out, handcuffed again and thrown into a truck. It is dark again. We get all of our belongings back except for our IDs. Men and women in black suits are yelling at us through the back of the truck asking if we have been tortured. We don't know if they are activists, reporters or legal support. We find out later that they are the legal delegation for INPEG, the group that called for the Prague Convergence. We are trying to let them know that we have been totured.

The police take us to an apartment building. On the way to the main lobby black suits ask us about our condition. The police shove us past them quickly. We realize we are in an old folks home; elderly people in bathrobes and slippers are scratching their heads as we are marched through.

We're taken to an upstairs room. We're some of the first to arrive. More people slowly filter in. A bunch of the cops are dressed head to toe in black leather, looking like SS officers. Regular cops shove us into chairs and open all the windows letting in freezing air.

The sun is coming up again; intense bright white. We're in really uncomfortable chairs, but we're glad to be sitting down. Some people are sitting on the floor. We're only allowed to whisper. Someone moves to close a window and a cop makes a motion to strike him. The cops laugh and joke about it in Czech.

More people are showing up. It seems like every group is in worse shape than the one before. Folks are hobbling in with broken ankles, feet, arms, collarbones, missing teeth. This is the most insane collection of bruises I've ever seen in one room. The dark skinned people have the worst of it.

Another funny cop joke was at the point of a knife. A cop would draw a knife and approach toward your throat. With a sudden lunge they would dive over your body and slice off your handcuffs. Each new group gets to experience this. We're punished if we try to let them know it's coming.

We still haven't been charged with anything. I have cracked ribs, broken fingers, the tendons of my left ankle are ripped, and I have a concussion.

Eventually there are over a hundred of us in this space. They separate us by gender. People are taken away. Some come back and tell us they've been strip-searched or cavity-searched on a higher floor. Some come back really shook up and they tell us they had the shit beaten out of them. Others don't come back.

The cops start telling some people, "Get the fuck out and don't come back." These people are allowed to leave for real. The crowd is getting smaller.

Finally they call my name and my friend's. I think it's our turn to get beat (again). The police start handing out IDs; they give us our passports. They tell us we have twenty-four hours to leave the country. If we don't leave, we're informed, they'll throw us back in jail.

"You really don't want that," one cop admonishes. We think, 'You're right. You people are fucking terrifying.'

pol potlatch as told to fran harris and paul hawkins

Direct Action Convergences 2000

Andrea del Moral

April 20, 1999–Feb. 6, 2000

México City, México: Students at Universidad Nacional de Autonomia de México strike against exponential tuition increase from 2 cents to US $65 per semester and for more control in their education. Students completely shut down the massive institution attended by 270,000. Strikers hold their own workshops and discussions, blocking use of the classrooms and offices by the administration. The strike is supported by two UNAM workers' unions. Students create an assembly and formulate demands.

On Mayday '99, the electricians' union joins in solidarity. They circulate a flyer publicizing the strike, and donate money to the students. A student explains the character of the strike: "The battle of force is over. The second battle is that of the imagination. This is a radical struggle to open broader spaces for dialogue and ideas. We're not fighting for ourselves, but for those who will follow us."

In June '99 the rector of UNAM, Francisco Barnés, agrees to halt the tuition increase, but internal departments are still allowed to charge fees. The strikers begin to faction along class lines; the insistent working class radicals vs. the more affluent moderates, who want to end the strike.

Less than a week after the WTO protest hundreds of radicals, including many UNAM strikers, march on the US embassy to protest police brutality and demand the release of political prisoners in Seattle. The marchers are brutalized by the police, but not before they break ten embassy windows.

In January of 2000 a vote following a meeting attended by thousands decides to end the strike. But a sizeable faction, desiring a complete transformation of the internal structure of UNAM (with money shifting from administrators' salaries to educational resources), still wants to continue. They refuse to abide by the vote. This internal conflict results in a large-scale riot at the UNAM High School 3 on February 1, 2000.

The strike is broken on February 6, 2000. Six hundred and forty-five protesters are arrested by 2260 cops. On February 8, striking students return to the university. They are met by the police. A melee follows, in which 37 students are injured and 251 are arrested. The charges against the students range from robbery, assault, and sabotage to menacing society, plundering, and terrorism. Over 100 students are imprisoned for over a month.

January 29

Davos, Switzerland: The World Economic Forum holds its annual meeting. It is attended by 2,000 "world leaders in business and politics." A diverse, multi-issue crowd of at least 1,300 descends upon the ski town to protest. They smash windows, vandalize a McDonald's, and damage some cars. Protestors attempt to cross the police line protecting the WEF meeting and are assaulted by riot cops. A number of protestors are injured and/or arrested by the police. Several police officers suffer head wounds.

Mayday

New York City, NY: This protest is the most multi-cultural in the recent history of New York City activism. The day begins with an early afternoon rally at Union Square which is attended by workers on half-day strike and supported by many unions, including the AFL-CIO. The event calls for an end to repressive policies against immigrant workers and their families. The Square is surrounded by a ring of riot cops acting as a watchful escort.

From the rally, people march to City Hall. There, artists stage puppet shows and street theatre celebrating Mayday and portraying such subjects as workers' struggle for the eight-hour day, and paying homage to the Haymarket martyrs, who were executed in the struggle. The event ends at rush hour. Police act aggressively toward puppetistas heading back to Brooklyn, but let up as the activists leave Manhattan.

Anticipating an action at the capitalist core of the city, police barricade Wall Street, obstructing traffic. The police, however, are the only action.

San Francisco, CA: The three-year old Reclaim Mayday coalition holds two roving street parties. The first is intercepted at the Levi's store, its launching spot, by police. Thirty people are arrested. The second draws a rowdy crowd to Justin Herman Plaza at noon. Fifteen hundred people are treated to performances by the SF Mime Troupe, and a range of musicians. Local unions are in attendance. Their members give speeches. Speakers denounce Occidental Petroleum and Fidelity Investments (for their omnicidal incursions on U'Wa land in Colombia), as well as other corporate criminals. The crowd then becomes mobile, visiting the GAP and Kaplan, McLoughlin, and Diaz, an architecture firm that designs prisons. Its ranks include two anarchist marching bands, San Francisco's Anti-Capitalist Drum Corps and the Infernal Noise Brigade.

Portland, OR: At 11 AM, two hundred rowdies march through Portland with a pirate ship decked out in red, green, and black flags. They tour several corporate sites, including NikeTown, whose window was smashed the night before. Activists put U-locks on the doors of nine businesses: three Starbucks, a Barnes & Noble, a Borders, and four banks. Later in the day eight hundred people parade through downtown in a legal march. They are escorted by 150 cops. The police are aggressive and attack protestors without provocation. They shoot beanbags and tear gas at protestors at close range and charge at individuals with their horses. As the event disperses, cops harass and intimidate the fragmenting crowd.

June 4–6

Windsor, ON, Canada: The Organization of American States meets to further plans for the Free Trade Area of the Americas. Hundreds of people come for direct action protests. The US-Canada border at Detroit is *de facto* shut down for days preceding and during the protest. The OAS meeting area is surrounded by a 10' tall fence of concrete blocks and mesh steel. The city teems with police, who surveille and intimidate activists. Two US citizens, David Solnit of Art & Revolution and Arthur Foelsche of the Independent Media Center, are arrested and detained on tenuous grounds of prior misdemeanor charges.[6] The night of June 3, before the 6 AM direct action, the spokescouncil decides to abandon its plans for direct action due to lack of numbers. The group decides to instead join the labor march, and to carry out small-scale actions alongside it. A few people hang a banner along the perimeter fence. People get arrested for blockading a delegates' bus. Police seek out practitioners of direct action, but for the most part, the activists escape persecution by melting into the crowd. Labor seems to be cool with playing this protective role.

June 10–12

Calgary, AB, Canada: Three thousand executives representing eighty companies meet at the World Petroleum Congress, a six-year-old oil industry organization. At the keynote address, given by the CEO of the BP Amoco Group, two activists drop a banner reading, "BP Amoco and PetroChina: Get Out of Tibet." Outside, a large rally protests the 590-mile pipeline planned by PetroChina to cut through Tibet. On Sunday the 10th, fifteen hundred people march through the streets of Calgary. One person is arrested for "obstructing a police officer." Two hundred people march in the streets on Monday. Two San Francisco activists from Project Underground and the Transnational Resource & Action Center are detained at the Calgary airport for their "political involvement in criticizing the WPC." The two were to speak at a teach-in about the oil industry.

June 30–July 1

Millau, France: An international crowd of fifty thousand demonstrate outside the hearing for members of Confederation Paysanne, who dismantled a McDonald's there in '99. The Millau Ten are found guilty.

September 11–13

Melbourne, Australia: The World Economic Forum, a global summit for the advancement of the World Capitalist Agenda, meets for their annual Asia-Pacific conference. Activists organize a week long "Carnival for Global Justice" that begins at 5:30 AM on September 11. They raise a tent city on South Bank, opposite the Crown Casino where the WEF meeting is taking place. Ten thousand surround the Crown Casino. One-third of the delegates are unable to get into the meeting. Several speaking engagements by WEF members, such as those by Bill

Andrea del Moral

Gates, are cancelled because of the overwhelming protestor presence.

September 21–23

San Francisco, CA: The National Association of Broadcasters is met by activists protesting the corporate media agenda. On Friday the 22nd, nine activists are arrested for disturbing the NAB meetings. Media Alliance Executive Director Andrea Buffa is hauled off after seizing the microphone at the opening breakfast. At 8AM four activists, united by U-locks, force their way into the Moscone Convention Center. Three lawyers are arrested for battery charges when pushing past police in an effort to see their recently arrested clients. Photographers from local media are initially given full access to the NAB conference, but when activists begin to disrupt, the independent press are denied entry.

After the morning's events, protestors go to Microsoft-owned radio station KYLD and demand an end to the FCC regulations that prohibit micropower radio.

On Saturday over five hundred people gather for a media and democracy rally. A Micropower Council of War convenes at New College of San Francisco.

September 25–29

Several solidarity actions occur around the globe during the week of mass action against the World Bank in Prague, Czech Republic:

Wellington, New Zealand: On the 26th, 200 people parade to Westpac Trust Bank, which funds uranium mining in Australia. The Committee for the Establishment of Civilization throws a street party. Nine people are arrested, four injured. By the end of the day, police are picking off people at random.

London, UK: Many activists from the UK go to Prague. Those who remain in London turn out a spoof paper, *The Financial Crimes,* which appears on the street on September 26. The paper critiques World Bank policy and the complicity of British financial institutions in the World Bank's work. On the 29th, the London anarchist forum stages a debate against the World Bank.

Moscow, Russia: A planned concert against capitalism and the IMF/World Bank is banned by police. So activists circulate fliers inviting people to gather at Engels statue at Kropotkinskaya metro station. Meanwhile, a small number of people meet with media at Majakovski metro station with a misleading press release about smashing up a McDonald's. The cops swarm the McDonald's and by the time they get it together to go to Engels statue a lively march is well underway. The noisy parade, described as "the most active and energetic demo Moscow's anarchist/libertarian scene has done in years" on the anarchist website www.ainfos.ca, consists of thirty people prancing to Moscow's World Bank headquarters with a banner that reads, "The World Bank is the enemy of the people." Protestors then make speeches inside the World Bank headquarters. Six speakers and banner hangers are arrested, five of whom are held overnight.

Kiev, Ukraine: Protests begin on September 25 with a large action near the Czech embassy. The event is covered by several major TV stations—a significant happening for Kiev. On the 26th, they demonstrate at the World Bank of Ukraine. They pass out "IMF credits" to people on the street: one or two kopecks and a loan agreement. They also plaster the underground public transit with labels reading: "More banks-fewer hospitals" and "Credits-heroin, IMF-drug pusher."

Saõ Paulo, Brazil: Anarchists begin their resistance at 9:30 AM on the morning of the 26th with a small protest of fifteen to twenty people. They hold a memorial for past Brazilian revolutionaries who have fought against capitalism and for freedom. At the end, they disperse into groups of three to scatter the mounting police presence.

Just after noon, fifteen hundred people, including scholars, ecologists, squatters, and revolutionary union members, converge and march through the city. The cops attempt to disperse the march by driving a van into the crowd at high speed. As a satisfying counterbalance, a protestor smacks a cop on the nose after the officer pops him for trying to retrieve a banner.

The crowd then strips the streets of banners for the upcoming mayoral elections. Protestors also trash propaganda from a leftist coalition, composed of capitalists, Maoists, Leninists, Stalinists, and Trotskyists. At XV Novembro Street, the crowd stops at Bo Isa de Valores building and spraypaint it. They then break a radio-tv van of the GloboNet corporation because of its support of the 20-year military regime in Brazil. Most of the fifteen hundred scatters when two police vans arrive. Two young women are arrested; one of them hits a cop in the face. Another cop attacks two protestors but is deterred by an anonymously thrown stone. As the cops retreat, one hundred protestors return to the street. The police then come back with gas bombs and fire guns. Protestors remain assertive, confronting and shoving police in an effort to unarrest their comrades. Seventeen more protestors are arrested in the attempt.

That evening, around 750 people gather at the Municipal Theatre Hall for a Samba Dance Against Capital. Twenty cop cars surround the event, so the crowd disperses and reconvenes in the Garden Republic for Art where artists perform folk music, poetry, street theatre, and dance. When the police show up, they injure members of the mainstream media, as well as performers.

Chennai, India: Tamilnadu, a women's collective from Chennai, and Jubilee 2000 gather for a three hour rally and speeches. The 450 person convergence is predominantly women.

Cork, Ireland: Sixty people carrying a coffin signifying the misery and death brought by capitalism block traffic in the center of the city. Many cabbies and other drivers show their support. The focus of the demonstration is on Ulster Bank, Bank of Ireland, and AIB, Irish banks involved with the World Bank and corrupt domestic politics. Protestors occupy the foyer of AIB building.

Malmo, Sweden: Protestors smash the windows of bank offices around Square Nydalatorget. Their press release explains their intention: to "strengthen the revolutionary anti-imperialist resistance—for communism."

Stockholm, Sweden: An evening protest brings 200 people to the workers' quar-

Andrea del Moral

ter. Marchers move through Sodermalm and Old Town. K9 police squads intercept and disperse the group before it can reach its planned destination.

Toronto, ON, Canada: Two hundred people gather at the US embassy. Police confine them to the sidewalks and work to prevent them from crossing streets. The protestors descend upon the stock exchange and condemn structural adjustment programs. The events end with a rally at City Hall. Only one person is arrested—he is selected out of the crowd for his involvement with the Ontario Coalition Against Poverty protests in June.

Montréal, PQ, Canada: 100–150 people of la Convergence des Luttes Anti-Capitalistes march to the stock exchange with a banner exhorting, "Smash capitalism before it smashes you!" Police block off routes to all nearby McDonald's. The protest goes to Hydro-Québec, the power company responsible for the displacement of Native people, the ruin of rivers in northern Québec, and corrupt investment policies. The rowdies continue to the World Commerce Center, then disperse into the Metro system to avoid the approaching riot squads.

Washington, D.C.: Thirty-five people sit in the street at rush hour. All are arrested. After the event, four hundred union members and activists hold a rally.

Lake Worth, FL: A banner is dropped over the freeway that says, "Globalize Resistance to Corporate Power; Shut Down the World Bank."

Hartford, CT: Hundreds of people gather at 2 PM and march on the federal building. Unions and activists with the Connecticut Global Action Network stage street theatre.

Portland, OR: About eighty people close Broadway by Pioneer Courthouse Square during rush hour. They throw eggs and get pepper-sprayed by the cops. Their numbers grow to 150-200 as they wind through downtown Portland. Elements in the crowd jump on cars, knock over trash cans, and block public transit from 5–8:45PM. Six are arrested.

Berkeley, CA: Five to six hundred people meet in downtown Berkeley at Center and University streets for a joint action by Critical Mass and Reclaim The Streets. The protest starts with a torchlit march on the new Berkeley jail. On University Avenue, activists hang a banner from a parking garage. The banner depicts a pirate ship dropping CEOs and landlords off the plank to sharks and reads: "Aye, to the plank with ye, money grubbin', resource lubbin', globalization lovin' varmin!" The march soon ends at the intersection where it started. A tripod is erected and a bonfire gets going while dance/rave music is pumped from a bicycle mounted sound system. After the crowd parties for a couple hours, the police extinguish the bonfire. Activists become mobile again, this time moving to a soundtrack of conscious hip hop and still illuminated by torches. They set a fire at McDonald's and smash the window of CalFed Bank and Citibank. One person is arrested and charged with a felony.

The march disperses after police begin to seal off protestors approaching

Telegraph Avenue. The Berkeley police department establishes a preemptive barricade at The Gap in anticipation of more property damage.

Bern, Switzerland: On September 29, the Swiss anarchist-syndicalist group FAUCH drops a banner on the Czech embassy demanding release of protestor-prisoners in Prague. For two hours the embassy officials are locked out, while FAUCH members hold a press conference from the balcony of the ambassador's office.

November 16–18

Cincinnati, OH: The Trans-Atlantic Business Dialogue, an informal group whose members include two hundred top U.S. and European business and government leaders, meets. Though the group has no official decision making power, it makes policy recommendations and is known as "the power behind the WTO." The protests against TABD takes similar form to those at other large protests in the previous year, with teach-ins and training.

The morning of the 16th begins with a press conference by the Coalition for a Humane Economy at Fountain Square. Approximately five hundred people attend, then march to Krogers supermarket headquarters to protest the company's refusal to support striking farm workers. That evening, at a symphony performance for TABD attendees, two men drop a banner that says, "End Corporate Rule." After they are kicked out of the music hall, they try to address fellow protestors, but are soon attacked by nearly twenty cops.

On Friday a legal mid-day rally and march draws about one thousand people. Roughly one quarter of the protestors are formed into an anti-capitalist black bloc. Around 1:30, the official event ends at the Omni-Netherlands Hotel, where the TABD is meeting. A black-clad splinter group of two to three hundred people pick up police barricades and head toward the waterfront. The police block the protestors and escort them back to Sawyers Point, where the day's activities began. Protestors are then divided into groups of four and permitted to leave one at a time. In the evening, an AFL-CIO picket of three to five hundred circles the TABD dinner, accompanied by nearly twice as many police.

Saturday, the final day of protest, begins at Fountain Square. Protestors have to pass a police checkpoint and patdown to enter the area. Police are decked out in brand new riot gear and carry pepper spray. They ticket many protestors for jaywalking. The police then deter the five to seven hundred people from their march destination—Krogers, where they are trying to drop off a papier-mâché pig. The group splinters and police use tear gas and arrests against them.

In the late afternoon, some TABD protestors join a Black Urban Defense rally against police brutality. Forty people are arrested. By evening, police threaten to arrest groups of five or more people standing in the street. Like so many major corporate gatherings since Seattle, the TABD conference ends in martial law.[14]

December 6–8
Nice, France: The Inter-Governmental Council, a secretive body of representatives from countries of the EU, meets. IGC policies allow anti-union laws in the

UK, repeal minimum income laws, and take the teeth out of collective bargaining and right to information and consultation laws. Items on the agenda at the Nice meeting include the expansion of the EU, and Article 133 of the Amsterdam Treaty, which binds all countries in the EU to all treaties that any member country has signed. Many protestors are blocked at borders, and protest there. Trains carrying protestors to Nice from other French cities are halted. Despite these effots to prevent mass protest, on December 6 a rally of eighty thousand workers floods Nice. From 6AM on December 7 socialists, anarchists, and communists engage in confrontation in the streets. The presence of radicals is significant, as six to seven thousand socialist/anarchists and nearly as many from the CRI-Communist Revolutionary League are in attendance. The police presence is heavy as well—an estimated fifteen thousand. They use tear gas and pepper spray on protestors.

battle of seattle

Holidays In The Sun
A Little Atrocity On The Mayan Riviera

Ramor Ryan

Neoliberal Paradise Found

There is a bus that leaves the indigenous town of Altamirano, Chiapas, near the Zapatista headquarters at Morelia, that sets out for Cancun full with temporary construction workers. The workers, Tseltal and Tojolabal campesinos, work 6 or 7 days a week for 12 hours a day, for the paltry sum of 40 pesos a day, about $4. They labor to construct the ever- expanding hotel industry and elite tourist playground. There are over 20,000 rooms in Cancun and the average price is around $100 a night.

Twenty-five years ago Cancun was a sleepy fisherman's village looking out over the beautiful Caribbean. Today it is more like a US colony modeled after Disneyland or a Hollywood movie set. The graceful shoreline is now choc-a-bloc with astonishingly ostentatious hotels of enormous proportions. Some are postmodern representations in the style of ancient Mayan pyramids, others are more reminiscent of gangster run Havana casinos of bygone eras; all cater to the rich, the vast majority of clients foreigners from the US and Europe. The sweeping avenue down the peninsula is a veritable wet dream for American shopping mall fanatics, with every brand store and logo commodity represented in abundance.

Jose Alfredo, a young Zapatista from a village near Altamirano returned a few months ago from his first stint of work at Cancun. "I thought I had left Mexico!" he commented, "I thought I was in another country." And he is right in one sense; Cancun is a model of a new kind of Global space. It is an embodiment of the global village as neoliberals would have it. A sanctuary for the wealthy where poverty does not exist. A utopia without hunger or illiteracy, or any of the everyday realities of life for the majority, not because there is some fine neoliberal solution, but because they are excluded. Cancun is a world of illusion where everything is shiny and happy, nothing can disturb the idea of this fanciful paradise. And just in case anybody is foolish or crazy enough to disagree or raise their voice in dissent, a huge security apparatus, both private and public, maintains a high profile. It is quite apt that the World Economic Forum chose this location for their latest reunion to discuss the liberalization of Latin American Markets and the consolidation of the neoliberal economic strategy for this region.

Enter the Clowns...

Globophobics are everywhere. Everywhere the globalizers have gone since the breakdown of the Seattle round in November of 1999, they have been pursued and harrassed by a plethora of protestors. The Cancun meeting continues with this successful strategy on behalf of the antiglobalization movement. A diversity of people have come to this absurd resort to organize and demonstrate, and possibly blockade and disrupt the proceedings. By their presence alone, the globophobics have affected the meeting. Various mouthpieces for the Economic Forum dispatch their press releases in defense of their doctrine, and try desperately to disarm the dissenting voice by engaging them in vacuous dialogue.

But what is to be done? How to effectively achieve the goal of disrupting the meeting? On the other side of southern Mexico the Zapatistas have been in rebellion since NAFTA came into force in '94. In many respects the Zapatista uprising is the moment when the movement against globalization found its first global audience, and it is perhaps the place where the tactics of that movement began. If agility, imagination, and cunning are tactics the movement has embraced with success then the Zapatistas are the template. The Zapatistas have renovated revolutionary action by using daring strategy; righteously and poetically serenading the populace and media while striking a pose with their guerrilla arms ever ready. Wary of the fact that the enemy, the Mexican state, has overwhelming force at their disposal, they have cleverly steered clear of straight-up military confrontation. The antiglobalization movement has been an attentive student of the Zapatistas but has missed some key lessons.

Today in Cancun, February 26, 2001, the numbers are low, only a few hundred protesters, but they climb steadily as the day unfolds. This disappointment is due in part to the location since Cancun is situated at the far end of the Yucatan peninsula, more than 1500km from Mexico City. The costs of arriving here are huge. As for the local community, the indigenous population of the town is small, as the workforce is, in classic neoliberal fashion, temporary, migratory and nonunion. Furthermore, most Mexican activists are organizing the mobilization in support of the Zapatista Caravan to Mexico City which unfortunately coincides with this event. Nevertheless the 500 or so who made the journey are aware they represent the millions nationally and globally who are not present.

A Festival of Resistance, or The Garden of Ghetsemene...

The first march on Monday the 26th is celebratory and peaceful in its manifestation. The protesters are grouped around four main organizations: F-26, Civil Disobedience, the student CGH (The General Strike Council, emanating from the recent marathon strike at the UNAM University), El Barzon (A large debtors union), as well as a bunch of black bloc anarchists and a cabal of Maoists. They are predominantly young and radical, dressed in punky and counterculture attire, peppered by the obligatory Zapatista ski masks and scarves. Boisterous and colorful, they march as far as the fortified police cordon at the entrance to the Tourist Zone, where they taunt security forces, a few cheekily exhibiting their backsides to the sullen lines of riot cops. Avenues around the city are lined by loitering police forces and riot squads, some with their gas masks at the ready. The ubiquitous helicopter hovers menacingly overhead. *La Migra* watch out for the participation of foreigners. Agent provocateurs mingle with the marchers, and every inch and every face is monitored and filmed.

Back at the Palapas, a quiet little grass park littered with old mangled trees that functions as base camp for the globophobics, the protesters assemble. Around campfires and a bunch of tents, they meet and organize all evening for the big day tommorow. The mood is intrepid but a little pessimistic. The numbers are dangerously low to attempt the professed aim of the mobilization—to block-ade and disrupt the meeting. Rumors abound of the arrival of hundreds more Barzon activists the next day, but this never materializes. Stupendously out-numbered—there are several thousand security elements in Cancun—still the 500 continue with their plans. Rubber inner-tubes are inflated and tied together to make mobile barricade defenses. The Civil Disobedience people (with support from F-26 and other people, making them the dominant protest force) are to attempt to break through the Police cordon like the Ya Basta! group at Prague, wearing white jumpsuits and fortifying their shoulders and arms with padding, and covering their heads with helmets to protect from beatings. Others plan to enter the Convention Hotel from the beach, masquerading as tourists, as the main body of the march battles with the police on the main road. Militant Maoists hold their own breakaway meeting, closed to outsiders. They have their own plans, disrupting the unity of the other groups. "Comrades!" screams an older masked man, to the assembled group of about 30 youths, "We are not afraid of the police or jail! Remember the glorious martyrs and prisoners!" The group breaks into another round of ultra-militant chanting about death to this or that. A corrosive assembly the previous night had revealed a serious division between these radicals hell bent on destructive ideas, and the majority, who preferred the tactic of nonviolent direct action for the protests.

Despite the industriousness of the preparations, the cheerful hum of the labors, there is an unmistakable mood of foreboding and fear. The local newspa-pers had contributed to fueling the tensions with their sensational reporting. *They Enter The Ring!* screams one front-page accompanied by a photo of masked up, fist-clenched militants. Others present the protestors as dangerous terror-ists—one version, (of the police searching arriving buses) indicates that explo-sives were found, but this can't be confirmed. Complete nonsense, of course, and they forget to inform their readers that the police also stole money and cameras from the buses. "They are going to fuck us up tomorrow!" said one 20-year-old philosophy student as he tried on his full-face motorcycle helmet. Even with the helmet, all the padding and his white jump-suit, he still looked terribly small and fragile. (The helmet would be seen the next day lying on the side of the road smashed in half by a police baton, and the youth in jail.) Others spoke confi-dently of Vicente Fox needing to keep his international image clean hence the police would be on better behavior than usual. Wishful thinking, as the local gov-ernor spoke of not tolerating any disorder in the streets of Cancun.

In the shadows of the trees on this warm tropical night, completely sur-rounded by patrolling cop pick-up trucks and undercover agents idling on every

Ramor Ryan

corner, they bravely prepare all night for battle, or better, for their suicide mission. Rebel dignity, pride and courage are the attributes of this raggle-taggle band of Mexican youth.

Tactics and Spontaneity

The 500 marched tentatively with much noise through the town. They arrived at a wide boulevard with a picturesque park between the two roads in and out of the Tourist Colony. A fortified army of police lines faced them behind two rows of solid metal fencing. This meant the Civil Disobedience plan of pushing through the police lines armed with their rubber tires was thwarted, as those metal fences were not for moving. In the moment's hesitation, the Maoists took the initiative, charging to the front and calling for a storming of the barricades nevertheless. This tactic is fearfully doomed, and the main body of the demonstration re-grouped to re-consider strategy, appealing for nonviolence. But already the forces are divided. The Maoists rushed up the police lines full of thunder and fury while the cops laughed. Their assault on the barricades falters a couple of meters short and a stand-off for an hour resumes as both sides exchanged insults and an occasional stick flies or a baton is swung. The Press horde crowded around with enthusiasm. Tourists stopped to watch. Their plans in disarray, the Ya Basta! grouping failed to come up with a coherent Plan B. They lingered in indecision. The main body of the march, following their lead, stalled and prevaricated. A few disrobed and attempted to dissolve the minor tension between the Maoists and the Police lines with their nakedness, while some others decide to stage a sit-down protest to block both sides of the road. After an hour or so, the traffic is held up for miles. Why the police didn't simply divert the traffic from the start is a mystery. Meanwhile a group of 30 had infiltrated the beach as far as the Hotel where the forum is held. There they are violently apprehended by a large contingent of riot cops and bundled off to jail. It was when the Civil Disobedience group began to leave, and the majority of people were sitting around the park tired and dehydrated, when the mood had become almost festive as a few hundred tourists and the press corps waited around for the next spectacle, that the barricades suddenly opened up.

Of Ultra-violence and Brutality

With an unbridled ferocity, the riot squads came storming out at full sprint. Hundreds of them flooded out. They swung wildly and indiscriminately at everyone in their path. First to be pummeled was the isolated group left sitting on the road. The still afternoon air became filled traumatically with screams of panic and pain, and a horrific battle-cry of the marauding cop gangs as they beat their shields...People fled hopelessly in every direction as the maddened thugs pursued them relentlessly. There was no resistance because there was none prepared. There was only running in absolute terror. It was simple savage punishment. Scenes of utter vomit-inducing brutality ensued. A tall cop beat a helpless youth on the ground with a 3-meter pole while his buddies delivered carefully aimed blows to the victim's head with their batons and boots. A silent couple clutched each other uselessly as a gang of thugs did a Rodney King on them. People with videos and cameras were singled out for beatings. The Civil Disobedience group, encumbered with their absurd rubber tires, got special punishment, while the Maoist contingent abandoned their militant posturing and fled frantically. A few valiant ones went in defense of their bloodied *companeros,* and were beaten heavily for their impudence. Some paltry stones flew and then the menacing sound of gas canisters being shot off was heard. The air filled with the poisonous fumes. The people fled in utter pandemonium. Heavily injured people were carried through the gas clouds. The picturesque grassy knoll resembled a furious medieval battle field. And the beatings went on and on, the cops frantically seeking fresh victims, or else any vanquished body languishing on the ground would do. The blare of ambulances interrupted the din of violence. The rout was complete. The neoliberals had triumphed heroically, their mercenary soldiers delighted with their crusading victory, their little slaughter of the Globophobics this sunny afternoon on the Mayan Riviera.

Tactical Follies

The lessons of Cancun lay in hospital beds and languished in cells around the city that night. With all their creative preparations and aestheticised resistance borrowed from Prague and elsewhere, the facts on the ground announced a grave miscalculation. The group of no more than a few hundred had employed tactics which had been developed, with varying degrees of success, by demonstrations of thousands strong. Massing before a much stronger force of tooled up cops, and dressed for battle or at least for confrontation, the outcome was surely predictable. With such meagre numbers it would perhaps have been wiser to avoid a head to head confrontation or the possibility of it in favor of guerilla style engagement by much smaller groups spread throughout the town. In this way, no group, whether they be the militant Maoists or the peaceniks, are able to determine the fate of everyone. Furthermore it would prevent the police mobilizing their formidable resources in one place and corralling the lambs for slaughter. Five hundred is not enough to close down or disrupt one of these summits if they organize as a block; this should have been recognized. But tactical victories could have been won with more mobile, autonomous and guerrilla style actions. This would at least have guaranteed fewer injuries and perhaps fewer arrests. Furthermore it would have enhanced the possibility of some people penetrating the cordon and reaching the hotel where the meeting was taking place and so offered the possibility of some disruption, the stated aim of the mobilization.

The Resurgence of the Struggle...

The attempted blockade was defeated but the media coverage was a victory. Images of the unprovoked ultra-violence flashed across the television networks. Newspapers the next day were filled with powerful photos of police violence under headlines of *Brutality! Police Riot!* and *Cowards And Savages.* The resignation of the Police chief was demanded. Trolleys filled with food arrived at the protesters' encampment as they bandaged up their wounds and searched to locate the 65 prisoners and the 15 hospitalized about whom the police would release no details. Locals rallied in support and warned protesters of new police movements. A solidarity demonstration was organized in the Capital. Even with small defeats, the movement grows. The next day popular pressure helped ensure the prisoners' release, and condemnation of the police came from every quarter, even, opportunistically, from PAN (the governing party) deputies and

Ramor Ryan

local representatives. A demonstration was called in front of the Town Hall. Not one uniformed cop appeared. They were withdrawn in disgrace. The authorities faltered under an avalanche of criticism and the journalists organized their own protest against the police brutality. Fox remained silent, his image tainted, returning a few days later on television to shed apologetic crocodile tears. The World Economic Forum finished up without a peep and the neoliberals hurried away from Cancun without releasing their usual celebratory communiqués. But, no doubt, business continued as usual.

The protesters mockingly charged the undefended Town Hall, as if to say, "Look! Here we are. . . still!" The message was clear; even if they batter them off the streets, the protesters won't go away. Cancun is a watershed for the movement. New strategies and tactics will emerge, and the neoliberal project continues to retreat under pressure.

Genova and the Antiglobalization Movement

Silvia Federici and George Caffentzis
August 2001

A Citizens' Arrest

These are some reflections on the demonstrations in Genova during the G8 meetings and the post-Genova debate. We were not in Genova on July 19-21, 2001 and were not involved in the process of preparing the demos; thus, there are aspects of this debate we cannot comment upon. We are responding, however, to the widespread realization that the July Genova days were a turning point for the antiglobalization movement and there are important lessons we in the movement must draw from it.

Two things happened in Genova that signal the development of a new political reality. First, 300,000 people from every part of Europe came together to challenge the legitimacy of the G8 meeting and practically attempt a citizen's arrest of it. On the first day of the demonstrations, moreover, 70, 000 immigrants and supporters marched—an unprecedented feat in Italy where immigrants politically are still relatively invisible.

What also happened in Genova is that in response to this challenge the Italian government and (more hiddenly) its G8 partners declared war on the anti-globalization movement, first by brutally attacking hundreds of peaceful demonstrators, and then by staunchly defending these attacks as perfectly legitimate, thus de facto backing a strategy of terror, and the abolition of all legal, civic, and human rights.

In the days and weeks following the Genova events, the Berlusconi government has not spared efforts, with the assistance of the many TV channels and newspapers which it now controls, to blame on the anti-global protesters the violence unleashed on them. Scenes of stone-throwing demonstrators confronting the police or methodically destroying shop-windows or putting cars on fire have been broadcast over and over, while the unprecedented sight of the hundreds of thousands who marched with chants and banners, have been censored. The goal has been to whip up a wave of moral indignation against the protesters high enough to make people forget the brutality and illegality of the treatment meted out to them.

Thus, it is very important for us, as we reflect on the meaning of the Genova demonstrations on the fate of our movement, to be clear on one basic fact: *What happened in Genova reflects a pre-meditated institutional plan to repress and terrorize the demonstrators, to convince them to never again participate in such protest. This plan was not shaped by how activists behaved.*

This could be seen by the shape of the events. The three days of demonstrations against the G-8, July 19-21, were planned, on the one side, by the new Berlusconi government and, on the other, by the Genoa Social Forum (GSF, a network of more than a thousand Italian and international antiglobalization associations, organizations and groups) and the Tute Bianche, an Italian organization that has specialized in non-violent blockades of meetings of the global "leaders." There were a number of meetings between the two sides that supposedly laid the ground rules for the confrontation. Three days of protest were planned. On the first, July 19, there was to be an international demonstration of immigrants, the second day was to be one of non-violent civil disobedience, and the third day was to be an international mass demonstration.

Even before the first demo, however, it was clear that the government was doing its best to create a sense of panic among the population to prevent people from going to Genova and to build the image of the anti-globalization demonstrators as terrorists. First there was the "bombs strategy". For a couple of days newspapers and TV news were filled with reports of bombs and/or mysterious packages being found in several parts of Italy, especially in Milan; then letter bombs arrived at the office of the Director of TV 4, one of Berlusconi's channels, and other companies. All in all there were 60 bomb scares(!!).

Meanwhile, hundreds of people were refused entrance at the borders (686 by the 18th), a move made possible by the fact that, for the duration of the summit, the Schengen Treaty (which guaranteed EU citizens freedom to cross all EU borders) was suspended. All those who arrived were meticulously screened, three buses of Greeks activists, with one of the organizing committees, were prevented from landing from the ship in Ancona. In addition, the gathering places in Genova were raided; innocuous, defensive material was confiscated and displayed on TV as if they were weapons; airports and train stations were closed.

But the most telling sign of what was to come what was done to Genova. By the 18th, Genova was a ghost-town as the area in which the G8 were to meet— the Zona Rossa—was enclosed in a true iron cage and people were practically forced to leave the city. It is now clear that the government did not want to have witnesses for the "action" planned. As in Prague, workers were forced to take their vacations during the summit, shop-keepers were told to keep their shops closed and leave because "vandals were coming." One Genovese out of three abandoned the city—in the end the only people left, especially in the Zona Rossa, were some elderly who had nowhere to go and could not even get to the streets because police patrols would push them back inside. Interviewed by the press they looked disoriented, disbelieving. "We look like tigers in a cage,"one said. "Not even in time of war we have seen anything like it." Others noted the eerie silence only broken by the buzz of the helicopters and the sound of the boots of the cops on the pavement— "the silence of a city after a coup d'etat," a paper wrote.

Everyone looked dismayed as scores of welders enclosed the Zona Rossa within a gated iron net. "Here democracy ends", "zone with limited rights" read the posters placed on the bars by some activists (and quickly removed by the police). So the signs of what was to come were there.

The next day, July 19th, however, passed without incident. In fact it was a glorious day. Immigrant organizations from all over Italy and other parts of Europe marched to protest the treatment meted out to them by the Italian government and the EU, and to present their demands: legal recognition, asylum rights, housing. It was wonderful in Italy, where immigrants are treated like pariahs and made object of a constant persecution, to see immigrants and Italians occupying the streets together, saying no to racism, demonstrating in their lives and struggles the effects of globalization and the political possibilities their presence in Europe opens up. (On the day before in Genova, a meeting of trade unionists from all over Europe was held, this too a first, and a sign, perhaps, that the trade unions may be beginning to realize the importance of international solidarity and coordination, even though the CGIL has refused to take a position against globalization. "Globalization must be agreed upon (*concertata*)—they said—not fought against.")

The "war" started on Friday, July 20th. By this time, despite the raids, the panic disseminated with the "bomb attempts- (a bomb was placed near the entry of the Carlini camp, where the Tute Bianche and other demonstrators had gathered), despite the high number of people rejected at the borders, the long checks to which individuals and busses were submitted, about 150, 000 had assembled. As in the anti-IMF/World Bank demonstrations in Prague, they were to demonstrate in different blocks, coming from the different gathering spots to then converge in the center of the town, where some groups had announced they would try to enter the Zona Rossa. But no one from the main demo made it there. From an early time in the morning a scenario started unfolding that continued through the next day. Demonstrators presumably belonging to the Black Bloc clashing with the police were chased in the direction of the other demonstrators, and soon policemen were attacking with tear gas and batons the whole march with a determination that was almost murderous.

This is no exaggeration and we urge people everywhere to read as many testimonies and reports as they can to verify this statement. Thousands of people, of all ages, peacefully marching were viciously beaten while strange demonstrators, clad in black and moving in paramilitary fashion were given free reign. For hours they were allowed to move from place to place, destroying things on their way—cars, windows; when the police charged them their goal was to push them towards the march, and in fact, through this tactic, the bulk of the demonstrators were assaulted. It is now agreed and documented that there were provocateurs and members of right-wing, nazi groups among the "Black Bloc" and the other demonstrators. As we heard over and over, a few hundred belligerants were free to move from place to place, rarely pursued by the cops and carabinieri, while the mass of the demo was savagely attacked.

That afternoon a policeman in a van shot Carlo Guiliani, a young demonstrator from Genova in the head. In the effort to get out of the hands of the furious crowd the driver of the van ran over Carlo's body twice.

As the news of Carlo's killing moved through the streets of Genova the battles, beatings and arrests continued. The arrested were sent to a number of jails for booking. One of the most infamous was Bolzenato which was, as one inmate put it, "truly a hell." The police in the prison were special mobile police officers sent from Rome who were trained to put down prison revolts. Cages for torture were built especially for the demo and those arrested were forced to sing fascist songs or little ditties like "1, 2, 3. . . viva Pinochet/ 4, 5, 6. . . kill the Jews/7, 8, 9. . . I don't care about little black kids" (it rhymes in Italian). People who had arrived already wounded were further attacked and women were threatened with rape. Those with dreads had their heads shaved and those with piercings had them ripped out.

The next day was scheduled to be the day of the international mass demonstration. The parade route had been previously announced and no attempt to penetrate the Red Zone had been organized that day. Most estimates put the number at about 300,000, one of the largest demonstrations in recent European history. The news of the savage attacks on peaceful demonstrators as well as Carlo Guilaini's killing had spread fast enough that many Italians who had previously planned not to take part in the demos came to protest what had happened the day before.

The GSF organizers were conscious of the danger of the police using the relatively marginal presence of the Black Bloc as an excuse to attack the mass demonstration. They attempted to distinguish the peaceful demonstrators from the Black Bloc by assigning a large number of clearly designated marshals to keep the ones intent on throwing stones at the police and smashing bank windows away from the cortege. This was not an empty gesture. There were times that people in the Black Bloc and the marshals clashed physically.

But these precautions and the previous agreements with the government did not help. The police literally pounced on the demonstrators. Thousands were attacked in the streets, tear gas was dropped on them from helicopters and even launched from boats. Mayhem was the police's order of the day.

With hundreds more arrests, hundreds more wounded, the day ended in the final display of terror: the attack on the Diaz school complex, which had been reserved with the approval of the local government as a place for sleeping. Ninety-three mostly young people were there when the police stormed in and beat most of them there, expertly, often to the edge of their lives. Some G8 leaders had clearly decided that this was to be the antiglobalization movement's Wounded Knee.

Immovable Objects with Batons: the G8 in Genova

It would be a mistake to read the police violence unleashed in Genova as the instinctive reaction of a fascistic government. True, Berlusconi's right-wing political history and the presence in his government of Alleanza Nationale, the modern reincarnation of the Mussulini's party, easily raise the spectre of a fascist coup. But it can be demonstrated that the repression carried out in Genova was concerted among the G8 leaders who were all present with their security forces during the police attacks, and well aware of it.

The attacks on demonstrators in Genoa were not the "excesses" of a fascistic government, but a well-calculated strategy, discussed and approved at the highest European and international levels.

First, the government, as mentioned before, while pretending to dialogue with the movement and expressing concern for the safety of the demonstrators, launched war against them.

Second, the plan for Genova was quite similar to that implemented in Quebec, and partly in Prague: force the local population to leave, isolate the demonstrators, fence off the meeting's zone, terrorize future demonstrators with preemptive raids, torture the arrested in the jail, scare everyone with heavy sentences and draconian laws. The government created the conditions for confrontation by treating the demonstrators as literal "plague-bearers" and transforming Genova from the lively city that it is into a military zone where police could operate with impunity.

Third, the complicity of the EU police services and US police has also been documented. We know now that three members of the Los Angeles Sheriff's Department went to Italy in June to give a hand in organizing the police response in Genova. Also documented is the collaboration between the police of the EU countries and the Italian police. Lists of names were sent to Italy by other EU governments signaling the arrival of certain activists, destined, it seems, to a special treatment; Greek activists believe that the Greek police informed their Italian colleagues about the buses where the Greek Genova organizing committee was traveling so that they could be prevented from landing in Ancona.

Most important, the diplomatic protests that have been presented to the Italian government by other government members of the EU have been totally inadequate considering the gravity of the violations of international law of which Italy has made itself responsible. The behavior of the Italian police and authorities towards foreign nationals has been so abominable that, in other times, it would have been a casus belli. Not only were hundreds and hundreds of peaceful demonstrators brutally beaten in the streets, often in ways that will maim them for life—but, in violation of the Geneva convention on prisoners and the EU convention on human rights, the following occurred:

(a) Demonstrators were mercilessly beaten by groups of policemen even when on the ground, and in no condition to inflict any harm or defend themselves;

(b) On Saturday evening, July 21, when the demos were over, hundreds of policemen conducted a punitive expedition, Chilean style, in the Diaz school complex where participants to the demos were sleeping. Many of them were foreign nationals. Of the 93 present, 66 exited on stretchers. Wounds inflicted included broken jaws—a young woman lost 14 teeth—broken ribs and punctured lungs;

(c) Dozens of arrested protesters, including many foreign nationals, were tortured in jail physically and psychologically;

(d) Arrested protesters, again including many foreign nationals, were kept incommunicado up to 96 hours—they were literally kidnapped by the Italian state;

(e) The foreign nationals arrested were made to sign statements in Italian (a language many could not read) and beaten when they asked for translators;

(f) Once released, even when cleared from all charges, foreign nationals were still forbidden from remaining in Italy. They were taken directly to the airport and put on a plane without documents and their belongings—despite the fact that lawyers and families were waiting for them outside the prisons. They were also informed that (in violation of the Schengen Treaty) they would not be allowed to return to Italy for another five years.

How could the European Parliament and the other government members of the EU have accepted this situation unless they had given it their dispensation? The G8 meeting was not some internal Italian affair; it was the meeting of a club of government leaders. Each of them must be held responsible for what happened there, both inside the Palazzo Ducale and outside. The Security Services of Schroeder, Jospin, Bush, and Blair were in Genova and must have given them first-hand reports as to what was unfolding. They were not pure bystanders.

Presently, some of the foreign governments are protesting and asking for explanations. But how could all of this have happened to begin with? Why is Italy not being expelled, or at least suspended from the EU? Why is Berlusconi not being denounced as a violator of human rights? And is it imaginable that the Italian government, which rarely acts in an independent fashion and always bends to the powerful, dared so openly to challenge the international agreements it has signed and threaten the lives of hundreds of EU nationals without a prior assenting nod by their governments?

Again, the answer must be *No!* We must make sure that the fact that the Berlusconi government is a right-wing government does not provide an alibi for the other EU countries that are equally responsible but glad perhaps to have the dirty work done by an already tainted partner. Blair publicly signaled his approval of Berlusconi's tactics before Genova by calling for a "robust" repressive response to the demonstrators. Schroeder called for a vigorous attack on "political hooligans" in the anti-globalization movement in the days after Genova. Indeed, the focus of the post-Genova intergovernmental discussion among EU members was of the creation of a EU-wide police body, with a site in every country, that would specialize in responding to the anti-globalization movement, and/or the creation of a special EU investigative corps, again concentrating on the anti-globalization movement.

There are, of course, limits to the EU governmental complicity. Appearances must be saved, and some lip service to human rights must be given. The very use of the human rights strategy as a way of speeding up the globalization process has now created a certain degree of inhibition (at least in Europe) in the use of force. Even the Berlusconi government, after several days of undiluted praise to the police has had to make some concessions. This is why it has been discovered that some "excesses" occurred, and some heads in the police force have rolled. But, all in all, we are witnessing a great political white-wash.

The Italian state's reaction in Genova was so violent and indiscriminate with the blessing of the G-8 because the G-8 and other globalization planners have nothing to give to the protest movement. They have nothing to negotiate so can only respond with repression.

That the peaceful were treated as violently as the belligerent is a telling sign that just being against capitalist globalization makes criminals of us. The global leaders cannot afford such a degradation of their legitimacy; they cannot differentiate, and make concessions because they have nothing to concede. The only language they can speak now is that of tear gas canisters, batons, groin kicks, and cigarette burns. The antiglobalization protest is a serious political challenge to their plans on many levels. They disrupts their meetings, give new confidence to Third World politicians who understand that capitalist globalization is a re-colonization process, undermine the New International Division of Labor, and, just a decade after the collapse of communism, re-propose the question of an alternative to capitalism as a matter of life and death for the majority of the world population.

The G8 cannot make concessions, since their Genova meeting occurred under the cloud of a pan-capitalist economic crisis—occurring not just in Asia, Russia, or Brazil, as in previous times, but in the heartland of advanced capitalism with simultaneous profits collapses in the US, Japan and the EU. This is why, despite the prayers of the Pope and Bono, and despite the condescending invitation to three African leaders, the issue of the Third World debt was not even put on the table. It was replaced by the question of a fund for AIDS in Africa, which is nothing more than a modest donation to the pharmaceutical companies to be administered by the World Bank.

Instead, the main topic of discussion for the G8 was the "economy" in the US, Japan, and Europe. Less than five months before the introduction of monetary unification, few countries in Europe have fulfilled the conditionalities nations must satisfy in order to join the unification stipulated almost a decade ago—few have reduced public spending, or managed to grow within the prescribed limits. Italy in particular has been the object of much deprecation by EU and IMF officers because of its large public debt and its population's resistance to pension and healthcare cuts. Thus, barely three months after the elections, the new government has "discovered" the public deficit is far larger than expected in the very days of the demonstration, as the police were beating and torturing the demonstrators, the government was preparing a legislative packet which is guaranteed to generate much protest and resistance in the Fall—a packet which decimates healthcare and reproposes the question of reducing pensions. We can well surmise that the ferocity of the repression in the streets of Genova and the sadistic behavior displayed by the police were also meant to be a warning for the Fall when the truth concerning the price of "European unity" is going to be revealed.

The state violence in Genova is an essential part of the devaluation of European labor that is now required by globalization.

When demonstrators in Genova said that they felt like they were in Chile or Argentina or they were being beaten like Rodney King in Los Angeles they expressed a deep intuition: *they were being treated by the police as if they were poor people in the Third World or blacks in the US, i.e., people whose labor has been so systematically devalued the police have no inhibitions in killing and maiming them.* This devaluation has taken place in the US and the Third World already (in the US with the quarter-century decline in real wages and the mass incarceration of black and Hispanic youth), but European capital has been hesitant to apply the same "Third World" and "American" methods to their own citizens. At best, this treatment has been reserved for the immigrants from Africa and the Middle East who have found themselves in the clutches of "Fortress Europe." European capital is now being told, however, by the IMF and its own planners that, if European unification is to overcome its own economic crisis, globalization "with a human face" must end. The European working class must be dramatically devalued, and a short-cut to devaluation is to treat anyone who resists the new economic policies not as a legitimate protester but as a criminal. The closest contemporary comparison to the way the Italian police responded to the protesters in Genova is the violent and unprovoked police behavior against anti-IMF/World Bank demonstrations in Third World nations like Nigeria, Jamaica and Bolivia.

The killing of Carlo Guiliani in the streets of Genova must then be seen as the beginning of a campaign intended to degrade and devalue European workers.

Genova and the Limits of the Seattle Experience

Even with the inevitable repression and the much grieved for death and maimings, the Genova demonstrations were in some respects an enormous success for the antiglobalization movement. Hundreds of thousands came from all over Europe to these demonstrations in the face of very open intimidation. Clearly the message of the movement is increasing in its range and power. Moreover, the mass immigrant march was an important first step in tying together the post-Seattle antiglobalization struggle in Europe with the much longer struggle against globalization in the Third World. After all, many immigrants were forced out their homes by globalization policies they struggled against in the streets of Africa, Asia and South America.

However, there is no doubt that at the end of the Genova demonstrations there was an wave of internal criticism and divisiveness within the movement which for some was much more demoralizing than Carlo's death and the hundreds of broken bones. It is important to voice some of this criticism in order to see that what is being criticized is not due of the personal failings of people of the GSF, the Tute Bianche or the genuine Black Bloc (Anarchists or autonomist Marxists as opposed to undercover police or neo-nazi thugs). It arises from a change in the struggle against globalization because a number of the tactics that proved so successful in Seattle are reaching their limit.

The major criticism lodged against the GSF is that it put too much trust in the negotiation with the government, underrating the hostility of the G8 against the anti-globalization movement and the previous examples of Washington D.C. and Quebec which testify to the growing tendency toward repression. GSF consequently failed to warn the participants of the risks they ran and to defend the march against surprise attack. The GSF also acted as if it represented the whole movement which it did not, with the result that again it did not prepare the demonstrators concerning the dangers they ran.

The common criticism lodged against the genuine Black Bloc-ers is that they failed to realize to what extent their tactics exposed them to being used by the government to attack the demonstration. As a result their tactics provoked revulsion among many of the demonstrators who found themselves facing a police charge and being severely beaten on account of both the Bloc's belligerence and the their readiness to flee after an action.

The main criticism lodged against Tute Bianche is that they insisted on entering the Red Zone even after it was clear that this would not be possible by any sort of civil disobedience, except at an unacceptably high cost. Even if they succeeded in a physical confrontation with the police, they could hardly have counted on the sympathy and applause of the Italian population, especially not the workers who, in Italy, as every other country, have a long history of physical confrontation with the police, but, precisely for this reason, are not likely to appreciate facing the risk of beating or arrest for sake of a purely symbolic gestures.

These criticisms, however just, have arisen, we believe, because two tactics which proved so successful in Seattle are reaching the limit of their effectiveness. First, the flexible, mass nonviolent blockade of globalizers' meetings inaugurated in Seattle—which has been quite successful until recently—is now in a crisis. Certainly as a result of the use of this tactic the globalizers' meetings since November 1999 cannot be held without the equivalent of city-wide shut-down in order to ensure that the meetings go ahead. At the same time, this type of blockade it is becoming problematic. The globalizers have shown that with thousands of police, tons of iron and barbed wire, and dozens of helicopters, they can have their meetings and make the protestors pay heavily in terms of the arrested, tortured, maimed and killed. The flexible blockade is not magical. Like any other tactic—e.g., the factory strike or the consumer boycott—it can be thwarted, just as strikes of factory workers can be defeated by the bringing in scabs, as has so often been done in the major factory worker confrontations with capital in the US during the 1980s and 1990s.

The Seattle demonstrations did succeed in disrupting a WTO meeting. But the globalizers are learning, and if their present ruminations are to be realized, they will be soon meet high on the Rockies (the next G8 meeting venue) or (as with the WTO's next shindig in Qatar) similarly inaccessible locations. Under these circumstances the goal of antiglobization demos must be rethought. More emphasis must be placed on the broader political aspects of the convergences— in the same way as in the 1980s, faced by the wide use of scabs by employers, unionists realized that no strike could win without a broad political preparation which often included making connections with workers in Asia or South America. This is being increasingly understood within the antiglobalization movement; it is learning that demonstrations against the WTO in fifty cities around the planet might be more effective than a purely symbolic attempt to blockade the globalizers' meeting in the middle of a desert, on top of a mountain, in the middle of sea or even in outer space! This does not mean, of course, that large antiglobalization demonstrations on the site of globalizers' meetings will be abandoned. On the contrary, the very possibility that such blockades could be called by the movement will forever change the nature of way capitalist globalizers will meet.

The second way Genova has also shown the limits of a tactic that proved so successful in Seattle involves the pluralistic approach to demonstrating. The pluralistic-style of organizing adopted in Genova seemed a promising, but ultimately problematic way of implementing the movement slogan, "One No, Many Yeses" (i.e., we can agree on rejecting capitalist globalization without agreeing beforehand on our alternative ways of fighting it or our post-capitalist ways of living). This approach was tried successfully in Seattle where there were simultaneously nonviolent blockaders, "Black Bloc" assaulters on Starbucks and Nike stores, and AFL-CIO members marching in a huge parade far from the confrontation zone. This model has been refined since then. In Prague pluralism was formalized, with the choice of three colors reflecting different ways of participating in the demonstration, while in Genoa there were five. This choice seemed to imply that there many different ways to confront Power and they could co-exist and even potentiate each other, as they did in Seattle.

This model assumes, however, that (a) the opposition will accept the rules of the game and modulate its response with respect to individual demonstrators according to the choice s/he made, and (b) that the demonstrators will also play by the rules. But neither assumption worked in Genova. The police, it appears, clubbed NGOers, feminists, enviromentalists, and Tute Bianche more than they did Black bloc-ers. This was not a momentary lapse on the part of the Italian police. It is now clear that from the viewpoint of the authorities all protestors of globalization are criminals.

Demonstrators were also unable to "honor" their colors and moved from one to another according to the situation. For example, many who had come to participate in a nonviolent demonstration physically confronted the police when attacked.

Again, this is not to say that "pluralism" in demonstrations is to be abandoned, but that the movement must be clear as to the extent and limits of this organizational tactic. The policies that govern one's participation in such demonstrations must also be clarified.

For demos are not just to be measured on a utilitarian basis, they are also prefigurations of the future world a movement wants to build, they offer protesters an opportunity to show concretely what the alternatives to capitalist globalization can be. This, ultimately, is the most powerful "weapon," the most effective means of consciousness-raising that the antiglobalization movement has, the one that would concretely show not only that this movement is capable of moving an immovable rock, but can build a new world. The first thing we can show the world (since it is watching) is that we can engage in common projects without irreducible conflict. If this is not possible, it will be a major defeat for the movment. In that case, the movement will loose its legitimacy as the bearer of alternative to capitalist globalization, a much more dangerous consequence than any police assault. In a word, what is crucial here is not just the police attack on the movement—which was all but inevitable in Genova given their use of provocateurs, neo-nazis and pre-emptive violence—but the movement's relation to itself. The powerful image of a movement that can bring together determined nonviolent blockaders and black blockers with unionists, enviromentalists, and NGOers and powerfully say *"No!"* to globalization is now being questioned under the pressure of an intense wave of repression. But the limits of Seattle's tactics are not the limits of the movement.

Finally, we should remember that though demonstrations like those in Seattle, Washington, Quebec and now Genova are important, the fate of the movement does not hinge on their success alone. This movement has far deeper and stronger roots in the daily confrontations of billions of people in Africa, Asia, and the Americas against the globalization agenda and its enforcers. A key question on the movement's horizon then is: how can this multiplicity of struggle in the Third World be expressed and amplified by the antiglobalization demonstrations in the metropoles of Europe and North America?

August 23, 2001

Silvia Federici and George Caffentzis

And Balanced With This Life, This Death
Genoa, the G8 and the battle in the streets

by Ramor Ryan

The Siege of Genoa

The walls went up around the old quarter of Genoa, enclosing the Group of 8 (G8) and their cohorts. Huge heavy walls of concrete and metal, like medieval fortifications or prison fences; walls to keep the people out, the world leaders penned in. Genoa is a beautiful renaissance city carved out of a treacherous mountain slope that seems as if it might slide irrevocably into the sea. Its pulsating streets, the mystery of its dense labyrinth and the expansive calm of the sea front are a surreal theater for the battle that would consume it.

Leading up to the summit, the authorities had closed down the airport, the main railway stations and severely restricted access by road. Aside from the center of town (the red zone), which was completely forbidden to citizens, the surrounding area (the yellow zone) was also restricted with people enduring random stop and searches. Local people fled the town in droves, and most businesses closed for the duration of the summit. The G8 had transformed Genoa from a thriving commercial and tourist metropolis to a war zone under a form of martial law.

As if to justify the extraordinary security measures, the media reported various bomb scares and explosive finds, all of which protesters viewed skeptically. No groups present claimed responsibility. These are not tactics used by the alternative globalization movement. The Italian military brought in an array of defensive missiles. War ships were stationed in the bay. A state of paranoid terror was created to dissuade protesters from coming, and to criminalize those who did.

On the Austrian border, activists from the group 'No Borders' were attacked; one woman lost 5 teeth. A boat full of protesters from Greece was held and the passengers attacked by riot police. Several hundred British protesters traveling by train were detained in France and a group of cyclists were held at the German border. Seventy migrants traveling from Germany to attend the

Migrants March on the Thursday prior to the G8 Summit were refused entry into Italy. People disembarking at airports in Milan and Turin were subjected to interrogation and searches. Cars were routinely pulled over and the occupants detained. Nevertheless, tens of thousands of outsiders would make it to Genoa and as many as 200,000 demonstrators attended the final demonstration .

The Genoa Social Forum—One No, Many Yeses.

The logistical setup for the protesters centered around the Genoa Social Forum (GSF), the organizing body representing over 800 diverse groups advocating an alternative to the current corporate globalization. Their slogan was *A Different World Is Possible.* They pointed out that the movement was not anti-globalization, but an alternative vision of globalization, one that does not put profits before people, free trade before free movement; a movement that seeks to eliminate the gap between rich and poor, the powerful and the powerless. In a word, to democratize the process of globalization.

The GSF was based in a huge parking lot on the sea front. From this Convergence Center, people were dispatched to camp in various stadiums and parks across the city, loosely based on group affiliation. A thriving Indymedia Center was located nearby. There were legal, medical and administrative centers demonstrating how the movement organizes itself autonomously. Cafe Clandestino provided free food and drink, while Manu Chao played a free late night concert before 25,000 ecstatic revelers the night before the summit began. A message from Sub-Commandante Marcos was boomed over the PA. How can one town hold so many Che Guevara t-shirts, Zapatista paliacates, Palestinian scarves?! The international connection, bridges between 1st and 3rd worlds, North and South, were everywhere to be seen, not just in the presence of Kurdish, African, Russian or Indian delegates, but also with Europeans who bring their foreign experiences home.

Gothenburg Revisited.

The paramilitary police raided the camping centers at dawn on the 20th, even before the summit began. From the start it was clear: heavy repression would be used to stifle protest with an iron fist. At the Carlini Stadium, temporary home to the strong Ya Basta faction, the loudspeakers woke us at 5:30 am. "The police have surrounded us, everybody defend the gates!"

Outside, lines of heavily armed paramilitary police stood ready. They demanded to enter to search for *arms and explosives.* Ya Basta is a non-violent direct action organization. "To show we have nothing to hide" and to diffuse the situation, the central committee allowed a delegation of cops in to search the premises. Many activists were furious to have to submit to this search, but the Ya Basta leaders prevailed. From early on, a split was emerging within the protesters' ranks between those who wished to resist the repression, and those who wanted to avoid confrontation. All around the city campsites are raided, causing distress, confusion, fear, and depriving people of sleep. Meanwhile houses of activists preparing to go to Genoa are raided in other cities; doors are kicked down, people detained. Five Germans are arrested while driving in a car close to the red zone.

The first mobilization takes place on Thursday 19 July. About 50,000 people gather for a Migrants' March. The day is warm and sunny and the streets throng with a peaceful, high-spirited multitude. There are no cops in sight, an dthe mood is light. The first demand—open the borders to people as well as goods. We are not against globalization, but against globalization that criminalizes and marginalizes migrants. Are the G8 listening? Do they care? At least it is reported that they are shifting their agenda to talk about debt relief (for people who never themselves borrowed the money which invariably benefits those nearest to the top of the pyramid) and an AIDS fund for Africa ($10 billion is requested, $1 billion is considered). The media is chocabloc full of street stories, scare stories, spectacular images, all fueling the tension. The stage is set: The New World Order, the Global Empire, protected by 20,000 police and military, besieged by the new Global protest movement. Graffiti appears on the walls."They make misery, we make history".

Death In Genoa.

Friday 20 July is a day of civil disobedience. The aim: to shut down the G8 by attempting to breach the fortifications enclosing the summit from a variety of positions. The tactics: direct action. The strongest contingent was the Ya Basta grouping, numbering more than 10,000 militants. Up at the Carlini Stadium, preparations began early with talks followed by training sessions. Resembling an army preparing for war, men and women, predominantly young and Italian, spent all morning taping up their fragile bodies with foam and padding. The atmosphere was tense, the mood defiant. It really seemed anything was possible. There was an ecstatic mood of celebration when we finally set off on the 4 km march to the city center. An endless sea of bopping helmets interspersed with a vast array of flags of every hue and color. At the front a long line of Ya Basta! militants pressed forward behind a wall of plastic shields.

News filtered through from around the city. Bad news. The Italian Trade Union group, COBAS, had been beaten badly before they had even gotten close to their target. In another part of the city, the Pink Block, a theatrical and prankster group of several thousands had also suffered heavy repression. A women's pacifist block had been attacked from the air by tear-gas firing helicopters. A strong section of Anarchists and 'Autonomes' had come close to the Red Zone but were now being brutally dispersed. The police were making pre-emptive strikes with tear gas and batons on every block. Only one of the roaming Black Bloc groups was not getting pounded, as they engaged in property destruction aimed at banks and multinational businesses. The only good news: one elderly man had, remarkably, penetrated the Red-Zone before been arrested.

Despite all the ominous reports, we swept down the wide boulevard confidently—we were so many! Like an unstoppable river! So many people prepared to use their bodies to break through, to defend themselves, to struggle. *El Pueblo Unido, Jamas Sera Vencido* they chanted. *Genova Libera! E-Z-L-N!* Rage Against The Machine blasted from the mobile P.A. as *Fuck You I Wont Do What You Tell Me!* was screamed along with by thousands. It was momentarily powerful and wonderful.

Two kilometers from the Red Zone, the police attacked us. First a frantic barrage of tear-gas canisters were lobbed over the front lines, deep into the heart of the demonstration. Nobody here had gas masks. The poisonous gas first blinds

Ramor Ryan

you, painfully, then disorientates you. It is immediate and devastating. The people, packed in tightly, panicked and surged backwards. Five Hundred heavily armed Riot squad cops stormed the front lines. In brutal scenes, the Ya basta militants crumbled despite brave resistance. All were battered. People screamed, turned, fled, falling over each other.

We retreated up the road. The sky was heavy with gas and helicopters hovered overhead. A water cannon blasted away, throwing bodies around like paper bags. What now? People looked to the Ya Basta! leadership, but there was no Plan B. The microphone that issued commands during the march was now silent. People retreated further and further, eventually sitting down. Meanwhile the front lines struggled to hold on, and the fighting was intense, the tear gas volleys raining down, the police hitting out viciously as the plastic shields shattered and the helmets cracked. Bleeding people were rushed to the back with head injuries including some inflicted when they had been shot in the face with tear gas canisters.

We were defeated before having even begun. The non-violent direct action tactics; an active defense crushed in the face of decisively brutal police tactics. As the majority of the march sat down further up the road, thousands of others streamed off into the side streets. The right-side was blocked by the railway track, while to the left lay a labyrinth of small enclosed streets. *Open new fronts! Break through police lines at 2, 3, 4 different points!* Spontaneous and enraged, thousands ran into the sidestreets. Meanwhile, the Ya Basta loudspeaker requested people to stay put on the road, far from the Red Zone.

Rebel Joy and Sorrow.

In a beautiful old barrio, the battle raged. Protesters charged up tight streets flinging stones at police lines. The police, protected head to toe, amassed behind shields and flanked by armored vehicles, responded with tear gas and by flinging back the rocks. The ferocious spirit of the protesters more than the paltry stones pushed back the police lines. Barricades were built with dumpsters, cars, anything at hand. The front lines would retreat nursing wounds and poisoned eyes. The more seriously injured were carried to ambulances. New people rushed to the front, while others tore up the pavement for ammunition. A tall gentleman fell back saying " We almost got through, we almost did it, we just need a few more people !"

Another surge, everyone rushed forward on 2 or 3 different streets. Some riot cops got stranded in their retreat and hand-to-hand fighting ensued. Those fighting are not necessarily in black, though some are masked. Some have helmets. It is not the Black Bloc, and there are no agent provocateurs. This is a militant energy driven by people who have said, *Ya Basta!, Fuck the police! Rage! Energy! Resolve!*

They move forward. Tear gas is everywhere. The police are retreating. An armored carabinieri truck is captured and the occupants flee. It is smashed up and set ablaze. This symbol of the hated oppressive state, is burning and everyone is cheering, filled with rebel joy. Someone sprays "We Are Winning!," the famous slogan that appeared in Seattle on the side of the carcass of the armored beast. Now they are almost in Piazza Alimondo. They are pushing the police back, two blocks, then three, further and further. Protesters are euphoric, storming forward, overwhelming the despised carabinieri. Approaching the despised wall of the G8; *"Here we are,"* they chant, *"we resist!"*

Hundreds strong, they poured into the expansive Piazza Alimondo. Two police vehicles drive recklessly into the crowd, one drives away, the other stalls; people rush toward the vehicle. Shots ring out. Rubber bullets? No, the ominous thud of live ammunition. The air heaved. The protesters stopped, reeled around, and fled.

Carlo Guiliani was 23 years old. A rebel. The papers belittled him, called him a "ne'er do well," a squatter. But we know him as a comrade and a revolutionary. He fought the paramilitary police bravely, fearlessly, pitting the little streets against the great. He was involved in the Zapata Social Center of Genoa. Carlo's death was not heroic, nor tragic. It was the consequence of his life, how he lived, how he resisted. Moments before he was shot in the face, Carlo probably felt the extraordinary rebel joy of this spontaneous uprising against power in the little side streets of Genoa. He died instantly, or else when the police drove over him, not once but twice, as if to make sure he was dead, really dead. For the police, Carlo had to die. Now they must kill us, because we are beginning to really threaten their power. Carlo was murdered. We are all Carlo.

The Ghost of Pinochet.

Saturday 21 July. This is how the police work. . . It is Saturday afternoon and there are as many as 200,000 people marching on Genoa against the eight most powerful economic powers in the world. It is not a combative march. As they swing onto the sea front, a group of agent provocateurs began throwing stones at the police. These are undercover cops, or secret police, or mercenaries or nazi's. They are used by the police the same way the paramilitaries are used by the state in Chiapas or in Belfast, or even how they used them in Italy in the 1970s. The police want to pick the time and place of the confrontation. They are ready and prepared. This was planned. This is how the police work: a few stones fall harmlessly into their ranks and they open up with tear-gas. The canisters fly deep into the multitude, immediately creating panic and chaos. People flee, young and old, parents with babies in their arms. But there are too many people, nowhere to run, they are hemmed in and poisoned from the gas. It is horrific.

This is how the people resist. . . The militants stream through the crowd to the front. There they attempt to build barricades and hold back the advancing cops. The sky fills with stones. They hold the police and those behind them have a few moments more to retreat. Those who needed to get away from the zone could. Communist party stewards directed people away, but many people stayed, indignant that the demonstration could be so brutally dispersed even before it could get to the piazza. Now is the hour of the Black Bloc and the insurrectionary anarchists. All afternoon the streets were mad with tear-gas, with stones, with burning banks, burning cars, barricades. The air was shrill with screams, of beatings, violence and fear.

Eventually the barricades were overrun. The police advanced ferociously, beating people indiscriminately. In a most surreal scene, cops in gray overalls beat up people on the beach, the Italian Riviera, while bathers looked on. Police in small boats launched tear-gas onto the beach. A helicopter overhead fired gas into the fleeing hordes. Further up, people jumped off the rocks into the sea. The huge march ended in absolute mayhem. Let it be recorded—200,000 overtly peaceful protesters were not allowed to demonstrate. "The Genoa Social Forum favored and covered the Black Bloc," said Italian Prime Minister Silvio Berlusconi by way of explanation the next day. We are all guilty. We are all Carlo Giulliani.

Attacking Indymedia

At midnight, the next police operation began. We were eating in a restaurant near the Indymedia Center. The quiet residential street was silent, the neighborhood sleeping. A long line of heavily armored men rushed by, masked and with their batons swinging. In single file, silent but for the thumping of their boots on the pavement. The next moment, a fleet of armored police vehicles rushes by. Suddenly a helicopter shattered the night sky. Finally, a long line of ambulances blasting their sirens passed by. All this in a couple of minutes, a surgical strike on the movement's offices. The police were extracting revenge. They crashed through the front gates of the Indymedia Center in an armored truck, then smashed up the computers, confiscated files and film and broke cameras, terrorizing the journalists inside.

Across the road in the school building being used by the GSF as offices and a dormitory for people who felt unsafe in the camping grounds, the real horror occurred. Police and plain-clothes cops—reportedly from the special paramilitary police unit , GOM—burst in and attacked everyone inside. Most were sleeping on the floor. Ninety-three people were injured, as the police closed the door and inflicted heavy punishment. Scores of people were eventually carried out on stretchers. Pools of blood remained on the floor, streaks of blood across the walls. Attacks on property cannot be equated to the legions of broken limbs, broken teeth, broken ribs and damaged skulls that a squad of police men inflicted on a somnambulant group of weary protesters as they lay on the floor of a school.

State Sponsored Terror

These men were following orders. Those who gave the orders get their general directives from a higher authority. The blame for this state terror lies at the feet of Berlusconi's regime, and ultimately, the G8. This is why we protest the G8. This is why comrades move from protest to resistance. The midnight attack on the school and Indymedia, the ensuing torture of the prisoners afterwards, was an attempt to terrorize the movement, to inflict extra-judiciary punishment on activists, and to instill mind numbing fear within the hearts and souls of protesters. In many ways, it was successful. Saturday night in Genoa was one of widespread fear and terror.

At the Carlini Stadium, bastion of the Ya Basta! movement, the officials ordered an immediate evacuation. "Like Saigon" reported one eye-witness. Hundreds of other activists not present at the time were left stranded. Plain clothes police swarmed in, and criminals were allowed in to rummage through peoples' belongings. That night, all over Genoa people fled from camping sites to roam the streets and alleys and back lanes of the city in fear, hunted like escaped convicts. It was the longest night. Eventually dawn came, but everything had changed.

Genoa was gutted. No city will host the G8 for a while. Thirty-four banks burnt. Eighty-three vehicles both police and civilian, destroyed, Forty-one businesses torched or looted, six supermarkets, twelve government offices illustrating the belief that some protesters have that targeting the economic organs of the enemy is the most effective tactic. (No buses were burnt, apparently because the bus drivers union was in solidarity with the protesters, ferrying everyone around for free the whole week). With Genoa in ruins, the G8 left quietly with a few promises to give some money to Africa (via drug companies). Italian Prime Minister Silvio Berlusconi blamed not just the Black Bloc and the anarchists, but the whole movement, rendering any distinction obsolete.

The GSF has since uncovered damning evidence of police collusion with agent provocateurs, and the inquiries into the night of terror at the school and the denunciations of torture afterwards continues, unrelenting. Two hundred people were arrested, six hundred injured. In the jails, the protesters were tortured while police mocked them with pictures of Mussolini and Nazis. They tortured them, as they have done in Seattle, Prague and Quebec. They tortured them as they did in Pinochet's Chile, in Argentina; everywhere activists have unsettled power, they terrorize them. They attempt to destroy the movement by spreading panic and fear. To break the back of the militants of this totally unarmed global protest movement.

A Summer's Day

A lovely tree filled piazza deep in the heart of Genoa. A pile of flowers. An endless flow of citizens pass by to pay their respects at the site of Carlo's murder. A memorial across the road beside an old church is overflowing with little gifts and offerings. Che Guevara images dominate amidst black, red and green flags, candles and flowers, cigarettes, beer bottles, tear gas canisters, Zapatista scarves, sunglasses, gloves. An array of notes and poems and good-bye letters from his friends. A photo of Carlo with his school class. He is the one with the shoulder length hair and the *Fuck Nike* t-shirt. Politically conscious at 16. People weep gently. Two squatter girls tie up a banner with the help of a posh older lady. A Mexican woman offers clasps from her coat to secure the banner. *"We with our hands,"* it read, *"they with their guns."*

Someone else leaves a poem, Shakespeare's Sonnet No. 18. "Shall I compare thee to a summers day?" On a summers day in Genoa, July 20,2001, Carlo fell. Let the July 20 Movement flourish.

WATERSHED:

TOWARDS A NEW MOVEMENT

part V:

The Vision Thing

Naomi Klein
The Nation, *July 10, 2000*

"This conference is not like other conferences."

That's what all the speakers at "Re-Imagining Politics and Society" were told before we arrived at New York's Riverside Church. When we addressed the delegates (there were about 1,000, over three days in May), we were to try to solve a very specific problem: the lack of "unity of vision and strategy" guiding the movement against global corporatism.

This was a very serious problem, we were advised. The young activists who went to Seattle to shut down the World Trade Organization and to Washington, DC, to protest the World Bank and the IMF had been getting hammered in the press as tree-wearing, lamb-costumed, drum-beating bubble brains. Our mission, according to the conference organizers at the Foundation for Ethics and Meaning, was to whip that chaos on the streets into some kind of structured, media-friendly shape. This wasn't just another talk shop. We were going to "give birth to a unified movement for holistic social, economic and political change."

As I slipped in and out of lecture rooms, soaking up vision galore from Arianna Huffington, Michael Lerner, David Korten and Cornel West, I was struck by the futility of this entire well-meaning exercise. Even if we did manage to come up with a ten-point plan—brilliant in its clarity, elegant in its coherence, unified in its outlook—to whom, exactly, would we hand down these commandments? The anti-corporate protest movement that came to world attention on the streets of Seattle last November is not united by a political party or a national network with a head office, annual elections and subordinate cells and locals. It is shaped by the ideas of individual organizers and intellectuals, but doesn't defer to any of them as leaders. In this amorphous context, the ideas and plans being hatched at the Riverside Church weren't irrelevant exactly, they just weren't important in the way they clearly hoped to be. Rather than changing the world, they were destined to be swept up and tossed around in the tidal wave of information—web diaries, NGO manifestoes, academic papers, homemade videos, *cris de coeur*—that the global anti-corporate network produces and consumes each and every day.

This is the flip side of the persistent criticism that the kids on the street lack clear leadership—they lack clear followers too. To those searching for replicas of the sixties, this absence makes the anti-corporate movement appear infuriatingly impassive: Evidently, these people are so disorganized they can't even get it together to respond to perfectly well-organized efforts to organize them. These are MTV-weaned activists, you can practically hear the old guard saying: scattered, nonlinear, no focus.

It's easy to be persuaded by these critiques. If there is one thing on which the left and right agree, it is the value of a clear, well-structured ideological argument. But maybe it's not quite so simple. Maybe the protests in Seattle and Washington look unfocused because they were not demonstrations of one movement at all but rather convergences of many smaller ones, each with its sights trained on a specific multinational corporation (like Nike), a particular industry (like agribusiness) or a new trade initiative (like the Free Trade Area of the Americas). These smaller, targeted movements are clearly part of a common cause: They share a belief that the disparate problems with which they are wrestling all derive from global deregulation, an agenda that is concentrating power and wealth into fewer and fewer hands. Of course, there are disagreements—about the role of the nation-state, about whether capitalism is redeemable, about the speed with which change should occur. But within most of these miniature movements, there is an emerging consensus that building community-based decision-making power—whether through unions, neighborhoods, farms, villages, anarchist collectives or aboriginal self-government—is essential to countering the might of multinational corporations.

Despite this common ground, these campaigns have not coalesced into a single movement. Rather, they are intricately and tightly linked to one another, much as "hotlinks" connect their websites on the Internet. This analogy is more than coincidental and is in fact key to understanding the changing nature of political organizing. Although many have observed that the recent mass protests would have been impossible without the Internet, what has been overlooked is how the communication technology that facilitates these campaigns is shaping the movement in its own image. Thanks to the Net, mobilizations are able to unfold with sparse bureaucracy and minimal hierarchy; forced consensus and labored manifestoes are fading into the background, replaced instead by a culture of constant, loosely structured and sometimes compulsive information-swapping.

What emerged on the streets of Seattle and Washington was an activist model that mirrors the organic, decentralized, interlinked pathways of the Internet—the Internet come to life.

The Washington-based research center TeleGeography has taken it upon itself to map out the architecture of the Internet as if it were the solar system. Recently, TeleGeography pronounced that the Internet is not one giant web but a network of "hubs and spokes." The hubs are the centers of activity, the spokes the links to other centers, which are autonomous but interconnected.

It seems like a perfect description of the protests in Seattle and Washington, DC. These mass convergences were activist hubs, made up of hun-

Watershed: Towards a New Movement

dreds, possibly thousands, of autonomous spokes. During the demonstrations, the spokes took the form of "affinity groups" of between five and twenty protesters, each of which elected a spokesperson to represent them at regular "spokescouncil" meetings. Although the affinity groups agreed to abide by a set of nonviolence principles, they also functioned as discrete units, with the power to make their own strategic decisions. At some rallies, activists carry actual cloth webs to symbolize their movement. When it's time for a meeting, they lay the web on the ground, call out "all spokes on the web" and the structure becomes a street-level boardroom.

In the four years before the Seattle and Washington protests, similar hub events had converged outside WTO, G7 and Asia Pacific Economic Cooperation summits in Auckland, Vancouver, Manila, Birmingham, London, Geneva, Kuala Lumpur and Cologne. Each of these mass protests was organized according to principles of coordinated decentralization. Rather than present a coherent front, small units of activists surrounded their target from all directions. And rather than build elaborate national or international bureaucracies, temporary structures were thrown up instead: Empty buildings were turned into "convergence centers," and independent media producers assembled impromptu activist news centers. The ad hoc coalitions behind these demonstrations frequently named themselves after the date of the planned event: J18, N30, A16, S26 and so on. When these events are over, they leave virtually no trace behind, save for an archived website.

Of course, all this talk of radical decentralization conceals a very real hierarchy based on who owns, understands and controls the computer networks linking the activists to one another—this is what Jesse Hirsh, one of the founders of the anarchist computer network Tao Communications, calls "a geek adhocracy."

The hubs and spokes model is more than a tactic used at protests; the protests are themselves made up of "coalitions of coalitions," to borrow a phrase from Kevin Danaher of Global Exchange. Each anti-corporate campaign is made up of many groups, mostly NGOs, labor unions, students and anarchists. They use the Internet, as well as more traditional organizing tools, to do everything from cataloguing the latest transgressions of the World Bank to bombarding Shell Oil with faxes and e-mails to distributing ready-to-download anti-sweatshop leaflets for protests at Nike Town. The groups remain autonomous, but their international coordination is deft and, to their targets, frequently devastating.

The charge that the anti-corporate movement lacks "vision" falls apart when looked at in the context of these campaigns. It's true that the mass protests in Seattle and DC were such a hodgepodge of slogans and causes, that to a casual observer, it was hard to decode the connections between Mumia's incarceration and the fate of the sea turtles. But in trying to find coherence in these large-scale shows of strength, the critics are confusing the outward demonstrations of the movement with the thing itself—missing the forest for the people dressed as trees. This movement is its spokes, and in the spokes there is no shortage of vision.

The student anti-sweatshop movement, for instance, has rapidly moved from simply criticizing companies and campus administrators to drafting alternate codes of conduct and building its own quasi-regulatory body, the Worker

Naomi Klein

Rights Consortium. The movement against genetically engineered and modified foods has leapt from one policy victory to the next, first getting many genetically modified foods removed from the shelves of British supermarkets, then getting labeling laws passed in Europe, then making enormous strides with the Montreal Protocol on Biosafety. Meanwhile, opponents of the World Bank's and IMF's export-led development models have produced bookshelves' worth of resources on community-based development models, debt relief and self-government principles. Critics of the oil and mining industries are similarly overflowing with ideas for sustainable energy and responsible resource extraction—though they rarely get the chance to put their visions into practice.

The fact that these campaigns are so decentralized is not a source of incoherence and fragmentation. Rather, it is a reasonable, even ingenious adaptation both to pre-existing fragmentation within progressive networks and to changes in the broader culture. It is a byproduct of the explosion of NGOs, which, since the Rio Summit in 1992, have been gaining power and prominence. There are so many NGOs involved in anti-corporate campaigns that nothing but the hubs and spokes model could possibly accommodate all their different styles, tactics and goals. Like the Internet itself, both the NGO and the affinity group networks are infinitely expandable systems. If somebody doesn't feel like they quite fit in to one of the 30,000 or so NGOs or thousands of affinity groups out there, they can just start their own and link up. Once involved, no one has to give up their individuality to the larger structure; as with all things online, we are free to dip in and out, take what we want and delete what we don't. It is a surfer's approach to activism reflecting the Internet's paradoxical culture of extreme narcissism coupled with an intense desire for external connection.

One of the great strengths of this model of laissez-faire organizing is that it has proven extraordinarily difficult to control, largely because it is so different from the organizing principles of the institutions and corporations it targets. It responds to corporate concentration with a maze of fragmentation, to globalization with its own kind of localization, to power consolidation with radical power dispersal.

Joshua Karliner of the Transnational Resource and Action Center calls this system "an unintentionally brilliant response to globalization." And because it was unintentional, we still lack even the vocabulary to describe it, which may be why a rather amusing metaphor industry has evolved to fill the gap. I'm throwing my lot in with hubs and spokes, but Maude Barlow of the Council of Canadians says, "We are up against a boulder. We can't remove it so we try to go underneath it, to go around it and over it." Britain's John Jordan, one of the founders of Reclaim the Streets, says transnationals "are like giant tankers, and we are like a school of fish. We can respond quickly; they can't." The US-based Free Burma Coalition talks of a network of "spiders," spinning a web strong enough to tie down the most powerful multinationals. A US military report about the Zapatista uprising in Chiapas even got in on the game. According to a study produced by RAND, the Zapatistas were waging "a war of the flea" that, thanks to the Internet and the global NGO network, turned into a "war of the swarm." The military challenge of a war of the swarm, the researchers noted, is that it has no "central leadership or command structure; it is multiheaded, impossible to decapitate."

Of course, this multiheaded system has its weaknesses too, and they were on full display on the streets of Washington during the anti-World Bank/IMF protests. At around noon on April 16, the day of the largest protest, a spokescouncil meeting was convened for the affinity groups that were in the midst of blocking all the street intersections surrounding the headquarters of the World Bank and the IMF. The intersections had been blocked since 6 AM, but the meeting delegates, the protesters had just learned, had slipped inside the police barricades before 5 AM. Given this new information, most of the spokespeople felt it was time to give up the intersections and join the official march at the Ellipse. The problem was that not everyone agreed: A handful of affinity groups wanted to see if they could block the delegates on their way out of their meetings.

The compromise the council came up with was telling. "OK, everybody listen up," Kevin Danaher shouted into a megaphone. "Each intersection has autonomy. If the intersection wants to stay locked down, that's cool. If it wants to come to the Ellipse, that's cool too. It's up to you."

This was impeccably fair and democratic, but there was just one problem—it made absolutely no sense. Sealing off the access points had been a coordinated action. If some intersections now opened up and other, rebel-camp intersections stayed occupied, delegates on their way out of the meeting could just hang a right instead of a left, and they would be home free. Which, of course, is precisely what happened.

As I watched clusters of protesters get up and wander off while others stayed seated, defiantly guarding, well, nothing, it struck me as an apt metaphor for the strengths and weaknesses of this nascent activist network. There is no question that the communication culture that reigns on the Net is better at speed and volume than at synthesis. It is capable of getting tens of thousands of people to meet on the same street corner, placards in hand, but is far less adept at helping those same people to agree on what they are really asking for before they get to the barricades—or after they leave.

For this reason, an odd sort of anxiety has begun to set in after each demonstration: Was that it? When's the next one? Will it be as good, as big? To keep up the momentum, a culture of serial protesting is rapidly taking hold. My inbox is cluttered with entreaties to come to what promises to be "the next Seattle." There was Windsor and Detroit on June 4 for a "shutdown" of the Organization of American States, and Calgary a week later for the World Petroleum Congress; the Republican convention will be in Philadelphia in July and the Democratic convention in LA in August; the World Economic Forum's Asia Pacific Economic Summit is on September 11 in Melbourne, followed shortly thereafter by anti-IMF demos on September 26 in Prague and then on to Quebec City for the Summit of the Americas in April 2001. Someone posted a message on the organizing e-mail list for the Washington demos: "Wherever they go, we shall be there! After this, see you in Prague!" But is this really what we want—a movement of meeting-stalkers, following the trade bureaucrats as if they were the Grateful Dead?

The prospect is dangerous for several reasons. Far too much expectation is being placed on these protests: The organizers of the DC demo, for instance, announced they would literally "shut down" two $30 billion transnational institutions, at the same time as they attempted to convey sophisticated ideas about the fallacies of neoliberal economics to the stock-happy public. They simply couldn't do it; no single demo could, and it's only going to get harder. Seattle's direct-action tactics worked because they took the police by surprise. That won't happen again. Police have now subscribed to all the e-mail lists. LA has put in a request for $4 million in new security gear and staffing costs to protect the city from the activist swarm.

In an attempt to build a stable political structure to advance the movement between protests, Danaher has begun to fundraise for a "permanent convergence center" in Washington. The International Forum on Globalization, meanwhile, has been meeting since March in hopes of producing a 200-page policy paper by the end of the year. According to IFG director Jerry Mander, it won't be a manifesto but a set of principles and priorities, an early attempt, as he puts it, at "defining a new architecture" for the global economy.

Like the conference organizers at the Riverside Church, however, these initiatives will face an uphill battle. Most activists agree that the time has come to sit down and start discussing a positive agenda—but at whose table, and who gets to decide?

These questions came to a head at the end of May when Czech President Vaclav Havel offered to "mediate" talks between World Bank president James Wolfensohn and the protesters planning to disrupt the bank's September 26-28 meeting in Prague. There was no consensus among protest organizers about participating in the negotiations at Prague Castle, and, more to the point, there was no process in place to make the decision: no mechanism to select acceptable members of an activist delegation (some suggested an Internet vote) and no agreed-upon set of goals by which to measure the benefits and pitfalls of taking part. If Havel had reached out to the groups specifically dealing with debt and structural adjustment, like Jubilee 2000 or 50 Years Is Enough, the proposal would have been dealt with in a straightforward manner. But because he approached the entire movement as if it were a single unit, he sent those organizing the demonstrations into weeks of internal strife that is still unresolved.

Part of the problem is structural. Among most anarchists, who are doing a great deal of the grassroots organizing (and who got online way before the more established Left), direct democracy, transparency and community self-determination are not lofty political goals, they are fundamental tenets governing their own organizations. Yet many of the key NGOs, though they may share the anarchists' ideas about democracy in theory, are themselves organized as traditional hierarchies. They are run by charismatic leaders and executive boards, while their members send them money and cheer from the sidelines.

So how do you extract coherence from a movement filled with anarchists, whose greatest tactical strength so far has been its similarity to a swarm of mosquitoes? Maybe, as with the Internet itself, you don't do it by imposing a preset structure but rather by skillfully surfing the structures that are already in place. Perhaps what is needed is not a single political party but better links among the affinity groups; perhaps rather than moving toward more centralization, what is needed is further radical decentralization.

When critics say that the protesters lack vision, what they are really saying is that they lack an overarching revolutionary philosophy—like Marxism, democratic socialism, deep ecology or social anarchy—on which they all agree.

That is absolutely true, and for this we should be extraordinarily thankful. At the moment, the anti-corporate street activists are ringed by would-be leaders, anxious for the opportunity to enlist them as foot soldiers for their particular cause. At one end there is Michael Lerner and his conference at the Riverside Church, waiting to welcome all that inchoate energy in Seattle and Washington inside the framework of his "Politics of Meaning." At the other, there is John Zerzan in Eugene, Oregon, who isn't interested in Lerner's call for "healing" but sees the rioting and property destruction as the first step toward the collapse of industrialization and a return to "anarcho-primitivism"—a pre-agrarian hunter-gatherer utopia. In between there are dozens of other visionaries, from the disciples of Murray Bookchin and his theory of social ecology, to certain sectarian Marxists who are convinced the revolution starts tomorrow, to devotees of Kalle Lasn, editor of *Adbusters,* and his watered-down version of revolution through "culture-jamming." And then there is the unimaginative pragmatism coming from some union leaders who, before Seattle, were ready to tack social clauses onto existing trade agreements and call it a day.

It is to this young movement's credit that it has as yet fended off all of these agendas and has rejected everyone's generously donated manifesto, holding out for an acceptably democratic, representative process to take its resistance to the next stage. Perhaps its true challenge is not finding a vision but rather resisting the urge to settle on one too quickly. If it succeeds in warding off the teams of visionaries-in-waiting, there will be some short-term public relations problems. Serial protesting will burn some people out. Street intersections will declare autonomy. And yes, young activists will offer themselves up like lambs—dressed, frequently enough, in actual lamb costumes—to the *New York Times* Op-Ed page for ridicule.

But so what? Already, this decentralized, multi-headed swarm of a movement has succeeded in educating and radicalizing a generation of activists around the world. Before it signs on to anyone's ten-point plan, it deserves the chance to see if, out of its chaotic network of hubs and spokes, something new, something entirely its own, can emerge.

Naomi Klein

Is There an Alternative to Globalization?

Questions and Answers from Olympia

This Q&A session transpired after George Katsiaficas gave a talk at Evergreen State College in Olympia, Washington on November 17, 2000.

Member of the Audience: *You mentioned earlier that our focus on antiglobalization has to be on a worldwide scale. Isn't this important when it's focusing on US intervention abroad? Can you maybe speak to a few instances of what you mean?*

George Katsiaficas: During the war in Kosovo, Belgrade was being bombed at the same time as the opening of the Socialist Scholars Conference, a yearly gathering of several thousand socialist scholars and activists in New York. The Friday night plenary featured Cornel West, Noam Chomsky, and other people had a lot to say. Yet, not a word was uttered from the stage about the US-led bombing of a heavily populated city. Even when some people from the audience raised the issue, Bogdan Denitch, the chair of the conference, deferred any discussion until a workshop first thing the next morning. Of course, the next morning the auditorium was packed. When I got there no more people were being allowed in. Boris Kagarlitsky, a Russian activist friend, was also outside. Noticing he was absolutely aghast, I asked him what was wrong. He announced that, to his great dismay, nobody on the stage was going to speak against the bombing. Only people who supported the bombing were invited to be speakers. If you think about it, even if you did support the US and European intervention you have to wonder why the critics were silenced.

The destruction of Belgrade is an example of globalization's self-righteousness. What's the character of globalization in the former Yugoslavia? Essentially, it's the Germans who are taking control of the area from the Russians and doing it with US money and US military power. The Germans, led by Joschka Fischer and the Green Party, have sent combat troops outside Germany for the first time since World War II. The national governments of Germany and the US were both able to implement their particular agenda by exaggerating the level of atrocities inside Serbia. I think of Noam Chomsky's excellent work on this subject, comparing how many people were killed in Colombia in the same period of time and asking why the US didn't even consider intervening to stop those murders. It's our allies who are committing many of those murders; that's why we don't hear about them. In contrast, the media was able to portray what was happening in Kosovo as of utmost important to US interests.

A: *Could you elaborate on the differences between the style of activism or the impression of activism in the Sixties and what we need to be doing now?*

GK: The Sixties movement was much more flamboyant. It was much more individually focused. Leaders like Huey Newton, Jerry Rubin and Ho Chi Minh were at the center of people's attention. Today, it's much more of a collective entity: antiglobalization protestors or the Direct Action Network are the focus rather than individual leaders. That's a real strength, not only because of the affirmation of the collective energies of people, but because it also means that the police can't as easily go after certain individuals to crush the movement. In the Sixties, very often any effective group had to spend hundreds of thousands of dollars and focus its attention on getting its leaders out of jail. Or its leaders were killed by the police. Fred Hampton of the Black Panther Party in Chicago was murdered while asleep after having been drugged by an FBI agent the night before. The twenty-eight dead Panthers made many people stop what they were doing and focus on fighting the repression against the Party. That re-focusing was immensely important in building interracial solidarity, but it also meant that the movement's own agenda suffered.

The movement today is much more able to understand problems of sexism, racism, homophobia, and anti-Semitism. Yet simultaneously, people can still get very sectarian today, as with some overzealous people in the violence/nonviolence debate after N30. I've heard stories of people being unmasked by nonviolent protestors so that they wouldn't be free to carry out their militant tactics. It's strange behavior. How do you explain away a nonviolent person putting their hands on somebody's neck?

A: *I'm wondering if you could talk more about finding common ground between people advocating mild tactics and people willing to use more militant ones. Also, you mentioned that you didn't think some of the more militant tactics would work here in the US because police would respond by using live ammo. What kind of militant tactics do you think would work here?*

GK: There is a real synergy among different levels of struggle. In Prague, for example, they divided into three groups: the Blues, the Yellows and the Pinks. Each group used different tactics. By separating, they were able to confuse the police; to the cops, all antiglobalization protesters are alike, right? The police didn't understand the differences within the movement.

The Battle of Seattle

Similarly, during the German Wackersdorf struggle against a nuclear reprocessing plant that would haven given Germany the ability to take waste from its many nuclear power plants and convert it into bomb-grade plutonium, the local farmers were extremely conservative but they united with punk rockers from Berlin and others to defeat the plant. German newspapers featured photos of punk rockers wearing black masks and farmers with pitchforks fighting side-by-side against the police. Pacifists were also extremely important. Because Wackersdorf was in the countryside, there was enough space for the pacifists to have demonstrations where they didn't get hurt and could be peacefully arrested by the hundreds while others could use different tactics. More militant people reached the fence and tried to breach it; the police had to be flown in by helicopters to stop them. It was like a major military campaign. Simultaneous actions stretched the police lines thin.

It was possible to articulate different ways for people to participate. I don't know that that happened in Seattle. This might have been why things became confused after Seattle. There hadn't been the discussion beforehand about how to separate out some of these actions. Could it have happened as in Germany? I don't know.

A: *One of the tactics that they tried in Seattle was separating different colored flags for basically arrest risk. There was a green flag, a really low arrest risk. And then there were three other different color flags. Red was the hottest.*

A: *I completely agree that, in terms of the internationalization of capital and its mobility, we need to be international in the way we organize. But that means putting forth an alternative productive, economic, political and organizing system. What do you see possibly as a regionalist alternative? How can you be bioregionalist and, at the same time, internationalist in the way you're organizing?*

GK: When you say bioregional, you raise an extremely important alternative to capitalist globalization. In my lifetime, if I saw *perestroika* in the United States, I'd be very happy. That should be our goal: to do away with the federal government in Washington and have several regional governments. I don't know exactly how many. The Soviet Union restructured their government, and they have suffered tremendously for it because there was no corresponding change in the rest of the world. They went from one country to 17. Could the United States have a similar devolution? It would be very hard. It was tried once before in the Civil War. This government will do anything to maintain control of the territory that it has been able to amass. By living bioregionally, by creating the networks, the ties, the economic ways for people to live productively and in harmony with the earth, by building up those networks from the grassroots, we create an infrastructure, and the infrastructure then leads to levels of struggle that I don't think we can understand without having the infrastructure in place.

It seems that, for instance, Olympia and Eugene have developed into major centers for the US movement. In the Sixties, Berkeley was a center. Today it's not so much of a focal point. What happened? It seems the revolutionary subject, as Marcuse said, emerges in the course of revolution. Regions are another way of organizing ourselves, and they would emerge in the course of making themselves real. We can't just have our alternative to capitalist globalization emerge full-blown from our brains. Some people have attempted to create models for how this country could be organized. I'm not sure that's the way. I think the way is for people to do it, to actually reorganize, live it.

A: *I want to respond to what you said about the Sixties as another person who came through the Sixties. Eugene was certainly a center in the Sixties and has remained a center. A lot of what you ascribe to the Sixties happened to a large degree spontaneously. Because of visible errors of leadership, of certain problems within the movements that were discussed, the movements as they continued don't have to reinvent the wheel, don't have to make those same mistakes over. What happened in the Sixties was very necessary, visibly, so people don't have to do that.*

There is today a much more spontaneous, diverse, non-specific leadership, much more broad-based. There isn't a leadership quality to what's going on now. That model isn't followed anymore. But if that hadn't happened in the Sixties, this might not and probably would not be happening in the same way. The way the Sixties movement was diffused and attacked because certain people were so visible doesn't have to happen again. That is not happening now, but I'm saying if that hadn't happened so visibly then, perhaps what's happening now wouldn't be happening in the same way with the same strength. And I do feel that because of what happened in the Sixties and those of us who came through it, our children and now their children, our grandchildren, have a very different consciousness because they saw it happening in their families. Someone like Abbie Hoffman maybe turned a page. Over time, more people turned the page than not but, also, there are always more people who take the next page freely. See what I'm saying? Not everyone signed away.

The Sixties as represented in the media are different than the Sixties to those who were actually participants. And believe me, the media have been very derogatory and very misrepresentational of many of us who were in the Sixties. We're regular people. We're family people. We were raising children. We were working. We were single mothers, whatever, and we haven't changed our points of view, and we didn't turn the page and sign over to something else. We continue to be here, and that's how I'm here at this meeting. [APPLAUSE]

GK: In fact, all the studies of the Central America activists showed how more than half were Sixties activists, and we kept the US from intervening in Central America more militantly than it did.

A: *One thing that I picked out of your* Subversion of Politics *book was how the Greens functioned as a recuperative force against the more militant tactics and the movement as a whole. You talked about them not as the movement in the government but the government in the movement. What I've been thinking about lately is how that pushes out into not only when you have representative democracy or you try to throw candidates out there but also just in how people are organized and how people function in a mental framework of the governmental idea in this activist circle. One way I hope that today's movement differs from the Sixties is that it grows out, that it refuses to work in this government. That way we won't be co-opted later on by having people become a Green Party or like a lot of the '68ers* *from Paris who are now in the government. Could you talk a little bit about governmental structures and how autonomous politics try to throw them out.*

GK: The first thing is not to rely on the police, and when I say that I don't just mean at demonstrations. It means in our everyday lives. How do we enact justice? What is justice? If something is happening, if someone has been raped and we know about it, shouldn't we do something? Why aren't there structures inside our circles to deal with issues of justice? Similarly, how do we deal with police infiltration? Again, people's impulse is to look the other way and to defer to the police. That is an abrogation of our responsibility. It is the beginning of relying on the government for everything, of letting the government run your life, run our lives. Of course, that's one of the most difficult pieces of freeing ourselves because the government won't allow dual power to happen. If you have a trial and hold this rapist or infiltrator, they're going to charge you with kidnapping, they're going to go all the way. So how do you enact these levels of dual power?

We begin with the police but I think we need to build up alternative institutions—schools, co-ops, bookstores, information centers, web sites, all of that. They have to be really autonomous. It has to be thought out as being built up in a self-reliant fashion to the greatest extent possible. There have to be these networks. That's the direction I think you're talking about—completely the opposite of the top-down globalization of the WTO, IMF and World Bank.

To some extent, such a process transpired in the cities of Europe where people squatted houses. It seemed to be the case, that as long as a house was illegal, it had a radical edge to it. And once it became legal, once it got a contract, even if it was a $1 a month rental contract, that edge was gone and people's lives became accommodated to the structures of schools, work, whatever. Even if people shared jobs, which people in a lot of these communes did so they would still have time for activism, even then, the problems that arose were not problems of the movement. I don't quite know why. I'd like to think that the dimension of illegality didn't have to be there for communes to be subversive and at the edge, that there didn't have to be a militant, confrontational edge. But what I've been able to witness is that those two seem to go together very often.

A: *In* Subversion of Politics, *you talk about the Greens and the more radical activists as being complementary even though there's a lot of debate and conflict between them. Do you feel like the same things can happen within the United States with the emerging Green Party and the radical movements? Beyond that, with the more conservative groups like the Sierra Club, do you see them as being complementary more than they are fractious? Do their contradictions outweigh their potential for synergy?*

GK: In my own understanding of this contradiction, I always come back to the German state of Lower Saxony. When the Greens were elected to the state government, they got the Ministry of Environmental affairs and the Ministry of Interior as their part of the package. At the same time, convoys of trucks carrying nuclear waste were coming into the Gorleben waste disposal site. To stop the trucks, protestors came to the area, dubbed the Free Republic of Wendland, a center of organic food production in Germany with lots of communes. They sat down in all the roads, thousands of people, and the Green minister, who herself had been a protestor there, was put in the position of having to order the police to arrest the protestors. She's from the Green Party who opposed nuclear power and who opposed, officially, the nuclear waste disposal site. But she did, in fact, order the arrest of her friends, comrades and other protestors after she got a call from the federal interior ministry saying: "You must do this, I'm ordering you." She was caught in that web; the Greens must act according to the law. If you go inside the government, that's what you agree to do—to obey the law.

Being outside the government means you have no obligation to obey the law. They may try to force you to do so, but it isn't an obligation. Being outside the government, your obligation is to the earth or to whatever you define as your center of consciousness and conscience.

Thanks to Allison, Brian, Joe, David, EPICA and people in Olympia whose energy generated these thoughts.

New Movements

Kevin Harris

The New Student Movement

Liza Featherstone
The Nation, *May 15, 2000*

"We have the university by the balls," said Nati Passow, a University of Pennsylvania junior, in a meeting with his fellow anti-sweatshop protesters. "Whatever way we twist them is going to hurt." Passow was one of thirteen Penn students—the group later grew to include forty—occupying the university president's office around the clock in early February to protest the sweatshop conditions under which clothing bearing the U-Penn logo is made. The Penn students, along with hundreds of other members of United Students Against Sweatshops nationwide, were demanding that their university withdraw from the Fair Labor Association, an industry-backed monitoring group, and instead join the Worker Rights Consortium, an organization independent of industry influence, founded by students in close cooperation with scholars, activists and workers' rights organizations in the global South.

At first the administration met the students with barely polite condescension. In one meeting, President Judith Rodin was accompanied by U-Penn professor Larry Gross, an earring-wearing baby boomer well-known on campus for his left-wing views, who urged the protesters to have more faith in the administration and mocked the sit-in strategy, claiming he'd "been there, done that." President Rodin assured them that a task force would review the problem by February 29, and there was no way she could speed up its decision. She admonished them to "respect the process."

Watching the Penn students negotiate with their university's president, it was clear they didn't believe any of her assurances. They knew there was no reason to trust that the administration would meet one more arbitrary deadline after missing so many others—so they stayed in the office. After eight days of torture by folk-singing, acoustic guitar, recorders, tambourines and ringing cell phones, as well as a flurry of international news coverage, Judith Rodin met the protesters halfway by withdrawing from the FLA. (To students' frustration, the task force decided in early April to postpone a decision about WRC membership until later this spring.)

The most remarkable thing about the Penn students' action was that it wasn't an isolated or spontaneous burst of idealism. Penn's was just the first anti-sweatshop sit-in of the year; by mid-April students at the universities of Michigan, Wisconsin, Oregon, Iowa and Kentucky, as well as SUNY-Albany, Tulane, Purdue and Macalester had followed suit. And the sit-in wasn't the protesters' only tactic: Purdue students held an eleven-day hunger strike. Other students chose less somber gestures of dissent. In late February the University of North Carolina's anti-sweatshop group, Students for Economic Justice, held a nude-optional party titled "I'd Rather Go Naked Than Wear Sweatshop Clothes." In late March, in an exuberant expression of the same principle, twelve Syracuse students biked across campus nude. The protests were a coordinated effort; members of United Students Against Sweatshops, which was founded three years ago and now has chapters at more than 200 schools, work closely with one another, a process made easier by the many listservs and websites that the students use to publicize actions, distribute information and help fuel turnout.

Though the largest, most successful—and before Seattle, the most visible—thread of the movement has focused on improving work conditions in the $2.5 billion collegiate apparel industry, university licensing policies have not been the only targets of recent anti-corporate agitation on campus. This year, from UC Davis to the University of Vermont, students have held globalization teach-ins, planned civil disobedience for the April IMF/World Bank meetings, protested labor policies at the Gap and launched vigorous campaigns to drive Starbucks out of university dining services. In snowy January, at the conservative Virginia Commonwealth University, twenty students slept outside the vice president's office for two nights to protest the university's contract with McDonald's (the school promised the fast food behemoth a twenty-year monopoly over the Student Commons). Students at Johns Hopkins and at Wesleyan held sit-ins demanding better wages for university workers. And at the end of March hundreds of students, many bearing hideously deformed papier-mâché puppets to illustrate the potential horrors of biotechnology, joined Boston's carnivalesque protest against genetic engineering.

With a *joie de vivre* that the American economic left has probably lacked since before WWI, college students are increasingly engaged in well-organized, thoughtful and morally outraged resistance to corporate power. These activists, more than any student radicals in years, passionately denounce the wealth gap, globally and in the United States, as well as the lack of democratic accountability in a world dominated by corporations. While some attend traditionally political schools like Evergreen, Michigan and Wisconsin, this movement does not revolve around usual suspects; some of this winter's most dramatic actions took place at campuses that have always been conservative, like the University of Pennsylvania, Virginia Commonwealth and Johns Hopkins. At this article's writing in late April, students were staging several significant anti-corporate protests every week. It is neither too soon, nor too naïvely optimistic, to call it a movement.

Few of these students resemble—either in appearance or tactics—the hooded anarchist kids who famously threw rocks through Starbucks windows in Seattle last November. They look as if they shop at the Gap (and most of them

The Battle of Seattle

do). Yet the movement does have an anti-hierarchical spirit; the Penn anti-sweat group, for example, made all decisions by consensus. Unlike their anarchist cohort, however, the student anti-corporatists have leaders and spokespeople—and most of them agree that if the movement is to maintain momentum, they will need many more. Fortunately, each major action seems to draw more people in, and new leaders are emerging fast—some students who were on the periphery of the Penn group when I visited the sit-in in early February, for example, have already assumed official leadership positions within the organization.

Much of the struggle concerns the corporatization of higher education. Universities are run increasingly like private firms, and have ever-more intimate relations with private industry. During one anti-sweat occupation in mid-April, for example, student activists at the University of Oregon led a campus tour of sites that illustrated the institution's numerous ties to corporations (one stop was the Phil Knight Library, named after Nike's president and CEO). A nation-wide student group called 180/Movement for Democracy and Education, based at the University of Wisconsin, articulates this problem, and its connection to other issues, more consistently than any other group, even leading teach-ins on how World Trade Organization policies affect higher education. But almost all of the current student struggles—whether over tuition increases, apparel licenses, socially responsible investing, McDonald's in the student union, the rights of university laundry workers, a dining-hall contractor's investment in private prisons or solidarity with the striking students in Mexico—focus on the reality of the university as corporate actor.

Battle lines are now being drawn on a number of campuses, including Penn and Wisconsin, over whether universities will give in to student demands and agree to join the Worker Rights Consortium. WRC members require their apparel licensees to comply with a strict code of conduct—guaranteeing workers a living wage and the right to organize unions—and mandate full public disclosure of wages, factory locations and working conditions. By denying industry any role in its governance and giving power instead to a board composed of administrators, students and human rights scholars and activists, the WRC provides a nascent model for the kind of university decision-making the students would like to see: a process free of corporate influence. It is also a model in which, so far, student activists have set the terms of discussion. No wonder so many university administrators, many of whom now like to be called "CEOs," have resisted it so savagely, even, in several cases, permitting quite forceful police treatment of peaceful protesters.

Yet many universities that once rebuffed the students' entreaties have since backed down, a testament to the skill and energy of the student organizers. The wave of sit-ins this spring was deliberately timed to precede the WRC's early April founding conference. Before the Penn sit-in, only a handful of institutions, none of which had substantial apparel-licensing contracts, belonged to the new organization; now forty-seven institutions belong, and the WRC founding meeting was attended by students or administrators from forty schools. The night before the meeting, the entire ten-school University of California system joined the organization and sent a representative to New York for the event. Some institutions joined without any building takeovers, choosing to avert bad publicity

Liza Featherstone

through graceful capitulation. "A lot of them joined without a sit-in because they thought there would be a sit-in the next day," says Maria Roeper, an anti-sweat activist taking a semester off from Haverford to coordinate the WRC.

Indeed, student activists have managed to put administrators on the defensive. On April 7 student anti-sweat protesters wearing duct tape over their mouths—to protest the fact that students have no say in campus decisions—met the University of Oregon president at the airport, frightening him so badly he left the baggage claim and hid in the bathroom. Even more striking, that same day, was the sight of dozens of suited university administrators at the WRC conference scurrying to "organize" among themselves. Many were pressured into WRC membership and worry that they won't have as much influence as they want over the new monitoring organization. Administrators were supposed to elect their representatives to the governing board at the founding meeting, but instead they asked for more time; they are now expected to do so later this spring, after holding their own meeting in Chicago. "It's only natural that they should want to do that," says Roeper. "The student group [USAS] did have a lot of power."

Industry, too, is getting nervous. Top officials of the Fair Labor Association, founded in 1996 by the Clinton Administration along with business representatives and some human rights groups, have been touring campuses, trying to convince students of their organization's good intentions. (Unlike the WRC, the FLA allows industry to choose its own monitors and doesn't include provisions for a living wage.) A week before the consortium's founding conference, Nike, which supports the FLA, canceled its contract with Brown University, objecting to the university's WRC membership. Nike has repeatedly denounced the WRC, calling it a "gotcha" monitoring system. "Nike is using Brown to threaten other schools," said Brown anti-sweat activist Nicholas Reville at the conference. More recently, Nike's Phil Knight, who had pledged $30 million to the University of Oregon for its sports stadium, indignantly withdrew the offer after the school announced its membership in the WRC.

In the recent history of student activism, the new emphasis on economics represents quite a shift. Ten years ago, there was plenty of student organizing, but it was fragmentary and sporadic, and most of it focused on what some, mostly its detractors, liked to call "identity politics," fighting the oppression of racial and sexual minorities, and of women. Admirable as they were—and effective in improving social relations on many campuses—there was little sense of solidarity among these groups, and they often seemed insular, bearing little relation to life outside the university.

That political moment is over, partly because in the larger world, organized feminism is in a lull and the mainstream gay movement now focuses on issues like inclusion in the military, gay marriage and hate-crimes legislation—moderate goals that don't speak to student idealism. By contrast, the economic left—especially the labor movement, and the burgeoning resistance to global capital—is enjoying a resurgence, both in numbers and in vision. The new student anti-corporatists are building strong relationships with unions, which are, in turn, showing remarkable dedication to the new generation. During February's Penn sit-in, a different union local brought the students dinner almost every night. "Seattle helped the unions see that the students were serious," explains Simon

Greer, Jobs With Justice's Workers' Rights board director. When the University of Wisconsin sent in the cops to drag away fifty-four peaceful anti-sweat protesters, George Becker, president of the United Steelworkers, issued a statement denouncing the administration's "oppressive actions."

The early-nineties struggles haven't vanished without a trace; indeed, it sometimes seems as if, through the anti-corporate movement, they have returned to their early-seventies roots as movements for radical liberation. Many of the leaders are women, and feminist analysis informs the movement's focus; the anti-sweat activists, for instance, frequently point out that most sweatshop workers are women. And although the struggle against homophobia has largely disappeared from the student progressive agenda, the tactics—militant, theatrical and often campy direct action—of early-nineties groups like ACT UP and Queer Nation have clearly influenced the new crew of student activists.

Anti-corporatism also has the potential to be a movement for racial justice. Farah Mongeau, a University of Michigan law student and member of UM's Students of Color Coalition, points out, "[Sweatshop labor] obviously affects people of color. People of color are the ones who work in the sweatshops." Yet, although many core organizers are South Asian, the anti-sweatshop movement is mostly white. Organizing by students of color is on the upswing, but its relationship to the anti-corporate groups can be uneasy. Some students of color say this is partly because white activists receive better treatment from those in power. At Michigan in February, SCC members protesting a racist secret society held a sit-in at the same time as the anti-sweat organization and resented the fact that while they were ignored for weeks, the predominantly white group got a meeting with the president immediately. Likewise, Justin Higgins, sophomore class president at North Carolina Central University, a historically black and working-class college, who in February had just joined the regional student anti-WTO/IMF coalition, said he wasn't planning to go to Washington, DC, and wasn't sorry to have missed Seattle. "If there had been black students [in Seattle]," Higgins said, "there would have been real bullets, not rubber bullets."

On the other hand, some less visible economic justice campaigns on campus have been more racially mixed: those fighting university tuition hikes, for instance. And the student movement's relationship with labor may help break down its whiteness. In its early stages, very few black students were involved in the Johns Hopkins action demanding higher wages for university workers, for example, though the low-wage workers at the school are predominantly people of color. But when local unions got involved in the sit-in, they were able to recruit members of the black student group. On other campuses, multiracial alliances between anti-corporate and prison activists are beginning to emerge. In early April students at ten campuses launched a boycott campaign against Sodexho-Marriott, which operates more than 500 campus dining halls, is the largest investor in US private prisons and is also currently facing censure from the National Labor Relations Board. In an April sit-in at SUNY-Albany, activists, in addition to sweatshop-related demands, insisted that the university drop Sodexho-Marriott if the company did not divest from private prisons, and improve its labor practices.

Part of the problem with early-to-mid-nineties student "identity politics" was an obsession with representation—only queers could talk about homophobia, only people of color could talk about racism—which seriously limited its constituency. Such first-person politics also restricted diverse activists' ability to work together and find common ground. Yet its premise—drawn from seventies feminism—that the personal is political laid the foundation for one of the core assumptions of the current anti-corporate movement, which is that because we are consumers, we are personally implicated in the depredations of capital. In the anti-sweat movement, students initially got involved because they were horrified to find out about the exploitation behind products that were a part of their everyday lives. Says Penn sophomore and USAS member Roopa Gona, "We're talking about *our* clothes." Student public-education campaigns about Starbucks—which, in mid-April, was pressured into buying Fair Trade Coffee—and genetically modified food also focus on buying power. The consumer experience is one that everyone has in common, rather than one that emphasizes power differences among students.

Exposing the sweatshop horror behind ubiquitous logos is subversive, especially in a culture completely hypnotized by them. The whole purpose of logos and brands is commodity fetishism; we are supposed to crave them but not question the conditions under which they were made. But, as Naomi Klein observes in her new book, *No Logo: Taking Aim at the Brand Bullies,* companies trafficking in image are particularly vulnerable when those images are tarnished. Obscure information-technology companies can quietly outsource their data-entry work to Mexican sweatshops, but companies like Disney, Starbucks and the Gap are different: Their prominence in consumers' hearts and minds makes it far easier for activists to publicize their wrongdoings. Like other contemporary anti-corporatists—those vandalizing and protesting under Golden Arches worldwide, for instance—students have expertly used big capital's catchy logos against it. And just like the Nike swoosh, "we can think of the university itself as a brand, a logo, that students consume," says veteran anti-sweat activist and University of North Carolina junior Todd Pugatch. Universities, especially prestigious ones or those with high-profile sports teams, depend on image, too. The recognizability of the University of Michigan's big yellow M, like that of McDonald's, can backfire if the logo comes to symbolize exploitation and corporate greed.

Still, brand targeting has limits. One of the ways in which contemporary capitalism maintains its hold on us is by defining everyone as consumers—rather than, say, citizens, workers, or activists. A crucial problem for the anti-corporate movement is how to appeal to a wider public without reducing politics to shopping. And students are realizing that simply as indignant shoppers, they can't be very effective. Boycotts in the apparel industry are futile because all major clothing companies use sweatshop labor, explains Laurie Eichenbaum, a Penn senior and USAS organizer who was wearing a red Old Navy fleece when I met her: "There is no good alternative." Saurav Sarkar, of Yale Students Against Sweatshops, says, "That's the most common misperception about us. People say, 'Oh, I don't want to stop buying clothes at the Gap.'" Crucial to the anti-corporate movement's gradual evolution beyond consumer consciousness and toward labor solidarity and broad structural change, as UNC's Pugatch observes, will be its relationship with workers, in the US labor movement as well as in the global South. If the WRC develops as the students hope, it will help give workers and unions a stronger voice in the apparel industry, rather than simply conferring a

Good Housekeeping-style seal of approval on "sweat-free" brands.

Despite this emerging vision, not all students come to anti-corporate activism with a radical outlook. "People are drawn in by the horror stories," says Maria Roeper, but then they start seeing how the whole system works. Students are also radicalized by their university's intransigence and by the realization that institutions only change when they're forced to do so. David Corson-Knowles, a Yale freshman and spokesperson for the Student Alliance to Reform Corporations, a national group founded at Yale, says he thinks his group will eventually convince the Yale Corporation—which has the CEO of Procter & Gamble on its board—to invest responsibly "because we're right." But in a group discussion in a coffee shop near campus, it's clear that students from the Student/Labor Action Coalition and the Yale chapter of United Students Against Sweatshops—older groups that have been struggling with the administration for longer and use more confrontational tactics—beg to differ. Yale SLAC activist Laurie Kimmington, a senior, says of the university's administrators, "They want to do nothing, as much as possible." Danielle Linzer, a Penn sophomore and STARC leader, admitted this might be the case. STARC, she acknowledged, had a "more conservative approach to reform" than United Students Against Sweatshops, but, she said, "we're a newer group, so we haven't yet been stalled the way they have."

All in all, it's impossible not to feel at least cautiously optimistic about this new movement. "We are training an entire generation to think differently about"—pause—"capitalism," says Kimmington. She glances at my notebook and at the STARC activists across the cafe table and giggles cheerfully. "Oops, maybe I shouldn't say that."

An Experiment in Media Democracy

Jeff Perlstein
of the Independent Media Center

The Independent Media Center was founded in the Fall of 1999 to provide an avenue for underrepresented groups to tell their own stories in their own voices, to get these voices out to the world quickly, and to move us all to action for social justice. This noncommercial, multimedia "people's newsroom" had an amazingly successful debut during the week of the World Trade Organization's ministerial talks in Seattle.

Activated just one day before the actions, the website (www.indymedia.org) received more than 1.5 million visitors from around the world during that week—easily eclipsing CNN's number of site visits for the same period. Hundreds of community radio and television stations rebroadcast the IMC's programming, sending the project's impact outward, beyond the digital divide, to break the corporate media's information blockade.

IMCs soon followed in Boston, Washington, DC, Los Angeles, and London—each with their own innovations and contributions to the evolving Indymedia network. In the 12 months since the project's debut, the network of IMCs has grown to over 40 locations in more than 10 countries, on four continents. The global site now receives over 10,000 visits on any given day—a significant accomplishment in the independent media realm in which limited distribution is so frequently cited as one of the biggest problems. But we'd be manifesting the values of the corporate media if we judged the merit of Indymedia in terms of numbers alone. Indymedia also seeks to be qualitatively democratic.

Putting the Democracy in Media Democracy

From the outset, the IMC project has been informed by the belief that a media project needs to be more than a site for creating and distributing progressive content. Physical and virtual spaces for interaction, dialogue, and transformation are the essential forums where a vital, vibrant, and true democracy can take place. Manuel Callahan has written that, "The IMC provided more than simply a site to produce alternative media and compete with the corporate media, but rather became a space for organizing, a space that was a refuge, and a space for convergence." This space is critical because under late capitalism we've witnessed the corporatization and commodification of most of our public spaces—parks and public lands, the airwaves, skylines, and even the Internet. The IMCs have sought to create such spaces for civil society to come together, free of commercial and governmental influence, to explore the possibility of creating the society we desire.

One way we've done this is by creating actual "community newsrooms" with virtual online counterparts (e.g. sf.indymedia.org, prague.indymedia.org). These autonomous nodes in the network address the unique needs of their local communities as they see appropriate. They are linked in virtual space through the global Indymedia website, which features content contributions from the participating IMCs and society at large. The Zapatistas provided a vital model for this mode of operation: affirm local struggles while simultaneously inviting an exploration of larger networks of struggle.

Participation, Indymedia Style

The Indymedia practice has been to invite broad and meaningful participation in every aspect of a project's day-to-day functions and its future direction. We've made invaluable use of email, listserves, online discussions, translation software, and live Internet Relay Chat technology to facilitate the flow of communication across town and across national borders. As for the as yet non-wired, they can participate via telephone or by meeting folks face-to-face at their local IMC.

One of the most celebrated features of the Indymedia website is the newswire's "open posting" capability, which allows anyone in the world with an Internet connection to publish a story directly on the front page. This "democracy wall" aspect of the site fosters a "claiming" of the project by the people and brings a compelling vibrancy to the content. Once at the site, visitors have access to a number of discussions and working groups on various aspects of the project itself.

Behind the scenes, facilitating this participatory media-making and distribution outlet, is an equally participatory team of tech volunteers. This international group is responsible for the design of the unprecedented "Active" software, and the ongoing innovation and maintenance of the Indymedia web infrastructure. Radically non-hierarchical, they collaborate online from their locations on different continents. Interested participants are always welcomed, invited to share suggestions and innovations, and put to work. Even the code used for the project reflects these values. The software is produced using Linux, an Open Source code that is non-proprietary and collaboratively updated by the international community of its users.

Process in Media Democracy

Since the project's beginning, there's been a firm commitment to an organizational structure and process that foster democracy and equity as much as possible—an embodiment of the vision of a just society that we're working toward with our media reportage and organization. In our attempt to live up to these ideals, the IMCs have tried to create structures that are nonhierarchical and use decision-making processes that are variations on the consensus model.

The global network structure is horizontal and composed of working groups that actively communicate with each other to share information. Each group is empowered to make decisions relating to its scope of responsibility, defined through dialogue with the larger network. Recently, a global "IMC-Communications" working group with representatives from most of the local IMCs worldwide was formed to better facilitate the flow of information and participation among the nodes in the network. Necessary elements of this horizontal model include frequent and clear communication, clear accountability, and, unfortunately for now, an Internet connection.

A number of the IMCs have made use of a "spokescouncil" (SC) composed of representatives from each of the local working groups. The SC meetings, which are open to working group participants, are an opportunity for face-to-face communication on decisions benefiting the local IMC, with input from each of the working groups. This particular format has been especially valuable when dealing with big events that require a high volume of decisions in a short time frame.

Used by most of the IMCs in some form, the consensus decision-making process is radical democracy in practice. It is based on a commitment to value the input of each and every participant and a belief that the group moves forward most strongly when all its members have consented to the decisions. Proposals for the group are put forward and all concerns, even those expressed by a small minority, are honored as needing resolution. This time- and energy-intensive dialogue can be made more efficient by a facilitator empowered by the group. It's this extra effort at dialogue, communication, and compromise that truly marks the IMCs as an experiment in media democracy.

Challenges and Opportunities

One complex question that has inspired much discussion is: What sort of an editorial policy, if any, should a media democracy project follow? Are there certain standards and criteria for posted stories? Who decides what they should be? What constitutes censorship? Should Indymedia censor "hate speech," and do we relate to this term differently, based on our different identities and histories?

IMCs have attempted to address aspects of this debate while also helping visitors to the website make the best use of the information posted. New "Opinion" and "Comments" sections allow an actual back-and-forth dialogue on the content. The Philadelphia IMC put into place an online ratings system to provide some guidance on the quality of the postings without destroying the open posting aspect of the newswire. Higher-rated pieces were featured at the top of the page. In true participatory fashion, anyone could sign on to the ratings team and have input in the process.

But in looking at the participatory aspect of the IMCs, it's vital that IMCs also critically examine the composition of the participants and the culture of the project. This may be Independent Media but by and for whom? Who's participating, who's not, and what are the obstacles to involvement? Is there only a question of access to technology —monumental in itself—or are there elements that discourage participation from under-represented constituencies?

Of the 40 local IMCs, almost all are in the Northern Hemisphere and a

Jeff Perlstein

majority are largely homogeneous groupings in terms of race, ethnicity, class, and gender. Is consensus meaningful considering who's not participating in the discussion?

We're faced with the challenge of creating spaces that don't mirror the existing systemic oppressions, hierarchies, and power relationships. But we're a part of this very system and can manifest these internalized privileges despite the very best intentions. Can we enact true democracy while inequitable systems are still in place? I'm not sure, but I believe we need to do more to actively and deliberately acknowledge and respect differences that emerge from our positions, identities, and histories. We need to continually examine how we're reproducing inequitable power relationships and take leadership from under-represented people on what can be done to foster a more just framework. We must be willing to act to restructure and reorganize.

We need to keep our eyes firmly fixed on the prize—justice and human dignity for all people. As media-makers we can play a role in realizing this vision. In fact, we must.

A New Movement

John Zerzan
Anarchy: A Journal of Desire Armed,
Fall/Winter 1999-2000

Not so many years ago the dominant orientation of anarchism was leftist. Anarchists have always stressed self-management of society, but what that society should be was pretty indistinguishable from what Marxists assume it should be. In other words, technology and mass production, rooted in division of labor and domestication, were standard beliefs for most anarchists.

In the course of the '90s there has been a fundamental shift, still underway, in what most anarchists see as the foundation of a free, healthy society. Self-managed factories and other forms of productionism and specialization are now widely understood as no advance at all. In this increasingly standardized, massified, anti-nature monoculture of a world, more and more anti-authoritarians realize that the answers go deeper than self-management of existing institutions.

A primitivist outlook, which indicts technology and civilization as well as capital, seems to be gaining ground in various parts of the world. As conditions visibly worsen at every level—the increasingly desolate individual psyche, ever more pathological and atrophied societies, the devastated natural world—we are driven to delve deeper in our analysis of a deeply toxic, future-less totality.

And there are signs that a new movement is beginning to emerge, signs of a militancy in outlook that just might overtake the general cynicism and pessimism.

David Ehrenfeld wrote in the January-February 1999 *Tikkun* that the days of the everywhere-triumphant Megamachine are in fact numbered. Rather surprising to see a mainstream magazine herald the fairly imminent collapse of technocapital, and in no uncertain terms. Ehrenfeld writes of the invincibility of the system as just an illusion compared to its real vulnerability.

Soon thereafter, the hitherto mainstream conservation quarterly *Food & Water* editorialized in its own surprising fashion. An editorial entitled "Objectifying Violence" concluded with the injunction to "Go forth and sabotage!"

Decades of mild, non-militant, write-your-congressperson advocacy has led only to an accelerating assault on nature, *Food & Water*'s editor reasoned, and he courageously faced up to this impotence. Needless to say enjoining the magazine's readers to commit acts of sabotage horrified many of them.

The Yuppie Eradication Project has drawn local, national, and even international media attention for its vandalistic efforts to protect San Francisco's Inner Mission district from complete gentrification. Trendy bars and expensive restaurants moved into the neighborhood, sending rents spiraling and creating an impossible hardship for the area's low-income residents.

Once suspected of being the handiwork of only a handful of people, YEP has drawn a hundred or more to recent meetings. Nocturnal attacks have spread to at least one additional San Francisco neighborhood.

The 30th anniversary Woodstock rock festival in late July ended in the looting and burning of tents, booths, and 12 semi trucks. At the end of August an anti-consumerism group bombed fast food outlets at a Moscow shopping mall, declaring that "a dead consumer's unfinished hamburger is a revolutionary hamburger." Also this summer, the rising militancy of animal liberationists was publicly noted, and the implications of its advances were understood by some. Richard Epstein, a University of Chicago law professor, observed that "there would be nothing left of human society if we treated animals not as property but as independent holders of rights."

In Eugene, anarchists have engaged in property damage for over a year, forcing public discussion of anarchy as the only real alternative to a cancerous, all-destroying global system. Breaking the rules in a sustained way has brought anarchy out of its former marginalized, suppressed position, and has raised radical alternatives in Eugene and, quite possibly, elsewhere soon. The June 18 "Reclaim the Streets" protest involved about three hundred who indeed reclaimed the streets, breaking business windows and skirmishing with police for several hours in an "Anarchist Rampage," as the local front page headline put it.

This activism is informed by a critique of the ensemble of domination, including technologized existence and its wellspring, civilization itself. The primitivist analysis is now widely discussed in such places as London, Istanbul, and Paris, inviting the suspicion that public contestation may be just around the corner.

What does not seem likely is a return to an anarchy dominated by the productionist/workerist/syndicalist perspectives of, say, Murray Bookchin and Noam Chomsky. A far more radical liberatory vision is taking shape, equal to the horrors around us and aware of whence they come. This outlook vastly deepens the insights of Marx, and is entirely fed up with the endless compromising and half-measures of leftism.

Addendum, January 2000

Since the anti-WTO "Battle of Seattle," a new movement is now clearly underway. A measure of its effectiveness, among many others, is the fact that virtually nowhere in the world can summit meetings (WTO, IMF, World Bank, NATO, etc.) be publicly held without incurring the wrath of militant protesters. Prague in September 2000 is only one graphic example, post-Seattle. The growing frequency and scope of Earth Liberation Front and Animal Liberation Front underground actions should also be cited.

Resurgent opposition is not red this time, as the left seems to continue to fade away. Rather, green and black are the colors of people's growing tendency to question and indict institutions at a fundamental level. Leftists still show zero interest in analyzing or challenging these institutions—such as division of labor, domestication, technology, civilization.

A radical women's movement is also re-emerging, a development that appeared too late to influence the movement of the 1960s. The struggle against male domination is primary, vital to the depth and success of today's effort. How far we contest domination in general will be determined by how far we move to gender equality. Moving together, the road to liberation may well be open before us.

At D-CON in Los Angeles, thousands of people of color took to the streets, braving intimidation by politicians and police. Will some of them mover closer to anarchy? A whites-only movement can never be strong or knowledgeable enough to prevail.

So much is at stake and so much is possible. Anarchy, the real name of contestation today, cannot be just another flavor of the left if we hope to succeed.

Color Blind

Activists of Color Bring the Economic War Home, But Is the Movement Missing the Message?

Andrew Hsiao
Village Voice, *July 25, 2000*

One weekend last summer, Jia Ching Chen found himself in the bucolic Santa Monica hills, dispensing advice to a roomful of young activists on some of the finer points of occupying a corporation's headquarters. For Chen, the talk itself was not all that new—as a longtime trainer for the Ruckus Society, the Berkeley-based group that in the last four years has schooled a couple of thousand activists in the arts of direct action protest, the 28-year-old Chen had led many similar workshops. Still, he says, he had never been more excited by a Ruckus event because, for the first time Chen could remember, he was not one of the only people of color in the room.

Indeed, that weekend's Democracy Action Camp—staged on the eve of the August 2000 Democratic convention in L.A.—brought together more than 40 African American, Latino, and Asian American activists with an equal number of white organizers, and was mirrored by a similar camp held on the East Coast to prep for the Republican convention in Philadelphia. For Chen, who has also raised hell with the Third Eye Movement—Bay Area "hip-hop organizers"—it was a rare instance when activist worlds collided. And the camps were "a trans-forming moment" for the notoriously hippy-hairy Ruckus, he says, a measure of how "we're really trying to address the racial and class divides."

He was talking, of course, about divides that were uncomfortably evident during the spectacular mass protests in Seattle and Washington, D.C against the WTO, the World Bank, the IMF, and global corporate domination. While the demonstrations electrified radicals across the country, the fact that the ranks of protesters were overwhelmingly white—especially pronounced after organized labor's early withdrawal at A16 (and the arrest of hundreds of young activists of color on the first day of the D.C. demos)—itself sparked months of internal protest. Many organizers working in black, Latino, and Asian communities were at once elated and disappointed by the demonstrations. Radical black scholar Robin D.G. Kelley spoke for many when he said, "The lack of people of color involved in those protests is a crisis." And for a time, discussion of the racial cast of the protests took on the tones of crisis management, confrontation, and denial. As Mark Rand, executive director of San Francisco's JustAct, noted last summer, "The e-mails have been flying, the listservs have been burning up." Widely circulated articles in *ColorLines*, the publication of the Oakland activist institute the Applied Research Center, prompted expansive—and often angry—electronic exchanges by posing the question, "Where was the color at A16?," and cataloguing "the reasons the Great Battle [of Seattle] was so white."

For many activists of color, those reasons began with the notion that "structural adjustment" abroad can seem abstract to people who "are getting our asses kicked daily," as Van Jones, the director of the Bay Area's Ella Baker Center for Human Rights, says. Meager resources certainly kept some people of color away from Seattle and Washington. And direct-action tactics have a different meaning in communities where many are undocumented or already have a perilous relationship with the police. Some activists of color who went to Seattle or D.C. came home complaining of an insider's culture of privileged militancy, while others pointed to the racial disconnect in movement ideologies. Activist-academic Vijay Prashad, who helps organize New York's annual Youth Solidarity Summer, for example, argues that the anarchist vibe of the anti-globalization movement turned off people of color, given how the state "is still seen as the arbiter of justice for our communities."

Meanwhile, some white organizers groused that communities of color were simply missing the movement, and perhaps—in their insistence on local, racial issues—the global economic point itself. Others said racial criticisms were based in an outmoded identity politics that has been transcended by the all-inclusive politics of economics. Besides, noted one lead organizer of A16, after Seattle the Mobilization for Global Justice made a number of efforts to diversify the ranks, hiring an outreach coordinator (the group's only paid staffer), visiting African American churches in Washington, and paying for buses of mostly black ACT UPers from Philadelphia. Njoki Njoroge Njehu, the U.S. director of the international 50 Years Is Enough Campaign, concluded an email defense of A16 outreach efforts with this pointed question: "For me, the question is to my sisters and brothers of color. Where were you on April 16?"

Framing the issue this way, however, as a matter of failed outreach (or of the limitations of activists of color) only sharpened for many the sense that the anti-global folks just didn't get it—and heightened the sense of missed opportunities. For if the last few years has brought an explosion of radical organizing against globalization, these same years have also featured a concurrent resurgence of activism among young people of color—around issues like police brutality, juvenile justice, and the death penalty. In California, for example, the fight against the draconian juvenile justice measure Prop. 21—designed to funnel teens into adult prisons by giving prosecutors the power to charge 14-year-olds in adult court—galvanized an array of multiracial youth groups, especially in the spring months of 2000 leading up to A16. But even in the Bay Area, home to anti-globalization stalwarts like Global Exchange and the Rainforest Network, "these two movements—anti-globalization and anti-prison industrial complex," as Mark Rand puts it, "have been like two ships passing in the night."

Ultimately, the anti-globalization movement's distance from communities of color led many to miss what's distinctive about new activism in these communities. Increasingly, young critics of the criminal-justice system recognize that the prison boom is connected to cuts in social spending and that more aggressive policing of schools, streets, and borders is the toxic by-product of neoliberalism. "They take an anti-corporate cut on the criminal-justice issue," says Van Jones. In March 2000, just before Prop. 21 passed, black, Latino, and Asian youth activists designed a campaign that involved storming the headquarters of corporations like Chevron, Pacific Gas & Electric, and Hilton, which had bankrolled the ballot initiative. One hundred seventy-five young people organized by the Third Eye Movement were arrested at the San Francisco Hilton in what Jones calls "the first hip-hop generation sit-in."

Hip-hop also provided the soundtrack for the Prison Moratorium Project's 40-city "No More Prisons" raptivists tour, whose targets include multinational Sodexho Alliance, a major underwriter of the private prison industry (and through its subsidiary, Sodexho-Marriott Services, a purveyor of cafeteria food on some 900 U.S. campuses). Meanwhile, to cite just one more example, L.A.'s immigrant-led Bus Rider's Union has wedded "an explicitly anti-corporate analysis," as lead organizer Cynthia Rojas puts it, to its campaign against " 'transit racism.' We've done solidarity work with the Zapatistas and connected our struggle to the enormous rise of money for prisons. Basically you're talking about capitalism."

These movements bring the economic war home, and by largely missing that message, the American anti-globalization movement has been fighting with one arm tied behind its back. As Van Jones puts it, "Outreach is a false issue, because the point isn't to make the movement look like a Benetton ad. The question is: How will this convergence actually change the movement?" Following Seattle and A16, movement groups retooled for R2K and D2K, trying to get the different currents of protest to meet at the Republican and Democratic conventions. There were plenty of unlikely and welcome convergences. In Philly, for example, out-of-town anti-globalists got a good taste of the Kensington Welfare Rights Union, one of the country's most creative and flat-out kick-ass movements of poor and homeless people, and—through its multistate marches, world summits, and international lawsuits—a pioneer in connecting the global corporate agenda to local battles. Meanwhile, says Philly organizer Amadee Braxton, cochair of the Black Radical Congress, R2K organizing, beginning with the Democracy Action Camp, helped young activists of color "struggling to find the language to describe structural adjustment at home" broaden their vocabulary. After all, it's not as if national black, Latino, and Asian leadership has taken an anti-capitalist, anti-imperialist turn: just as big labor's critique of globalization was blunted by its embrace of Al Gore, so did the NAACP's fondness for the ex-vice president put it inside the Democratic convention, not outside with young protesters of all colors.

Still, for some, there was a disconnected, menu-like quality to the protests at the conventions, partly exacerbated by the decision to devote particular days to specific themes. And it's unclear how activist groups have changed. That they will have to change, probably profoundly—if they truly want convergence—is unquestionable. Consider the road traveled by JustAct. Just a few years ago, JustAct was known as the Overseas Development Network, founded by two brothers from Bangladesh but the very image of what Rand describes as "a mildly progressive organization of mostly white, middle-class students that came into its own in the era of 'We Are the World.'" Then, Rand jokes, he made the mistake of hiring "some young rabble-rousers—working-class youth of color who were very engaged in survival struggles in their communities." Now the organization has been transformed (beginning with its full moniker, JustAct: Youth Action for Global Justice). It has twin concerns: global youth organizing and the more than 70 percent of American young people who don't attend four-year colleges.

The metamorphosis has been painful, involving "bitter arguments and many tear-filled meetings"—and not a few stormy resignations--says Rand, but it has wrought an impressively diverse staff interested in linking local and global struggles. The group helped mobilize multi-racial contingents at Seattle, A16, and D2K. Jia Ching Chen, who traveled a similar route from international human rights issues into criminal-justice activism, is now one of JustAct's organizers. A one-man bridge between movements, he was arrested at the San Francisco Hilton, in Seattle, and in L.A.

But even as the anti-globalization movement could learn from JustAct's difficult evolution, organizers in communities of color could gain by studying the struggles of radical outfits like New York's CAAAV: Organizing Asian Communities, which from a mid-'80s origin as an anti-bias group has added a transnational class analysis to its grassroots presence—and which was one of the groups that sent a contingent of activists of color to A16 and R2K. Both currents could gain from an enlarged sense of each other's movements—and, perhaps, a less diminished understanding of shared histories. As Robin Kelley points out, the rise of people-of-color-led international efforts in the supposedly identity-heavy '80s and '90s—like Central American solidarity groups and the South African divestment campaign—are seemingly forgotten by many today.

Teamsters, turtles—and raptivists? "Our capacities have been weakened because of our blind spots," Van Jones notes. "If we can bring both currents together, we'll have a flood. And the corporations will have a big problem."

From Seattle to South Central:

What the Movement Needs to Do Next

Juan Gonzalez
In These Times, *September 18, 2000*

Around the time the Democrats opened their convention at the Staples Center downtown, Margarita Reyes and her husband, Carlos, were catching an afternoon sandwich inside the tiny shoe and clothing store they own near the intersection of Florence and Normandie Avenues. The corner sits at the center of a story most politicians—both New Democrats and New Republicans—would like America to forget.

It was at Florence and Normandie in April 1992 that a crowd of angry blacks gathered after hearing that a Simi Valley jury had acquitted the cops who were caught on videotape brutally beating Rodney King. What followed was the nation's worst riot of the 20th century. By the time it was over, the arson and looting had spread throughout the sprawling city of Los Angeles and more than fifty people were dead and thousands had been arrested.

I spent several days back then reporting from the middle of those riots, interviewing looters as they carried off their wares, people fighting to defend their homes and businesses, cops trying to keep the peace, and residents so enraged at the verdict that peace no longer mattered. An enormous sadness fell over me as I wandered through streets so thick with smoke I could barely see, past the ruins of entire shopping centers, and as I talked to stunned families trying to salvage a few possessions from their burned-down homes.

Even before the rioting, this had been a neighborhood beset by drug trafficking and violence, long abandoned by the scores of factories that once provided its residents with jobs and some measure of hope. At the time, the rest of the country saw it as a black riot, even though the biggest group of people arrested during the disturbances was Hispanic, most of them immigrants picked up by police and National Guard troops for violating curfew or petty looting.

South Central, like the rest of this city, and like so much of our nation, was

Todo el pueblo latino
en
Protesta a la DNC
Convencion Nacional Democrata
LEVANTATE
POR LA
JUSTICIA
Festival de Resistencia
Accion Directa
No Violencia!
Lunes a Jueves
Agosto 14-17
Reune
cada dia
en Pershing Square
en el centro
de LA
Marcha
Agosto 14
4pm
en Pershing Square
SI A LAS NECESIDADES HUMANAS
NO A LA AVARICIA CORPORATIVA

El Pistolero Sin Pistol: DAN Community outreach in LA

a place undergoing a startling transformation. It was not only poor, but longtime black residents were moving out and being rapidly replaced by Mexican and Central American immigrants—newcomers fleeing a poverty and desperation in their homelands that could make the worst ghetto in this country seem like paradise.

Only eight years later, that transformation is even more pronounced. You see it in the businesses around Florence and Normandie. Margarita Reyes, who is from El Salvador, and her husband, who is from Guatemala, opened their store only three months ago. Up the street is the Cuba/Mexico Night Club. There is Pancho's convenience store, and Rosa's Party Supplies, and Hilda's Hair Salon, and Club Las Hadas—all owned by Latinos. None existed there before the riot. And so it goes all over Los Angeles, where Hispanics now comprise 45 percent of all residents. The same scenario is being repeated throughout the country. The number of Hispanics turning out to the polls, joining labor unions and getting involved in American civic life in general has skyrocketed.

Paul Mauldin, a black man and longtime resident, was busy repairing an engine at the Baby I'm Back Auto Care Shop, just down the street from the Reyes' clothing store. Mauldin, 47, moved to Los Angeles from Tyler, Texas in 1977. "All the blacks are moving to Riverside or San Bernardino," he says. "Nothing but Spanish moving in."

Not much has improved in South Central for either group since the riot. Most of those who had no insurance when their homes and businesses were destroyed have fled. Any progress has come from those who stayed to rebuild, and from the new immigrants, who were glad for a chance to buy or rent an abandoned store at a cheap price. City Hall and the politicians in Washington didn't put much money into the neighborhood. "You see any new housing since the riot?" asks George Stevens, a retired city worker whose family has lived in South Central for fifty years. "Nothing's changed for the poor man."

After decades of broken promises, local blacks are deeply bitter. They seethe at a Clinton-era prosperity that whizzed past South Central like traffic on the freeway. I asked Mauldin about the Democrats and the convention downtown. "I don't pay them no mind," he says. "Never voted in my life. Never heard one of them say something made me want to." The Latino newcomers, on the other hand, haven't had time to become disillusioned. Margarita Reyes became a citizen only this year; her husband is still a permanent resident. She concedes she hasn't followed Gore or Bush and doesn't know what either of them stands for. "It's my first chance to vote in November," she says. "I'm looking forward to it."

Over at the Staples Center, the Democrats, allegedly the party of working people, spent the week raising more money from big corporate donors and putting on a glitzy performance for television that blissfully ignored the growing number of workers so turned off to politics they refuse to vote; or those, like Reyes, who can't tell Bush and Gore apart. In South Central, and in the neighborhoods like it across America—those places where people make less than $20,000 a year—barely two out of ten adults vote these days. These are neighborhoods neither party has ever really cared about, except for those moments when they explode and spoil the show.

South Central's alienation is in stark contrast to the fiery protests outside both the Republican and Democratic conventions. Despite many attempts by the corporate media to ignore or minimize the dissidents, or to ridicule them as a hodgepodge of advocates for unrelated causes, the street protests and the less confrontational but equally passionate Shadow Conventions displayed an amazing unanimity in their themes: condemnation of how corporate control of American politics is destroying democracy; of how global capital and the national militaries that protect its expansion threaten the quality of life on our planet and impoverish the majority of its people; of how the war on crime and drugs has become an undeclared racial assault on black and brown America.

The WTO protests in Seattle last year, of course, were the watershed moment, when this international movement of peoples against the New World Order—a movement that had been developing for years—emerged from the shadows and stunned corporate CEOs and world political leaders alike. Officialdom was unprepared for the willingness of thousands to resort to civil disobedience and to disrupt the normal functioning of a city by undergoing mass arrests. It was taken aback by the cleverness and creativity, by the fervor and devotion of so many young people, who, despite being been born and bred in the ultimate individualist consumer society, chose to rebel against the immoral underpinnings of that society—things like child labor in Third World sweatshops or the destruction of the environment and animal life by global companies drunk with greed.

Our country has seen vibrant social and revolutionary movements rise and fall in the past. This new generation of activists can avoid the pitfalls that crippled or doomed past efforts by learning from the mistakes of those who came before them.

Already, after Seattle and the Washington IMF protests, after Philadelphia and Los Angeles, familiar danger signs have appeared. The past should teach us something. Some, enthralled by the spectacular success of Seattle, keep trying to repeat it. Some become enamored of big national showdowns, of the mere power to momentarily disrupt and of the sudden media attention, this being the sugar-coated bullet of modern capitalism. As the size and novelty of national actions ebb and flow—and they inevitably do—some may be tempted to resort to more drastic "vanguard actions" as a substitute, as a means of galvanizing the attention of the very corporate media they condemn, instead of opting to redirect more time back in the neighborhoods, schools and workplaces they came from, educating and organizing more recruits.

Others tend to overlook or pay lip service to the big disconnect that still exists between the new movement, which is largely white and middle-class, and the millions of black, Hispanic and working-class Americans who may sympathize with some of the movement's issues, but don't yet see ways they can become a part of it. While there was more involvement by Third World youth in Los Angeles than in prior protests, I saw disturbing signs of class and racial bias even among some of the most committed protesters in Philadelphia and L.A.

There was, for instance, the young activist outside the West Philadelphia puppet-making center that police raided, arresting seventy people inside who had committed no crime. A phalanx of young cops, most of them black, had been posted outside the warehouse while commanders negotiated the surrender of those inside. The raid itself was inexcusable and a clear violation of basic civil rights, but the cops on the detail were courteous and well-behaved. I listened in astonishment as the young white activist began to berate the black cops, calling them traitors to the memory of Martin Luther King, defenders of racism and oppression, and a variety of other names.

The movement must expand to America's heartland, or it will slowly wither and die

As someone who has spent years chronicling the harrowing experiences of untold numbers of black and Latino cops within urban police departments in this country, I have no doubt that the average black officer encounters and often battles against far more racism than that young radical could ever hope to imagine. Not to recognize that even within the most repressive agencies and institutions of our society there are many men and women of good will battling for justice—people who could be potential allies—is an arrogance and immaturity the new movement cannot afford.

In fact, the movement seems unduly obsessed with generating media attention to how police are treating it. To those of us who grew up and still live in black and brown neighborhoods in this country or emigrated from the Third World, it is hardly noteworthy that some cops can be brutal, especially when they toss you in jail. Nor is it surprising that when you challenge police authority in disruptive protests at high-profile national events, police departments will use clubs, horses, tear gas and rubber bullets. The police brutality exhibited in the various national protests during the past year should be condemned, but it hardly compares to the vicious repression and even murders suffered by civil rights and radical groups such as Southern Christian Leadership Conference, SNCC, the Black Panthers, the Republic of New Afrika, the Young Lords, the Brown Berets and others in the '60s and '70s, or those that still exist in Africa, Asia and Latin America today.

What is far more troubling, and what must be relentlessly exposed, is the trend toward using obscenely high bails, unconstitutional bans on assembly, pre-emptive strike arrests and conspiracy charges to prevent the growing movement from being able to organize itself or engage in future mass mobilizations, for the right of assembly is a basic right of any democracy.

Despite its weaknesses, this new movement is maybe the best thing to happen to this country's radicals in a quarter century. It has already shaken up corporate America and the political establishment, and it has shown an amazing ability to get out its message directly to the American people by nurturing new independent media centers that have started to make the first cracks into the corporate stranglehold on mass media.

American capitalism, however, has proven to be a resilient system. Those in power were surprised by Seattle, but they are awake now, and they will use ever more sophisticated tactics to isolate and divide the many groups and causes that made Seattle possible.

The movement, on the other hand, must expand to America's heartland, or it will slowly wither and die. Expansion requires more time spent in local hometowns, educating and winning over those who now might disagree with its aims. It means airing the contradictions over tactics, methods, strategies and goals between the movement's various components through teach-ins, forums, publications and the Internet, while guarding against the intolerance, splintering and factional fights that over the years have doomed so many radical movements in American society. It means building real and equal partnerships with activists and leaders in Third World communities as well as the labor movement, not just speaking rhetoric about fighting racism and defending workers.

It means, above all, firmly grasping that the road to fundamental change in American society lies not simply in disrupting our downtowns, but in awakening, organizing and providing some vision of a better world to our South Centrals.

Juan Gonzalez

Kevin Harris

Spiritual Warfare

Hakim Bey
November 2000

1

As I understand it, corporate law is based on the ancient legal fiction of the King's Two Bodies. The individual king dies but the KING never dies, and certain properties belong to the archetype but not to the mortal sovereign. For example the mortal king cannot sell or alienate lands belonging to the immortal King, the realm itself. But the mortal king partakes of the unique rights of his immortal doppelganger, for instance in the privilege of granting monopolies. The monopolies (such as the East India Company, or the Chinese salt monopolies) formed the germs of the modern corporation. But the truly modern corporation could only come into being when the concept of the monopoly was opened up and combined with the concept of the royal body in a single entity. Thus in law a corporation enjoys far more privilege and far less responsibility ("limited liability") than any mere fleshly human being. A corporation would seem rather to be a discorporation, a spiritual disincarnate undying being with vast powers on the material plane. Sounds like a demon, doesn't it? In a single century corporation law has succeeded in pulling off an occult stunt that makes Satanism look like a harmless hobby for disgruntled employees.

Banking is another highly spiritual activity, rooted in the fact that the original banks were temples. In the late fourth millennium Sumerian temples were loaning money-commodity currencies: cattle, barley, silver—at rates as high as 33.3% per year. The tradition of the Jubilee (known to the Bible), the periodic forgiveness of debts, appears first in Sumeria. The economy would've collapsed without such safety valves. The modern bank solved this problem by obtaining the monopoly on money-creation. The invention of coins in Lydia, 7th century B.C.E., facilitated this fiat magic. By lending (at interest) ten times its reserves, the bank simply creates the money needed to pay off the debts owed to it. The Federal Reserve Bank (a private bank with a monopoly) actually coins money and lends it to the government. Most states have been in debt to private banks for centuries.

The key to such magic was to cut off all connection between commodities (e.g. barley or silver) and money. Money freed of its anchor in real goods can float upwards forever, compounding itself unto eternity. The history of money reveals an ever-more-attenuated connection with gross materiality, till in 1973 even the (highly magical) link with gold was dissolved by the alchemist Nixon. At this point money began a wild spiralling apotheosis that still goes on. At present over 95% of all money has no actual connection with any material substance. It is not productive capital but "pure" capital—not wealth, only money. Money begets money, as Ben Franklin gloated—the sexuality of the Dead. Pure spirituality, and yet endowed with absolute power over materiality and life itself. Money: not just the "bottom line" but the only line, the final Enclosure—the disappearance of the Outside.

In short, money is another demon. The landscape of our tired old Enlightenment indeed seems haunted by spectres (or "hobgoblins," as in the first English translation of the *Communist Manifesto*). Corporations and banks need to be understood in the light of the history of religions. Strange spooks inhabit the belfry of "neo-liberalism" in its amok triumphalism. We need a hermetic critique of institutions. We want a science of hieroglyphics to help us penetrate the tranced labyrinth of text and image that conceals (at its center) the sheer non-being of corporations and banks, and the purely magical nature of money.

Ideology now appears to us as yet another spook. Ideology betrayed us, not (like banks and corporations) by winning, but by losing the struggle for paradigmatic hegemony in the last millennium. If the Dialectic is going to be kick-started again in the 21st century, Ideology's not going to be doing the kicking. The movement of the social needs to be resurrected, not just resuscitated. Something miraculous is demanded. Something "impossible."

2

Biotechnics presents yet another scary supernatural scenario. But "Frankenfoods" and six-toed babies, or any possible failure of genetic manipulation frighten me far less than its actual successes. In a world where every decision made by science is determined (predetermined) by "money interests" (i.e. the interests of money and the interest on money), then we have a world where science and humanity retain no interests in common. Who precisely is going to "benefit" from the imminent end of human reproduction as we've known it? What 3% of the world will look like movie/TV stars (who already look like mutants)—and what 97% will resemble unsuccessful graduates of Chernobyl's Wormwood High?

And why do Americans seem to care so much about who owns what piece of recorded music (recordings which are nothing more than the digital tombstones of once-live performances), and so little about who owns the "intellectual copyright" of the DNA of, say, rice? Bioengineering in alliance with Pure Capital has already re-shaped our lived reality; the "killer apps" and "terminal genes" are mere details. This is the Future; we're living in it now. And not one SciFi writer predicted it.

3

Nothing's happening. As I write we have a Schrodinger's President situation here in the U.S. We can't open the box because it might kill the cat; but we can't not open the box. There are ever thinner and thinner slices of unreality. What you see happening is what's actually happening—i.e. nothing. No conspiracies, no depth, no illusions. Nothing is hidden, no datum goes unprocessed. All information, all the time; infinity-wide and a micron deep. All light, no shadow.

The medium for this ecstasy of information is of course the media. Unified on a global scale for the first time since writing was invented around six thousand years ago, the media—TV, radio, movies, print, internet, image-commodities, education, music—all propagate the same sameness, the same hysterical greed for an ever-less-seductive fetishism, the same thin scrim over an abyss of boredom. And the boredom itself is the flimsy curtain that only barely contains our terror, anger, shame. Thinner and thinner slices.

"Alternative media" means stuff that can't compete in the free market. Governments are no longer interested in subsidizing it, and in fact it has near-zero influence on what passes for the consensus. The whole vitality of an avant-garde depends on the existence of an Outside toward which it strives. But there is no more Outside. Only failure. Do we have to make failure our Outside?

This would constitute a way of renunciation and even asceticism: a deliberate unknowing or refusal of knowlege. The monasteries of the Dark Ages were points of light on a map of sepulchral gloom. A crisis of epistemology was overcome by keeping knowlege secret. Maybe in these Lite Ages we need monasteries of darkness to tide us over and preserve our last secrets till the unending day of the plague has passed. If ever. No doubt a counsel of despair. But I can't see any way to avoid the work of negativity. If not the monastery then. . . the barbarian horde.

4

The First World and the Second World have both collapsed; CapitalISM died at the same moment as Communism. Only Pure Capital survives. There is no Third World and there is no Third Way. On the one side, humanity; on the other side, money. This is no longer a question of mere tactics, "molecular" or otherwise. Conceptually this is confrontation, strategy, war.

But how do you wage war against disincarnate entities? Malay Black Djinn Curse? Exorcism? Probably futile. Could there exist some form of warfare capable of being waged on the invisible plane? A guerilla response to the Pure War of Pure Capital? A strategy, yes—but what? As F. Jameson says, it appears to be "impossible to imagine an alternative" to Capital. Perhaps we have less need for a new Marx or Kropotkin, and more for a new Von Clauswitz or Sun Tzu.

5

I can't help thinking that somehow or other Luddism still has a role to play. The original Luddites were not Primitivists; they wanted a technology that could support the social relation, not destroy it in the name of profit and/or efficiency. What we used to call "appropriate technology" in the 1960s and '70s. In the intoxication of the Internet and other groovy new technologies a great many radicals appear to have abandoned their old commitment to such "machine smashing"

Hakim Bey

notions as renewable resources, biodiversity, or the social responsibility of science. It's not theory but personal experience that forces on me the impression of "the best minds" of the era slumped before the Screen, lost in cyberspace, tranced into the belief that what happens there is really happening. And yet already the Market is bored with its new toys; NASDAQ trembles and even biotech stocks are looking dull. Nothing's happening—except for drifts of dead daytraders falling like November leaves. Boring, boring. Not even money is interesting anymore.

Despite the fact that Luddism is historically a movement of the Left, some ideologues have dismissed it as reactionary because it is not a "progressive" movement. Indeed if "Left" demands the Enlightenment and its "cruel instrumentality of Reason" (i.e. not rationality but rationalism), if "Left" implies a single world culture based on the machine and its demands, then some might say the time has come to move "beyond Left and Right" and even to look for allies amongst other so-called reactionaries. It's hard to find common ground with the Left these days because it's hard to locate any Left at all. (The Green Party doesn't count; does the Green Party have a coherent critique of Capital?) Left would be nice. Hell, even "young" Marx looks good now that all the old marxists are dead. As for the Right, is it possible that there may exist some true conservatives who are not racists, chauvinist nationalists, apologists for neo-liberalism, fashion fascists nor heavy metal diabolists? Conservatives interested in the conservation of things like wilderness and farms, human values, community and other such old fashioned virtues? Maybe both Left and Right are empty categories, null sets. Can biophilia unite humans against the frigid antibiosis of Capital's machinery? I have my doubts but I'm trying to resolve them and find a way out of despair. Meanwhile could we finally just forget the ancient floor plan of the French Assembly and simply address ourselves instead to those remnants who still feel that humanity is something more than a dwindling market niche?

6

According to P. Virilio, a globe united by one technology, one economy, one Image, has become a setting for the One Big Accident. Maybe it's already happened: the failure of ideology, of the movement of the social—the end even of the Spectacle and its replacement by sheer Simulacrum. If not the end of History then the idea of the end of the idea of History. Theology and materialism both in the trashbin; physics and metaphysics alike—6000 years of immiserabilism—culminating in the victory of those "other bodies," alien and inhuman, demons of our inner emptiness. Any strategy of resistance then—however "impossible"—would have to develop a kind of rough empiricism capable of transcending the false consciousnesses of both materialism and immaterialism. This process of discovery might provide useful tasks for those monasteries of darkness where hermetic critique and hieroglyphic theory will be studied—tasks of both negation and creation.

From my perspective religion and spirituality are two different things. Religion in Sumer and Egypt appropriated spirituality from shamanism and neolithic paganism. Religion used its supposed monopoly of grace to reinforce separation and hierarchy. From this point of view ideology might appear simply as secularized theology, since its end result is the same.

Spirituality (for want of a better word) strikes me as an empirical thing, since—like countless others—I've experienced it through psychotropic plants and chemicals, and by other means no less natural or unnatural. I find it interesting that Global Capital seems unable to digest and commodify the "power plants" and phantastica; over and above the economic advantages of the war on drugs there remains a residue of sheer psychic hysteria about the repression that somehow suggests real power is at stake. And real power is rare outside the sphere of money. We should take note of such esoteric power flows. We need every possible advantage.

A resistance based on empiricism, it seems to me, will have to consider the apparent actuality of spirit. At this point I must admit that I'm waiting for a sign, like some very minor Old Testament prophet. I can't predict, but I have the feeling that this sign will somehow involve what I'm calling spirituality. For this reason I expect the sign to appear not in America or any of the other "included zones" but perhaps in what used to be called the Fourth World, the world of tribes, foresters and peasants (and shamans and pagans), the excluded zones where the frontline battles of Global Capital are being fought. If both religion and ideology have betrayed us then the sign cannot take the form of religion or ideology. Somehow the sign will combine elements of difference and also solidarity, and present a real opposition to sameness as well as separation. This sounds quite paradoxical, and therefore suggests the spirituality of the sign. Above all I believe the sign will arise spontaneously, and that it cannot be cooked up as an intellectual exercise or artwork. And 1 have absolutely no idea what it will be. Or if it will be.

7 (addendum)

What does all this mean in terms of possible strategy—or even tactics—"after Seattle," etc., etc.? How does this "waiting for a sign" relate to the struggle against the WTO, IMF, World Bank, NAFTA, GATT, major corporations, superfunds... not to mention the usual old straightforward enemies like governments and armies?, and new ambiguous enemies like the NGOs?

I'd like to make a plea for theory, which doesn't by any means imply ideology. Theoria originally signifies "vision," and includes both sight and "Visionary experience." Since the decay of post-deconstruction, post-modernism and post everything else, theory has fallen on hard times. Theory now requires the kind of empiricism evoked in the previous paragraphs; it needs psychotropic madness and spontaneity as well. But above all theory needs to clarify the issue of Capital, and this is a work of negation. The protesters in Seattle or Prague are by no means united in their understanding of Capital. The reformist element actually believes in "Capital with a human face," and shares no common language with the anarchists, etc. As a result alliances made around the emotions of confrontation tend to dissolve when strategic issues are raised. Populism would be a welcome phenomenon, and might have some appeal to reform and even to productive capital, as well as to the resistance. But populism in the Green Party style has no future except lost elections. Until a viable form of populism appears I think non-authoritarians might as well work on sharpening their theory of Capital.

Another crying need is for real strategic thinking. New and unusual forms of the old "demo" caught the Seattle police by surprise, but the actions against the Democratic and Republican conventions were failures because these tactics were anticipated by police. (The anti-convention actions also failed, I suspect, because no one really cares about politics. The best tactic would have been to deliberately stay away from the conventions, not to demonstrate at all, but to denounce them as boring shams.) Each move on the part of Capital's forces requires a new tactical response from the resistance, and these new tactics can only arise out of strategic thinking. Elementary Von Clauswitz.

Meanwhile, in closing, a salute to French farmer José Bové. He did more for the cause by driving his tractor into a McDonald's than all Web pages and NGOs combined. And hail to Vandana Shiva as well. She and her Indian women are very nearly a "sign" in themselves.

On Populism and the Antiglobalization Movement

James O'Connor
Capitalism, Nature, Socialism, *October 15, 2000*

Poverty[1] Nobody *defends* mass poverty in the world because there is no defense. Yet mass poverty persists. Most economists believe that the cure for poverty is faster economic growth. An increasing rate of growth in the U.S. in the last half (compared with the first half) of the 1990s reduced the percentage of American families living in poverty. A century and a half of industrial capitalism in the North (neoliberal economists argue) has reduced poverty to "manageable" levels. This means, first, that the poor have become politically manageable, and, second, that poverty is no longer a scandal. Hence no special programs are needed to elevate families economically beyond welfare reform.

Until the appearance of the antiglobalization movement—to some the "anti–corporate globalization" movement[2]—the World Bank and IMF were confident that increased economic growth in general and in the South in particular would reduce poverty in the latter, as U.S. growth has decreased poverty here. Everyone knows that they failed miserably, that conditions in the South beginning with the debt crisis and Structural Adjustment Programs in the late 1970s/early 1980s have deteriorated badly compared with the "golden age" of nationalist, semisocialist development during the 1950s and 1960s. Exactly how much the Bank/IMF are to blame for the disasters in Latin America in the 1980s and in Africa during the 1980s and 1990s no one can say. But the antiglobalist movement is predicated on the fact that the Bank and Fund (and U.S. foreign policy) soon became a big part of the problem, not the solution.

The movement has increasingly protested IMF and World Bank policies that movement leaders rightly believe increase, not decrease, world poverty. This movement is well-organized and tenacious and has good leadership; the movement is also growing in numbers and militancy and has become global in scope.

In the U.S., politically, it is a populist movement, not a class-based movement, which is probably a plus at the moment.[3] The movement, finally, has become influential enough to force the World Bank to change its theory of poverty and its alleviation. The Bank today still regards economic growth as indispensable to "poverty reduction" and still rejects the radical idea that poverty can be reduced by redistributing wealth and income. Their new idea is that a larger share of the increments to growth (the extra capital that growth produces) should be allocated to targeted antipoverty projects. Most movement leaders would reject this theory or policy as too timid. They are rightly convinced that any significant reduction of poverty presupposes a redistribution of wealth and income, from the North to the South, from local corrupt elites to local workers, small farmers and unemployed, and from global corporations to the hundreds of millions of people living in poverty today.

Movement leaders are quite clear that the redistribution of wealth and income presupposes a redistribution of political power, which, of course, is where the Bank, IMF and WTO draw the line. Thus the ongoing struggle against global political elites, global corporations, and global institutions such as the Bank. This struggle is bound to continue until the movement has achieved a national and international power shift in its favor.

At this point movement folk whose stock in trade are ideas have different visions for the future. Some stress bulking up the UN to give it real power over the global corporations and elites. Some want to reform the IMF et al., while others want to abolish the international economic agencies. Some want "people-centered alternatives" while many in the South want better terms of trade, market opening in the North, technology transfer, and so on. Some imagine a global Keynesianism while others stress international labor solidarity. Whatever the envisioned future, movement spokespeople seem to agree on one thing—they won't quit until wealth and income have been redistributed to the point at which world poverty is or nearly is abolished. In CNS-talk, they are "reds" because they demand that wealth be redistributed but not yet "green" because they don't also demand that at the same time wealth be systematically *redefined*—from commodity wealth to ecological production, distribution and consumption.

Meanwhile the global corporations (and financial markets and other basic features of capitalism about which populists say little) and the U.S. imperialist state which stands behind the corporations and markets, and the IMF et al., which serve this state—all these forces will fight the movement tooth and nail. If history is any guide, popular power comes after World Wars and during economic crises and hard times—and nobody wants either war or depression. But just because something has never happened before doesn't mean that it can't happen, or be made to happen in the future.

Populism and Globalization The antiglobalization movement wears many political and ideological masks, so many that "movements" might be more accurate than "movement." In the South the movement is often nationalist, often radically so. At home U.S. nationalism is another name for U.S. imperialism, which the antiglobalist movement in North America does not yet explicitly acknowledge. Yet while the slogan "end U.S. imperialism" has been conspicuously absent at protest demonstrations, most in the U.S. movement oppose the U.S.-dominated IMF, WTO, and World Bank and also support market opening, improve terms of trade, technology transfer and more radical demands (such as the decommodification of water and other basics) placed on the North by the movement (and by many governments) in the South.

North and South the movement today is fundamentally populist (as noted). This means among other things that it is not (yet?) based on the interests and demands of any one economic class or alliance of classes. While global capital plays the "class card" at every turn, antiglobalization sentiment is divided into (among other ways) left populist and right populist castes. In the U.S., left populism (secular and internationalist) is organized within the movement itself while right-wing populism (antisecular and nationalist) is not internationally organized. In the South, right populism, fundamentalism, and nationalism (i.e. anti-U.S. imperialism) are much better organized. This is particularly true in Saharan Africa and the Middle East, on the edges of prosperous Europe, and in South Asia, on the border of the Southeast Asian "emerging market economies." Right-wing populism in the South seems to be weakest in Brazil and South Africa—big industrial countries distant from the North and also from regions where fundamentalism is strong—where class-based antiglobalism (which for obvious reasons is also powerfully antiracist North imperialism) is relatively well-organized. European right populism—anti-immigrant nativist workers, tradespeople, truckers, open racists, and political extremists, et al.—is better organized than in the States but not as well as in the countries and regions in the South where right populism is a factor. The South, of course, has tens of millions of left populist villagers, fisherfolk, landless movements, workers' movements, women's movements in towns and countryside, indigenous peoples, scientists, intellectuals and others under attack on two fronts: first, by the forces of neoliberal globalism, second, by local right-wing populist parties and movements. My own opinion is that at some point most everybody will be taking sides on globalization (for or against, reform or revolution) and hence that antiglobalist politics North and South (and East) are likely to be difficult (to put it mildly) for some time to come.

One important fact of life in antiglobalist politics is that right populists in the South are anti-imperialist while their opposite numbers in the North are pro-imperialist. Of equal importance, right populists in the South are people of color and antiracist while their counterparts in the North are (often proudly) racist. In most countries I would guess that right populists regard themselves as patriotic. This all means that the likelihood of a right-wing global populist movement is zero while the odds are much better for an international populism of the left. This is important because the political terrain of both capital and antiglobalist movements is itself global.

One globalist (imperialist) project is to create a strong globalist comprador bourgeoisie in as many countries in the South as possible; thus one reason for the urgency often expressed by the globalizing elites. The means of implementing this project are many and varied. Tying a country's currency to the dollar is one way. Structural Adjustment Programss are another, as they change not only economic structures in the South but also the class composition and political alignments in SAPed countries. A successful SAP project helps transform a local business class into a globalist comprador class, which is best able to rule or govern a

James O'Connor

country the way that the U.S. wants the country to be ruled (without the need for obvious or dramatic interventionism on the part of the U.S. government and military). Neoimperialist political rule involves above all destroying all traces of older models of nationalist economic and social development in the South and also opposing new regionalist models based on political economic polycentrism (Samir Amin's term). It should be clear to everyone at this point that the purpose of U.S. policy as outlined by neoliberal globalists is to replace any and all national projects with the single globalist development model organized by Washington and Wall Street (see "House Organ," *CNS,* September, 2000).

Unfortunately for the latter there is no way that the U.S. imperial state (or national security state) can expand and evolve in ways that will allow it to keep up with (much less regulate) the expansion of global capital, on the one hand, and the growing antiglobalist movement, on the other. This is indicated by the short life of the Washington Consensus (unrevised version); the attacks on neoliberal thinking from outside and inside the major international institutions; the inability of the World Bank and IMF to hold their hardline stances when confronted with major economic crises (e.g. 1997–1998) and the loss of legitimacy they suffered when their crisis-management policies were exposed as recession-producing policies; the confession that free markets alone aren't able to do away with mass poverty in the South; and the pathetic yet dangerous attempts on the part of big corporations to make money off global warming and ozone depletion (and the rest) instead of confronting the environmental (social) crisis directly. Recall it took a landed gentry, the stewards and trustees of yore—FDR being the best-known, to confront the Great Depression on a broad front—and only near the end of FDR's first term at that.

The fact that neoliberal practice has slipped away from neoliberal theory shouldn't be underestimated. This and other failures of empire create good chances for left antiglobalism since they put into question the legitimacy of the hegemonic or ruling ideas of our time, as well as the real intentions of the globalists (make money and more money into infinity). As I wrote in a previous article, "High Stakes," neoliberalism is a castle in the air. Harmless economic nonsense on paper, neoliberal economics becomes a psychotic enterprise when the globalists try to occupy the castle and make it home. This is what Emma Bovary did, in her own way, which ended in her painful suicide. This will also be neoliberal globalism's fate absent some very (unlikely?) deep reforms of the system. As noted, some put forth the idea of a global New Deal,

> Right populists in the South are anti-imperialist while their opposite numbers in the North are pro-imperialist. Of equal importance, right populists in the South are people of color and antiracist while their counterparts in the North are (often proudly) racist. In most countries I would guess that right populists regard themselves as patriotic. This all means that the likelihood of a right-wing global populist movement is zero while the odds are much better for an international populism of the left.

which for me is harder to imagine than systemic crisis and collapse.

Yet the failures create openings for left antiglobalist forces. Perhaps most important is to heed the call of the nationalist, left populists in the South: continue to attack the Washington consensus and neoliberal model of global development; help breathe new life into older models of nationalist development and newer models of regional polycentric development; support trade and investment rules, technology transfers and other South demands that will help restore or reinvent nationalist socio-economic, ecological development; demand that ecological rationality, equity, and social justice come before efficiency and profit. Abolish the WTO and radically reform the IMF and World Bank, possibly via UN General Assembly control of these and other global institutions.

Every country has the right to develop its resources, human and ecological, in accordance with its own needs and desires. No country should be forced into the monocultural model of globalist development, as designed by Wall Street and the U.S. Treasury. Not even our own country. That should be basic. As history has shown, self-determination is a very imperfect solution; however, it's a better solution than neoliberal imperialism and its castles in the air.

Potted History The antiglobalization movement has a short and as yet unrecorded history. Some say that the movement began in the late 1970s, at the birth of neoliberalism, in the first stage of the Third World debt crisis, IMF Structural Adjustment Programs (SAPs), and the IMF riots in Africa, Latin America, and Asia. The word "globalization," however, wasn't commonly used until the late 1980s and early 1990s. Others seem to date the origins of the movement to the alternative summit in Rio 1992, but this was a meeting of NGOs, not a protest demonstration by social movements.[4] The genesis of the movement might be dated to any one (or all) of a dozen major protests at IMF, World Bank, G7 and other international meetings during the 1990s, the Madrid "Fifty Years are Enough" demonstrations arguably the most successful. In almost all accounts, however, Seattle 1999 appears time and again as a real turning point, the first movement victory in the streets.[5]

This reading of the 1990s risks missing the movement's two significant victories against MAI internationally and "fast track" at home (the latter being antiglobalist, if not anticorporate),[6] which were achieved by a combination of NGO lobbying, pressure group politics, internetworking, and street protests, together with some inside deal-making between organized labor and the Clinton administration with respect to "fast track." Historians may see these victories as the real precursors of the antiglobalization movement, first, because they were victories, second because they were accomplished by the vanguard of the movement, those who could see further into the future than anyone else at the time.

Yet my own favorite origins story is Seattle if only because the media still systematically lies about what actually happened on the streets and in the jails of that fabled city late last year. Most Americans doubtless believe that the Seattle demonstrators fomented a "riot," when in fact most confined their participation to a peaceful march. The "rioters" were police beating up militants engaged in nonviolent resistance (a few dozen self-described anarchists could not be said to be "rioting" when they broke a few windows). Shades of the early civil rights movement, when nonviolent sit-ins, marches, and demonstrations were

James O'Connor

met by spontaneous and organized police brutality, which time and again came back to haunt the forces of racism during the later stage of the movement culminating in the Civil Rights Act of 1964.

Since Seattle, antiglobalist (and anti-corporate) demonstrations have multiplied in number and also with respect to the targets demonstrators choose to protest. In Washington, D.C., Philadelphia, Los Angeles, Bangkok, Formosa, Melbourne, and Prague (among other places) there was a kind of wedding (if not wedding, an engagement) between antiglobalist forces, on the one hand, and civil rights, welfare rights, anti-police brutality, feminist, environmentalist and other domestically-oriented movements, on the other hand—ad hoc as these were. For example, organized groups from the nominally domestic environmental justice movement protested in Seattle and antiglobalist forces showed up in Philadelphia and Los Angeles, where environmental justice issues were among the most paramount ("nominally domestic" because the movement—called by some the movement for environmental and economic justice and by others the movement for environmental and social justice—has been working with EJ groups in other countries for some time). The Independent Media Centers, established in dozens of cities, exemplified what a truly democratic, yet organized and professional, media could look like. More than making up for the absence of big labor and mainstream environmental organizations in Philly and L.A. were living wage, welfare rights, and other local groups and movements (noted above).

The result has been that more people doubtless understand in various ways the linkages or internal relationships between the big corporations and globalization, and between global and local issues, American foreign and domestic policy, and economics and politics, generally. The drum beat faster in Seattle and half a million or more demonstrators around the world have picked up the beat since Seattle.

Antiglobalization protests have paid dividends, at least a down payment on a long overdue debt by global corporations and elites to the world's poor, small farmers and tradespeople, sweatshop workers, unemployed, village women, countless others. Or if not a down payment, the promise of one. As noted above, World Bank and IMF chiefs and others who constitute the global elite are acting as if the movement has caused them to see the light and undergo a change of heart. Suddenly, "poverty reduction," "living wages," "an end to sweatshops," "better health care and education," and a World Bank one billion dollar AIDS relief project for Africa and other movement causes are proposed by the elites as their very own aims or goals ("House Organ," CNS, June, 2000). As also noted, neoliberal economists in power are finding more exceptions to the policy implications of monitarist/neoclassical economic theory than Alfred Marshall ever dreamt of, while second-tier global officials whisper about the need to reintroduce capital controls to prevent another financial crisis of the 1997–98 type. Sometimes it seems that half of the entire French establishment is wondering if globalization is worth the candle.

In practice, there has been more pleasing rhetoric than plausible policy changes: this despite the facts that two billion people live on less than two dollars a day world-wide and the elite's discreet admission that the rising tide lifts all boats theory of development has badly designed rigging and leaky logic. In practice, also: more militarized police trampling more boldly on the civil liberties of protest demonstrators here and abroad have mocked the basic tenets of liberal democracy.

For their part, the individuals and groups and NGOs who have organized a decade or more of protests, and the ideologies which movement rhetoric is based upon—all speak to one central point: world economy and politics as we know them are much too important to be left to the economists and politicians—unecological, inequitable, unjust, and undemocratic as these economics and politics are. More people here and elsewhere increasingly regard the world that global capital is making as a hopelessly alienated and reified place unfit for real human beings. The economists' language of efficiency, profits and "consumer choice" is no match for the best ideals and practices of the antiglobalist movement. And more women and oppressed minorities are especially adamant in their opposition to the world that ideologues of global capital imagine as some kind of New Jerusalem.

For their part, despite stated good intentions, sincere or not, global corporations and financial groups and institutions and political elites will do everything and anything they think is necessary to preserve the "global way of life"— the totalitarianism of the single globalist development model, which most in the ruling class and political elite probably regard as the culmination of the idea of Progress, invented hundreds of years ago by their real and imagined North European forerunners. Not merely their profits but their whole way of life is at stake. They believe that this way of life is the best possible way and hence regard anyone who opposes it not only as a political enemy but also as suffering a mental or moral disorder. This is a dangerous group of people: unable to grasp neoliberal globalization as a castle in the air which will drive more people mad, they label "insane" those who refuse to live in their dream-world.

Politics and Populism Revisited. I think that we can expect (and should encourage) the antiglobalist movement to become more political, not only with respect to (as at present) political *means* to ecological, economic, and social goals, but also with regard to political *ends*. Since Seattle, in less than a year, movement issues and demands are becoming more multidimensional and all-inclusive, presented as ensembles of problems and solutions interrelated in various ways, unable to be resolved at any other level than the political (which, dialectically, makes local experiments in alternative working and living all the more important). This is especially so given that domestic issues of racism and police brutality are connected in more people's minds with global issues arising from corporate rule, the rule of international finance markets, and the subordination of use value by exchange value. The difference between what corporate and political elites say they will do (reduce poverty) and what they actually do (increase poverty), will also help to politicize the movement (in the sense of developing political goals). The fact that antiglobalization protests of traditional and new types engender more police violence and suspension of civil liberties, is also a politicizing factor. Because many mainstream North NGOs seem to want to believe elite promises and also seem to downplay police brutality, there might possibly occur a split between NGOs (especially government-sponsored, corporate-funded NGOs) and movement organizers and activists who are less credulous and more intellectually sophisticated (in the critical thinking sense) than

James O'Connor

the typical NGO official. I think this can be regarded as a good rather than bad thing, a positive development, because NGOs are by definition already compromised in various ways while the movement itself may be likened to a flow of creative and critical human energy, thinking and doing, directed at what most see as an oppressive and exploitative system of corporate/U.S. Treasury/central bank/IMF, et al., rule. I don't believe that the elites see the NGOs as the real threat to their world capitalist project, but rather the unpredictable, centerless movement. Alex Demirovic's theory of NGOs and social movements is important precisely because of the kinds of distinctions he finds between the two.[4] Years ago, Alex denoted theoretically what today is working itself out in different variations in practical terms, for everyone who cares to see.

There are reasons why the idea of debating, developing and adopting political goals will be regarded by all kinds of people as unrealistic, falsely utopian, and possibly harmful or dangerous. There are many differences between the antiglobalization movements in the South and the North in terms of what they want, how they organize themselves, and the language and goals of resistance. There are the different relationships that different parts of the movement have with the existing political systems world-wide, including different assessments of the possible scope and limits of liberal democracy, and different definitions of the word "democracy" itself. There is the awful deadening effect of bourgeois politics as usual in today's world of neoliberal globalization. Above all, there is the terrible fear of any action or organization that proposes any "totalizing" solutions to the problem of globalization. To say that the movement's political aims will be democratic, pluralistic, anti-sexist, pro-oppressed minorities, ecological, ad infinitum would be (and is) seen in many circles as a bad joke. Yet I think that the movement itself will be forced to adopt a project with definite political ends, an international and internationalist project as the only viable way to oppose globalization successfully, including defining and implementing as much as possible independent alternatives.

The last problem I'll mention seems to be more intractable than it really is. This is the division, noted above, between right-wing populism and the populism of the left in the U.S. I have often read that on the subject of foreign trade and investment right and left populism speak the same language—that both are antiglobalist in the sense that both reject "free trade" and liberalized foreign investment. Superficially, the fit between right populists and U.S. organized labor seems even tighter: American workers tend to support the regulation of international business and also to be socially conservative. This is Pat Buchanan's political formula and on the surface not so distant from Ralph Nader's political positions in 1996.[7]

In fact the similarity between right and left populists begins and ends with the slogans "Stop the export of jobs" and "Fair trade not free trade" (although most right populists seem to be self-defined protectionists while left populists are not, or if they are they keep it to themselves). Right populists around the world, including in the US, are cultural reactionaries and, unlike many if not most populist small farmers a century ago, left populists today are mainly cultural liberals. For right populists, cultural conservatism fits nicely with their uncritical nationalism, while left populists tend to be multi-cultural and internationalist. Right populists are often small business people being squeezed by big corporations and left populists (exceptions are noted above) are militantly anticorporate, but the former ally themselves with the latter only when the labor or trade union issue is tabled. Right populist businesspeople are as anti-union as left populists are pro-union (thus the only question of interest in any coalition of the two in relation to a particular issue, say, "free trade," is, which side has the power to dump the other side from the coalition when the stakes change and the issue of unionism and worker power comes up, as it always does). Right populists hate the WTO and IMF because they appear to represent a shift of power from the American nation-state to international bodies; left populists feel the same way not because the WTO and IMF are international bodies but because they make U.S. foreign policy more undemocratic than it already is and because they exploit and oppress the South. In sum, there are not a lot of things that right-wing nationalists and left-wing internationalists and democrats (small "d") can or do agree on. This is partly because of differences in ideology and political sensibility and partly because their constituencies are very different: the right speaks to small business under attack from big business (for example, small farmers in the U.S. today who have to sell their crops to one of a handful of giant food companies) while the left speaks more to the poor, unemployed, workers getting less than a living wage, and some trade unionists (for example, public sector unions under attack by top elected officials who are paid to organize work-force downsizing or to prepare a public utility or social service for privatization). Populism of all kinds appeals to the little guy against the big guy but today the little guy has many names, including (as noted) public sector workers. In sum, left populism and right populism are very different with respect to the issues of nationalism vs. internationalism, cultural conservatism vs. social liberalism, and business vs. labor. Right populism isn't a terribly big danger in the U.S. for the simple reason that the U.S. is the imperial hegemon, that is, nationalism equals imperialism under the stars and stripes.

Circling back to the subject of political goals for the antiglobalist movement: the Green Party? the U.S. Labor or Socialist parties? a fifth international of red-green organizations and parties? a movement to split the U.S. Democrats into center left and center right components? an IMF-LEFT, established by South countries organized regionally or in polycentric forms, financially backed perhaps by...? a World Forum for Capital Controls, which repoliticizes international capital movements? a World Collective of farmer-to-consumer networks, explicitly seeking to reduce and eliminate the power of the U.S.-based global food companies? a Global Counsel on Immigration that politically eliminates the super-exploitation of immigrant workers employing the immigrants' own organized political power? a reconstituted UN, in which the Security Counsel is confined to administrative tasks, politics the monopoly of the General Assembly?

So many political goals have been cited, trial ballooned, mentioned in passing, received scholarly attention, etc. I don't know what they will be, but I think I know what they in fact are today, whether the participants are aware of it or not: the idea that capital today is politicized, that the WTO, for example, is a political form of capital (and a big capitalist mistake, as Nader said years ago, since it makes what is fundamentally a private relationship—capitalist free trade—into a public and political relationship which needs to legitimize itself to the global public, and thus presents itself as a political target). It's clear that all movement struggles pertaining to the conditions of production (health and education, the use of place and space, environment, community, etc.) are by definition political struggles. This is so because the state either produces or regulates the conditions of production (because these conditions are not produced as commodities, only treated as if they are commodities). This is the idea, in short, of struggles within and against the state, to democratize the state, an idea shared by some theory-minded radicals, while ridiculed as an oxymoron by more traditional leftists. I'm not sure that the antiglobalist movement will acknowledge that much of its activity aims to democratize (or abolish) the state, e.g. the WTO, and I'm even less sure that the movement will some day choose other, perhaps more politically potent or interesting, political goals. I am pretty sure that without such goals, there will be lots more corporate and state greenwashing, today compounded by World Bank "redwashing," or the make-believe that this eminently capitalist institution either wants to or is able to abolish poverty worldwide.

This is not such a difficult task as the World Bank and IMF make it out to be. What's difficult is to prioritize "economic growth"—capitalist accumulation—as the indispensable condition for "poverty reduction," as the WB and IMF do and will continue to do. Translated, this means that "there will be no redistribution of wealth, monetary, physical, ecological, or any other kind; the best we can do is to increase growth rates then target the poor for a goodly share of the increments to growth." How? Of course, by turning the poor into human capital! However, if you think about it, poverty can be abolished in a few months, assuming the political will and the economic and ecological resources. First step, make poverty abolition the basic goal of international politics. Second step, allocate some billions of dollars of World Bank, IMF, regional development bank, and other monies to the task at hand. Third step, employ these monies, not for human capital or any other kind of capital, but to use local biomass for building homes, schools, and the rest; paying (well) public health and medical technicians, teachers of the "pedagogy of the oppressed" variety, psychologists of the Fanon-type, planners of the Kerala or Gaviota variety, and organizers of the type presently engaged in the antiglobalist movement (including NGO people of course). And more, but you get the idea. *Then,* choose investment projects, not in terms of EIRs that seek to minimize damage to local or regional ecologies but rather to *maximize* ecological values, community values, cultural values, public health values, and so on: a simple reversal of existing capitalist values and investment criteria. Not "safe food" but "nourishing food." Not "adequate housing" but "excellent housing." Not "mass transport" but "public transit of different types that are a pleasure to utilize." Obviously, not "chemical-laced" agriculture but "pesticide-free agronomy." Not "food monopolies" but "farm-to-market global distribution." The tragedy is that so many people *know* "what is to be done," based on tens of thousands of local and regional experiments and practices, from the allocation of water to the production and allocation of steel (in the U.S. during WWII, for example), yet we can do little to make a world in which use value subordinates exchange value (and concrete labor subordinates abstract labor) given the present-day monopoly of power by capital, capital markets, the capitalist state, and capitalist international agencies. Just suppose the IMF, WB, et al., were reduced to the status of the IHO, ILO, and other branches of the "international peoples' state," while the latter's power was expanded to the level of the present-day WB and IMF. That would be something, wouldn't it? The problem of course is not a technical one, a practical problem, but a political problem, the problem of capitalist power, in and outside the markets. No movement can challenge capitalist power with success without adopting its own political aims and socio-economic alternatives.

There is every need for an internationalist political terrain, an anti-imperialist terrain (which in our world means an antiwhite rule terrain, as the North Europeans here and overseas still rule the world). World War I broke up their continental empires, Russia's excepted, and WW II broke up their overseas empires, the US's remains. Not yet has domination by European whites remains and the white settler capitalist powers been overthrown by the "lesser" ethnicities and people of color.

1. This is the fourth of a series of sketches on "global capital and its antimonies." All four can be found on the CNS/CPE website: http://gate.cruzio.com/~cns/.

2. The "anti–corporate globalization" movement because U.S. movement leaders (theorists? spokespeople?) seek an alliance between organized labor and the big environmental organizations. Neither organized labor nor mainstream environmentalists are "anti-corporate," the first because labor needs corporations for jobs, good wages and benefits, and so on, the second because so many enviro leaders are connected to the big corporations as well as dependent on big money for project grants, etc. Both, however, are ant–corporate globalization, labor because corporate globalization policies mean job losses and lower pay, and the enviros because they oppose many types of corporate investments and production systems in the South as harmful to the environment.

3. How do you know a populist declaration or document when you see one? My own method is to look for key words. Most if not all documents originating within the populist antiglobalist movement use expressions such as "global corporations," "undemocratic and elitist" (applied to the IMF, et al.), "peoples of the world," "non-governmental organizations," and "people-centered alternatives." These same documents don't use words such as "capitalism" and "capital" and "finance capital" and "capital markets" (that discipline the corporations). The word "exploitation" (e.g., of labor) is used to apply to the South but not the North. "U.S. imperialism" is taboo outside of sectarian party circles, as is "imperialism" of any type. In movement analyses and declarations from the South, "nationalism" is used, not so in statements from the North. Finally, movement publicists fail to distinguish between NGOs and social movements. The above is, of course, a personal reading.

4. For the differences between NGOs and social movements, see Alex Demirovic, "NGOs and Social Movements: A Study in Contrasts," CNS, 9, 3, September, 1980.

5. More precisely, the conflicts within the WTO (U.S. versus Europe, South versus North) combined with the street protests (which older participants say they hadn't seen the likes of since the anti-Vietnam war movement in the late 1960s) to produce a stalemate in WTO member negotiations. Stymied on the agricultural and some other fronts, the WTO is at present cooking up even more outrageous trade rules in Geneva, in secret, pertaining to global trade in services and intellectual property rights.

6. Much of organized labor in the U.S., for example, is definitely antiglobalist but hardly anti-corporate, as noted above.

7. Black and feminist groups put Nader on the carpet for ignoring civil right issues and women's issues such as abortion rights four years ago. Nader's standard response to civil rights questions has been, "Ask my running mate." When last September he was attacked by the National Organization of Women (NOW) for neglecting women's issues (obviously a Gore-inspired move to stop women from voting for Nader in 2000), Nader reminded everyone of his

political support of women, including abortion rights. As two major campaign speeches in Santa Cruz made clear, Nader is obviously no social conservative and just as obviously plays up his main theme of corporate greed and corruption and the role of the "public citizen" in fighting same. Nader is thus a left populist with nothing in common with the likes of Buchanan, yet his machine will seek votes among small businesspeople in the Heartland who seem to agree with him on economics, even though they no doubt disagree with him on most social issues. The question is, do they really agree on economics or does it just seem that they do? (see above).

Glossary

Iain A. Boal

The compiler salutes that small band of writers drawn to the critical glossary as a literary form: first, contrarian lexicographers such as Ambrose Bierce (The Devil's Dictionary) and Charles Bufe (The Heretic's Handbook of Quotations); poets, too, of a committed imagination with an accurate ear for the demoralization of the dialect of the tribe—and here I think, for example, of Benjamin Péret, W.H. Auden, Allen Ginsberg, and Tom Paulin; but most to the purpose, a pair of critics, one American and the other Welsh—Kenneth Burke and Raymond Williams—who composed what the former called "a dictionary of pivotal terms" and the latter dubbed "a vocabulary of culture and society". These glossarians were far from nostalgic for some Adamic speech, for the "true meaning" of a word; nor did they intend to combat, in the manner of reactionary linguistic watchdogs, loose usage with precision, let alone vulgarisms with a style book. It is, in fact, the active range of meanings that matters, since the immense complexity and contradiction within terms like "environment" and "violence" register deep conflicts in the social order.

Language, on this view, does not just label things in the world; it helps to constitute it. The naming of parts, the framing of questions, the refusing to explain, are at once the prerogative and the springs of power. Much more crucial to the powerful, however, than their assertions—say, "Sam is suffering from drapetomania"—are the presuppositions that underlie discourse. It was one thing, in the ante-bellum South, to query the medical diagnosis of Sam's drapetomania, defined as a "pathological propensity to attempt to escape"; it was quite another to challenge the institutions of slavery and medicine that conspired to pathologize the seeking of freedom. Defunct vocabularies, and labels such as drapetomania, abandoned by the classifying classes as either obsolete (vis-à-vis some new regime of stigmata) or embarrassing (after a struggle by those so labeled), are particularly revealing of the strategic links between language and institutional sites of power. The anti-capitalist movement, standing on terrain not of its own choosing, too often retorts in an idiom satisfactory to the sovereign.

Raymond Williams' explorations in historical semantics are much the better known, but his Keywords was anticipated, a generation earlier, by Kenneth Burke when he launched a critique of the left's political lexicon in the face of corporate-fascist reaction to capital's big twentieth century emergency. Burke recommended "intellectual vagabondage" that would constitute "a grave interference with the cultural code" of industrial modernity; he proposed sabotage of the system by defending inefficiency, pessimism, dissipation, mockery, distrust, hypochondria and treason. One communist called Burke's negative aesthetic "the philosophy of the petit bourgeois gone mad", and Burke didn't much disagree. In view of the millennial coronation of business culture Kenneth Burke's 1931 "Program" in Counter-Statement repays a fresh reading.

Then in April 1935, at the time of the popular front and the bienio negro in Spain, Burke gave a brief address to the first American Writers' Congress in New York on "Revolutionary Symbolism in America". He told his audience that, when they weren't talking into the mirror, they were using a patronizing language that was sure to fail, simply because idealizing "the workers" in the same breath as insisting on the absolute degradation of work under capitalism was a rhetorical disaster. Burke went on to recommend "the people" rather than "workers" as a mode of address, even though he was aware that, in a society riven by hierarchies of class, gender, race and the rest, "the people" has its own problems, to say the least; any totalizing term is necessarily ideological. So hostile was the reaction— he was accused of proposing the rhetorical methods of Hitler—that Burke later hallucinated excrement dripping from his tongue.

Another totalization—there is none greater—stamped the days of Seattle, both on the streets and in the suites. I mean, of course, the "globe" (and its derivatives), under which sign the committees of capital and their opponents converged. "Globalization", which began as business school jargon, became a cant word during the nineties, but students of imperialism were frankly unimpressed by the purported novelty of the phenomenon; already in 1848 two pamphleteers had remarked that the "need of a constantly expanding market for its products chases the bourgeoisie over the whole surface of the globe. It must nestle everywhere, settle everywhere, establish connections everywhere." Actually, the connections are still distinctly patchy; much of Africa lies unwired, and one in three of the globe's population has never yet heard a phone ring.

But this is just to rehearse the banality that capitalist development is uneven. More to the point—and it goes some way to account for the disturbances in Seattle and since—is the fact that structural adjustment at home in the US has been dismantling the remains of the New Deal compromise, as well as the dividends of the civil rights, feminist, peace and environmental movements. The pattern of events at Seattle confounded, no surprise, the rump of professional revolutionaries, stranded since the mock-epic of the Cold War, no less than the stenographers of power in the accredited media. Not that the program of the liberal NGOs and the self-anointed leaders of Seattle's motley crew—"Reform the corporations!" "A place at the table!"—is other than in bad taste. Still, it would be wise to hear the critic who observed that, although political writing is always instrumental as well as utopian, its time of instrumentality—its time as a weapon—sometimes lies a little in the future. As to what might be entailed in the forging of a political language adequate to the business currently at hand, the following glossary is offered as a gesture, though readers should bear in mind that its remit is confined to the vocabulary of capitalist globalization and its detractors.

> *"It is not only by shooting bullets in the battlefields that tyranny is overthrown, but also by hurling ideas of redemption, words of freedom, and terrible anathemas against the hangmen that people bring down dictators and empires."*
> —*Emiliano Zapata*

Activist

Label used, often without qualification, by those campaigning for "social change", suggesting a liberal confidence in the general direction of history, as if the Pol Pots and Kissingers of the world weren't themselves active in the business of social change. The bane of hard-core activists is "passivity" in their targeted communities (q.v.) and the ivory tower; anti-intellectualism is the theory, activism the practice. Still, they have a point: "doing theory" in the academy can be a nasty sight.

Anarchist

Pierre-Joseph ("property is theft") Proudhon was among the first to embrace this term of abuse—Roget's Thesaurus places it in the company of terrorist, savage and fanatic—but peaceable anarchists, in the tradition of William Godwin, Pietr Kropotkin and Emma Goldman, have greatly outnumbered advocates of "negotiation by dynamite," which remains the specialty of governments. Still, anarchists have understood that, however much they carry in their hearts a world organized on principles of mutual aid and free association, the current owners show no signs of leaving quietly, and for that reason Buenaventura Durruti once remarked: "The bourgeoisie may blast and ruin their own world before they leave the stage of history. We are not in the least afraid of ruins." If the tactics of Seattle's enragés – the symbolic breaking of corporate property - showed one (masked) face of anarchism, the other was the classic anarchist organizational form of non-hierarchical affinity groups.

Autonomy

A term with wide currency among the opposition to capitalist globalization—cf. Italian autonomia, German autonomen, Zapatista autonomismo, and "temporary autonomous zones" (TAZ). Not to be understood in the abstract formalist Kantian sense of autonomy as obedience to reason, but in Cornelius Castoriadis' sense of movement away from heteronomy in general ("being in someone else's project", whether state, parent or boss) towards self-activity. Unsurprisingly, the idea attracts its share of those in fear of any dependency—cowboys, loners and

Iain A. Boal

authoritarians in flight from mother.

Biopiracy

Athough the term slanders pirates (see Marcus Rediker's Between the Devil and the Deep Blue Sea) it is intended as a corrective to what the genetic-industrial complex (Monsanto et al.) calls bio-prospecting. Refers to the privatization of plant and other organic material (fungi, animal DNA, human body and blood products, etc.) from the global South, home to 95% of the world's genetic resources, by way of the Northern patent mills. There is a deep continuity with the post-Columbus plunder of specimens by naturalist agents of empire and the 19th century global system of botanical laboratories (e.g., Kew Gardens, Jardin des Plantes).

Biotechnology

The new frontier whose salesmen and stock analysts glimpse whole continents of (com)modified life waiting to be staked out. The synergy between DNA technologists, silicon robotics and venture capital has produced a pre-emptive patent rush, rapid monopolization of life forms licenced by the courts, and a Niagara of hype (Green revolution redux and even immortality). These new enclosures (q.v.) are meeting popular resistance worldwide; the struggle is on to prevent the privatization of the world's germplasm (the essential means of production for farmers), not to mention the viralization of life by the vectors of transgenic DNA.

Black Bloc

The roving, uncivil, complement to the sit-down blockaders at Seattle, sharing a commitment to direct action in the streets, but viewing sedentary disobedience as privileged, moralizing and needlessly sacrificial. Named after their black clothing, a parody of the dress code of solemn bourgeois ritual. Its origins lie in European anarchist and autonomist tendencies, removed from the American legacy of civil-rights (Gandhian and Quaker-style) pacifism. The tactic of corporate property damage and their open masquerade have made the black bloc grist for the mills of the spectacle and, apparently, state provocateurs.

Borders

Be careful what you ask for. "World without borders" has now joined those other counter-cultural bumper slogans— "Think globally, act locally", "Flexible work hours!"—as the basic vocabulary of neo-liberalism. The hip academy's love affair with "transgressing borders" has put them in interesting company—the German Wehrmacht and the WTO. The dismantling of barriers is, of course, highly selective in favor of goods and capital rather than people, a fact well understood by workers trying to enter fortress Europe or to cross the Rio Grande from the South, and by travelers to Quebec and Genoa.

Capitalism

From Latin root capit- "head"; for connections not merely etymological between capital punishment and the punishment of capital, see Peter Linebaugh's The London Hanged. The economic order that, like its ruling class, will rarely speak its name, preferring the codewords "market", "democracy", and "freedom". Capitalism is organized around the production of commodities by commodities, from which follows the subversion of markets, the annulling of democracy, and the subordination of freedom.

Civil Society
"Community", "stakeholder", "participation", "transparency", "empowerment" — these are the grisly fetish words of foundation officers, non-profit apparatchiks and boardrooms everywhere, echoed in the field by the NGO cadres busy producing "locals". These liberal shibboleths, that cluster under the heading of "civil society", name simulacra of the social and disclose only its disappearance. Not for the first time; at the turn of the 19th century, Romantic schoolmasters and antiquarians—the clerisy of European nationalisms—celebrated the "folk" at the very moment its extinction was assured by enclosure of the commons and the criminalization of custom. It was the proto-Romantic Rousseau who remarked: "The first person who, having fenced off a plot of ground, took it into his head to say this is mine and found people simple enough to believe him, was the true founder of civil society."

Coase's Theorem
The notorious December 1991 World Bank memo, written by Lawrence Summers, later U.S. Treasury Secretary, argued that "the economic logic behind dumping a load of toxic waste in the lowest wage country is impeccable" because "under-populated countries in Africa are vastly under-polluted, their air quality is probably vastly inefficiently low compared to Los Angeles or Mexico City". Brazil's Secretary of the Environment wrote to Summers about the leaked memo: "Your reasoning is perfectly logical but totally insane" and was fired soon after. The reasoning referred to was in fact a pure example of the logic behind Coase's Theorem, which relates market efficiency, property, transaction costs and "exernalities", and underpins much of neo-liberal legal and economic doctrine, as well as WTO and IMF policies. Ronald Coase is the economist responsible for tradeable pollution rights by dreaming of a world of zero transaction costs where everything can be smoothly brought to market, and no ethical distinction made between the harm done by an oil refinery to those living downwind and the harm done to its owners by downwinders being in the way; it's just a cost-benefit matter requiring only clear and absolute private property rights (no common goods) and enough police to enforce them. The World Bank's "impeccable" Coasian logic means that there is no right to clean water, air or soil but merely the right to pay to keep them clean or to be compensated for their fouling. Too bad about those not at the bargaining table—above all, the unborn (or stillborn) generations. Luckily economists have long prepared us to discount the future; Coase once said that the future valuation of property was put at risk by "such cataclysmic events as the abolition of slavery". Coase won the Nobel Prize for Economics in 1991.

Commons
See under "Enclosure".

The law locks up the man or woman,
That steals the goose from off the common,
But lets the greater felon loose,
That steals the common from the goose.

Iain A. Boal

Community

The maximum shibboleth. A mantra used affirmatively across the entire political and cultural landscape; NPR once interviewed a spokesman from "the organized crime community". There is an implied antithesis to "the state" (with its suggestion of power, authority and central decision), in favor of the local and the face-to-face. The results can be grotesque: the release of asylum and hospital inmates to "the community" often means, in reality, warm ventilation grates. The "communitarian" right would rather nobody noticed that the shattering of communities is a direct effect of capital moving away in obedience to the logic of the very system they endorse.

Corporation

From corpus,"body". The body of the Catholic church was the ur-corporation, as the monastery was the prototype for other key institutions in the West—the asylum, the hospital, the university, the factory. By a legal fiction the business corporation was given a deathless personality—an idea related to the theory of the "divine right of kings" by which the monarch has two bodies, one that decays, one that doesn't ("The king is dead; long live the king"). The laws of the corporation inversely mirror the laws of criminal conspiracy. When individuals combine in pursuit of capital, they are afforded more protection than they enjoy in their own persons (e.g., limits to both civil and criminal liability, special treatment re taxation); when individuals combine against capital, they have less protection than they have on their own—mere association is criminalized, since the very act of combining is seen as a threat. That is, two or more people agreeing to commit a misdemeanor—whether or not they ever go through with it—is considered by the state a felony, because the greater threat is the sheer coming together in opposition to those interests the state serves.

Democracy

System of periodic ratification of political masters by ballot; meanwhile, the major decisions — who whom, for what, how — remain in the hands of the few. Democracy is the ideological keystone of the West's charter myth, and historically consistent, by its own account, with slavery (Athens), monarchy (England) and plutocracy (United States).

Development

Perhaps the key term of modernity, drawing into a single nexus the discourses of real estate, childhood and colonialism, for the future realization of added value. By the colonization of infancy and the infantilization of the colonies, labor and land (human and natural capital) are made ready for "improvement", the older word that "development" replaced, etymologically derived from <pros> "profit".

Direct Action

A mode of politics that tactically—and for some, strategically—shortcircuits official channels of "representation", often by interrupting business as usual, and deploying a variety of means, open and clandestine: street manifestations, blockades, trespass, sit-ins, banner hanging, squatting, sabotage, crop-trashing, pie-throwing. The debate since Seattle about property damage and the activity of the black bloc—whether it is tactically effective ("helps break the spell of the commodity" versus "allows demonization of the movement as mindless vandalism"), and whether it constitutes violence ("to treat property as sacred and inviolable is to think like the state, and anyway what about the silent violence of structural adjustment or redlining") rehearses old tensions between pacifist and "physical force" traditions in abolitionist, nationalist and anti-colonial struggles.

Direct Action Network (DAN)

DAN Emerged from the direct action training camp two months before Seattle, organized by the Ruckus Society, offspring of Greenpeace commando training crossed with Earth First! forest defense techniques, and adapted to non-wilderness, urban contexts—street blockades, lockdowns, tall building banner-hangs—combined with political puppetry, street theatre, culture-jamming and net-based bypassing of capitalist media. See under "Direct action".

Diversity

The key term of US multiculturalism, a liberal doctrine endorsed by big business and government for the management of "difference" in response to the civil rights, feminist, and gay liberation movements. The doggerel read at Clinton's first inauguration, "On the Pulse of Morning", confirmed the ascendancy of multicultural nationalism; contrast the previous inaugural verse (at Kennedy's induction), "The Gift Outright", Robert Frost's white puritan poem of blood sacrifice and western conquest. Although capitalist globalization is spoken of as a homogenizing force (viz. extinction of languages and species, death of customary lifeways, Weberian harmonization), it co-opts and even encourages the proliferation of identities—gender, ethnic and consumer—consistent with profit-taking. Biodiversity, that mantra of environmentalists, is, to say nothing of its merits, multiculturalism projected onto the realm of nature; by the same token, the native plant movement draws, willy-nilly, from the wellsprings of xenophobia and anti-immigrant rhetoric. To speak of nature is always already to be in the space of the social.

Economy

The alpha and omega of our epoch. The mere utterance of the words, "the bottom line", is supposed to halt discussion. The disembedding of the "economy" from its social and moral matrix has been a long and savage process; its first paid professor was the Reverend Malthus in 1800. As often, it was in a work of imagination, not theory—in Daniel Defoe, rather than Adam Smith—that one encounters the first classic projection of homo economicus. What is Robinson Crusoe, that lonely, primitive accumulator and idol of economists, but a cost-benefit calculating machine? Such is the neurotic Protestant imago that the technicians of the WTO dream of universalizing.

Enclosure

The exclusion (sometimes physically by hedges and fences) of commoners and peasants from the means of life, in order to "free" them for wage labor under capitalist modernity. Enclosure meant not only the extinction (by force and later by acts of parliament) of customary "rights of common" to soil, grazing, firewood, timber, and the cultivated and uncultivated bounty of the earth, but, at least as important, the breaking of communal consciousness and autonomy. The commodification of land and labor was capitalism's essential founding process, written "in letters of blood and fire". The buying and selling of commodities could then be generalized; property and price come to mediate all relations with nature and humanity. The structural adjustment programs of the IMF, and the WTO's intellectual property regimes, amount to new (as well as old) forms of enclosure—privatization of water and public land, auctioning of the electromagnetic spectrum, the patenting of seeds, etc.

Environment

When taken to mean external surroundings, "environment" reinforces the old split between humanity and nature, between inside and outside, which at least has the merit of not positing a fascist metaphysics of identity (blood and soil, thinking with the body, woman equals nature). Environments are constituted by the life-activity of their inhabitants; without the active involvement of its denizens, no expert has any business claiming even to identify an environment.

Environmentalists

Corporate capital's stormy petrels, warning of bad weather. That Mobil and environmentalists both like to operate under the sign of NASA's " whole earth" image reveals how green politics is a version of global managerialism. The Malthusian assumptions and the eugenic and racist roots of environmentalism (population control, native plant fanaticism, defence of wilderness that was someone else's home) are barely below the surface.

Fair trade

The alternative to "free trade" on offer from the loyal opposition, led by Global Exchange, a San Francisco travel agency and crafts importer.

Free trade

Traditional slogan of imperial monopolists and protectionists...for export only.

Genetically Modified Organism (GMO)

See under "Biotechnology."

Gibson's Law

"For every PhD there is an equal and opposite PhD." Scientists flatly contradicting each other became a common sight during the mad cow outbreak, and caused a crisis of legitimacy in Europe, which will only deepen with each surprising plague. Because scientists are increasingly licensed by industry, we are bound to hear more kitsch assertions like "The chances of GM pollen drift are zero", and "There can no prions in the milk".

Global South

The old West/East division, based on the political geography of the capitalist-communist bloc system, is giving way to North/South terminology, reflecting the post-Cold War configuration of a Northern capitalist core (to use the metaphor of world-system theory) and a Southern periphery. The obvious limitations of these hemispheric spatial terms led, in the first case, to the coining of "tiers monde"/"third world" for countries "non-aligned" with the two blocs, and recently to the attachment of "global" to "South" to capture the fact that capitalism's uneven development creates conditions typically associated with the South inside the Northern heartlands.

Globalization

Business school jargon that gained general currency in the 1990s, to describe the dismantling of barriers to the movement of capital and the loss of local and national sovereignties to the interests of transnational firms, helped along by developments in telecommunications and the collapse of the two-bloc world. Globes were originally "emblems of sovereignty" (1614), that became playthings of merchant princes and navigators, familiar as props in Renaissance portraiture. It was the task of cartography to project the globe into two dimensions; without the resulting maps and charts the business of empire and planetary capitalist hegemony would be literally unthinkable.

Human rights

Liberal discourse lately favored by the managers of the new world order, not least the military humanists of NATO and the Pentagon who use it, arbitrarily of course, as a trojan horse for intervention worldwide, by land, sea, air and, soon no doubt, space—mercy by any means necessary.

International Monetary Fund (IMF)

Created by the US and Britain at the 1944 Bretton Woods conference to provide loans to countries with short-term liquidity problems, and to buffer the irrationality of markets by enshrining capital controls in Article VI. Since the defeat of this original scheme of John Maynard Keynes and Dexter White, the IMF has been turned into a major global instrument for the disciplining of movements toward local autonomy by savage "conditionalities" on loans.

Independent Media Center (IMC)

Hub of non-corporate news gathering and dissemination, taking advantage of the new technics of communications (digital cameras, satellites, wireless telephony, the internet). The mushrooming of IMCs, modeled on the Seattle experience, is a response to the continuing enclosures and concentration of the capitalist media.

Internet

The child of Victorian telegraphy, even down to the utopian hype—in 1852 a Saint-Simonian disciple announced: "A perfect network of electric filaments will afford a new social harmony." The space-pulverizing machinery of the virtual brings, along with new connections, intensified separation, plus low-grade depression and digital palsy, that nasty relative of the televisual body ("couch potato"). Its liberatory refunctioning as a tool for "organizing from below" flourishes in the shade of its dominant use as essential support for the global transmission of administrative, military and commercial intelligence, and the

Iain A. Boal

enhanced surveillance of labor.

Intellectual Property Rights (IPR)

Their origins lie in the history of the printing press and questions of copyright ownership; the new technologies of communication, replication and the rise of corporate patents and branding have brought trade related intellectual property rights (TRIPs) sharply into focus, and onto the main agenda of the WTO. It is symptomatic that the fortune of today's Croesus is amassed by licensing intellectual property (software, patents) rather than by owning oil wells or steelmills, in the style of 19th century robber barons. The managers and brokers of capital prefer these purified forms of property; they can circulate at the speed of light.

Libertarian

Historically the contrast was with "determinist" (vis-a-vis free will); later used by anarchists (e.g., Noam Chomsky) to distance themselves from authoritarian socialists in their various guises (Stalinist, Leninist, Trotskyist, Maoist, Castroite); recently the party of market fetishists, automatic weapons collectors and the anti-tax lobby.

Luddite

The most powerful swearword of capital ("mindless, destructive, resister of progress"), now doing double-duty since "communist" has, for the moment, lost its charge. Still, all the sabotage in history would not even register in the scales compared to capitalism's scheduled destruction. Both the left and the right told the same lie about the historical luddites, that they were primitivist and backward looking, as if those skilled weavers at the dawn of industrial modernity were against the future rather than its foreclosure by immiseration, factory discipline and the gallows.

Market

More accurately described by the French historian Braudel as the "anti-market". Capitalism from its birth has been about oligopolies and monopolies. The necessary contrast to the glory of old marketplaces, fairs, bazaars, and agoras is the "container", the tilt-up warehouse, and the supermarket.

Multitude

Key term of the philosopher Spinoza, the anti-Hobbes of early modernity, now dusted off for the digital epoch by certain critics of globalization. The argument goes: if capitalism at its dawning produced a multitude, and the factories of the industrial revolution a proletariat, the social factory of the cybernetic economy is producing a new (global, wired) multitude. Some in the current anti-capitalist movement recognize themselves in this neo-Spinozist scheme, and hope that the power of the new antinomian multitude will constitute the gravedigger this time.

Neoliberalism

Post-60's version of classical liberalism's gospel of the market and the "hidden hand". For forty years the strategy developed during the crisis of the 1930s to prevent anti-capitalist movements from taking power—national Keynesianism—

was hegemonic in the West, in the form of welfare safety nets, income redistribution, domestic industry protection, state-financed public works, and capital controls. The assault on national Keynesianism came in the shape of globalizing neo-liberalism, propagated in reactionary think-tanks (funded by oil and armaments fortunes) in response to the revolutionary events of the sixties and the falling rate of profit. The immediate intellectual roots lay in the work of an English accountant Ronald Coase (q.v.), with von Hayek the bridge to classical liberalism, the University of Chicago its academic home, and Thatcher and Reagan its door-to-door salesforce. Neo-liberals wish to bury the memory of their system's savior—"capitalism in itself", observed Keynes in 1924, "is in many ways objectionable"—by claiming that "there is no alternative" to unregulated global flows of money and goods, the sale of public assets, the overriding of workplace and environmental protections, and a recomposed planetary division of labor; in sum, the removal of any fetters on the rate of exploitation.

Non-governmental Organizations (NGOs)
The mendicant orders of late capitalism. By one calculation they numbered a mere nine in 1907, most famously the Red Cross. The Biafran famine in the mid 1960s, where international state action proved spectacularly inadequate, was the watershed, and by the late nineties NGO's numbered in the thousands. They are thriving on famine, disease, and war, and in the spaces (north as well as south) created by structural adjustment—forced privatization, market deregulation, and the hollowing out of state agencies.

Non-violent Direct Action (NVDA)
See under "violence" and "direct action".

Pacifism
The rejection of all forms of organized violence. Dismissed right, left and center —by generals, revolutionaries and pragmatic liberals alike—as hopelessly unrealistic, thought pacifists are unimpressed by what passes for political realism and look for routes to a peaceable world that interrupt the codes of violence. The "peace process", however, usually means war by other means, and pacifists operating under its banner might reflect on Tacitus' remark about the fate of Carthage: the Romans "made a desert and called it peace".

Police
Institutionalized by Napoleon in France and by Robert Peel in 18th London to enforce the wage-form and the criminalization of custom. The more modern the police force, the more medieval-looking the body armor—though the weaponry is the scientific fruit of corporate laboratories.

Policy
Etymological variant of "police".

Primitivism
A branch of romanticism (Enlightenment's unruly sibling) having deep American roots, with recent developments in Detroit and Eugene. Rejects industrial civi-

lization and, in austere versions, even agriculture; in the limit case, human language itself is considered a technology of alienation. Associated in the public mind with the Unabomber, whom the press portrayed as society's mad outcast, but his manifesto reveals not only a widely held apocalyptic view of modern science and technology, but in some ways a traditional white American male profile, viz. anti-urbanism, misogyny and a fascination with violence and homemade explosives.

Privatization

Etymological kin to "deprivation", though any memory of why that might be—namely, that "privacy" was a prideful abstention from a life in common—is long gone. The transvaluation has taken four hundred years, and can be marked by the junkbond artist Ivan Boesky's notorious speech to Berkeley's Haas (Levi Strauss) Business School when he announced "Greed is good", and was cheered to the rafters. The privatization of everything is often imagined to be the ideal of free marketeers, but their real game involves the maximum socialization of costs in the sink of nature and labor.

Risk

The entry under "Risk" in the Dictionary of the Social Sciences has a single cross-reference, to "Profit". That is at least honest, since the rhetoric of risk, which now drives medicine, law, portfolio management, criminology, social welfare, education, public health, technology impact, environmental policy, banking, industrial hygiene, urban planning, military strategy and genomics, emerged during the 17th century in the milieu of Lloyd's coffeehouse, where the new capitalist dealers in risk (sale of annuities, stock jobbing, marine insurance) were busy undermining the moral economy with the logic of the market and the counting house. Modern apologists of risk, such as Tony "Third Way" Giddens, inform us that new technologies make for an unavoidably dangerous world, and therefore the real menace comes from riskophobes and untrusting luddites facing backwards.

Seattle

Poster city of the "new economy", home of Microsoft, Boeing, and Starbucks, the firms that connect its workforce, fly the top layer around, and keep them awake and flexible. Seattle is a classic example of the denaturing by containerization of the old waterfronts of the Atlantic and Pacific littoral, whose passing has been recorded in Alan Sekula's photo-documentary Fish Story. The Chamber of Commerce is living with the fear that the name of their city will always conjure up, not a vision of the new economy, but its nemesis.

Science

Since harnessing fundamental chemistry to colonial warfare and atomic physics to state arsenals, science seems more menace than hope, the scientist more Frankenstein than Prometheus. Industry science is often intended actually to produce ignorance—about cigarettes, asbestos, global warming, GM crops—turning the skepticism of critical inquiry to corporate advantage, in order to buy time; a Brown and Williamson (tobacco company) memo admitted: "Doubt is our product". Science, once and still emancipatory vis-à-vis the mystification of clerics, has become capital's way of knowing the world.

Sixties

The long shadow of that crowded decade continues to haunt both the soixante-huitards and those who insist it was all a chimera. That it was a revolutionary conjuncture, and a global one, should be of interest this time around. For evidence see Ronald Fraser's 1968, Sonya Sayres et al. The Sixties Without Apology, Michael Watts' 1968 and All That, and Chris Marker's two-part documentary Le Fond de L'Air est Rouge.

Sovereignty

Supreme authority. The parcellized power of feudal lords became absolute under monarchical and nation-states systems; late capitalism is re-parcellizing and punching holes in state sovereignty (e.g., Native American casino enclaves) in the interests of flexible accumulation. Most conspicuously, the sovereignty of WTO rules now trumps national laws enacted for the protection of the environment and workers.

Terrorism

The strategic use of violence against civilians—typically by states but also by those thinking like a state, however marginal and poor in resources. Terrorism seeks to kill and maim, but also more widely to demoralize, to spread the message that no one is safe. Terrorism is an act of communication. It aims to breed rumor, grab headlines, burn an image of pain and horror into the citizenry's collective skull. The tactic is cost-effective, and has had successes. Colonial occupiers have given up and gone home in the face of it. Whether victimization and the sowing of mass paranoia can ever provide the basis for a "revolution"—that is, the release and refocusing of repressed social energies—is another question. Whereas terror is often disavowed (though inherent to rapine, slavery, inquisitions and colonialism), terrorism lives on the oxygen of publicity. It took modern form with the Jacobins' spectacular use of Dr Guillotin's enlightenment machine for rational decapitation. The next fin-de-siècle burst of "propaganda by the deed"—political assassinations, bombings and incendiarism, often in fact the work of agents provocateurs in the service of the state's need to justify the deployment of its hegemonic violence—turned out to be just a curtain-raiser for the twentieth century which witnessed the apotheosis of terrorism. Its emblematic instruments have been, in the industrialized North, the car-bomb, and, in the Third World, disappearances and the death-squad. But twentieth century terrorism's hallmark was bombardment from the air, the Damoclean threat of mass death aimed at the inhabitants of cities—Guernica, London, Dresden, and the ground zero of globalized atomic terror, Hiroshima. For keepers of nuclear stockpiles to declare a "war on terrorism" places them very deep in Orwell's debt. In political rhetoric, the epithet "terrorist" is projected only onto others—enemies so designated by authorities wherever; in the US, the term is rapidly proliferating to implicate all resistance to capitalist globalization, foreign and domestic. Thus fast-track free trade legislation, corporate bail-outs and environmental de-regulation are called "counter-terrorism" measures. Not for the first time is "terrorist" (cf. "luddite" and "communist") being forged as a weapon in

Iain A. Boal

capitalism's arsenal.

Utopia

Thomas More's 16th century book forever lent its name to projections of an ideal world. They are, typically, static blueprints—More's original Utopia, though it contained a savage critique of early capitalist enclosures, was really a nostalgic retrospect for a dying patriarchal feudal order. We are currently living in the utopia of 1930s automobile company executives, who gave us fair warning in the GM pavilion of the 1939 World's Fair. Although Ursula Le Guin's The Lathe of Heaven, P.M.'s Bolo Bolo, and William Morris's News from Nowhere shine out as beacons in a dismal genre, it grows harder to envisage the far side of capitalism, the more everyday life is colonized by the imagineers of the commodity world.

Violence

Chief of the state monopolies—indeed, no state is conceivable without it, though it will be called "force", not "violence". The stenographers of domination systematically conflate necessary ethical distinctions between the violence of the oppressor and the oppressed, between harm to persons and harm to property, between institutionalized violence (right and left) as opposed to the improvised violence of insurrections. Violence routinized is a mirror of the state, as non-violence advocates are quick to point out; on the other hand, non-violence fetishized is often a mark of privilege.

Virtual

The electronic sublime heralded fifty years ago by the barkers of the cybernetic revolution have finally arrived under the sign of the "virtual". Video screens constitute the myth space of modernity, which thus far mostly offers playworlds where wargaming meets Fordist speed-up. It is no surprise that relationships at a remove are often welcomed when the spaces of everyday life—depending on gender, race, class and age—are surveilled, dangerous or denatured, with the chances of pleasurable encounters close to vanishing. The virtual life is, however, always on the cusp of boredom, which is fascination's other face.

War

The health of the state.

World Bank

Properly the World Bank Group. Emerged out of the International Bank for Reconstruction and Development (IBRD), set up at the Bretton Woods meeting in 1944 to funnel low-interest loans for the rebuilding of war-ravaged Europe, and to head off communism. It later evolved into the prime agency for Third World aid and development, or what the Wall Street Journal called "promoting socialism". During the 1970s McNamara oversaw a massive growth in the World Bank's resources; on his watch the "structural adjustment" loan was devised as a vehicle for imposing, as they say, "free-market liberalization". In recent years, by hiring on some of its milder critics, the World Bank is able to play good cop to the IMF's bad cop.

World Trade Organization (WTO)

1995 successor organization to GATT (General Agreement on Tariffs and Trade). Its early origins lie in the ITO (International Trade Organization) set up in 1948 in Havana to coordinate the international trading system in the wake of the crisis of the 1930s. GATT was a system of member-state negotiations ("rounds") concluding in contracts that fixed tarrifs in industrial products at national borders. The Uruguay Round ended in 1995 with the establishment of a permanent international bureaucracy, the World Trade Organization (WTO), having a much larger scope that does not stop at borders, and includes agriculture, intellectual property rights (IPR), trade in services, and investment measures. It is structured in the image of the private tyrannies it serves, capitalist firms.

Iain A. Boal

Notes On Contributors

Katharine Ainger is an editor of *The New Internationalist*. She is a member of an editorial collective writing *We Are Everywhere: The Irresistible Rise of Global Anti-Capitalism*.

Stanley Aronowitz is a Distinguished Professor of Sociology at the Graduate Center, City University of New York. Long involved in the labor movement and in education, he is founder of the Center for Worker Education at the City College of New York. He is the author of over 18 books, including, most recently *The Knowledge Factory: Dismantling the Corporate University and Creating True Higher Learning* (Beacon 2000).

Associazione Ya Basta! is a network writing the original Ya Basta!, mostly based in milan and Italy's Veneto region, and a parallel, slightly more recent— 1998—movement of *tute bianche* (white overalls).

David Barsamian is the Director of Alternative Radio in Boulder, Colorado. His most recent book is *Propaganda and the Public Mind* (South End Press 2001), a collection of interviews with Noam Chomsky.

Hakim Bey is the author of *T.A.Z. Temporary Autonomous Zones* and *Millenium* (Autonomedia 1996), among other books.

Iain Boal teaches in the Geography Department at the University of California at Berkeley. He is the co-editor, with James Brook, of *Resisting the Virtual Life* (City Lights 1995) and the author of *The Long Theft* (forthcoming from City Lights).

Daniel Burton Rose is an activist and writer based in the East Bay. He is the co-editor of The Celling of America: An Inside Look at the U.S. Prison Industry (Common Courage Press: 1998). An award winning journalist he has written for *Vibe, Z Magazine, San Francisco Bay Gaurdian, Dollars and Sense, Middle East Report,* and *The MultiNational Monitor,* among other publications.

George Caffentzis is a coordinator of the Committee for Academic Freedom in Africa, a member of the Midnight Notes collective and coeditor of *Auroras of the Zapatistas: Local and Global Struggles of the Fourth World War* (Autonomedia 2001).

Manuel Callahan is a member of Accion Zapatista (www.utexas.edu/students/nave/), a collective dedicated to supporting the Zapatista struggle and promulgating Zapatismo as a revolutionary project. He lives in Austin, Texas.

Noam Chomsky is a longtime political activist, writer and professor of linguistics at MIT. His latest books are *The Common Good* (Odonian Press 1998) and *The New Military Humanism* (Common Courage Press 1999).

Alexander Cockburn and **Jeffrey St. Clair** are the authors of *Five Days that Shook the World* (Verso 2000). Together they edit the radical muckraking newsletter *CounterPunch*.

James Davis is an Irish filmmaker living in New York. His most recent work is *Safety Orange,* a documentary about the US criminal Justice system. He can be reached at debonaire@mindspring.com.

Andrea del Moral lives in Oakland, CA. She writes poetry and prose, and works on inciting freedom through urban agriculture projects, theatre, and dance.

Barbara Ehrenreich is the author of numerous books, including *Nickel-and-Dimed: On (Not) Getting By In America* (Metropolitan Books). A social critic and journalist, she has written for a wide array of newspapers and magazines, and is currently a columnist for *The Progressive*.

Barbara Epstein teaches in the History of Consciousness Program at UC Santa Cruz. She is the author of *Political Protest and Cultural Revolt: Nonviolent Direct Action of the 1970s and 1980s* (University Of California Press 1991).

Liza Featherstone is a Manhattan-based journalist. She is the author of *Students Against Sweatshops: the Making of a Movement* (Verso).

Silvia Federici is a coordinator of the Committee for Academic Freedom in Africa and a co-editor of *A Thousand Flowers: Social Struggles Against Structural Adjustment in African Universities* (Africa World Press, 2000).

Juan Gonzalez is a award-winning columnist for *The New York Daily News* and a frequent contributor to *In These Times*. He is the author of *Roll Down Your Windows: Stones from a Forgotten America* (Verso, 1995) and *Harvest of an Empire: A History of Latinos in America* (Viking, 2000).

Jay Griffiths is the author of *Pip Pip: A Sideways Look at Time*. She has written for *The Guardian, The Observer*, and the *London Review of Books,* among other publications.

Stephanie Guilloud is an Olympia, Washington based activist. She's the editor of *Through the Eyes of the Judged* and *Voices of the WTO*.

fran harris is a poet and activist living in Brooklyn, NY.

Kevin Harris is an illustrator, graphic artist, and printer. He's influenced by deerpaths and detritus. kevin@cea.edu.

Paul Hawkin is an anarchist activist from the midwest

Andrew Hsiao is an editor with The New Press and a writer with the *Village*

Voice. He lives in Brooklyn.

Boris Kagarlitsky is a political scientist and activist living in Moscow. He was a political prisoner under Brezhnev (1982–83), a member of the Moscow City Soviet (1990–93), advisor to the Chair of the Federation of Independent Trade Unions of Russia (1992–94), and is now a senior research fellow at the Institute of Comparative Political Studies of the Russian Academy of Sciences. His books include *Return of Radicalism* (Pluto Press 2000) and *Twilight of Globalization* (Pluto Press 2000).

George Katsiaficas is the editor of *New Political Science.* He is the author of *The Imagination of the New Left: A Global Analysis of 1968* (South End Press: 1987), *The Subversion of Politics: European Autonomous Social Movements and the Decolonization of Everyday Life* (Humanities Press 1997), and, with Kathleen Cleaver, edited *Liberation, Imagination and the Black Panther Party* (Routledge 2001). He is currently based at Chonnam National University in Kwangju, Korea.

Eliot Katz is the author of *Unlocking the Exits* (Coffee House Press 1999) and a coeditor of *Poems for the Nation* (Seven Stories Press 2000), a collection of contemporary political poems compiled by Allen Ginsberg.

L.A. Kauffman's column on radical activism, *Free Radical: Chronicle of the New Unrest,* is on the web at www.free-radical.org. She's writing a history of radical direct action movements from the early '70s to the present.

Naomi Klein is the author of *No Logo: Taking Aim at the Brand Bullies* (Picador 1999). She is based in Toronto, Ontario.

Eric Krebbers and **Merijn Schoenmaker** are members of the Dutch organization De Fabel van de Illegaal.

David Kubrin has been a political activist and organizer since the late 1950s. He has taught history at Dartmouth college, and the University of Wisconsin, and currently teaches science at a San Francisco middle school. During the '80s he was a member of Matrix, an anarchist, pagan affinity group involved in actions at Diablo Canyon, Vandenberg Force Base, Livermore labs, and elsewhere.

George Lakey is a member of Training for Change (www.trainingforchange.org) in Philadelphia. A nonviolent activist for over forty years, his books include *A Manual for Direct Action* and *Strategy for a Living Revolution.*

Mark Laskey is an anarchist activist from Boston, Massachusetts. He's a member of the Northeastern Federation of Anarcho-Communists and works in the Sabate Anarchist Collective, the editorial collective for NEFAC's theoretical and agitational magazine.

David Lindorff is a progressive journalist based in the Philadelphia area, and is the author of *Marketplace Medicine: The Rise of the For-Profit Hospital Chains* (Bantam 1992) and is currently writing a book on the case of death-row inmate Mumia Abu-Jamal for Common Courage Press. He writes for *Salon,* the *Nation, In These Times, Businessweek* and other publications.

Kari Lydersen is a Chicago-based journalist. She's a stringer for the *Washington Post* and contributes frequently to *In These Times* and *Street Sheet.*

Josh MacPhee is a graphic artist and activist living and working in Chicago. He runs Just Seeds (justseeds@hotmail.com or P.O. Box 476971, Chicago, IL. 60647). He's workin on a book about street stencils for New Mouth of the Dirty South.

Rachel Neumann is a writer, teacher, editor and activist. She lives in Brooklyn, New York.

James O'Connor, a Professor Emeritus at the University of California at Santa Cruz, is a co-founder and editor of *Capitalism, Nature and Socialism: A Journal of Socialist Ecology.* He's the Director of the Center for Political Ecology, also in Santa Cruz. He is the author of six books, including *Natural Causes: Essays in Ecological Marxism* (Guilford Press 1998).

Geov Parrish is an anarchist and pacifist organizer, media activist, and tax resistance counselor. He is a radio commentator and weekly political columnist for *The Seattle Weekly* and the radical zine *Eat the State!*

Jeffrey Perlstein is a co-founder of the The Independent Media Center in Seattle and Indymedia.org. He wishes to thank and pay respect to all those who've participated in Indymedia, those who continue to participate, and all those who paved the way. He currently resides in the Bay Area.

Colin Rajah is director of programs at JustAct, an organization based in San Francisco that promotes youth education and activism for global justice.

Jim Redden is the author of *Snitch Culture* (Feral House 2001).

Tim Russo is a freelance photo and media activist based in Southern Mexico since 1994. He has worked extensively with a collective of media activists, NGOs and solidarity groups in establishing the Chiapas Independent Media Center (chiapas.indymedia.org). He has also been the KGNU Mexico correpsondent for nearly six years.

Ramor Ryan was born in Dublin town. In keeping with old Irish traditions of rebellion and exile, he now lives between Chiapas, Mexico and New York City. He is working on a book chronicalling his travels.

Jaggi Singh is a writer, independent journalist and political activist based in

Montreal.

Organized in 1966, the **Surrealist Movement in the United States** is based in Chicago but includes dozens of participants from coast to coast. Its critics have called it too anarchist, too Marxist, too political, not political enough, and much too influenced by Bugs Bunny. You can decide for yourself by checking its website: www.surrealism-usa.org.

Seth Tobocman is and artist/activist and co-founder of *World War Three Illustrated*. His books are *You Don't Have to Fuck People over to Survive* (Soft Skull, 1999) and *War in the Neighborhood* (Autonomedia, 2000)

Kristine Wong is a Chinese-American activist and writer. A longtime environmental justice and community health organizer, educator, and trainer, she has lived and worked in the San Francisco Bay Area and Seattle.

Eddie Yuen is a PhD candidate in the Sociology program at the University of California at Santa Cruz. He teaches at Brooklyn College, City University of New York.

John Zerzan is a Eugene, Oregon based writer and activist. His books include *Against Civilization* (Uncivilized Books 1999), *Future Primitive* (Autonomedia 1999), and *Elements of Refusal* (Left Bank Books 1998).

Information Resources

Alternative Radio
P.O. Box 551
Boulder, CO 80306
(800) 444-1977
www.alternativeradio.org

Anarchy:
A Journal of Desire Armed
C.A.L. Press
PO Box 1313
Lawrence, KS 66044

Black-Clad Messenger and Revolt!
Anarchist Action Collective
P.O. Box 11331
Eugene, OR 97440
Send postage and/or donation

Capitalism, Nature, Socialism:
A Journal of Socialist Ecology
P.O. Box 8467
Santa Cruz, CA 95961
www.cruzio.com/~cns

Colorlines
Subscription Department
P.O. Box 3000
Denville, NJ 07834-9206
(888) 458-8588

CounterPunch
3220 N St. NW PMB 346
Washington, D.C. 20007-2829
(800) 840-3683
$40/year, $30 low income
www.counterpunch.org

Eat the State!
PO Box 85541
Seattle, WA 98145
$29/ 40 issues

In These Times
2040 N. Milwaukee Ave.
Chicago, IL 60647
$36.95/year ($59 for Institutions)
(800) 827-0270
www.inthesetimes.org

Left Business Observer
250 W. 85th Street
New York, NY 10024-3217
$22/11 issues ($55/institutions,
high income)
(212) 874-4020
www.panix.com

My Enemy's Enemy
Anti-Fascist Forum
P.O. Box 6326 Station A
Toronto, Ontario
M5W1P7
Canada

The Nation
P.O. Box 55149
Boulder, CO 80332-5149
$52/yr
(800) 333-8536
www.thenation.com

The Progressive
P.O. Box 421
Mount Morris, IL 61504-0421
$32/yr $21/yr student rate
(800) 827-0555
www.progressive.org

Voices from the WTO
TESC Bookstore
2700 Evergreen Parkway
Olympia, WA 98505
$6.75 per copy
plus $2 shipping and handling
(360) 866-6000 ext.6215

Z Magazine
18 Millfield St.
Woods Hole, MA 02543
$30/yr $25/yr low income
(508) 457-0626
www.zmag.org